Advance Praise for *REST in Practice*

"Jim, Savas, and Ian manage to make the notoriously abstract concepts behind RESTful integration useful and applicable in day-to-day work, as well as easy to understand. If you're looking into how to do web-based integration simply and effectively, this is where you should start."

—Mark Nottingham
Principal Technical Yahoo!, Yahoo

"It is no coincidence that since Jim, Savas, and Ian started their frequent presentations and writings on the importance and applicability of hypermedia in distributed systems, the landscape of REST's practical usage started to change. Restfulie is an example how influential their ideas have been."

—Guilherme Silveira
Tech Lead at Caelum and Restfulie Project Leader

"While there are by now many books that describe basic REST and HTTP principles, this book raises the bar by exploiting the web architecture's benefits for more advanced use cases, such as hypermedia-driven processes. A perfect mix of theory and practice."

—Stefan Tilkov
CEO, InnoQ

"REST is different from traditional approaches to application design and development. It's important to clearly understand REST and build on successful examples. *REST in Practice* meets this need head-on. Its authors are all excellent technologists and communicators, and have done a great job tackling this challenging subject."

—Eric Newcomer
Chief Architect, Investment Banking Division, Credit Suisse

"*REST in Practice* unifies a grounded, pragmatic approach to building real-world services with crystal-clear explanations of higher-level abstractions. The result is a book that teaches you both how and why to develop services with flexible, negotiable, discoverable interfaces."

—Michael T. Nygard
Author of *Release It!*

"REST can appear confusing and inaccessible, filled with jargon and with precious few really good examples. Luckily, this book does a superb job of taking the difficult and misunderstood parts of REST and describing them so they appear both simple and obvious. Along the way, it also shows how to build upon REST and the Web to solve real-world problems."

—Colin Jack
Senior Software Developer

REST in Practice

Jim Webber, Savas Parastatidis, and Ian Robinson

O'REILLY®

Beijing · Cambridge · Farnham · Köln · Sebastopol · Tokyo

REST in Practice

by Jim Webber, Savas Parastatidis, and Ian Robinson

Published by O'Reilly Media, Inc., 1005 Gravenstein Highway North, Sebastopol, CA 95472.

O'Reilly books may be purchased for educational, business, or sales promotional use. Online editions are also available for most titles (*http://my.safaribooksonline.com*). For more information, contact our corporate/institutional sales department: (800) 998-9938 or *corporate@oreilly.com*.

Editor: Simon St.Laurent	**Indexer:** Lucie Haskins
Production Editor: Rachel Monaghan	**Cover Designer:** Karen Montgomery
Copyeditor: Audrey Doyle	**Interior Designer:** Ron Bilodeau
Proofreader: Rachel Monaghan	**Illustrator:** Robert Romano
Production Services: Newgen North America	

Printing History:

September 2010:   First Edition.

ISBN: 978-0-596-80582-1

[M]

CONTENTS

Foreword

FROM THE VERY START OF WHEN I GOT INVOLVED IN COMPUTING, there's been the desire to have software systems designed as components that can be freely combined. The wide-scale connectivity of the Internet fueled this desire, and added the desire to have components operate over networks that introduce issues of latency and unknown reliability. In this world many systems have been tried, and many have failed—usually with a whimper.

A great example of success is the World Wide Web. Its success has penetrated both business operations and popular culture. It provides opportunities for people to pull together information from many sources, with hardly any prearranged collaboration—and at a global scale.

The Web, as we currently know it, isn't the be-all and end-all of computing, but many people believe it offers an important lesson on how to construct systems of networked components. Many people take advantage of its protocol, HTTP, to connect systems. But some people think we should go further, using HTTP not as a convenient tunnel, but to embrace the way the Web works as a foundation for systems collaboration.

This thinking gathers together under the name of "REST." It refers to Roy Fielding's PhD thesis, which is far more often referred to than it is read. There is a growing notion that following the principles of REST offers a fruitful path to making networked components work, one that is built upon the success of the Web itself.

That vision is attractive, but there is much to be done to reach it. We have to take the principles of REST and see how to apply them to the everyday problems of systems integration. This is the task the authors of this book have taken on: to take REST from an attractive vision to implemented systems. They've done much to teach me about thinking in resources, how to use HTTP idioms, and the importance of hypermedia controls. As a result, this book will give you a thorough grounding in applying the core elements of RESTful thinking.

As we all should know, REST is not the answer to all questions. There are many situations where a REST approach is an appropriate approach, but many where it is not. As it's early days in using this style for integration problems, we are still feeling our way around these boundaries. But in order to explore these boundaries properly, it's vital to have a proper understanding of what REST is about. Without that, you run the risk of trying pseudo-REST and drawing the wrong conclusions. This book can help you avoid that fate.

—Martin Fowler
August 2010

Preface

THE WEB HAS REVOLUTIONIZED THE WAY WE ACCESS AND SHARE INFORMATION. In just two decades, it has become *the* global platform for delivering and consuming services.

The pervasiveness and ubiquity of the Web stems from the way it combines architectural simplicity with a small set of widely accepted technologies. The Web provides scalability, security, and reliability for those systems that embrace its simple tenets, and it does so using commodity tools and platforms.

Our goal in this book is twofold: to demystify the Web as an application platform and to showcase how web architecture can be applied to common enterprise computing problems. Throughout the chapters, we make it a point to demonstrate how services can leverage the Web both inside and outside enterprise boundaries. Our vision is of an information platform that is open and available to other systems, which eschews integration in favor of composition, and yet implements valuable business behaviors: a distributed, hypermedia-driven application platform.

You don't have to know REST or HTTP in detail in order to understand this book. We'll take you from simple integration through to sophisticated business protocols, all with detailed code examples that you can adapt for your own ends.

Should I Read This Book?

Like most of us, you're probably already building something that feeds into the Web, and you've probably used tools and patterns for the Web that seem pretty useful. Then you've tackled typical enterprise problems and wondered why it can't be as nice as the web stuff.

You're seeing the benefits of the Web all around and you start to question whether your enterprise's expensive middleware offers a good return on investment, or whether it will ever scale to meet your users' demands.

You might be a developer who wants to understand the Web's principles in more detail, and likes to learn through code examples. You've heard terms such as *URIs*, *HTTP*, and *Atom*, and you want to learn more about them, including the type of support you can get from popular programming platforms.

You may even be an enthusiast who has heard about REST and wants to know what it is all about. You want to learn more about "hypermedia" and the REST architectural style so that you can build resource-oriented systems and implement sophisticated business protocols atop the Web.

This book will help.

Should I Skip This Book?

If you are looking to learn how to design websites or how to write JavaScript applications, this book will not offer you much, though there's plenty for competent AJAX developers to leverage from our approach to building backend services.

If you are looking to build mashups or systems for people to use directly, this book is probably not for you. We've focused on machine-to-machine interactions. In fact, this book is full of machines talking to one another through the Web.

We rather like it that way.

Resources

The book is accompanied by a website: *http://restinpractice.com*. There you'll find working code samples from the book, links to other resources, errata, and community information. We will make every effort to continuously update the site with more information.

What Did You Think About the Book?

We are very interested in your thoughts on this book, positive or negative. You can head to Amazon and share your thoughts by writing a review. Alternatively, O'Reilly would be more than happy to hear your views at:

   http://www.oreilly.com/catalog/9780596805821/

Errata

While we have made every effort to keep the book error-free, we have probably missed a few things. Errata give readers a way to let us know about typos, errors, and other problems with the book. You can head to the book's URI at O'Reilly in order to let us know. We'd really appreciate it:

http://www.oreilly.com/catalog/9780596805821/

Alternatively, you can reach us directly. Our contact details can be found on the book's website:

http://restinpractice.com

We will post corrections on both websites as soon as possible after confirming the identified issue. O'Reilly can also fix errata in future printings of the book and on Safari, so you can help make the book even better. We'll credit your assistance on the website and in any future editions too!

Conventions Used in This Book

The following font conventions are used in this book:

Italic
> Indicates Internet addresses, such as domain names and URIs, and new items where they are defined

`Constant width`
> Indicates method, variable, and class names in programs; also, XML element and attribute names, and HTTP idioms

`Constant width bold`
> Indicates emphasis in program code lines

NOTE

This icon signifies a tip, suggestion, or general note.

WARNING

This icon indicates a warning or caution.

Using Code Examples

This book is here to help you get your job done. In general, you may use the code in this book in your programs and documentation. You do not need to contact us for permission unless you're reproducing a significant portion of the code. For example, writing a program that uses several chunks of code from this book does not require permission. Selling or distributing a CD-ROM of examples from O'Reilly books *does* require permission. Answering a question by citing this book and quoting example code does not require permission. Incorporating a significant amount of example code from this book into your product's documentation *does* require permission.

We appreciate, but do not require, attribution. An attribution usually includes the title, authors, publisher, copyright holder, and ISBN. For example: "*REST in Practice* by Jim Webber, Savas Parastatidis, and Ian Robinson (O'Reilly). Copyright 2010 Jim Webber, Savas Parastatidis, and Ian Robinson, 978-0-596-80582-1."

If you feel your use of code examples falls outside fair use or the permission given here, feel free to contact us at *permissions@oreilly.com*.

How to Contact Us

We have tested and verified the information in this book to the best of our ability, but you may find that features have changed (or even that we have made a few mistakes!). Please let us know about any errors you find, as well as your suggestions for future editions, by writing to:

> O'Reilly Media, Inc.
> 1005 Gravenstein Highway North
> Sebastopol, CA 95472
> 800-998-9938 (in the U.S. or Canada)
> 707-829-0515 (international/local)
> 707-829-0104 (fax)

O'Reilly has a web page for this book, where we list errata, examples, and any additional information. You can access this page at:

> *http://www.oreilly.com/catalog/9780596805821/*

The book also has its own website at:

> *http://restinpractice.com*

To comment or ask technical questions about this book, send email to:

> *questions@restinpractice.com*

For more information about our books, conferences, Resource Centers, and the O'Reilly Network, see our website at:

> *http://www.oreilly.com*

Safari® Books Online

Safari Books Online is an on-demand digital library that lets you easily search over 7,500 technology and creative reference books and videos to find the answers you need quickly.

With a subscription, you can read any page and watch any video from our library online. Read books on your cell phone and mobile devices. Access new titles before they are available for print, and get exclusive access to manuscripts in development and post feedback for the authors. Copy and paste code samples, organize your favorites, download chapters, bookmark key sections, create notes, print out pages, and benefit from tons of other time-saving features.

O'Reilly Media has uploaded this book to the Safari Books Online service. To have full digital access to this book and others on similar topics from O'Reilly and other publishers, sign up for free at *http://my.safaribooksonline.com*.

Acknowledgments

We would like to thank all our community reviewers for their feedback and advice over the course of this book project. They all *volunteered* their time to help us write this book over several years: Solomon Duskis, Rafael de F. Ferreira, Glen Ford, Martin Fowler, Colin Jack, Ken Kolchier, Sriram Narayan, Eric Newcomer, Barry Norton, Chris Read, Ryan Riley, Guilherme Silveira, Halvard Skogsrud, Nigel Small, Monika Solanki, Stefan Tilkov, Jon Tirsen, Spiros Tzavellas, Steve Vinoski, Lasse Westh-Nielsen, and Herbjörn Wilhelmsen.

Our O'Reilly reviewers also deserve to be called out for their very useful and prompt feedback: William Martínez Pomares and Zach Kessin.

Our great appreciation and warm thanks go to our editor, Simon St.Laurent.

Special thanks to Mark Baker, who inspired us to write this book, educated us along the way, and never gave up on us.

This book wouldn't have been possible without the constant love and support of our families and friends. Special thanks go to Kath, Mary, Lottie, Tiger, and Elliot. It's been a long road.

Our deepest thanks to you all.

CHAPTER ONE

The Web As a Platform for Building Distributed Systems

THE WEB HAS RADICALLY TRANSFORMED THE WAY we produce and share information. Its international ecosystem of applications and services allows us to search, aggregate, combine, transform, replicate, cache, and archive the information that underpins today's digital society. Successful despite its chaotic growth, it is the largest, least formal integration project ever attempted—all of this, despite having barely entered its teenage years.

Today's Web is in large part the human Web: human users are the direct consumers of the services offered by the majority of today's web applications. Given its success in managing our digital needs at such phenomenal scale, we're now starting to ask how we might apply the Web's underlying architectural principles to building other kinds of distributed systems, particularly the kinds of distributed systems typically implemented by "enterprise application" developers.

Why is the Web such a successful application platform? What are its guiding principles, and how should we apply them when building distributed systems? What technologies can and should we use? Why does the Web model feel familiar, but still different from previous platforms? Conversely, is the Web always the solution to the challenges we face as enterprise application developers?

These are the questions we'll answer in the rest of this book. Our goal throughout is to describe how to build distributed systems based on the Web's architecture. We show how to implement systems that use the Web's predominant application protocol,

HyperText Transfer Protocol (HTTP), and which leverage REST's architectural tenets. We explain the Web's fundamental principles in simple terms and discuss their relevance in developing robust distributed applications. And we illustrate all this with challenging examples drawn from representative enterprise scenarios and solutions implemented using Java and .NET.

The remainder of this chapter takes a first, high-level look at the Web's architecture. Here we discuss some key building blocks, touch briefly on the REpresentational State Transfer (REST) architectural style, and explain why the Web can readily be used as a platform for connecting services at global scale. Subsequent chapters dive deeper into the Web's principles and discuss the technologies available for connecting systems in a web-friendly manner.

Architecture of the Web

Tim Berners-Lee designed and built the foundations of the World Wide Web while a research fellow at CERN in the early 1990s. His motivation was to create an easy-to-use, distributed, loosely coupled system for sharing documents. Rather than starting from traditional distributed application middleware stacks, he opted for a small set of technologies and architectural principles. His approach made it simple to implement applications and author content. At the same time, it enabled the nascent Web to scale and evolve globally. Within a few years of the Web's birth, academic and research websites had emerged all over the Internet. Shortly thereafter, the business world started establishing a web presence and extracting web-scale profits from its use. Today the Web is a heady mix of business, research, government, social, and individual interests.

This diverse constituency makes the Web a chaotic place—the only consistency being the consistent variety of the interests represented there; the only unifying factor the seemingly never-ending thread of connections that lead from gaming to commerce, to dating to enterprise administration, as we see in Figure 1-1.

Despite the emergent chaos at global scale, the Web is remarkably simple to understand and easy to use at local scale. As documented by the World Wide Web Consortium (W3C) in its "Architecture of the World Wide Web," the anarchic architecture of today's Web is the culmination of thousands of simple, small-scale interactions between agents and resources that use the founding technologies of HTTP and the URI.*

---

* "Architecture of the World Wide Web, Volume One," *http://www.w3.org/TR/webarch/*.

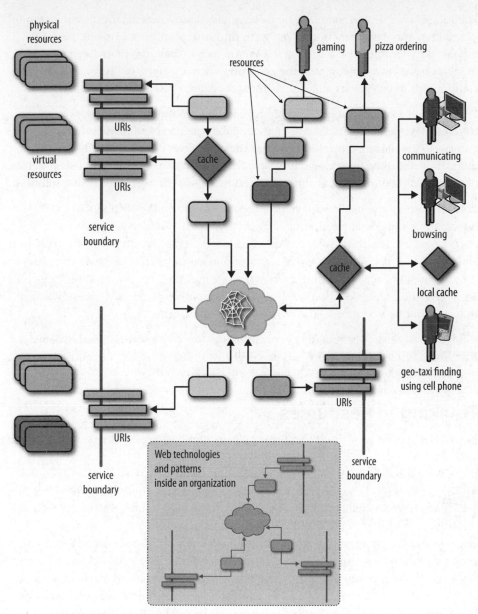

Figure 1-1. *The Web*

The Web's architecture, as portrayed in Figure 1-1, shows URIs and resources playing a leading role, supported by web caches for scalability. Behind the scenes, service boundaries support isolation and independent evolution of functionality, thereby encouraging loose coupling. In the enterprise, the same architectural principles and technology can be applied.

Traditionally we've used middleware to build distributed systems. Despite the amount of research and development that has gone into such platforms, none of them has managed to become as pervasive as the Web is today. Traditional middleware technologies have always focused on the computer science aspects of distributed systems: components, type systems, objects, remote procedure calls, and so on.

The Web's middleware is a set of widely deployed and commoditized servers. From the obvious—web servers that host resources (and the data and computation that back them)—to the hidden: proxies, caches, and content delivery networks, which manage traffic flow. Together, these elements support the deployment of a planetary-scale network of systems without resorting to intricate object models or complex middleware solutions.

This low-ceremony middleware environment has allowed the Web's focus to shift to information and document sharing using hypermedia. While hypermedia itself was not a new idea, its application at Internet scale took a radical turn with the decision to allow broken links. Although we're now nonplussed (though sometimes annoyed) at the classic "404 Page Not Found" error when we use the Web, this modest status code set a new and radical direction for distributed computing: it explicitly acknowledged that we can't be in control of the whole system all the time.

Compared to classic distributed systems thinking, the Web's seeming ambivalence to dangling pointers is heresy. But it is precisely this shift toward a web-centric way of building computer systems that is the focus of this book.

Thinking in Resources

Resources are the fundamental building blocks of web-based systems, to the extent that the Web is often referred to as being "resource-oriented." A resource is anything we expose to the Web, from a document or video clip to a business process or device. From a consumer's point of view, a resource is anything with which that consumer interacts while progressing toward some goal. Many real-world resources might at first appear impossible to project onto the Web. However, their appearance on the Web is a result of our abstracting out their useful *information* aspects and presenting these aspects to the digital world. A flesh-and-blood or bricks-and-mortar resource becomes a web resource by the simple act of making the information associated with it accessible on the Web. The generality of the resource concept makes for a heterogeneous community. Almost anything can be modeled as a resource and then made available for manipulation over the network: "Roy's dissertation," "the movie *Star Wars*," "the invoice for the books Jane just bought," "Paul's poker bot," and "the HR process for dealing with new hires" all happily coexist as resources on the Web.

Resources and Identifiers

To use a resource we need both to be able to identify it on the network and to have some means of manipulating it. The Web provides the Uniform Resource Identifier, or URI, for just these purposes. A URI uniquely identifies a web resource, and at the same time makes it addressable, or capable of being manipulated using an application protocol such as HTTP (which is the predominant protocol on the Web). A resource's URI distinguishes it from any other resource, and it's through its URI that interactions with that resource take place.

The relationship between URIs and resources is many-to-one. A URI identifies only one resource, but a resource can have more than one URI. That is, a resource can be identified in more than one way, much as humans can have multiple email addresses or telephone numbers. This fits well with our frequent need to identify real-world resources in more than one way.

There's no limit on the number of URIs that can refer to a resource, and it is in fact quite common for a resource to be identified by numerous URIs, as shown in Figure 1-2. A resource's URIs may provide different information about the location of the resource, or the protocol that can be used to manipulate it. For example, the Google home page (which is, of course, a resource) can be accessed via both *http://www.google.com* and *http://google.com* URIs.

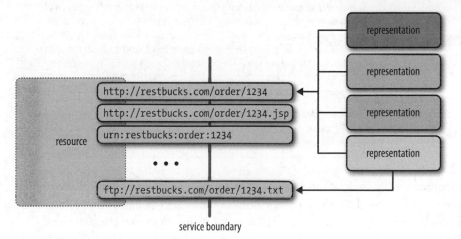

Figure 1-2. *Multiple URIs for a resource*

A URI takes the form *<scheme>:<scheme-specific-structure>*. The *scheme* defines how the
rest of the identifier is to be interpreted. For example, the *http* part of a URI such as
http://example.org/reports/book.tar tells us that the rest of the URI must be interpreted
according to the HTTP scheme. Under this scheme, the URI identifies a resource at
a machine that is identified by the hostname *example.org* using DNS lookup. It's the
responsibility of the machine "listening" at *example.org* to map the remainder of the
URI, *reports/book.tar*, to the actual resource. Any authorized software agent that understands the HTTP scheme can interact with this resource by following the rules set out
by the HTTP specification (RFC 2616).

In addition to *URI*, several other terms are used to refer to web resource identifiers.
Table 1-1 presents a few of the more common terms, including *URN* and *URL*, which
are specific forms of URIs, and *IRI*, which supports international character sets.

---

* RFC 1738, Uniform Resource Locators (URLs): *http://www.ietf.org/rfc/rfc1738.txt*.

Table 1-1. *Terms used on the Web to refer to identifiers*

Term	Comments
URI (Uniform Resource Identifier)	This is often incorrectly referred to as a "Universal" or "Unique" Resource Identifier; "Uniform" is the correct expansion.
IRI (International Resource Identifier)	This is an update to the definition of *URI* to allow the use of international characters.
URN (Uniform Resource Name)	This is a URI with "urn" as the scheme, used to convey unique names in a particular "namespace." The namespace is defined as part of the URN's structure. For example, a book's ISBN can be captured as a unique name: *urn:isbn:0131401602*.
URL (Uniform Resource Locator)	This is a URI used to convey information about the way in which one interacts with the identified resource. For example, *http://google.com* identifies a resource on the Web with which communication is possible through HTTP. This term is now obsolete, since not all URIs need to convey interaction-protocol-specific information. However, the term is part of the Web's history and is still widely in use.
Address	Many think of resources as having "addresses" on the Web and, as a result, refer to their identifiers as such.

URI Versus URL Versus URN

URLs and URNs are special forms of URIs. A URI that identifies the mechanism by which a resource may be accessed is usually referred to as a URL. HTTP URIs are examples of URLs.

If the URI has *urn* as its scheme and adheres to the requirements of RFC 2141 and RFC 2611,* it is a URN. The goal of URNs is to provide globally unique names for resources.

* *http://www.ietf.org/rfc/rfc2141.txt* and *http://www.ietf.org/rfc/rfc2611.txt*

Resource Representations

The Web is so pervasive that the HTTP URI scheme is today a common synonym for both identity and address. In the web-based solutions presented in this book, we'll use HTTP URIs exclusively to identify resources, and we'll often refer to these URIs using the shorthand term *address*.

Resources must have at least one identifier to be addressable on the Web, and each identifier is associated with one or more *representations*. A representation is a transformation or a view of a resource's state at an instant in time. This view is encoded in one or more transferable formats, such as XHTML, Atom, XML, JSON, plain text, comma-separated values, MP3, or JPEG.

For real-world resources, such as goods in a warehouse, we can distinguish between the actual object and the logical "information" resource encapsulated by an application or service. It's the information resource that is made available to interested parties through projecting its representations onto the Web. By distinguishing between the "real" and the "information" resource, we recognize that objects in the real world can have properties that are not captured in any of their representations. In this book, we're primarily interested in representations of information resources, and where we talk of a resource or "underlying resource," it's the information resource to which we're referring.

Access to a resource is always mediated by way of its representations. That is, web components *exchange* representations; they never access the underlying resource directly— the Web does not support pointers! URIs relate, connect, and associate representations with their resources on the Web. This separation between a resource and its representations promotes loose coupling between backend systems and consuming applications. It also helps with scalability, since a representation can be cached and replicated.

> ── **NOTE** ──────────────────────────────
>
> The terms *resource representation* and *resource* are often used interchangeably. It is important to understand, though, that there is a difference, and that there exists a one-to-many relationship between a resource and its representations.

There are other reasons we wouldn't want to directly expose the state of a resource. For example, we may want to serve different views of a resource's state depending on which user or application interacts with it, or we may want to consider different quality-of-service characteristics for individual consumers. Perhaps a legacy application written for a mainframe requires access to invoices in plain text, while a more modern application can cope with an XML or JSON representation of the same information. Each representation is a view onto the same underlying resource, with transfer formats negotiated at runtime through the Web's *content negotiation* mechanism.

The Web doesn't prescribe any particular structure or format for resource representations; representations can just as well take the form of a photograph or a video as they can a text file or an XML or JSON document. Given the range of options for resource representations, it might seem that the Web is far too chaotic a choice for integrating computer systems, which traditionally prefer fewer, more structured formats. However, by carefully choosing a set of appropriate representation formats, we can constrain the Web's chaos so that it supports computer-to-computer interactions.

Resource *representation formats* serve the needs of service consumers. This consumer friendliness, however, does not extend to allowing consumers to control how resources are identified, evolved, modified, and managed. Instead, services control their resources and how their states are represented to the outside world. This encapsulation is one of the key aspects of the Web's loose coupling.

The success of the Web is linked with the proliferation and wide acceptance of common representation formats. This ecosystem of formats (which includes HTML for structured documents, PNG and JPEG for images, MPEG for videos, and XML and JSON for data), combined with the large installed base of software capable of processing them, has been a catalyst in the Web's success. After all, if your web browser couldn't decode JPEG images or HTML documents, the human Web would have been stunted from the start, despite the benefits of a widespread transfer protocol such as HTTP.

To illustrate the importance of representation formats, in Figure 1-3 we've modeled the menu of a new coffee store called Restbucks (which will provide the domain for examples and explanations throughout this book). We have associated this menu with an HTTP URI. The publication of the URI surfaces the resource to the Web, allowing software agents to access the resource's representation(s).

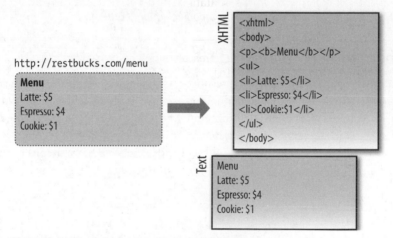

Figure 1-3. *Example of a resource and its representations*

In this example, we have decided to make only XHTML and text-only representations of the resource available. Many more representations of the same announcement could be served using formats such as PDF, JPEG, MPEG video, and so on, but we have made a pragmatic decision to limit our formats to those that are both human- and machine-friendly.

Typically, resource representations such as those in Figure 1-3 are meant for human consumption via a web browser. Browsers are the most common computer agents on the Web today. They understand protocols such as HTTP and FTP, and they know how to render formats such as (X)HTML and JPEG for human consumption. Yet, as we move toward an era of computer systems that span the Web, there is no reason to think of the web browser as the only important software agent, or to think that humans will be the only active consumers of those resources. Take Figure 1-4 as an example. An order resource is exposed on the Web through a URI. Another software agent consumes the XML representation of the order as part of a business-to-business process. Computers interact with one another over the Web, using HTTP, URIs, and representation formats to drive the process forward just as readily as humans.

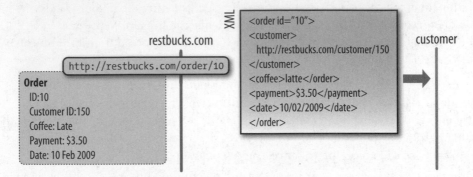

Figure 1-4. *Computer-to-computer communication using the Web*

Representation Formats and URIs

There is a misconception that different resource representations should each have their own URI—a notion that has been popularized by the Rails framework. With this approach, consumers of a resource terminate URIs with *.xml* or *.json* to indicate a preferred format, requesting *http://restbucks.com/order.xml* or *http://example.org/order.json* as they see fit. While such URIs convey intent explicitly, the Web has a means of negotiating representation formats that is a little more sophisticated.

— NOTE —

URIs should be opaque to consumers. Only the issuer of the URI knows how to interpret and map it to a resource. Using extensions such as *.xml*, *.html*, or *.json* is a historical convention that stems from the time when web servers simply mapped URIs directly to files.

In the example in Figure 1-3, we hinted at the availability of two representation formats: XHTML and plain text. But we didn't specify two separate URIs for the representations. This is because there is a one-to-many association between a URI and its possible resource representations, as Figure 1-5 illustrates.

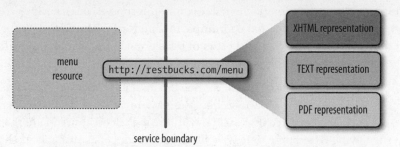

Figure 1-5. *Multiple resource representations addressed by a single URI*

Using *content negotiation*, consumers can negotiate for specific representation formats from a service. They do so by populating the HTTP Accept request header with a list of media types they're prepared to process. However, it is ultimately up to the owner of a resource to decide what constitutes a good representation of that resource in the context of the current interaction, and hence which format should be returned.

The Art of Communication

It's time to bring some threads together to see how resources, representation formats, and URIs help us build systems. On the Web, resources provide the subjects and objects with which we want to interact, but how do we act on them? The answer is that we need verbs, and on the Web these verbs are provided by HTTP methods.*

The term *uniform interface* is used to describe how a (small) number of verbs with well-defined and widely accepted semantics are sufficient to meet the requirements of most distributed applications. A collection of verbs is used for communication between systems.

> **NOTE**
>
> In theory, HTTP is just one of the many interaction protocols that can be used to support a web of resources and actions, but given its pervasiveness we will assume that HTTP is *the* protocol of the Web.

In contemporary distributed systems thinking, it's a popular idea that the set of verbs supported by HTTP—GET, POST, PUT, DELETE, OPTIONS, HEAD, TRACE, CONNECT, and PATCH—forms a sufficiently general-purpose protocol to support a wide range of solutions.

> **NOTE**
>
> In reality, these verbs are used with differing frequencies on the Web, suggesting that an even smaller subset is usually enough to satisfy the requirements of many distributed applications.

---

* Commonly, the term *verb* is used to describe HTTP actions, but in the HTTP specification the term *method* is used instead. We'll stick with *verb* in this book because *method* suggests object-oriented thinking, whereas we tend to think in terms of resources.

In addition to verbs, HTTP also defines a collection of response codes, such as 200 OK, 201 Created, and 404 Not Found, that coordinate the interactions instigated by the use of the verbs. Taken together, verbs and status codes provide a general framework for operating on resources over the network.

Resources, identifiers, and actions are all we need to interact with resources hosted on the Web. For example, Figure 1-6 shows how the XML representation of an order might be requested and then delivered using HTTP, with the overall orchestration of the process governed by HTTP response codes. We'll see much more of all this in later chapters.

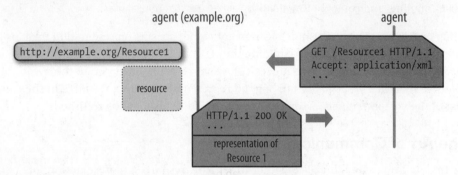

Figure 1-6. *Using HTTP to "GET" the representation of a resource*

From the Web Architecture to the REST Architectural Style

Intrigued by the Web, researchers studied its rapid growth and sought to understand the reasons for its success. In that spirit, the Web's architectural underpinnings were investigated in a seminal work that supports much of our thinking around contemporary web-based systems.

As part of his doctoral work, Roy Fielding generalized the Web's architectural principles and presented them as a framework of constraints, or an *architectural style*. Through this framework, Fielding described how distributed information systems such as the Web are built and operated. He described the interplay between resources, and the role of unique identifiers in such systems. He also talked about using a limited set of operations with uniform semantics to build a ubiquitous infrastructure that can support any type of application.* Fielding referred to this architectural style as *REpresentational State Transfer*, or REST. REST describes the Web as a distributed hypermedia application whose linked resources communicate by exchanging representations of resource state.

---

* *http://www.ics.uci.edu/~fielding/pubs/dissertation/top.htm*

Hypermedia

The description of the Web, as captured in W3C's "Architecture of the World Wide Web"*
and other IETF RFC† documents, was heavily influenced by Fielding's work. The architectural abstractions and constraints he established led to the introduction of *hypermedia
as the engine of application state*. The latter has given us a new perspective on how the Web
can be used for tasks other than information storage and retrieval. His work on REST
demonstrated that the Web is an application platform, with the REST architectural style
providing guiding principles for building distributed applications that scale well, exhibit
loose coupling, and compose functionality across service boundaries.

The idea is simple, and yet very powerful. A distributed application makes forward progress by transitioning from one state to another, just like a state machine. The difference
from traditional state machines, however, is that the possible states and the transitions
between them are not known in advance. Instead, as the application reaches a new
state, the next possible transitions are discovered. It's like a treasure hunt.

NOTE

We're used to this notion on the human Web. In a typical e-commerce solution such
as Amazon.com, the server generates web pages with links on them that corral the
user through the process of selecting goods, purchasing, and arranging delivery.

This is hypermedia at work, but it doesn't have to be restricted to humans; computers are just as good at following protocols defined by state machines.

In a hypermedia system, application states are communicated through representations
of uniquely identifiable resources. The identifiers of the states to which the application
can transition are embedded in the representation of the current state in the form of
links. Figure 1-7 illustrates such a hypermedia state machine.

---

* *http://www.w3.org/TR/webarch/*
† IETF: Internet Engineering Task Force; RFC: Request for Comments. See *http://www.ietf.org*.

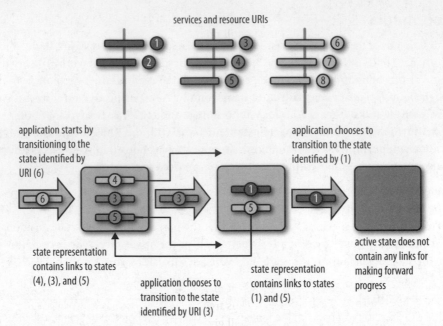

services and resource URIs

application starts by
transitioning to the
state identified by
URI (6)

application chooses to
transition to the state
identified by (1)

state representation
contains links to states
(4), (3), and (5)

application chooses to
transition to the state
identified by URI (3)

state representation
contains links to states
(1) and (5)

active state does not
contain any links for
making forward
progress

Figure 1-7. *Example of hypermedia as the engine for application state in action*

This, in simple terms, is what the famous *hypermedia as the engine of application state* or *HATEOAS* constraint is all about. We see it in action every day on the Web, when we follow the links to other pages within our browsers. In this book, we show how the same principles can be used to enable computer-to-computer interactions.

REST and the Rest of This Book

While REST captures the fundamental principles that underlie the Web, there are still occasions where practice sidesteps theoretical guidance. Even so, the term *REST* has become so popular that it is almost impossible to disassociate it from any approach that uses HTTP.* It's no surprise that the term *REST* is treated as a buzzword these days rather than as an accurate description of the Web's blueprints.

The pervasiveness of HTTP sets it aside as being special among all the Internet protocols. The Web has become a universal "on ramp," providing near-ubiquitous connectivity for billions of software agents across the planet. Correspondingly, the focus of this book is on the Web as it is used in practice—as a distributed application platform rather than as a single large hypermedia system. Although we are highly appreciative of Fielding's research, and of much subsequent work in understanding web-scale systems, we'll use the term *web* throughout this book to depict a warts-'n-all view, reserving the REST terminology to describe solutions that embrace the REST architectural style. We do this

* RFC 2616: *http://www.w3.org/Protocols/rfc2616/rfc2616.html*.

because many of today's distributed applications on the Web do not follow the REST architectural tenets, even though many still refer to these applications as "RESTful."

The Web As an Application Platform

Though the Web began as a publishing platform, it is now emerging as a means of connecting distributed applications. The Web as a platform is the result of its architectural simplicity, the use of a widely implemented and agreed-upon protocol (HTTP), and the pervasiveness of common representation formats. The Web is no longer just a successful large-scale information system, but a platform for an ecosystem of services.

But how can resources, identifiers, document formats, and a protocol make such an impression? Why, even after the dot-com bubble, are we still interested in it? What do enterprises—with their innate tendency toward safe middleware choices from established vendors—see in it? What is new that changes the way we deliver functionality and integrate systems inside and outside the enterprise?

As developers, we build solutions on top of platforms that solve or help with hard distributed computing problems, leaving us free to work on delivering valuable business functionality. Hopefully, this book will give you the information you need in order to make an informed decision on whether the Web fits your problem domain, and whether it will help or hinder delivering your solution. We happen to believe that the Web is a sensible solution for the majority of the distributed computing problems encountered in business computing, and we hope to convince you of this view in the following chapters. But for starters, here are a number of reasons we're such web fans.

Technology Support

An application platform isn't of much use unless it's supported by software libraries and development toolkits. Today, practically all operating systems and development platforms provide some kind of support for web technologies (e.g., .NET, Java, Perl, PHP, Python, and Ruby). Furthermore, the capabilities to process HTTP messages, deal with URIs, and handle XML or JSON payloads are all widely implemented in web frameworks such as Ruby on Rails, Java servlets, PHP Symfony, and ASP.NET MVC. Web servers such as Apache and Internet Information Server provide runtime hosting for services.

Scalability and Performance

Underpinned by HTTP, the web architecture supports a global deployment of networked applications. But the massive volume of blogs, mashups, and news feeds wouldn't have been possible if it wasn't for the way in which the Web and HTTP constrain solutions to a handful of scalable patterns and practices.

Scalability and performance are quite different concerns. Naively, it would seem that if latency and bandwidth are critical success factors for an application, using HTTP is not a good option. We know that there are messaging protocols with far better performance characteristics than HTTP's text-based, synchronous, request-response behavior. Yet this is an inequitable comparison, since HTTP is not just another messaging protocol; it's a protocol that implements some very specific application semantics. The HTTP verbs (and GET in particular) support caching, which translates into reduced latency, enabling massive horizontal scaling for large aggregate throughput of work.

NOTE

As developers ourselves, we understand how we can believe that asynchronous message-centric solutions are the most scalable and highest-performing options. However, existing high-performance and highly available services on the Web are proof that a synchronous, text-based request-response protocol can provide good performance and massive scalability when used correctly.

The Web combines a widely shared vision for how to use HTTP efficiently and how to federate load through a network. It may sound incredible, but through the remainder of this book, we hope to demonstrate this paradox beyond doubt.

Loose Coupling

The Web is loosely coupled, and correspondingly scalable. The Web does not try to incorporate in its architecture and technology stack any of the traditional quality-of-service guarantees, such as data consistency, transactionality, referential integrity, statefulness, and so on. This deliberate lack of guarantees means that browsers sometimes try to retrieve nonexistent pages, mashups can't always access information, and business applications can't always make immediate progress. Such failures are part of our everyday lives, and the Web is no different. Just like us, the Web needs to know how to cope with unintended outcomes or outright failures.

A software agent may be given the URI of a resource on the Web, or it might retrieve it from the list of hypermedia links inside an HTML document, or find it after a business-to-business XML message interaction. But a request to retrieve the representation of that resource is never guaranteed to be successful. Unlike other contemporary distributed systems architectures, the Web's blueprints do not provide any explicit mechanisms to support information integrity. For example, if a service on the Web decides that a URI is no longer going to be associated with a particular resource, there is no way to notify all those consumers that depend on the old URI–resource association.

This is an unusual stance, but it does not mean that the Web is neglectful—far from it. HTTP defines response codes that can be used by service providers to indicate what has happened. To communicate that "the resource is now associated with a new URI," a service can use the status code 301 Moved Permanently or 303 See Other. The Web always tries to help move us toward a successful conclusion, but without introducing tight coupling.

Business Processes

Although business processes can be modeled and exposed through web resources, HTTP does not provide direct support for such processes. There is a plethora of work on vocabularies to capture business processes (e.g., BPEL,* WS-Choreography†), but none of them has really embraced the Web's architectural principles. Yet the Web—and hypermedia specifically—provides a great platform for modeling business-to-business interactions.

Instead of reaching for extensive XML dialects to construct choreographies, the Web allows us to model state machines using HTTP and hypermedia-friendly formats such as XHTML and Atom. Once we understand that the states of a process can be modeled as resources, it's simply a matter of describing the transitions between those resources and allowing clients to choose among them at runtime.

This isn't exactly new thinking, since HTML does precisely this for the human-readable Web through the `<a href="...">` tag. Although implementing hypermedia-based solutions for computer-to-computer systems is a new step for most developers, we'll show you how to embrace this model in your systems to support loosely coupled business processes (i.e., behavior, not just data) over the Web.

Consistency and Uniformity

To the Web, one representation looks very much like another. The Web doesn't care if a document is encoded as HTML and carries weather information for on-screen human consumption, or as an XML document conveying the same weather data to another application for further processing. Irrespective of the format, they're all just resource representations.

The principle of uniformity and least surprise is a fundamental aspect of the Web. We see this in the way the number of permissible operations is constrained to a small set, the members of which have well-understood semantics. By embracing these constraints, the web community has developed myriad creative ways to build applications and infrastructure that support information exchange and application delivery over the Web.

Caches and proxy servers work precisely because of the widely understood caching semantics of some of the HTTP verbs—in particular, GET. The Web's underlying infrastructure enables reuse of software tools and development libraries to provide an ecosystem of middleware services, such as caches, that support performance and scaling. With plumbing that understands the application model baked right into the network, the Web allows innovation to flourish at the edges, with the heavy lifting being carried out in the cloud.

---

* *http://docs.oasis-open.org/wsbpel/2.0/OS/wsbpel-v2.0-OS.html*
† *http://www.w3.org/TR/2004/WD-ws-cdl-10-20041217/*

Simplicity, Architectural Pervasiveness, and Reach

This focus on resources, identifiers, HTTP, and formats as the building blocks of the world's largest distributed information system might sound strange to those of us who are used to building distributed applications around remote method invocations, message-oriented middleware platforms, interface description languages, and shared type systems. We have been told that distributed application development is difficult and requires specialist software and skills. And yet web proponents constantly talk about simpler approaches.

Traditionally, distributed systems development has focused on exposing custom behavior in the form of application-specific interfaces and interaction protocols. Conversely, the Web focuses on a few well-known network actions (those now-familiar HTTP verbs) and the application-specific interpretation of resource representations. URIs, HTTP, and common representation formats give us reach—straightforward connectivity and ubiquitous support from mobile phones and embedded devices to entire server farms, all sharing a common application infrastructure.

Web Friendliness and the Richardson Maturity Model

As with any other technology, the Web will not automatically solve a business's application and integration problems. But good design practices and adoption of good, well-tested, and widely deployed patterns will take us a long way in our journey to build great web services.

You'll often hear the term *web friendliness* used to characterize good application of web technologies. For example, a service would be considered "web-friendly" if it correctly implemented the semantics of HTTP GET when exposing resources through URIs. Since GET doesn't make any service-side state changes that a consumer can be held accountable for, representations generated as responses to GET *may* be cached to increase performance and decrease latency.

Leonard Richardson proposed a classification for services on the Web that we'll use in this book to quantify discussions on service maturity.* Leonard's model promotes three levels of service maturity based on a service's support for URIs, HTTP, and hypermedia (and a fourth level where no support is present). We believe this taxonomy is important because it allows us to ascribe general architectural patterns to services in a manner that is easily understood by service implementers.

The diagram in Figure 1-8 shows the three core technologies with which Richardson evaluates service maturity. Each layer builds on the concepts and technologies of the

* Richardson presented this taxonomy during his talk "Justice Will Take Us Millions Of Intricate Moves" at QCon San Francisco 2008; see *http://www.crummy.com/writing/speaking/2008-QCon/*.

layers below. Generally speaking, the higher up the stack an application sits, and the more it employs instances of the technology in each layer, the more mature it is.

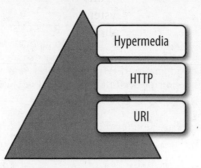

Figure 1-8. *The levels of maturity according to Richardson's model*

Level Zero Services

The most basic level of service maturity is characterized by those services that have a single URI, and which use a single HTTP method (typically POST). For example, most Web Services (WS-*)-based services use a single URI to identify an endpoint, and HTTP POST to transfer SOAP-based payloads, effectively ignoring the rest of the HTTP verbs.*

> ── **NOTE** ──────────────────────────────
>
> We can do wonderful, sophisticated things with WS-*, and it is not our intention to imply that its level zero status is a criticism. We merely observe that WS-* services do not use many web features to help achieve their goals.†

XML-RPC and Plain Old XML (POX) employ similar methods: HTTP POST requests with XML payloads transmitted to a single URI endpoint, with replies delivered in XML as part of the HTTP response. We will examine the details of these patterns, and show where they can be effective, in Chapter 3.

Level One Services

The next level of service maturity employs many URIs but only a single HTTP verb. The key dividing feature between these kinds of rudimentary services and level zero services is that level one services expose numerous logical resources, while level zero services tunnel all interactions through a single (large, complex) resource. In level one services,

---

* The suite of SOAP-based specifications and technologies, such as WSDL, WS-Transfer, WS-MetadataExchange, and so forth. Refer to *http://www.w3.org/2002/ws/* as a starting point. We'll discuss Web Services and their relationship to the Web in Chapter 12.

† The report of the "Web of Services" workshop is a great source of information on this topic: *http://www.w3.org/2006/10/wos-ec-cfp.html*.

however, operations are tunneled by inserting operation names and parameters into a URI, and then transmitting that URI to a remote service, typically via HTTP GET.

> **NOTE**
>
> Richardson claims that most services that describe themselves as "RESTful" today are in reality often level one services. Level one services can be useful, even though they don't strictly adhere to RESTful constraints, and so it's possible to accidentally destroy data by using a verb (GET) that should not have such side effects.

Level Two Services

Level two services host numerous URI-addressable resources. Such services support several of the HTTP verbs on each exposed resource. Included in this level are Create Read Update Delete (CRUD) services, which we cover in Chapter 4, where the state of resources, typically representing business entities, can be manipulated over the network. A prominent example of such a service is Amazon's S3 storage system.

> **NOTE**
>
> Importantly, level two services use HTTP verbs and status codes to coordinate interactions. This suggests that they make use of the Web for robustness.

Level Three Services

The most web-aware level of service supports the notion of hypermedia as the engine of application state. That is, representations contain URI links to other resources that might be of interest to consumers. The service leads consumers through a trail of resources, causing application state transitions as a result.

> **NOTE**
>
> The phrase *hypermedia as the engine of application state* comes from Fielding's work on the REST architectural style. In this book, we'll tend to use the term *hypermedia constraint* instead because it's shorter and it conveys that using hypermedia to manage application state is a beneficial aspect of large-scale computing systems.

GET on Board

Can the same principles that drive the Web today be used to connect systems? Can we follow the same principles driving the human Web for computer-to-computer scenarios? In the remainder of this book, we will try to show why it makes sense to do exactly that, but first we'll need to introduce our business domain: a simple coffee shop called Restbucks.

CHAPTER TWO

Introducing Restbucks: How to GET a Coffee, Web Style

WHILE DEVELOPING THIS BOOK, we wondered how we would describe web-based distributed systems in an accessible scenario. We weren't really keen on the idea of yet another e-commerce or trading application. We thought it would have been too boring. We certainly wouldn't want to read a book like that, so why write one?

Instead, we chose a modest scenario that doesn't try to steal the focus from the technical discussion or try to become the star of the book. We didn't want to engage in long explanations about complex problem domains. So, in that spirit, this is the only chapter where we'll discuss our domain in depth. The other chapters will deal with technical concepts.

The inspiration for our problem domain came from Gregor Hohpe's brilliant observation on how a Starbucks coffee shop works. In his popular blog entry, Gregor talks about synchronous and asynchronous messaging, transactions, and scaling the message-processing pipeline in an everyday situation.*

We liked the approach very much, and as believers that "imitation is the sincerest form of flattery," we adopted Gregor's scenario at the heart of this book. We freely admit that our need for good coffee while writing also encouraged us to focus on our own little coffee megastore: Restbucks.

---

* *http://www.enterpriseintegrationpatterns.com/ramblings/18_starbucks.html*

Restbucks: A Little Coffee Shop with Global Ambitions

Throughout this book, we'll frame our problems and web-based solutions in terms of a coffee shop called Restbucks, which grows from modest beginnings to become a global enterprise. As Restbucks grows, so do its needs for better organization and more efficient use of resources for operating at larger scale. We'll show how Restbucks operations can be implemented with web technologies and patterns to support all stages of the company's growth.

While nothing can replace the actual experience of waiting in line, ordering, and then tasting the coffee, our intention is to use our coffee shop to showcase common problems and demonstrate how web technologies and patterns can help solve them, within both Restbucks and systems development in general. The Restbucks analogy does not describe every aspect of the coffee shop business; we chose to highlight only those problems that help support the technical discussion.

Actors and Conversations

The Restbucks service and the resources that it exposes form the core of our discussion. Restbucks has actors such as customers, cashiers, baristas, managers, and suppliers who must interact to keep the coffee flowing.

In all of the examples in this book, computers replace human-to-human interactions. Each actor is a program that interacts through the Web to drive business processes hosted by Restbucks services. Even so, our business goals remain: we want to serve good coffee, take payments, keep the supply chain moving, and ultimately keep the business alive.

Interactions occur through HTTP using formats that are commonly found on the Web. We chose to use XML since it's widely supported and it's relatively easy for humans to parse, as we can see in Figure 2-1. Of course, XML isn't our only option for integration; others exist, such as plain text, HTML forms, and JSON. As our problem domain becomes more sophisticated in later chapters, we'll evolve our formats to meet the new requirements.

Figure 2-1. *XML-based exchange between a customer and a waiter*

As in real life, things won't always go according to plan in Restbucks. Coffee machines may break, demand may peak, or the shop may have supply chain difficulties. Given the importance of scaling, fault reporting, and error handling in integration scenarios, we will identify relevant web technologies and patterns that we can use to cope with such problems.

Boundaries

In Restbucks, we draw boundaries around the actors involved in the system to encapsulate implementation details and emphasize the interactions between systems. When we order a coffee, we don't usually care about the mechanics of the supply chain or the details of the shop's internal coffee-making processes. Composition of functionality and the introduction of façades with which we can interact are common practices in system design, and web-based systems are no different in that respect. For example, in Figure 2-2 the customer doesn't need to know about the waiter–cashier and cashier–barista interactions when he orders a cup of coffee from the waiter.

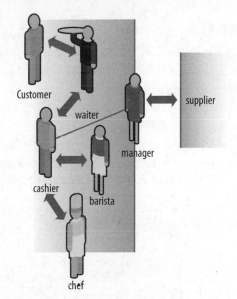

Figure 2-2. *Boundaries help decompose groups of interactions*

The Web's principles, technologies, and patterns can be used to model and implement business processes whether they are exposed across the boundaries of the Restbucks service or used for internal functionality. That is, the Web pervades Restbucks' infrastructure, providing connectivity to both external partners and customers and internal systems!

The Menu

Restbucks prides itself on the variety of products it serves and allows customers to customize their coffee with several options. Table 2-1 shows some of the products and options offered. Throughout the book, we'll see how these options manifest themselves in service interactions and the design decisions regarding their representation.

Table 2-1. *Sample catalog of products offered by Restbucks*

Product name	Customization option
Latte	Milk: skim, semi, whole
Cappuccino	Size: small, medium, large
Espresso	Shots: single, double, triple
Tea	
Hot chocolate	Milk: skim, semi, whole
	Size: small, medium, large
	Whipped cream: yes, no
Cookie	Kind: Chocolate chip, ginger
All	Consume location: take away, in shop

Sample Interactions

Let's set the scene for the remainder of the book by examining some of the typical interactions between the main actors. Subsequent chapters build on these scenarios, expand them further, and introduce new ones.

Customer–Barista

Restbucks takes its first steps as a small, neighborhood coffee shop. A barista is responsible for everything: taking orders, preparing the coffee, receiving payment, and giving receipts. Figure 2-3 shows the interaction between a customer and a barista.

Figure 2-3. *A simple interaction between a customer and a barista*

If we want to model the interactions of Figure 2-3 on the Web, we have to consider the representation of the order (its format), the communication mechanism (HTTP), and the resources themselves (addressed by URIs). However, we're not immune to classic problems in distributed systems. For example, we still have to address the following issues:

Notification

We need mechanisms for sending notification. For example, we need to be able to signal that a coffee is ready.

Handling communication failures

We need a solution for handling failures that occur during the flow of an interaction, including timeouts.

Transactions

We have to consider the implementation of transactions. For example, we need to consider whether we will optimistically accept orders even though we may not be able to fulfill a small number of them in exception cases (such as running out of coffee beans).

Scalability

We need to consider how to cope with large volumes of customers or repeated requests.

At the outset, Restbucks employs only a single barista. As a result, every customer has to wait in line, as shown in Figure 2-4. This approach doesn't scale well for a busy shop, nor does it scale for web-based systems where we often need to scale individual services or components independently to manage load.

Figure 2-4. *Customers will have to wait*

Customer–Cashier–Barista

Although Restbucks stems from modest roots, its coffee quality and increasingly positive reputation help it to continue to grow. To help scale the business, Restbucks decides to hire a cashier to speed things up. With a cashier busy handling the financial aspects of the operation, the barista can concentrate on making coffee. The customer's interactions aren't affected, but Restbucks now needs to coordinate the cashier's and barista's tasks with a low-ceremony approach using sticky notes. The interactions (or protocol) between the cashier and the barista remain hidden from customers. Now that we've got two moving parts in our coffee shop, we need to think about how to encapsulate them, which leads to the scenario shown in Figure 2-5.

Figure 2-5. *A cashier helps the barista*

By implementing this scheme, Restbucks decouples ordering and payment from the coffee preparation. In turn, it is possible for Restbucks to abstract the inner workings of the shop through a façade. While the customer gets the same good coffee, Restbucks is free to innovate and evolve its implementation behind the scenes.

Decoupling payments and drink preparation allows Restbucks to optimize available resources. The barista can now look at the queue of orders and make decisions for the optimal preparation sequence. Furthermore, decoupling tasks allows Restbucks to scale operations by adding more cashiers and baristas independently as demand increases. We will see that the Web makes adding capacity straightforward.

Toolbox

Although Restbucks is contrived to provide a simple problem domain, we will be using real web technologies. We will choose the appropriate URIs for identifying resources, identify the formats that meet business and technical requirements, and apply the necessary patterns for modeling and implementing interactions. With that in mind, it's time to see some examples of how web technologies might be used to model interactions.

Restbucks Formats

We discussed formats for resource representations in general terms in Chapter 1, but here we'll introduce formats that Restbucks uses in its business. All Restbucks resources are represented by XML documents defined in the `http://restbucks.com` namespace and identified on the Web as the media types `application/xml` and `application/vnd.restbucks+xml` for standard XML processing and Restbucks-specific processing, respectively.*

NOTE

We've chosen XML-based formats deliberately for this book since they're easily understood and readable by humans. However, we shouldn't see XML as the only option. As we discussed in Chapter 1, real web services use myriad other formats, depending on the application.

Example 2-1 shows an order represented in XML, with the different specialties and options drawn from the Restbucks menu. We've chosen element names for the XML representations that are easy for humans to understand, even though that is not strictly necessary for machine-to-machine communication. However, we believe there's value in making representations—like source code—as self-descriptive as possible, so we'll pay the modest price of a few more bytes per interaction to keep the representations human-friendly.

---

* For now, it's easiest to think of both of these as simply XML documents. However, in Chapter 5, when we think about hypermedia and REST, we'll need to differentiate more critically.

Example 2-1. *A Restbucks order resource represented in XML format*

```
POST /order HTTP/1.1
Host: restbucks.com
Content-Type:application/vnd.restbucks+xml
Content-Length: 243

<order xmlns="http://schemas.restbucks.com/order">
  <location>takeAway</location>
  <item>
    <name>latte</name>
    <quantity>1</quantity>
    <milk>whole</milk>
    <size>small</size>
  </item>
</order>
```

A cashier service receiving the order in Example 2-1 will lodge the order and respond with the XML in Example 2-2, which contains the representation of a newly created order resource.

Example 2-2. *Acknowledging the order with a custom XML format*

```
HTTP/1.1 200 OK
Content-Length: 421
Content-Type: application/vnd.restbucks+xml
Date: Sun, 3 May 2009 18:22:11 GMT
<order xmlns="http://restbucks.com" xlmns:atom="http://www.w3.org/2005/Atom">
  <location>takeAway</location>
  <item>
    <name>latte</name>
    <quantity>1</quantity>
    <milk>whole</milk>
    <size>small</size>
  </item>
  <cost>3.00</cost>
  <currency>GBP</currency>
  <atom:link rel="payment" type="application/xml"
href="http://restbucks.com/order/1234/payment"/>
</order>
```

A customer receiving a response such as that in Example 2-2 can be assured that its order has been received and accepted by the Restbucks service. The order details are confirmed in the reply and some additional information is contained, such as the payment amount and currency, a timestamp for when the order was received, and a <link> element that identifies another resource with which the customer is expected to interact to make a payment.

Modeling Protocols and State Transitions

Using `<atom:link>` elements to describe possible next steps through a service protocol should feel familiar; after all, we're quite used to links and forms being used to guide us through HTML pages on the Web. In particular, we're comfortable with e-commerce sites guiding us through selecting products, confirming delivery addresses, and taking payment by stringing together a set of pages into a workflow. Unwittingly, we have all been driving a business protocol via HTTP using a web browser!

It's remarkable that the Web has managed to turn us humans into robots who follow protocols, but we take it for granted nowadays. We even think the concept of computers driving protocols through the same mechanism is new, yet this is the very essence of building distributed systems on the Web: using hypermedia to describe protocol state machines that govern interactions between systems.

Although hypermedia-based protocols are useful in their own right, they can be strengthened using microformats, such as hCard.† If we embed semantic information about the next permissible steps in a protocol inside the hypermedia links, we raise the level of abstraction. This allows us to change the underlying URIs as the system evolves without breaking any consumers, as well as to declare and even change a protocol dynamically without breaking existing consumers.

---

* See *http://tools.ietf.org/html/rfc4287*.

† See *http://microformats.org*. Microformats and other semantics-related technologies will be discussed in Chapter 10.

Of course, we *can* break existing consumers, but only if we remove or redefine something on which they rely. We're safe to add new, optional protocol steps or to change
the URIs contained within the links, provided we keep the microformat vocabulary
consistent.

Figure 2-6 shows an example of a protocol state machine as it evolves through the
interactions between the customer, cashier, and barista. The state machine will not
generally show the total set of permissible states, only those choices that are available during any given interaction to take the consumer down a particular path. If the
customer cancels its order, it will not be presented with the option to pay the bill or
add specialties to its coffee. The description of an application's state machine might be
exposed in its entirety as part of metadata associated with a service, if the service provider chooses to do so. However, a state machine might change over time, even as a
customer interacts with the service.

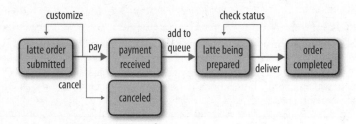

Figure 2-6. *Modeling state machines dynamically*

Here Comes the Web

Restbucks provides a domain that allows us to think of the Web as a platform for
building distributed systems. We'll continue to expand Restbucks' domain throughout the book as more ambitious scenarios are introduced. Expect to see the addition of
third-party services, security, more coordination of interactions, and scalability measures. Along the way, we'll dip into topics as diverse as manageability, semantics, notifications, queuing, caching, and load balancing, all neatly tied together by the Web.

But to start with, we're going to see how we can integrate systems using the bedrock
of web technologies: the humble URI.

CHAPTER THREE

Basic Web Integration

UNDERSTANDING EVERY ASPECT OF THE WEB'S ARCHITECTURE can be a challenging task. That task, coupled with the everyday pressure to deliver working software, means we are often time-poor. Fortunately, we can start to use some web techniques immediately, at least for simple integration problems.

> —— **WARNING** ————————————————————
>
> Although the techniques we cover in this chapter are simple, they come with an enormous health warning. If you find yourself using them, it's probably an indication that you should reconsider your design and use some of the techniques described in later chapters instead.

We will learn more sophisticated patterns and techniques as requirements become more challenging. The approaches we're going to consider in this chapter are simple to pick up. For now, we're going to focus on two simple web techniques for application integration: URI tunneling and Plain Old XML (POX). These techniques allow us to quickly integrate systems using nothing more than web servers, URIs, and, for POX, a little XML.

Lose Weight, Feel Great!

Many enterprise integration projects (wrongly) begin with middleware. Architects invest significant efforts in making sure the middleware products they choose support the latest features for reliable messaging, security, transactions, and so on. The chosen platform is then dropped onto development teams, whose working life is subsequently spent trying to figure out what to do with all the software they've been told to use.

Of course, there's an element of caricature in these sentiments, yet sometimes, while we're working on enterprise systems, there's a nagging doubt about whether we really need all these clever middleware capabilities. Sometimes, while reflecting over the business drivers for the solution, we realize that the features, cost, and complexity inherent in enterprise solutions are really overkill for our purposes.

Choosing to base your system on the Web may raise some pointed questions. After all, any respectable software project includes a middleware product. However, it's also customary for projects to overrun cost and time; and although only anecdotal evidence supports the claim, working with large, complex middleware is often a factor in project underperformance. Conversely, the projects we've worked on using approaches based on HTTP have rarely disappointed. We believe this is a function of low-ceremony, highly commoditized tools that are highly amenable to contemporary iterative software delivery.

The fact is that not all integration problems need middleware-based solutions. Going lightweight can significantly reduce the complexity of a system and reduce its cost, risk, and time to deployment. Going lightweight also allows us to favor simpler technology from commodity development platforms. And leveraging HTTP gives us straightforward application-to-application connectivity with very little effort, not least because HTTP libraries are so pervasive in modern computer systems.

NOTE ───────────────────────────────────

As web-based integration becomes more popular, it's inevitable that increasingly ambitious middleware tools will come to market. However, we hold to the principle that we should start with the simplest possible system architecture, and add middleware to the mix only if it implements something that would be risky or costly to implement for ourselves. Throughout this book, we hope to show that "risky" or "costly" software is really the opposite of what the Web offers.

A Simple Coffee Ordering System

One of the best ways to understand how to apply a new technique is to build a simple system. For our purposes, that system is the Restbucks coffee ordering service, which allows remote customers to lodge their coffee orders with the Restbucks server. Our goal here is to understand how application code and server infrastructure fit within the overall solution.

Choosing Integration Points for a Service

Though services and service-oriented architecture often seem arcane, in reality a service is nothing more than a technical mechanism for hosting some business logic. The way we allow others to consume services—business logic—over a network is the core topic of this book, and we think the Web is the right kind of system to support networks of collaborative business processes.

While the Web gives us infrastructure and patterns to deal with connecting systems together, we still need to invest effort in designing services properly so that they will be robust when exposed to remote consumers and easy to maintain as those consumers become more demanding.

Choosing integration points is not difficult; we look for appropriate modules in our software through which we expose business-meaningful functionality. To illustrate, let's look at the example in Figure 3-1. Although the example is (deliberately) simplistic, it shows a logical architecture, with customer software agents interacting with Restbucks to place orders. To support this scenario, we have to expose existing Restbucks functionality for external consumption by mapping the internal domain model onto the network domain (and absolutely not exposing the internal details directly, because that is the path that leads to tight, brittle coupling).

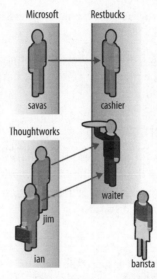

Figure 3-1. *Customers from other companies interact with Restbucks employees*

NOTE

Integration-friendly interfaces tend to be at the edges of the system (or at least on the periphery of major modules), rather than deep inside the domain model or data access tiers. In that spirit, we should look for interfaces that encapsulate recognizable concepts from the problem domain with reasonably coarse granularity.

We've learned from building service-oriented systems that good integration points tend to encapsulate business-meaningful processes or workflows. Generally, we don't want to expose any technical or implementation details. It's often worth writing façades (adapting Fowler's Remote Façade pattern*) to support this idiom if no existing

---

* *http://martinfowler.com/eaaCatalog/remoteFacade.html*

interfaces or integration points are suitable. For Restbucks services, we will look for the following kinds of integration points:

- Methods that encapsulate some (coarse-grained) business concept rather than low-level technical detail

- Methods that support existing presentation logic, such as controllers in the Model-View-Controller* pattern

- Scripts or workflows that orchestrate interactions with a domain model

Conversely, we avoid integration points such as:

- Data access methods, especially those that are transactional

- Properties/getters and setters

- Anything that binds to an existing presentation tier such as reusing view logic or screen scraping

These aren't hard-and-fast rules, and you may find solutions where this guidance doesn't apply. In those cases, be pragmatic and do the simplest thing that will work without compromising the solution.

A Simple Service Architecture

We'll be using HTTP requests and responses to transfer information between the customers and Restbucks. To keep things simple from a client programming point of view, we'll abstract the remote behavior of the cashier behind a local-looking façade that we've termed the *client-side cashier dispatcher*.

NOTE

Hiding remote behavior from a consuming application is known to be a poor idea.[†] Still, we've deliberately written examples in this chapter to highlight that HTTP is all too often abused for remote procedure calls.

Hiding remote activity is usually a poor design choice that may have surprisingly harsh consequences at runtime when an operation that appears local malfunctions because of hidden remote activity over the network.

In Figure 3-2, network code that customer objects use is encapsulated behind the dispatcher's interface (a waiter in real life), which gives a necessary clean separation of concerns between plumbing code and our application-level objects. On the server side,

---

* *http://en.wikipedia.org/wiki/Model-view-controller*

† Waldo et al. argue in their seminal paper, "A Note on Distributed Computing," that abstracting away remote behavior is an anti-pattern, and we agree. The "remoteness" of a service is one of the important nonfunctional characteristics that we have to cater to if we're going to build good systems.

we follow suit with a server-side cashier dispatcher, which isolates server-side objects from the underlying network protocol.

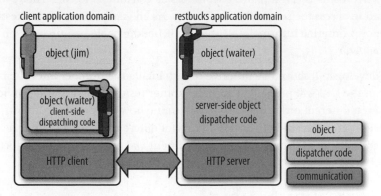

Figure 3-2. *HTTP remote procedure call architecture*

Figure 3-2 shows a very simple architecture that uses a tiered approach to system integration. It can be built using common components from *any* decent development framework, even using different platforms. Since both the customer client application and the cashier service agree on HTTP as the wire protocol, they can very easily interoperate.

We still need to write some code to turn this design into a working solution, but it will only be a little plumbing between the dispatchers and web client, and between the server APIs and the business logic. However, before we get down to coding, we need to understand one more technique used to design and share service contracts with consumers: URI templates.

URI Templates

Often in distributed systems, service providers offer machine-readable metadata that describes how clients should bind to and interact with services. For example, you would normally use interface definition languages (IDLs) such as Web Services Description Language (WSDL) for WS-* Web Services, or CORBA-IDL when implementing CORBA systems. On the Web, various metadata technologies are used to describe service contracts, including URI templates, which describe syntactic patterns for the set of URIs that a service supports.

When used properly, URI templates can be an excellent tool for solution designers. As we discuss in later chapters, they are particularly useful for internal service documentation.

WARNING ───

When used poorly, URI templates increase coupling between systems and lead to brittle integration. In subsequent chapters, we'll see how *hypermedia* greatly reduces the necessity to share URI templates outside services.

Intuitive URIs

A service advertising URI templates encourages its consumers to construct URIs that can be used to access the service's functionality. As an example, let's take Restbucks, which exposes ordering information through URI-addressable resources, such as *http://restbucks.com/order/1234*.

To a web developer, it should be intuitive that changing the number after the final / character in the URI will probably result in another resource representation being returned for a different order. It's easy to determine how to vary the contents of a simple URI programmatically to access a range of different resources from the service. Intuitive URIs are great things—they convey intent *and* provide a level of documentation for services.

From Intuitive URIs to URI Templates

While intuitive URIs are encouraged, intuition alone isn't enough. As implementers of web services, we need to provide richer metadata for consumers. This is where URI templates come into their own, since they provide a way to parameterize URIs with variables that can be substituted at runtime. In turn, they can therefore be used to describe a service contract.*

Since we want to help Restbucks' customers use our services as easily as possible, we would like to provide a description of how these services can be accessed through a URI. A URI template fits the bill here. An example of a URI template that describes valid URIs for the service is `http://restbucks.com/order/{order_id}`.

The markup in curly braces, `{order_id}`, is an invitation to Restbucks customers to "fill in the gaps" with sensible values. By substituting those parameters, customers address different coffee orders hosted at Restbucks. In most cases, this is as far as we might go with URI templates, and in fact, many web services are documented with just a handful of similar URI templates.†

> ──── **NOTE** ────
>
> Calculating a URI from a URI template and a set of variables is known as *expansion*, and the URI template draft specifies a set of rules governing it. Those rules include how to substitute variables with values, including dealing with some of the quirkier aspects of internationalized character sets.

---

* This is actually a little white lie for now. We will see in later chapters that service contracts aren't just constituted from URIs and URI templates, but from a conflation of URIs, the HTTP uniform interface, and media types.

† Plus a handful of verbs and status codes with some explanatory text.

Of course, we're not limited to single variables in our URI templates, and it's common to represent hierarchies in URIs. For example, the `http://restbucks.com/order/{year}/{month}/{day}` template supports accessing all of the orders for a given date, allowing consumers to vary the year, month, and day variables to access audit information.

In addition to variable substitution, URI templates support several more sophisticated use cases that allow advanced URI template expansions. The URI Template specification contains a set of worked examples for each operator, which is useful if you are dealing with sophisticated URI structures. However, we only use simple variable substitution in this book, which covers the majority of everyday uses.

Using URI Templates

One of the major uses for URI templates is as human- and machine-readable documentation. For humans, a good URI template lays out a map of the service with which we want to interact; for machines, URI templates allow easy and rapid validation of URIs that should resolve to valid addresses for a given service and so can help automate the way clients bind to services.

> ––––– **NOTE** ––
>
> In practice, we prefer URI templates as a means of internal documentation for services, rather than as contract metadata. We find that URI templates are fine as a shorthand notation for communication within the context of a system, but as a mechanism for describing contracts, we think they risk introducing tight coupling. In the next chapter, we'll show why, but for now, we'll accept that they have drawbacks and use them anyway.

We can put URI templates into practice immediately, staring with the most basic HTTP integration option: URI tunneling.

URI Tunneling

When we order coffee from Restbucks, we first select the drinks we'd like, then we customize those drinks in terms of size, type of milk (if any), and other specialties such as flavorings. Once we've decided, we can convey our order to the cashier who handles all incoming orders. Of course, we have numerous options for how to convey our order to a cashier, and on the Web, URI tunneling is the simplest.

URI tunneling uses URIs as a means of transferring information across system boundaries by encoding the information within the URI itself.* This can be a useful technique, because URIs are well understood by web servers (of course!) and web client software. Since web servers can host code, this allows us to trigger program execution

---

* In more robust integration schemes, URIs identify only resources, which can then be manipulated using HTTP verbs and metadata.

by sending a simple HTTP GET or POST request to a web server, and gives us the ability to parameterize the execution of that code using the content of the URI. Whether we choose GET or POST depends on our intentions: retrieving information should be tunneled through GET, while changing state really ought to use POST.

On the Web, we use GET in situations where we want to *retrieve* a resource's state representation, rather than deliberately *modify* that state. When used properly, GET is both *safe* and *idempotent*.

By safe, we mean a GET request generates no server-side side effects for which the client can be held responsible. There may still be side effects, but any that do occur are the sole responsibility of the service. For example, many services log GET requests, thereby changing some part of their state. But GET is still safe. Server-side logging is a private affair; clients don't ask for something to be logged when they issue a GET request.

An idempotent operation is one that generates absolute side effects. Invoking an idempotent operation repeatedly has the same effect as invoking it once. Because GET exhibits no side effects for which the consumer can be held responsible, it is naturally idempotent. Multiple GETs of the same URI generate the same *result*: they retrieve the state of the resource associated with that URI at the moment the request was received, even if they return different *data* (which can occur if the resource's state changes in between requests).

When developing services we *must* preserve the semantics of GET. Consumers of our resources expect our service to behave according to the HTTP specification (RFC 2616). Using a GET request to do something other than retrieve a resource representation—such as delete a resource, for example—is simply an abuse of the Web and its conventions.

POST is much less strict than GET; in fact, it's often used as a wildcard operation on the Web. When we use POST to tunnel information through URIs, it is expected that changes to resource state will occur. To illustrate, let's look at Figure 3-3.

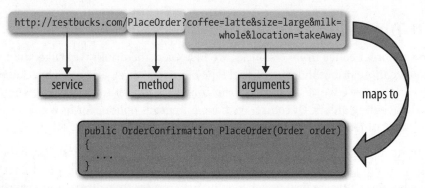

Figure 3-3. *Mapping method calls to URIs*

Figure 3-3 shows an example of a URI used to convey order information to the ordering service at *http://restbucks.com* in accordance with the URI template http://restbucks.com/PlaceOrder?coffee={type}&size={size}&milk={milk}&location={location}. On the server side, this URI is matched against the template and is deconstructed, and an instance of the class `Order` is populated based on the values extracted from the URI path. The `Order` instance is then dispatched into a method called `PlaceOrder()`, which in turn will execute the business logic for that order. Once the `PlaceOrder` method has completed, it will return an order ID that is serialized into the response, as shown in Figure 3-4.

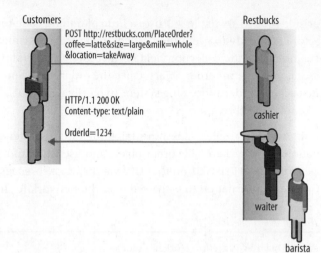

Figure 3-4. *HTTP request/response for URI tunneling*

Knowing the URI structure, response format, and expected behavior allows us to write code to support simple remote interactions. As it happens, using URI tunneling means our code turns out to be very simple. First, let's take a look at how we might build this on the server side in .NET code in Example 3-1.

Example 3-1. *Extracting business objects from a URI*

```
public void ProcessPost(HttpListenerContext context)
{
  // Parse the URI
  Order order = ParseUriForOrderDetails(context.Request.QueryString);
  string response = string.Empty;
  if (order != null)
  {
    // Process the order by calling the mapped method
    var orderConfirmation = RestbucksService.PlaceOrder(order);
    response = "OrderId=" + orderConfirmation.OrderId.ToString();
  }
  else
  {
    response = "Failure: Could not place order.";
  }
```

```
    // Write to the response stream
    using (var sw = new StreamWriter(context.Response.OutputStream))
    {
      sw.Write(response);
    }
  }
}
```

The .NET server-side code in Example 3-1 uses a little plumbing code to bind to an `HttpListener` before it is ready to use. When called, the `ProcessPost` method parses out order information from the collection held in the `context.Request.QueryString` property and uses it to create an order object. Once the order has been created, it's dispatched to some backend order processing system (typically a barista!), and the order confirmation is returned to the caller.

The client code shown in Example 3-2 is also straightforward to understand. It simply extracts information out of a client-side `Order` object and uses that information to form a URI. It then performs an HTTP POST on that URI via the `HttpWebRequest` instance, which causes the order information to be passed over the network to the server.

Example 3-2. *URI-tunneling client*

```
public OrderConfirmation PlaceOrder(Order order)
{
  // Create the URI
  var sb = new StringBuilder("http://restbucks.com/PlaceOrder?");
  sb.AppendFormat("coffee={0}", order.Coffee.ToString());
  sb.AppendFormat("&size={0}", order.Size.ToString());
  sb.AppendFormat("&milk={0}", order.Milk.ToString());
  sb.AppendFormat("&location={0}", order.ConsumeLocation.ToString());

  // Set up the POST request
  var request = HttpRequest.Create(sb.ToString()) as HttpWebRequest;
  request.Method = "POST";
  // Send the POST request
  var response = request.GetResponse();

  // Read the contents of the response
  OrderConfirmation orderConfirmation = null;
  using (var sr = new StreamReader(response.GetResponseStream()))
  {
    var str = sr.ReadToEnd();
    // Create an OrderConfirmation object from the response
    orderConfirmation = new OrderConfirmation(str);
  }

  return orderConfirmation;
}
```

When the remote server responds, the client software simply parses the contents of the HTTP response and creates an OrderConfirmation object before continuing processing.

NOTE

Although we use the same name for the OrderConfirmation class in both the client and the service, there is no requirement for the client and the service to share a type system. In fact, we generally advise against sharing types across service boundaries since it introduces tight coupling, which prevents independent evolution of the coupled systems.

Is URI Tunneling a Good Idea?

Services that use URI tunneling are categorized as level one services by Richardson's maturity model. Figure 3-5 highlights that URIs are a key concept in such services, but no other web technologies are embraced. Even HTTP is only used as a transport protocol for moving URIs over the Web.

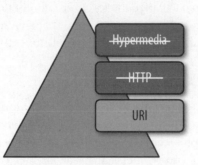

Figure 3-5. *URI tunneling is only at level one in Richardson's maturity model*

Though tunneling remote method calls through URIs is not a sophisticated way of integrating systems, sometimes it can be web-friendly. First, we have URIs, and naming resources through URIs is the first step toward any web-friendly solution. Second, if an HTTP GET request doesn't change any state on a service, we're within the guidelines of the Web Architecture, which suggests that GET should be "safe." For example, the URI *http://restbucks.com/GetOrder?orderId=1234* could either represent a URI-encoded operation called GetOrder or equally identify a resource (a coffee order) through an ugly (verb-embedded-in-URI) convention. From the point of view of a consumer of the service, this is indeed the observable behavior.

However, in the general case, URI tunneling isn't web-friendly because URIs are used to encode operations rather than identify resources that can be manipulated through HTTP verbs. Ordering a coffee is a demonstration of how URI tunneling can be used to violate the *safe and idempotent* nature of HTTP GET. For example, a client executing GET (instead of POST) on *http://restbucks.com/PlaceOrder?id=1234&coffee=latte* expects that a new coffee order (a resource) will be created as a result, whereas if we follow good web practices, GET requests to a URI shouldn't result in new resources being created as a side effect—the result is neither safe (it changes server state) nor idempotent (it cannot be repeated without further side effects).*

> **WARNING**
>
> Where we use URIs as the conduit for transferring information to services, often instead of building a level one service, *we end up building many level zero services*. For instance, the set of URIs permitted by `http://restbucks.com/GetOrder?orderId={id}` is really nothing more than a shorthand for many level zero services, all of which support a single URI and a single verb.

Although it might be tempting to offer services based on URI tunneling, we must be aware that consumers of those services will expect to be able to GET URIs without going against the Web Architecture guidelines. Violating the widely shared understanding of GET will lead to trouble!

Using POST instead of GET goes some way toward alleviating the problem of unintended side effects, though it doesn't change the level zero mindset of a service. POST requests are understood to have side effects by the Web so that any intermediaries (such as caches) don't get confused. Either way, the trade-offs in URI tunneling are not nice!

POX: Plain Old XML over HTTP

For all its ingenuity (and potential drawbacks too), URI tunneling is a little out of the ordinary for enterprise integration—using addresses to convey business intent is, after all, strange. Our second web-based approach to lightweight integration puts us squarely back in familiar territory: messaging. The Plain Old XML (POX) web-style approach to application integration uses HTTP requests and responses as the means to transfer documents, encoded in regular XML, between a client and a server. It's a lot like SOAP, but without the SOAP envelope or any of the other baggage.

POX is appealing as an approach because XML gives us platform independence, while the use of HTTP gives us practically ubiquitous connectivity between systems. Furthermore, compared to the URI tunneling approach, dealing with XML allows us to use more complex data structures than can be encoded in a URI, which supports more sophisticated integration scenarios.

That's not to say that POX is on a par with enterprise message-oriented middleware, because clearly it isn't. We have to remember that POX is a pattern, not a platform, and POX can't handle transacted or reliable message delivery in a standard way.

---

* This is a simplification. In reality, resources may be created, but the client issuing the GET request is not accountable for them. If your service supports resource creation—and remember, in some cases, these may be physical resources such as payments—on GET requests, you are responsible for them, not your clients!

However, for integration problems that don't need such advanced features, XML over HTTP has the virtue of being a simple and highly commoditized solution.

In the remainder of this chapter, we'll revisit our ordering system and show how it can be developed using the POX approach. We'll see how to use web servers and request-response XML message exchanges to enable remote procedure calls between systems, and we'll also take the time to understand the strengths and weaknesses of the approach.

Using XML and HTTP for Remote Procedure Calls

POX uses HTTP POST to transfer XML documents between systems. On both sides of the message exchange, the information contained in the XML payload is converted into a format suitable for making local method calls.

It's often said of POX that, like URI tunneling, it too tunnels through the Web. Since POX uses HTTP as a transport protocol, all application semantics reside inside the XML payload and much of the metadata contained in the HTTP envelope is ignored. In fact, POX uses HTTP merely as a synchronous, firewall-friendly transport protocol for convenience. POX would work just as well over a TCP connection, message queues, or even SOAP as it does over HTTP.

While POX isn't rocket science, it can form the basic pattern for constructing distributed systems that are relatively simple to build and easy to deploy, as shown in Figure 3-6.

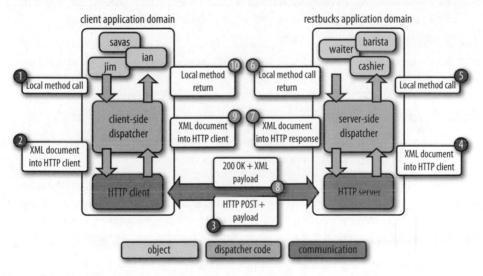

Figure 3-6. *Canonical POX interaction*

Figure 3-6 shows the typical execution model of a POX-based solution:

1. A POX invocation begins with an object in the customer's system calling into a dispatcher that presents a local interface to the remote Restbucks service.

2. The dispatcher converts the values of parameters it receives from the application-level object into an XML document. It then calls into an HTTP client library to pass the information over the network.

3. The HTTP client POSTs the XML payload from the dispatcher to the remote service.

4. The web server hosting the ordering service accepts the incoming POST and passes the request's context to the server-side dispatcher.

5. The server-side dispatcher translates the XML document into a local method call on an object in the Restbucks service.

6. When the method call returns, any returned values are passed to the dispatcher.

7. The dispatcher creates an XML document from the returned values and pushes it back into the web server.

8. The web server generates an HTTP response (habitually using a 200 status code) with the XML document from the dispatcher as the entity body. It sends the response over the same HTTP connection used for the original request.

9. The HTTP client on the customer's system receives the response and makes the XML payload available to the client-side dispatcher.

10. The client-side dispatcher extracts values from the XML response into a return value, which is then returned to the original calling object, completing the remote call.

POX isn't a hard pattern. Indeed, all this should be familiar given that most RPC systems have a very similar design, so let's press on with applying what we know.

POX Away!

Now that we're comfortable with the approach, the next stage is to determine the APIs that we're going to expose as integration points on the server side.

Let's consider this in terms of server-side methods such as `public OrderConfirmation PlaceOrder(Order order) { ... }`. Given this method signature, our challenge is to figure out what information needs to flow between the client and server. Once we know that, then we need to design XML messages for the remote call we want to support.

We'll expose this method to remote clients in a similar way to URI tunneling: by making it part of the URI to which clients will POST XML-encoded arguments. For example, the method `PlaceOrder()` can be exposed through the URI *http://restbucks. com/PlaceOrder*. Unlike URI tunneling, though, the order information will be sent as an XML document in the HTTP request from the customer. The result of the method call, the `OrderConfirmation` instance, is serialized as an XML document and sent back as the payload of an HTTP response with 200 OK as its status, as we see in Figure 3-7.

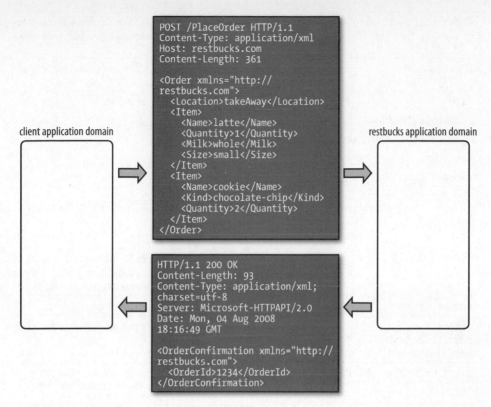

```
POST /PlaceOrder HTTP/1.1
Content-Type: application/xml
Host: restbucks.com
Content-Length: 361

<Order xmlns="http://
restbucks.com">
  <Location>takeAway</Location>
  <Item>
    <Name>latte</Name>
    <Quantity>1</Quantity>
    <Milk>whole</Milk>
    <Size>small</Size>
  </Item>
  <Item>
    <Name>cookie</Name>
    <Kind>chocolate-chip</Kind>
    <Quantity>2</Quantity>
  </Item>
</Order>
```

```
HTTP/1.1 200 OK
Content-Length: 93
Content-Type: application/xml;
charset=utf-8
Server: Microsoft-HTTPAPI/2.0
Date: Mon, 04 Aug 2008
18:16:49 GMT

<OrderConfirmation xmlns="http://
restbucks.com">
  <OrderId>1234</OrderId>
</OrderConfirmation>
```

client application domain

restbucks application domain

Figure 3-7. *POX wire-level protocol*

Figure 3-7 shows a typical interaction with the Restbucks ordering service. The request message for our service is an HTTP POST with an XML document representing an order as the payload. There's nothing in this exchange that comes as a surprise to us here since we're familiar with XML, and the headers are commonplace in our everyday use of the World Wide Web. Still, it's illustrative to take a closer look, starting with the headers:

POST /PlaceOrder HTTP/1.1	This tells the web server hosting the Restbucks service that the incoming request is a POST and is directed at the /PlaceOrder resource (bound to a method call in the service implementation) using HTTP 1.1.
Content-Type: application/xml	This indicates that the body content is XML intended for machine consumption.
Host: restbucks.com	This is the hostname of the machine providing the service.
Content-Length: 361	This is the size (in bytes) of the body content.

The XML document contained in the body is quite simple too. Let's take a look at that now:

`<Order xmlns=... >`	This is an `Order` serialized into XML. The service will use this XML content to create and populate objects when it receives the message.
`<Location />`	This is the place where the order will be consumed, either `inStore` or `takeAway`.

`<Item>`
  `<Name>latte</Name>`
  `<Quantity>1</Quantity>`
  `...`
`</Item>`
	Finally, we have the items we're ordering.

We can break down the response from the server along similar lines. First, there are the HTTP headers:

`HTTP/1.1 200 OK`	The request was processed happily by the service at least as far as the HTTP part is concerned. Nothing related to the network protocol failed and nothing threw a top-level exception.
`Content-Length: 93`	This indicates the length of the reply in bytes.
`Content-Type: application/xml; charset=utf-8`	This indicates that we can expect our response to be XML-encoded as UTF-8.
`Server: Microsoft-HTTPA-PI/2.0`	This indicates the type of web server that handled the request (in this case, Microsoft's development server).
`Date: Mon, 28 Jul 2008 19:18:03 GMT`	This is the timestamp when the response was generated.

Finally, we have the body of the response:

`<OrderConfirmation xmlns= "http://restbucks.com">`
  `<OrderId>1234</OrderId>`
`</OrderConfirmation>`
	This is the confirmation that the order was processed on the server side, with an ID that uniquely identifies the order.

Using this approach, creating a simple XML remote procedure call solution using `POST` is well within our grasp. Implementing the solution is just a matter of writing the business logic, and deploying any plumbing code needed onto a web server. As we'll see in the next section, that's straightforward to do.

Server-side POX implementation in .NET

To show just how straightforward POX can be, let's start off by looking at the server-side implementation. Unlike the URI tunneling example, where most of the effort was spent writing XML plumbing code between the web server and methods on business objects, here we'll delegate that work to a framework (see Example 3-3). For this example, we've chosen Microsoft's Windows Communication Foundation (WCF), which supports exposing resources via HTTP and is widely used in enterprise environments.

Example 3-3. *Server-side POX implementation with WCF*

```
[ServiceContract(Namespace = "http://restbucks.com")]
public interface IRestbucksService
{
  [OperationContract]
  [WebInvoke(Method = "POST", UriTemplate="/PlaceOrder")]
  OrderConfirmation PlaceOrder(Order order);
}
```

The code in Example 3-3 follows the typical WCF idiom of separating the contract from the implementation of the service (which we are not showing for the sake of brevity*). WCF allows us to express a set of addressable resources using URI templates and HTTP methods set at compile time.

In this case, we have a service contract expressed as in the IRestbucksService interface. The PlaceOrder method of the interface is annotated with the OperationContract attribute, which indicates to WCF that the method will become part of the service contract and be exposed over the network. Since this is a POX solution, we use the WebInvoke attribute on the PlaceOrder() method to indicate to WCF that this method is going to handle HTTP POST messages to the /PlaceOrder URI. Under the covers, the WCF framework will help us to handle message dispatching, serialization, and deserialization.

All that is left to do now is to implement the IOrderingService interface with our business logic and put the necessary deployment configuration options in the *app.config* file to run the service.

Server-side POX in Java

For the Java RestbucksService, we've chosen to go back to basics and use the Servlet API rather than a higher-level framework. In doing so, we hope to show that, just like URI tunneling, we don't need much in the way of frameworks or libraries to get POX services working (see Example 3-4).

Example 3-4. *Java POX service using the HTTP servlet*

```
public class RestbucksService extends HttpServlet {

  protected void doPost(HttpServletRequest request,
                        HttpServletResponse response)
                          throws ServletException, IOException {

    // Initialization code omitted for brevity
    try {
      BufferedReader requestReader = request.getReader();
      PrintWriter responseWriter = response.getWriter();
```

* Go to *http://restinpractice.com* to find full examples.

```
                String xmlRequest = extractPayload(requestReader);
                Order order = createOrder(xmlRequest);
                OrderConfirmation confirmation = restbucksService.place(order);
                embedPayload(responseWriter, confirmation);
            } finally {
                // Cleanup code omitted for brevity
            }
        }
    }
```

The Java implementation shown in Example 3-4 uses the RestbucksService (which extends the base HttpServlet class) to listen for HTTP POST requests via the overridden doPost method. The doPost method is invoked on receiving an HTTP POST at a URI registered with the servlet container.

Inside the doPost method, we call extractPayload(...) to handle the translation of XML found in the HTTP requests to Java objects. Internally, that method merely uses XPath expressions to extract values from the request, and using those values creates domain objects for computation. On the return path, the embedPayload(...) method does the reverse by serializing an OrderConfirmation object into the HTTP response.

All the interaction with the HTTP aspects of the system is done through the servlet framework classes. It is the requestReader and responseWriter objects that provide access to the underlying network messages. Using the requestReader, we're able to extract information from request payloads. Using the requestWriter, we're able to compute response messages for the consumer.

NOTE ──

Servlets aren't the only way to write POX (or any other kind of web) services. In later chapters, we'll use more recent frameworks such as JAXB (for serialization) and JAX-RS (for our HTTP API) to build Java-based services. It's interesting to see how we trade off control for simplicity in those frameworks compared to our servlet implementation.

───

Client-Side POX Implementation

Constructing a client API to consume POX services is well supported in modern development platforms. We already know the simple protocol that the service supports because we designed it (or where we're consumer third-party services we'll have read the service's documentation, XML templates, WADL, or WSDL), and so the next task is to implement that protocol atop an HTTP client library and encapsulate it behind a set of friendly method calls.

Using the .NET WebClient to invoke the ordering service

Numerous options are available to us for developing clients for our ordering service. For this example, we're going to make use of an object-to-XML (de)serializer and the default HTTP client implementation from the .NET platform.

For our .NET client, all we have to do is to create the appropriate XML payload and then use a WebClient object to send our request message to the service via an HTTP POST. Once the service responds, we pick out the XML from the response and use it to set any return values. The PlaceOrder method shown in Example 3-5 is a typical client-side implementation.

Example 3-5. *.NET client-side POX bindings*

```
public OrderConfirmation PlaceOrder(Item[] items)
{
  // Serialize our objects
  XmlDocument requestXml = CreateXmlRequest(items);
  var client = new WebClient();

  var ms = new MemoryStream();
  requestXml.Save(ms);

  client.Headers.Add("Content-Type", "application/xml");
  ms = new MemoryStream(client.UploadData("http://restbucks.com/PlaceOrder",
                        null, ms.ToArray()));
  var responseXml = new XmlDocument();
  responseXml.Load(ms);
  return CreateOrderConfirmation(responseXml);
}
```

---

* WADL (Web Application Description Language) can be used to describe XML over HTTP interfaces. We'll show how WADL can be used in the next chapter. If you're too curious to wait until then, see *https://wadl.dev.java.net/wadl20060802.pdf*.

There are a few interesting aspects to the code in Example 3-5. First, we encapsulate the creation of an XML request in the CreateXmlRequest() method. The generated XML document is converted to a byte stream, which is then given to the UploadData() method of our WebClient instance, resulting in an HTTP POST request. If you recall the server implementations, both the verb and the URI are used to dispatch and deserialize the message, so the client must provide both of these.

The next point of interest is that we add the header Content-Type: application/xml to the HTTP envelope to help the receiving web server identify the content as XML, rather than name-value pairs, JSON, or other formats. After sending the HTTP POST via the UploadData(...) method, we finally load the payload of the response to an XmlDocument instance and deserialize it to an OrderConfirmation object. Although this isn't a particularly sophisticated way to process the response, it highlights the fact that we don't need any fancy frameworks (though such frameworks exist, and may be helpful) to make POX work—just commodity XML and HTTP processing.

> **NOTE**
>
> It goes without saying that in production code, we'll need to check for any reported errors from the service. Also, we need to make sure the returned XML payload is indeed deserializable to an OrderConfirmation object. It's all part of the fun of writing robust software.

Using the Apache Commons HttpClient in Java

In the Java implementation, we follow the same pattern that we used for .NET using the HttpClient from the Apache Commons library to handle the HTTP parts of the solution. In Example 3-6, we see how the HttpClient is used to POST string-constructed XML payloads to the service.

Example 3-6. *Java client for the ordering service*

```
public class OrderingClient {

  private static final String XML_HEADING = "<?xml version=\"1.0\"?>\n";
  private static final String NO_RESPONSE = "Error: No response. ";

  public String placeOrder(String[] items) throws Exception {

    String request = ... // XML request string creation omitted for brevity
    String response = sendRequestPost(request, "http://restbucks.com/PlaceOrder");

    Document xmlResponse =
      DocumentBuilderFactory.newInstance().newDocumentBuilder()
        .parse(new InputSource(new StringReader(response)));
    // XML response handling omitted for brevity
  }
```

```
    private String sendRequestPost(String request, String uri)
                                   throws IOException, HttpException {
      PostMethod method = new PostMethod(uri);
      method.setRequestHeader("Content-type", "application/xml");
      method.setRequestBody(XML_HEADING + request);
      try {
       new HttpClient().executeMethod(method);
       return new String(method.getResponseBody(),"UTF-8");
      } finally {
       method.releaseConnection();
      }
    }
   }
```

In the placeOrder() method of Example 3-6, the order information is serialized to a string representation of an XML document that is used as the payload of the HTTP request. The implementation of the sendRequestPost method provides the actual connectivity to the service. Each business method, such as placeOrder, uses sendRequest-Post to interact with the remote service.

NOTE ───

In both the Java and .NET clients, any notion of timeliness is omitted for the sake of clarity. In any production code, the client will have to deal with the latency of interacting with the remote service, and be prepared to time out if the service doesn't respond quickly enough. Otherwise, a crashed service will cause the client to lock too!

The body of the sendRequestPost method acts as our client-side dispatcher. It sets the content type header and fills the body of the HTTP request with the XML content. It places the XML payload of a request into an HTTP POST message and extracts the response message from the service before releasing the connection, leaving the placeOrder method free to deal with business logic.

XML-RPC

At this point, it's worth mentioning another HTTP and XML remoting technology, called XML-RPC.* The premise of XML-RPC is to support simple remote procedure calls across different kinds of systems using XML as a common intermediate format.

As such, XML-RPC falls under the POX umbrella because it uses HTTP POST and XML to make remote calls. XML-RPC attempts to standardize the way in which such information is represented in the HTTP request and response payloads so that different applications don't have to invent their own formats and mappings to type systems. As a result,

* *http://www.xmlrpc.com/*

reusable components/frameworks are available to hide the plumbing details and provide comfortable programming abstractions.

—— **NOTE** ——————————————————————————————

XML-RPC defines an interoperable, lowest-common-denominator type system in terms of XML structures. This type system can easily be mapped into those of common enterprise platforms such as .NET and Java. However, the architectural style is equivalent to POX and suffers from the same drawbacks. Equally, we do not advise deploying XML-RPC, though in niche situations where some form of POX is unavoidable, at least there is tool support and documentation for XML-RPC that may swing the balance in its favor.

For comparison, Example 3-7 shows how a request to call the `PlaceOrder()` method might look when conveyed as the payload of an XML-RPC request.

Example 3-7. PlaceOrder() method call represented in XML-RPC

```
<methodCall>
  <methodName>PlaceOrder</methodName>
  <params>
    <param>
      <value>
        <string>1234</string>
      </value>
    </param>
    <param>
      <array>
        <data>
          <struct>
            <member>
              <name>Name</name>
              <value>
                <string>latte</string>
              </value>
            </member>
            <member>
              <name>Quantity</name>
              <value>
                <int>1</int>
              </value>
            </member>
  ...
  <!-- The rest of the XML is omitted... It looks very similar -->

</methodCall>
```

What About When Things Go Wrong?

The POX approach is popular because it's lightweight and almost universally interoperable, but it is not an especially robust pattern.

POX services are given a level zero rating by Richardson's maturity model. Figure 3-8 highlights that none of the fundamental web technologies is prevalent in such services. Instead, level zero services use HTTP for a transport protocol and a single URI as a well-known endpoint through which XML messages can be exchanged.

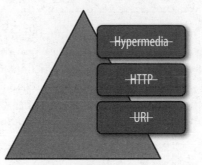

Figure 3-8. *POX services are level zero in Richardson's maturity model*

Although POX, like URI tunneling, lacks sophistication, it does have some useful characteristics. For example, since POX uses HTTP as a transport protocol, it's often very firewall-friendly and, as we have seen, straightforward to implement.

However, the POX approach ignores the Web as a platform and merely uses it as a tunnel for tunneling remote calls. The scalability, reliability, and robustness characteristics, which are inherent in the Web's architecture, are not necessarily available to POX-based solutions. As a result, POX solutions tend to be limited to simpler integration problems. If POX is to be used for mission-critical scenarios, significant additional effort is required to deal with failure cases where messages go missing and services fail (and may potentially recover).

Although it's a simple approach and one that is comfortingly familiar, POX, like URI tunneling, has extremely limited applicability. Our advice in general is to avoid POX like the plague!

We Are Just Getting Started

URI tunneling and POX over HTTP integration emphasize simplicity and accessibility over robustness. While proprietary systems such as Java RMI and .NET remoting may be more robust than passing XML documents or URIs around, the web-based approaches are often simpler and more widely supported.

Using URIs or XML for transferring messages over HTTP directly enables platform-independent integration. This is important in the enterprise context, given that most enterprises have a heterogeneous range of systems to support. Since URI and XML processing components are commonplace, using these tools for simple integration projects is an appealing, low-ceremony option—provided that we understand each approach's strengths and weaknesses, as we've discussed.

As you might expect, URI tunneling and POX are not the only strategies available to developers when building distributed systems on the Web. You probably wouldn't be reading this book if that were the case! Embracing functionality provided by the Web can alleviate many of the more difficult issues around reliability that we've covered in this chapter. In the next chapter, we'll start to look past using HTTP as a transport protocol and begin to think about how to use the Web as a platform for building distributed systems.

CHAPTER FOUR

CRUD Web Services

IN THE PRECEDING CHAPTER, we saw how GET and POST can be used to tunnel information to remote services through URIs and how POST can be used to transfer XML documents between services. However, as more interesting distributed system scenarios emerge, we rapidly reach the limit of what we can accomplish with those verbs. We need to expand our vocabulary in order to support more advanced interactions.

In this chapter, we'll introduce two new HTTP verbs to our repertoire: PUT and DELETE. Alongside GET and POST, they form the set of verbs required to fully support the Create, Read, Update, Delete (CRUD) pattern for manipulating resources across the network.

> ── **NOTE** ─────────────────────────
> From here onward, we consider the network and HTTP as an integral part of our distributed application, not just as a means of transporting bytes over the wire.

Through CRUD, we'll take our first steps along the path to enlightenment using HTTP as an application protocol instead of a transport protocol, and see how the Web is really a big framework for building distributed systems.

Modeling Orders As Resources

In Restbucks, orders are core business entities, and as such, their life cycles are of real interest to us from a CRUD perspective. For the ordering parts of the Restbucks business process, we want to create, read, update, and delete order resources like so:

• Orders are created when a customer makes a purchase.

• Orders are frequently read, particularly when their preparation status is inquired.

- Under certain conditions, it may be possible for orders to be updated (e.g., in cases where customers change their minds or add specialties to their drinks).

- Finally, if an order is still pending, a customer may be allowed to cancel it (or delete it).

Within the ordering service, these actions (which collectively constitute a protocol) move orders through specific life-cycle phases, as shown in Figure 4-1.

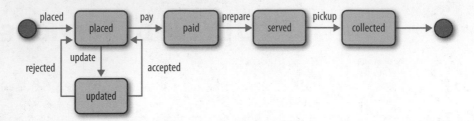

Figure 4-1. *Possible states for an order*

Each operation on an order can be mapped onto one of the HTTP verbs. For example, we use POST for creating a new order, GET for retrieving its details, PUT for updating it, and DELETE for, well, deleting it. When mixed with appropriate status codes and some commonsense patterns, HTTP can provide a good platform for CRUD domains, resulting in really simple architectures, as shown in Figure 4-2.

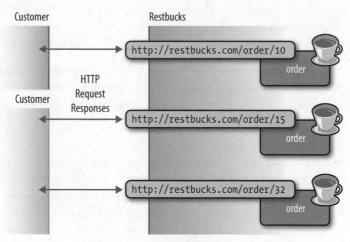

Figure 4-2. *CRUD ordering service high-level architecture*

While Figure 4-2 exemplifies a very simple architectural style, it actually marks a significant rite of passage toward embracing the Web's architecture. In particular, it highlights the use of URIs to identify and address orders at Restbucks, and in turn it supports HTTP-based interactions between the customers and their orders.

Since CRUD services embrace both HTTP and URIs, they are considered to be at level two in Richardson's maturity model. Figure 4-3 shows how CRUD services embrace URIs to identify resources such as coffee orders and HTTP to govern the interactions with those resources.

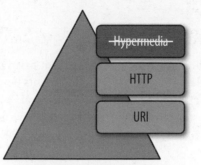

Figure 4-3. *CRUD services reach level two on Richardson's maturity model*

Level two is a significant milestone in our understanding. Many successful distributed systems have been built using level two services. For example, Amazon's S3 product is a classic level two service that has enabled the delivery of many successful systems built to consume its functionality over the Web. And like the consumers of Amazon S3, we'd like to build systems around level two services too!

Building CRUD Services

When you're building a service, it helps to think in terms of the behaviors that the service will implement. In turn, this leads us to think in terms of the contract that the service will expose to its consumers. Unlike other distributed system approaches, the contract that CRUD services such as Restbucks exposes to customers is straightforward, as it involves only a single concrete URI, a single URI template, and four HTTP verbs. In fact, it's so compact that we can provide an overview in just a few lines, as shown in Table 4-1.

Table 4-1. *The ordering service contract overview*

Verb	URI or template	Use
POST	/order	Create a new order, and upon success, receive a `Location` header specifying the new order's URI.
GET	/order/{orderId}	Request the current state of the order specified by the URI.
PUT	/order/{orderId}	Update an order at the given URI with new information, providing the full representation.
DELETE	/order/{orderId}	Logically remove the order identified by the given URI.

The contract in Table 4-1 provides an understanding of the overall life cycle of an order. Using that contract, we can design a protocol to allow consumers to create, read, update, and delete orders. Better still, we can implement it in code and host it as a service.

Creating a Resource with POST

We first saw HTTP POST in Chapter 3, when we used it as an all-purpose transfer
mechanism for moving Plain Old XML (POX) documents between clients and servers.
In that example, however, the semantics of POST were very loose, conveying only that
the client wished to "transfer a document" to the server with the hope that the server
would somehow process it and perhaps create a response document to complete the
interaction.

As the Restbucks coffee ordering service evolves into a CRUD service, we're going to
strengthen the semantics of POST and use it as a request to create an order resource
within the service. To achieve this, the payload of the POST request will contain a
representation of the new order to create, encoded as an XML document. Figure 4-4
illustrates how this works in practice.

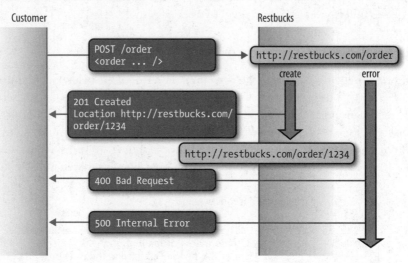

Figure 4-4. *Creating an order via POST*

In our solution, creating an order at Restbucks requires that we POST an order representation in XML to the service.* The create request consists of the POST verb, the
ordering service path (relative to the Restbucks service's URI), and the HTTP version.
In addition, requests usually include a Host header that identifies the receiving host of

---

* We've adopted the convention used in *RESTful Web Services* (*http://oreilly.com/catalog/9780596529260/*)
  by Leonard Richardson and Sam Ruby (O'Reilly), where POST is used for creation and the server
  determines the URI of the created resource.

the server being contacted and an optional port number. Finally, the media type (XML in this case) and length (in bytes) of the payload is provided to help the service process the request. Example 4-1 shows a network-level view of a POST request that should result in a newly created order.

Example 4-1. *Creating a coffee order via POST*

```
POST /order HTTP/1.1
Host: restbucks.com
Content-Type: application/xml
Content-Length: 239

<order xmlns="http://schemas.restbucks.com/order">
  <location>takeAway</location>
  <items>
    <item>
      <name>latte</name>
      <quantity>1</quantity>
      <milk>whole</milk>
      <size>small</size>
    </item>
  </items>
</order>
```

Once the service receives the request, its payload is examined and, if understood, dispatched to create a new order resource.

> **—— NOTE ——————————————————————————**
>
> The receiving service may choose to be strict or lax with respect to the syntactic structure of the order representation. If it is strict, it may force compliance with an order schema. If the receiving service chooses to be lax (e.g., by extracting the information it needs through XPath expressions), its processing logic needs to be permissive with respect to the representation formats that might be used.
>
> Robust services obey Postel's Law,* which states, "be conservative in what you do; be liberal in what you accept from others." That is, a good service implementation is very strict about the resource representations it generates, but is permissive about any representations it receives.

If the POST request succeeds, the server creates an order resource. It then generates an HTTP response with a status code of 201 Created, a Location header containing the newly created order's URI, and confirmation of the new order's state in the response body, as we can see in Example 4-2.

---

* See *http://en.wikipedia.org/wiki/Jon_Postel#Postel.27s_Law*.

Example 4-2. *Response to successful order creation*

```
HTTP/1.1 201 Created
Content-Length: 267
Content-Type: application/xml
Date: Wed, 19 Nov 2008 21:45:03 GMT
Location: http://restbucks.com/order/1234

<order xmlns="http://schemas.restbucks.com/order">
  <location>takeAway</location>
  <items>
    <item>
      <name>latte</name>
      <quantity>1</quantity>
      <milk>whole</milk>
      <size>small</size>
    </item>
  </items>
  <status>pending</status>
</order>
```

The Location header that identifies the URI of the newly created order resource is important. Once the client has the URI of its order resource, it can then interact with it via HTTP using GET, PUT, and DELETE.

While a 201 Created response is the normal outcome when creating orders, things may not always go according to plan. As with any computing system—especially distributed systems—things can and do go wrong. As service providers, we have to be able to deal with problems and convey helpful information back to the consumer in a structured manner so that the consumer can make forward (or backward) progress. Similarly, as consumers of the ordering service, we have to be ready to act on those problematic responses.

Fortunately, HTTP offers a choice of response codes, allowing services to inform their consumers about a range of different error conditions that may arise during processing. The Restbucks ordering service has elected to support two error responses when a request to create a coffee order fails:

- 400 Bad Request, when the client sends a malformed request to the service

- 500 Internal Server Error, for those rare cases where the server faults and cannot recover internally

With each of these responses, the server is giving the consumer information about what has gone wrong so that a decision can be made on how (or whether) to make further progress. It is the consumer's job to figure out what to do next.

> ——— **NOTE** ————————————————————————
>
> 500 Internal Server Error as a catchall error response from the ordering service isn't very descriptive. In reality, busy baristas might respond with 503 Service Unavailable and a Retry-After header indicating that the server is temporarily too busy to process the request. We'll see event status codes and how they help in building robust distributed applications in later chapters.

When the ordering service responds with a 400 status, it means the client has sent an order that the server doesn't understand. In this case, the client shouldn't try to resubmit the same order because it will result in the same 400 response. For example, the malformed request in Example 4-3 doesn't contain the drink that the consumer wants, and so cannot be a meaningful coffee order irrespective of how strict or lax the server implementation is in its interpretation. Since the <name> element is missing, the service can't interpret what kind of drink the consumer wanted to order, and so an order resource cannot be created. As a result, the service must respond with an error.

Example 4-3. A malformed order request

```
POST /order HTTP/1.1
Host: restbucks.com
Content-Type: application/xml
Content-Length: 216

<order xmlns="http://schemas.restbucks.com/order">
  <location>takeAway</location>
  <items>
    <item>
      <quantity>1</quantity>
      <milk>whole</milk>
      <size>small</size>
    </item>
  </items>
</order>
```

On receiving the malformed request, the server responds with a 400 status code, and includes a description of why it rejected the request,* as we see in Example 4-4.

---

* This is demanded of us by the HTTP specification.

Example 4-4. *Response to a malformed order request*

```
HTTP/1.1 400 Bad Request
Content-Length: 250
Content-Type: application/xml
Date: Wed, 19 Nov 2008 21:48:11 GMT

<order xmlns="http://schemas.restbucks.com/order">
  <location>takeAway</location>
  <items>
    <item>
      <!-- Missing drink type -->
      <quantity>1</quantity>
      <milk>whole</milk>
      <size>small</size>
    </item>
  </items>
</order>
```

To address this problem, the consumer must reconsider the content of the request and ensure that it meets the criteria expected by the ordering service before resubmitting it. If the service implementers were being particularly helpful, they might provide a textual or machine-processable description of why the interaction failed to help the consumer correct its request, or even just a link to the service's documentation. The ordering service won't create an order in this case, and so retrying with a corrected order is the right thing for the consumer to do.

In the case of a 500 response, the consumer may have no clear understanding about what happened to the service or whether the request to create an order succeeded, and so making forward progress can be tricky. In this case, the consumer's only real hope is to try again by repeating the POST request to lodge an order.

> **NOTE**
>
> In the general case, consumers can try to recompute application state by GETting the current representations of any resources whose URIs they happen to know. Since GET doesn't have side effects (that consumers can be held accountable for), it's safe to call repeatedly until a sufficiently coherent picture of the system state emerges and forward or backward progress can be made. However, at this stage in our ordering protocol, the consumer knows nothing other than the entry point URI for the coffee ordering service, *http://restbucks.com/order*, and can only retry.

On the server side, if the ordering service is in a recoverable state, or may eventually be, its implementation should be prepared to clean up any state created by the failed interaction. That way, the server keeps its own internal order state consistent whether the client retries or not.

Implementing create with POST

Now that we have a reasonable strategy for handling order creation, let's see how to put it into practice with a short code sample (see Example 4-5).

Example 4-5. *A Java servlet implementation for creating a coffee order*

```java
protected void doPost(HttpServletRequest request, HttpServletResponse response) {
  try {
    Order order = extractOrderFromRequest(request);
    if(order == null) {
      response.setStatus(HttpServletResponse.SC_BAD_REQUEST);
    } else {
      String internalOrderId = saveOrder(order);
      response.setHeader("Location", computeLocationHeader(request,
                         internalOrderId));
      response.setStatus(HttpServletResponse.SC_CREATED);
    } catch(Exception ex) {
        response.setStatus(HttpServletResponse.SC_INTERNAL_SERVER_ERROR);
    }
  }
}
```

The Java code in Example 4-5 captures the pattern we're following for processing a POST request on the service side. We extract an order from the POST request content and save it into a database. If that operation fails, we'll conclude that the request from the consumer wasn't valid and we'll respond with a 400 Bad Request response, using the value SC_BAD_REQUEST. If the order is successfully created, we'll embed that order's URI in a Location header and respond with a 201 status (using the SC_CREATED value) to the consumer. If anything goes wrong, and an Exception is thrown, the service returns a 500 response using the SC_INTERNAL_SERVER_ERROR value.

Reading Resource State with GET

We've already seen how GET can be used to invoke remote methods via URI tunneling, and we've also seen it being used to recover from 500 response codes during order creation. From here onward, we'll be using GET explicitly for retrieving state information—resource representations—from services. In our case, we are going to use GET to retrieve coffee orders from Restbucks that we've previously created with POST.

Using GET to implement the "R" in CRUD is straightforward. We know that after a successful POST, the service creates a coffee order at a URI of its choosing and sends that URI back to the consumer in the HTTP response's Location header. In turn, that URI allows consumers to retrieve the current state of coffee order resources, as we see in Figure 4-5.

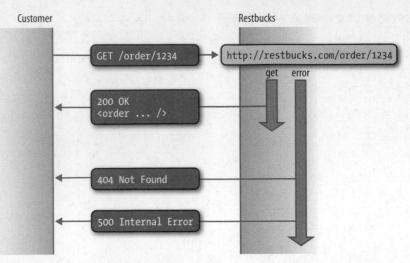

Figure 4-5. *Reading a coffee order with GET*

Performing GET on an order's URI is very simple. At the HTTP level, it looks like Example 4-6.

Example 4-6. *Requesting an order via GET*

```
GET /order/1234 HTTP/1.1
Host: restbucks.com
```

If the GET request is successful, the service will respond with a 200 OK status code and a representation of the state of the resource, as shown in Example 4-7.

Example 4-7. *Reading an order with GET*

```
HTTP/1.1 200 OK
Content-Length: 241
Content-Type: application/xml
Date: Wed, 19 Nov 2008 21:48:10 GMT

<order xmlns="http://schemas.restbucks.com/order">
  <location>takeAway</location>
  <items>
    <item>
      <name>latte</name>
      <quantity>1</quantity>
      <milk>whole</milk>
      <size>small</size>
    </item>
  </items>
</order>
```

The response from the server consists of a representation of the order created by the original POST request, plus some additional information such as the status, and a collection of useful metadata in the headers. The first line includes a 200 OK status code and a short textual description of the outcome of the response informing us that our GET operation was successful. Two headers follow, which consumers use as hints to help parse the representation in the payload. The Content-Type header informs us that the payload is an XML document, while Content-Length declares the length of the representation in bytes. Finally, the representation is found in the body of the response, which is encoded in XML in accordance with the Content-Type header.

A client can GET a representation many times over without the requests causing the resource to change. Of course, the resource may still change between requests for other reasons. For example, the status of a coffee order could change from "pending" to "served" as the barista makes progress. However, the consumer's GET requests should not cause any of those state changes, lest they violate the widely shared understanding that GET is safe.

Since Restbucks is a good web citizen, it's safe to GET a representation of an order at any point. However, clients should be prepared to receive different representations over time since resource state—that is, the order—changes on the server side as the barista prepares the coffee. To illustrate the point, imagine issuing the GET request from Example 4-6 again a few minutes later. This time around, the response is different because the order's status has changed from paid to served (in the <status> element), since the barista has finished preparing the drink, as we can see in Example 4-8.

Example 4-8. *Rereading an order with GET*

```
HTTP/1.1 200 OK
Content-Length: 265
Content-Type: application/xml
Date: Wed, 19 Nov 2008 21:58:21 GMT

<order xmlns="http://schemas.restbucks.com/order">
  <location>takeAway</location>
  <items>
    <item>
      <name>latte</name>
      <quantity>1</quantity>
      <milk>whole</milk>
      <size>small</size>
    </item>
  </items>
  <status>served</status>
</order>
```

In our CRUD ordering service, we're only going to consider two failure cases for GET. The first is where the client requests an order that doesn't exist, and the second is where the server fails in an unspecified manner. For these situations, we borrow inspiration from the Web and use the 404 and 500 status codes to signify that an order hasn't been found or that the server failed, respectively. For example, the request in Example 4-9 identifies an order that does not (yet) exist, so the service responds with the 404 Not Found status code shown in Example 4-10.

Example 4-9. Requesting an order that doesn't exist via GET

```
GET /order/123456789012345667890 HTTP/1.1
Host: restbucks.com
```

Example 4-10. Ordering service does not recognize an order URI and responds with 404 Not Found

```
HTTP/1.1 404 Not Found
Date: Sat, 20 Dec 2008 19:01:33 GMT
```

The 404 Not Found status code in Example 4-10 informs the consumer that the specified order is unknown to the service.* On receipt of a 404 response, the client can do very little to recover. Effectively, its view of application state is in violent disagreement with that of the ordering service. Under these circumstances, Restbucks consumers should rely on out-of-band mechanisms (such as pleading with the barista!) to solve the problem, or try to rediscover the URI of their order.

If the consumer receives a 500 Internal Server Error status code as in Example 4-11, there may be a way forward without having to immediately resort to out-of-band tactics. For instance, if the server-side error is transient, the consumer can simply retry the request later.

Example 4-11. Ordering service indicates unexpected failure with a 500 response

```
HTTP/1.1 500 Internal Server Error
Date: Sat, 20 Dec 2008 19:24:34 GMT
```

This is a very simple but powerful recovery scenario whose semantics are guaranteed by the behavior of GET. Since GET requests don't change service state, it's safe for consumers to GET representations as often as they need. In failure cases, consumers simply back off for a while and retry the GET request until they give up (and accept handing over control to some out-of-band mechanism) or wait until the service comes back online and processing continues.

---

* If we wanted to be more helpful to the consumer, our service could provide a helpful error message in the HTTP body.

Implementing read with GET

The code in Example 4-12 shows how retrieving an order via GET can be implemented using JAX-RS* in Java.

Example 4-12. *Server-side implementation of GET with JAX-RS*

```
@Path("/order")
public class OrderingService {
  @GET
  @Produces("application/xml")
  @Path("/{orderId}")
  public String getOrder(@PathParam("orderId") String orderId) {
    try {
      Order order = OrderDatabase.getOrder(orderId);
      if (order != null) {
        // Use an existing XStream instance to create the XML response
        return xstream.toXML(order);
      } else {
        throw new WebApplicationException(Response.Status.NOT_FOUND);
      }
    } catch (Exception e) {
      throw new WebApplicationException(Response.Status.INTERNAL_SERVER_ERROR);
    }
  }
  // Remainder of implementation omitted for brevity
}
```

In Example 4-12, the root path where our service will be hosted is declared using the @Path annotation, which in turn yields the /order part of the URI. The getOrder(...) method is annotated with @GET, @Produces, and @Path annotations that provide the following behaviors:

- @GET declares that the getOrder(...) method responds to HTTP GET requests.

- @Produces declares the media type that the method generates as its return value. In turn, this is mapped onto the HTTP Content-Type header in the response. Since the ordering service uses XML for order resource representations, we use application/xml here.

- @Path declares the final part of the URI where the method is registered, using the URI template {/orderId}. By combining this with the root path declared at the class level, the service is registered at the URI /order/{orderId}.

---

* Oracle Corp. website. "JAX-RS (JSR 311): The Java API for RESTful Web Services"; see *http://jcp.org/en/jsr/detail?id=311.*

The orderId parameter to the getOrder(...) method is automatically bound by JAX-RS using the @PathParam annotation on the method's orderId parameter to match the @Path annotation attached to the method. Once this is all configured, the JAX-RS implementation extracts the order identifier from URIs such as *http://restbucks.com/order/1234* and makes it available as the String parameter called orderId in the getOrder(...) method.

Inside the getOrder(...) method, we try to retrieve order information from the database keyed by the orderId parameter. If we find a record matching the orderId, we encode it as an XML document using XStream* and return the document. This relinquishes control back to JAX-RS, which in turn packages the XML-encoded order into an HTTP response and returns it to the consumer. If we can't find the order in the database, the implementation throws a WebApplicationException with the parameter NOT_FOUND, which results in a 404 Not Found response code being returned to the consumer. If something unpredicted goes wrong, such as the loss of database connectivity, we throw a WebApplicationException but with a 500 Internal Server Error status code indicated by the INTERNAL_SERVER_ERROR code. Either way, JAX-RS takes care of all the plumbing for us, including the creation of a well-formed HTTP response.

NOTE

It's interesting that the JAX-RS implementation for GET in Example 4-10 deals with a substantial amount of plumbing code on our behalf when compared to the bare servlet implementation in Example 4-3. However, it's also important to note that we don't have to use frameworks such as JAX-RS to build CRUD services, since servlets (and other HTTP libraries) can work just as well.

Updating a Resource with PUT

For the uninitiated, HTTP can be a strange protocol, not least because it offers two ways of transmitting information from client to server with the POST *and* PUT verbs. In their landmark book,† Richardson and Ruby established a convention for determining when to use PUT and when to use POST to resolve the ambiguity:

- Use POST to create a resource identified by a service-generated URI.

- Use POST to append a resource to a collection identified by a service-generated URI.

- Use PUT to create or overwrite a resource identified by a URI computed by the client.

This convention has become widely accepted, and the Restbucks ordering service embraces it by generating URIs for orders when they're created by POSTing to the well-known entry point: *http://restbucks.com/order*. Conversely, when updating orders via PUT, consumers specify the URIs. Figure 4-6 shows how using different verbs disambiguates the two different cases and simplifies the protocol.

---
* *http://xstream.codehaus.org/*
† *RESTful Web Services* (*http://oreilly.com/catalog/9780596529260/*), published by O'Reilly.

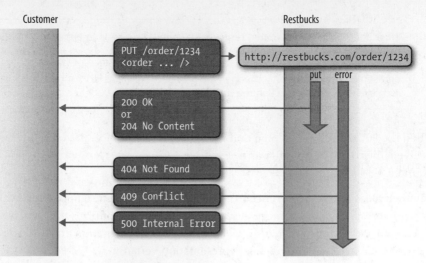

Figure 4-6. *PUT request and responses*

In Figure 4-6, consumers know the URI of the order they want to update from the Location header received in the response to an earlier POST (create) request. Using that URI, a consumer can PUT an updated order representation to the ordering service. In accordance with the HTTP specification, a successful PUT request won't create a new resource or produce a new URI. Instead, the state of the identified resource will be updated to reflect the data in the request representation.

Example 4-13 shows how a request for an update looks on the wire. While the HTTP headers should look familiar, in this case the HTTP body contains an XML representation of the original order with the contents of the <milk> element for the cappuccino changed to be skim rather than whole.

Example 4-13. *Updating an order*

```
PUT /order/1234 HTTP/1.1
Host: restbucks.com
Content-Type: application/xml
Content-Length: 246

<order xmlns="http://schemas.restbucks.com/order">
  <location>takeAway</location>
  <items>
    <item>
      <milk>skim</milk>
      <name>cappuccino</name>
      <quantity>1</quantity>
      <size>large</size>
    </item>
  </items>
</order>
```

When the PUT request is accepted and processed by the service, the consumer will receive either a 200 OK response as in Example 4-14, or a 204 No Content response as in Example 4-15.

Whether 200 is used in preference to 204 is largely an aesthetic choice. However, 200 with a response body is more descriptive and actively confirms the server-side state, while 204 is more efficient since it returns no representation and indicates that the server has accepted the request representation verbatim.

Example 4-14. Successful update with a 200 response

```
HTTP/1.1 200 OK
Content-Length: 275
Content-Type: application/xml
Date: Sun, 30 Nov 2008 21:47:34 GMT

<order xmlns="http://schemas.restbucks.com/order">
  <location>takeAway</location>
  <items>
    <item>
      <milk>skim</milk>
      <name>cappuccino</name>
      <quantity>1</quantity>
      <size>large</size>
    </item>
  </items>
  <status>preparing</status>
</order>
```

Example 4-15. Successful update with a 204 response

```
HTTP/1.1 204 No Content
Date: Sun, 30 Nov 2008 21:47:34 GMT
```

On receiving a 200 or 204 response, the consumer can be satisfied that the order has been updated. However, things can and do go wrong in distributed systems, so we should be prepared to deal with those eventualities.

The most difficult of the three failure response codes from Figure 4-6 is where a request has failed because of incompatible state. An example of this kind of failure is where the consumer tries to change its order after drinks have already been served by the barista. To signal conflicting state back to the client, the service responds with a 409 Conflict status code, as shown in Example 4-16.

Example 4-16. *Order has already been served as a take-away*

```
HTTP/1.1 409 Conflict
Date: Sun, 21 Dec 2008 16:43:07 GMT
Content-Length:271

<order xmlns="http://schemas.restbucks.com/order">
  <location>takeAway</location>
  <items>
    <item>
      <milk>whole</milk>
      <name>cappuccino</name>
      <quantity>1</quantity>
      <size>large</size>
    </item>
  </items>
  <status>served</status>
</order>
```

In keeping with the HTTP specification, the response body includes enough information for the client to understand and potentially fix the problem, if at all possible. To that end, Example 4-16 shows that the ordering service returns a representation of the current state of the order resource from the service. In the payload, we can see that the <status> element contains the value served, which indicates that the order cannot be altered. To make progress, the consumer will have to interpret the status code and payload to determine what might have gone wrong.

> **NOTE**
>
> We might reasonably expect that either 405 Method Not Allowed or 409 Conflict would be a valid choice for a response code in situations where PUTting an update to a resource isn't supported. In this instance, we chose 409 since PUT may be valid for some updates that don't violate business rules. For example, it might still be permitted to change the order from drink-in to take-away during the order's life cycle since it's just a matter of changing cups.

As with errors when processing POST and GET, a 500 response code is equally straightforward when using PUT—simply wait and retry. Since PUT is idempotent—because service-side state is *replaced wholesale* by consumer-side state—the consumer can safely repeat the operation as many times as necessary. However, PUT can only be safely used for absolute updates; it cannot be used for relative updates such as "add an extra shot to the cappuccino in order 1234." That would violate its semantics.

―――――― NOTE ――

PUT is one of the HTTP verbs that has idempotent semantics (along with GET and
DELETE in this chapter). The ordering service must therefore guarantee that PUTting
the same order many times has the same side effects as PUTting it exactly once.
This greatly simplifies dealing with intermittent problems and crash recovery by
allowing the operation to be repeated in the event of failure.

If the service recovers, it simply applies any changes from any of the PUT requests to
its underlying data store. Once a PUT request is received and processed by the ordering
service, the consumer will receive a 200 OK response.

Implementing update with PUT

Now that we understand the update process, implementation is straightforward, especially with a little help from a framework. Example 4-17 shows an implementation of
the update operation using the HTTP-centric features of Microsoft's WCF. The service
contract—the set of operations that will be exposed—is captured by the IOrderingService
interface. In turn, the IOrderingService is adorned by a [ServiceContract] attribute that
binds the interface to WCF so that the underlying framework can expose implementing classes as services.* For our purposes, the most interesting aspect of this code is the
[WebInvoke] attribute, which, when used in tandem with an [OperationContract] attribute, declares that the associated method is accessible via HTTP.

Example 4-17. *WCF ServiceContract for updating an order with PUT*

```
[ServiceContract]
public interface IOrderingService
{
    [OperationContract]
    [WebInvoke(Method = "PUT", UriTemplate = "/order/{orderId}")]
    void UpdateOrder(string orderId, Order order);

    // Remainder of service contract omitted for brevity
}
```

The [WebInvoke] attribute takes much of the drudgery out of plumbing together
URIs, entity body payloads, and the methods that process representations.
Compared to lower-level frameworks, the WCF approach removes much boilerplate
plumbing code.

---

* WCF implements the same model for all kinds of remote behavior, including queues and WS-*
Web Services. This lowest-common-denominator approach seeks to simplify programming distributed systems. Unfortunately, it often hides essential complexity, so use it with care!

In Example 4-17, the [WebInvoke] attribute is parameterized so that it responds only to the PUT verb, at URIs that match the URI template /order/{orderId}. The value supplied in {orderId} is bound at runtime by WCF to the string parameter orderId, which is then used to process the update.

When invoked, the representation in the HTTP body is deserialized from XML and dispatched to the implementing method as an instance of the Order type. To achieve this, we declare the mapping between the on-the-wire XML and the local Order object by decorating the Order type with [DataContract] and [DataMember] attributes, as shown in Example 4-18. These declarations help the WCF serializer to marshal objects to and from XML. Once the WCF serializer completes the deserialization work, all we need to implement is the update business logic, as shown in Example 4-19.

Example 4-18. *Marking up an order for use with WCF*

```
[DataContract(Namespace = "http://schemas.restbucks.com/order", Name = "order")]
public class Order
{
  [DataMember(Name = "location")]
  public Location ConsumeLocation
  {
    get { return location; }
    set { location = value; }
  }

  [DataMember(Name = "items")]
  public List<Item> Items
  {
    get { return items; }
    set { items = value; }
  }

  [DataMember(Name = "status")]
  public Status OrderStatus
  {
    get { return status; }
    set { status = value; }
  }
  // Remainder of implementation omitted for brevity
}
```

Example 4-19. *WCF implementation for updating an order*

```csharp
public void UpdateOrder(string orderId, Order order)
{
  try
  {
    if (OrderDatabase.Database.Exists(orderId))
    {
      bool conflict = OrderDatabase.Database.Save(order);
      if (!conflict)
      {
        WebOperationContext.Current.OutgoingResponse.StatusCode =
        HttpStatusCode.NoContent;
      }
      else
      {
        WebOperationContext.Current.OutgoingResponse.StatusCode =
        HttpStatusCode.Conflict;
      }
    }
    else
    {
      WebOperationContext.Current.OutgoingResponse.StatusCode =
      HttpStatusCode.NotFound;
    }
  }
  catch (Exception)
  {
    WebOperationContext.Current.OutgoingResponse.StatusCode =
    HttpStatusCode.InternalServerError;
  }
}
```

The code in Example 4-19 first checks whether the order exists in the database. If the order is found, it is simply updated and a 204 No Content status code is returned to the consumer by setting the WebOperationContext.Current.OutgoingResponse.StatusCode property.

If there's a conflict while trying to update the order, a 409 Conflict response and a representation highlighting the inconsistency will be returned to the consumer.

NOTE

It's worth noting that the only identifier we have for the order comes from the URI itself, extracted by WCF via the {orderId} template. There's no order ID embedded in the payload, since it would be superfluous. Following this DRY (Don't Repeat Yourself) pattern, we avoid potential inconsistencies between the domain model and the resources the service exposes, and keep the URI as the authoritative identifier, as it should be.

If we can't find the entry in the database, we'll set a 404 Not Found response to indicate the order resource isn't hosted by the service. Finally, if something unexpected happens, we'll catch any Exception and set a 500 Internal Server Error status code on the response to flag that the consumer should take some alternative (recovery) action.

Removing a Resource with DELETE

When a consumer decides that a resource is no longer useful, it can send an HTTP DELETE request to the resource's URI. The service hosting that resource will interpret the request as an indication that the client has become disinterested in it and may decide that the resource should be removed—the decision depends on the requirements of the service and the service implementation.

NOTE

Deleting a resource doesn't always mean the resource is physically deleted; there are a range of outcomes. A service may leave the resource accessible to other applications, make it inaccessible from the Web and maintain its state internally, or even delete it outright.

Figure 4-7 highlights the use of DELETE in the Restbucks ordering service where DELETE is used to cancel an order, if that order is in a state where it can still be canceled. For example, sending DELETE to an order's URI prior to preparation should be successful and the client should expect a 204 No Content response from the service as a confirmation.

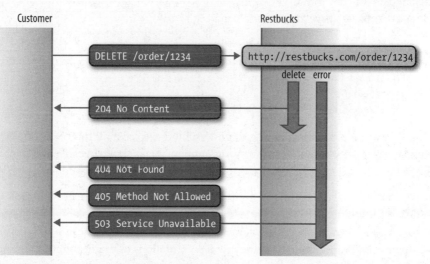

Figure 4-7. *DELETE request and responses*

Conversely, if the order has already been prepared, which means it can't be deleted, a 405 Method Not Allowed response would be used. If the service is unavailable to respond to our DELETE request for some other reason, the client can expect a 503 Service Unavailable response and might try the request again later.

On the wire, DELETE requests are simple, consisting only of the verb, resource URI, protocol version, and HOST (and optional PORT) header(s), as shown in Example 4-20.

Example 4-20. *Removing an order with DELETE*

```
DELETE /order/1234 HTTP/1.1
Host: restbucks.com
```

Assuming the ordering service is able to satisfy the DELETE request, it will respond affirmatively with a 204 No Content response, as shown in Example 4-21.

Example 4-21. *Order successfully removed*

```
HTTP/1.1 204 No Content
Date: Tue, 16 Dec 2008 17:40:11 GMT
```

> **NOTE**
>
> Some services may elect to return the final state of the deleted resource on the HTTP response. In those cases, 204 isn't appropriate, and a 200 OK response along with Content-Type and Content-Length headers and a resource representation in the body is used.

Failure cases tend to be intricate with DELETE requests, since they might have significant side effects! One such failure case is shown in Example 4-22, where the client has specified a URI that the server cannot map to an order, causing the ordering service to generate a 404 Not Found response.

Example 4-22. *The requested order doesn't exist*

```
HTTP/1.1 404 Not Found
Content-Length: 0
Date: Tue, 16 Dec 2008 17:42:12 GMT
```

Although this is a simple response to understand—we see it all too often on the human Web, after all—it's troubling from a programmatic perspective because it means the consumer has stale information about order resource state compared to the service.

We might take one of several different recovery strategies when we get a 404 Not Found response. Ordinarily, we might prefer a human to resolve the problem through some out-of-band mechanism. However, in some situations, it may be practical for the consumer to recompute application state by retrieving representations of the resources it knows about and attempt to make forward progress once it's synchronized with the service.

Restbucks archives all orders after they have been served for audit purposes. Once archived, the order becomes immutable, and any attempts to DELETE an archived order will result in a 405 Method Not Allowed response from the ordering service, as shown in Example 4-23.

Example 4-23. *Order has been archived*

```
HTTP/1.1 405 Method Not Allowed
Allow: GET
Date: Tue, 23 Dec 2008 16:23:49 GMT
```

The response in Example 4-23 informs the client that while the order resource still exists, the client is not allowed to DELETE it. In fact, the Allow header is used to convey that GET is the only acceptable verb at this point in time and that requests using any other verb will be met with a 405 Method Not Allowed response.

> **NOTE**
>
> The Allow header can be used to convey a comma-separated list of verbs that can be applied to a given resource at an instant.

An implementation for DELETE using the HttpListener from the .NET Framework is shown in Example 4-24. Like the servlet implementation in Example 4-5, this example shows that it's possible to develop services with just an HTTP library, and that we don't always have to use sophisticated frameworks.

Example 4-24. *Using HttpListener to delete an order*

```
static void DeleteResource(HttpListenerContext context)
{
  string orderId = ExtractOrderId(context.Request.Url.AbsolutePath);

  var order = OrderDatabase.Retrieve(orderId);

  if (order == null)
  {
    context.Response.StatusCode = HttpStatusCode.NotFound;
  }
  else  if (order.CanDelete)
  {
    OrderDatabase.archive(orderId);
    context.Response.StatusCode = HttpStatusCode.NoContent;
  }
  else
  {
    context.Response.StatusCode = HttpStatusCode.MethodNotAllowed;
  }

  context.Response.Close();
}
```

In Example 4-24, an HTTPListenerContext instance provides access to the underlying HTTP request and response messages. Using the request URI, we extract an order identifier and then determine whether it corresponds to a valid order. If no order is found, we immediately set the HTTP response to 404 and call Close() on the response object to return control to the web server, which in turn returns a well-formed 404 Not Found response message to the consumer.

If we can find the resource, we check whether we're allowed to delete it. If we are, we logically remove the associated order before returning a 204 No Content response to the client. Otherwise, we set the response code to 405 and let the client know they can't delete that resource.

Safety and Idempotency

We saw in Chapter 3 that GET is special since it has the properties of being both safe and idempotent. PUT and DELETE are both idempotent, but neither is safe, while POST is neither safe nor idempotent. Only GET returns the same result with repeated invocations and has no side effects for which the consumer is responsible.

With GET, failed requests can be repeated without changing the overall behavior of an application. For example, if any part of a distributed application crashes in the midst of a GET operation, or the network goes down before a response to a GET is received, the client can just reissue the same request without changing the semantics of its interaction with the server.

In broad terms, the same applies to both PUT and DELETE requests. Making an absolute update to a resource's state or deleting it outright has the same outcome whether the operation is attempted once or many times. Should PUT or DELETE fail because of a transient network or server error (e.g., a 503 response), the operation can be safely repeated.

However, since both PUT and DELETE introduce side effects (because they are not safe), it may not always be possible to simply repeat an operation if the server refuses it at first. For instance, we have already seen how a 409 response is generated when the consumer and service's view of resource state is inconsistent—merely replaying the interaction is unlikely to help. However, HTTP offers other useful features to help us when state changes abound.

Aligning Resource State

In a distributed application, it's often the case that several consumers might interact with a single resource, with each consumer oblivious to changes made by the others. As well as these consumer-driven changes, internal service behaviors can also lead to a resource's state changing without consumers knowing. In both cases, a consumer's understanding of resource state can become misaligned with the service's resource state. Without some way of realigning expectations, changes requested by a consumer based on an out-of-date understanding of resource state can have undesired effects, from repeating computationally expensive requests to overwriting and losing another consumer's changes.

HTTP provides a simple but powerful mechanism for aligning resource state expectations (and preventing race conditions) in the form of *entity tags* and *conditional request headers*. An entity tag value, or ETag, is an opaque string token that a server associates with a resource to uniquely identify the state of the resource over its lifetime. When the resource changes—that is, when one or more of its headers, or its entity body, changes—the entity tag changes accordingly, highlighting that state has been modified.

ETags are used to compare entities from the same resource. By supplying an entity tag value in a conditional request header—either an If-Match or an If-None-Match request header—a consumer can require the server to test a precondition related to the current resource state before applying the method supplied in the request.

NOTE ──────────────────────────────────

ETags are also used for cache control purposes, as we'll see in Chapter 6.

To illustrate how ETags can be used to align resource state in a multiconsumer scenario, imagine a situation in which a party of two consumers places an order for a single coffee. Shortly after placing the order, the first consumer decides it wants whole milk instead of skim milk. Around the same time, the second consumer decides it, too, would like a coffee. Neither consumer consults the other before trying to amend the order.

To begin, both consumers GET the current state of the order independently of each other. Example 4-25 shows one of the consumer's requests.

Example 4-25. *Consumer GETs the order*

```
GET /order/1234 HTTP/1.1
Host: restbucks.com
```

The service's response contains an ETag header whose value is a hash of the returned representation (Example 4-26).

Example 4-26. *Service generates a response with an ETag header*

```
HTTP/1.1 200 OK
Content-Type: application/xml
Content-Length: 275
ETag: "72232bd0daafa12f7e2d1561c81cd082"

<order xmlns="http://schemas.restbucks.com/order">
  <location>takeAway</location>
  <items>
    <item>
      <milk>skim</milk>
      <name>cappuccino</name>
```

```
        <quantity>1</quantity>
        <size>large</size>
      </item>
    </items>
    <status>pending</preparing>
</order>
```

NOTE

The service computes the entity tag and supplies it as a quoted string in the ETag header prior to returning a response. Entity tag values can be based on anything that uniquely identifies an entity: a version number associated with a resource in persistent storage, one or more file attributes, or a checksum of the entity headers and body, for example. Some methods of generating entity tag values are more computationally expensive than others. ETags are often computed by applying a hash function to the resource's state, but if hashes are too computationally expensive, any other scheme that produces unique values can be used. Whichever method is used, we recommend attaching ETag headers to responses wherever possible.

When a consumer receives a response containing an ETag, it can (and should) use the value in any subsequent requests it directs to the same resource. Such requests are called *conditional requests*. By supplying the received entity tag as the value of an If-Match or If-None-Match conditional header, the consumer can instruct the service to process its request only if the precondition in the conditional header holds true.

Of course, consumers aren't obliged to retransmit ETags they've received, and so services can't expect to receive them just because they've been generated. However, consumers that don't take advantage of ETags are disadvantaged in two ways. First, consumers will encounter increased response times as services have to perform more computation on their behalf. Second, consumers will discover their state has become out of sync with service state through status codes such as 409 Conflict at inconvenient and (because they're not using ETags) unexpected times. Both of these failings are easily rectified by diligent use of ETags.

An If-Match request header instructs the service to apply the consumer's request only if the resource to which the request is directed *hasn't changed* since the consumer last retrieved a representation of it. The service determines whether the resource has changed by comparing the resource's current entity tag value with the value supplied in the If-Match header. If the values are equal, the resource hasn't changed. The service then applies the method supplied in the request and returns a 2xx response. If the entity tag values don't match, the server concludes that the resource has changed since the consumer last accessed it, and responds with 412 Precondition Failed.

Continuing with our example, the first consumer does a conditional PUT to update the order from skim to whole milk. As Example 4-27 shows, the conditional PUT includes an `If-Match` header containing the ETag value from the previous GET.

Example 4-27. The first consumer conditionally PUTs an updated order

```
PUT /order/1234 HTTP/1.1
Host: restbucks.com
If-Match: "72232bd0daafa12f7e2d1561c81cd082"

<order xmlns="http://schemas.restbucks.com/order">
  <location>takeAway</location>
  <items>
    <item>
      <milk>whole</milk>
      <name>cappuccino</name>
      <quantity>1</quantity>
      <size>large</size>
    </item>
  </items>
  <status>pending</preparing>
</order>
```

Because the order hadn't been modified since the first consumer last saw it, the PUT succeeds, as shown in Example 4-28.

Example 4-28. The conditional PUT succeeds

```
HTTP/1.1 204 No Content
ETag: "6e87391fdb5ab218c9f445d61ee781c1"
```

Notice that while the response doesn't include an entity body, it does include an updated ETag header. This new entity tag value reflects the new state of the order resource held on the server (the result of the successful PUT).

Oblivious to the change that has just taken place, the second consumer attempts to add its order, as shown in Example 4-29. This request again uses a conditional PUT, but with an entity tag value that is now out of date (as a result of the first consumer's modification).

Example 4-29. *The second consumer conditionally PUTs an updated order*

```
PUT /order/1234 HTTP/1.1
Host: restbucks.com
If-Match: "72232bd0daafa12f7e2d1561c81cd082"

<order xmlns="http://schemas.restbucks.com/order">
  <location>takeAway</location>
  <items>
    <item>
      <milk>skim</milk>
      <name>cappuccino</name>
      <quantity>2</quantity>
      <size>large</size>
    </item>
  </items>
  <status>pending</preparing>
</order>
```

The service determines that the second consumer is trying to modify the order based on an out-of-date understanding of resource state, and so rejects the request, as shown in Example 4-30.

Example 4-30. *The response indicates a precondition has failed*

```
HTTP/1.1 412 Precondition Failed
```

When a consumer receives a 412 Precondition Failed status code, the correct thing to do is to GET a fresh representation of the current state of the resource, and then use the ETag header value supplied in this response to retry the original request, which is what the second consumer does in this case. Having done a fresh GET, the consumer sees that the original order had been modified. The second consumer is now in a position to PUT a revised order that reflects both its and the first consumer's wishes.

Our example used the If-Match header to prevent the second consumer from overwriting the first consumer's changes. Besides If-Match, consumers can also use If-None-Match. An If-None-Match header instructs the service to process the request only if the associated resource *has changed* since the consumer last accessed it. The primary use of If-None-Match is to save valuable computing resources on the service side. For example, it may be far cheaper for a service to compare ETag values than to perform computation to generate a representation.

> ───── **NOTE** ───
>
> If-None-Match is mainly used with conditional GETs, whereas If-Match is typically used with the other request methods, where race conditions between multiple consumers can lead to unpredictable side effects unless properly coordinated.

Both If-Match and If-None-Match allow the use of a wildcard character, *, instead of a normal entity tag value. An If-None-Match conditional request that takes a wildcard entity tag value instructs the service to apply the request method only if the resource doesn't currently exist. Wildcard If-None-Match requests help to prevent race conditions in situations where multiple consumers compete to PUT a new resource to a well-known URI. In contrast, an If-Match conditional request containing a wildcard value instructs the service to apply the request only if the resource does exist. Wildcard If-Match requests are useful in situations where the consumer wishes to modify an existing resource using a PUT, but only if the resource hasn't already been deleted.

NOTE ──

As well as ETag and its associated If-Match and If-None-Match headers, HTTP supports a timestamp-based Last-Modified header and its two associated conditional headers: If-Modified-Since and If-Unmodified-Since. These timestamp-based conditional headers act in exactly the same way as the If-Match and If-None-Match headers, but the conditional mechanism they implement is accurate only to the nearest second—the limit of the timestamp format used by HTTP. Because timestamps are often cheaper than hashes, If-Modified-Since and If-Unmodified-Since may be preferable in solutions where resources don't change more often than once per second.

In practice, we tend to use timestamps as cheap ETag header values, rather than as Last-Modified values. By using ETags from the outset, we ensure that the upgrade path to finer-grained ETags is entirely at the discretion of the service. The service can switch from using timestamps to using hashes without upsetting clients.

Consuming CRUD Services

Services are one side of distributed systems, but to perform useful work they need consumers to drive them through their protocols. Fortunately, many frameworks and libraries support CRUD Web Services, and it's worthwhile to understand a little about what they offer.

A Java-Based Consumer

In the Java world, we might use the Apache Commons HTTP client* to implement the Create part of the protocol by POSTing an order to the ordering service, as shown in Example 4-31.

Example 4-31. *Client-side order creation in Java*

```
public String placeOrder(Order order, String restbucksOrderingServiceUri)
                    throws BadRequestException, ServerFailureException,
                           HttpException, IOException {
```

---

* *http://hc.apache.org/httpcomponents-client/index.html*

```
      PostMethod post = new PostMethod(restbucksOrderingServiceUri);
      // Use an existing XStream instance to generate XML for the order to transmit
      RequestEntity entity = new ByteArrayRequestEntity(
                                 xstream.toXML(order).getBytes());
      post.setRequestEntity(entity);

      HttpClient client = new HttpClient();

      try {
        int response = client.executeMethod(post);

        if(response == 201) {
          return post.getResponseHeader("Location").getValue();
        } else if(response == 400) {
          // If we get a 400 response, the caller's gone wrong
          throw new BadRequestException();
        } else if(response == 500 || response == 503) {
          // If we get a 5xx response, the caller may retry
          throw new ServerFailureException(post.getResponseHeader("Retry-After"));
        }
        // Otherwise abandon the interaction
        throw new HttpException("Failed to create order. Status code: " + response);
      } finally {
        post.releaseConnection();
      }
    }
```

The implementation in Example 4-31 shows the construction of a POST operation on the ordering service, using a PostMethod object. All we need to do is to populate the HTTP request with the necessary coffee order information by setting the request entity to contain the bytes of an XML representation of the order. To keep things simple for ourselves, we use the XStream library to encode the order resource representation in XML.

Having populated the HTTP request, we instantiate an HttpClient and execute the PostMethod, which POSTs the order to the Restbucks ordering service. Once the method returns, we examine the response code for a 201 Created status and return the contents of the Location header, which will contain the URI of the newly created order. We can use this URI in subsequent interactions with Restbucks. If we don't get a 201 response, we fail by throwing an HTTPException, and assume that order creation has failed.

A .NET Consumer

On the .NET platform, we can opt for the framework's built-in XML and HTTP libraries. The code in Example 4-32 represents how a client can send an order update to the Restbucks ordering service via HTTP PUT.

Example 4-32. *.NET client code for order update via PUT*

```
public void UpdateOrder(Order order, string orderUri)
{
  HttpWebRequest request = WebRequest.Create(orderUri) as HttpWebRequest;
  request.Method = "PUT";
  request.ContentType = "application/xml";

  XmlSerializer xmlSerializer = new XmlSerializer(typeof(Order));
  xmlSerializer.Serialize(request.GetRequestStream(), order);

  request.GetRequestStream().Close();

  HttpWebResponse response = (HttpWebResponse)request.GetResponse();

  if (response.StatusCode != HttpStatusCode.OK)
  {
    // Compensation logic omitted for brevity
  }
}
```

In Example 4-32, we use an HTTPWebRequest instance to handle the HTTP aspects of
the interaction. First we set the HTTP verb PUT via the Method property and subsequently set the Content-Type header to application/xml through the ContentType
property. We then write an XML-serialized representation of the order object that
was given as an argument to the UpdateOrder() method. The XmlSerializer transforms the local object instance into an XML document, and the Serialize() method
writes the XML to the request's stream. Once we're done populating the request
stream, we simply call Close(). Under the covers, the framework sets other headers
such as Content-Length and Host for us, so we don't have to worry about them.

To send the request we call the GetResponse() method on the request object, which
has the effect of transmitting an HTTP PUT to the URI supplied as an argument to
the updateOrder() method. The response from the ordering service is returned as an
HttpWebResponse and its StatusCode property triggers any further processing.

One final job that we need to undertake is to mark up the Order type so that the
XmlSerializer knows how to transform Order instances to and from XML representations. The code snippet in Example 4-33 shows the .NET attributes that we need to
apply for our client-side plumbing to be complete.

Example 4-33. *An XML-serializable order*

```
[XmlRoot(Namespace = "http://schemas.restbucks.com/order")]
[XmlType(TypeName = "order")]
public class Order
{
```

```
[XmlElement(ElementName = "location")]
public Location ConsumeLocation
{
  get; set;
}


// Remainder of type omitted for brevity
}
```

Consuming Services Automatically with WADL

Although the patterns for writing clients in .NET and Java are easy to understand and implement, we can save ourselves effort—and, in some cases, generate code automatically—using service metadata. Up to this point, much of the work we've done in building our ordering service and its consumers has been plumbing code. But for some kinds of services,* a static description can be used to advertise the addresses and representation formats of the resources the service hosts. This is the premise of the Web Application Description Language, or WADL.

A WADL contract is an XML document that describes a set of resources with URI templates, permitted operations, and request-response representations. As you'd expect, WADL also supports the HTTP fault model and supports the description of multiple formats for resource representations. Example 4-34 shows a WADL description of the Restbucks ordering service.

Example 4-34. *Ordering service WADL example*

```
<?xml version="1.0" encoding="utf-8"?>
<application
  xmlns:xsd=http://www.w3.org/2001/XMLSchema
  xmlns="http://research.sun.com/wadl/2006/10"
  xmlns:ord="http://schemas.restbucks.com/order">

  <grammars>
    <include href="order.xsd"/>
  </grammars>

  <resources base="http://restbucks.com/">
    <resource path="order">
      <method name="POST">
        <request>
          <representation mediaType="application/xml" element="ord:order"/>
        </request>
```

---

* CRUD services are great candidates for describing with WADL. Hypermedia services—as we will see in the next chapter—use different mechanisms to describe the protocols they support.

```
        <response>
          <representation status="201"/>
          <fault mediaType="application/xml" element="ord:error" status="400"/>
          <fault mediaType="application/xml" element="ord:error" status="500"/>
        </response>
      </method>
    </resource>
    <resource path="order/{orderId}">
      <method name="GET">
        <response>
          <representation mediaType="application/xml" element="ord:order"/>
          <fault mediaType="application/xml" element="ord:error" status="404"/>
          <fault mediaType="application/xml" element="ord:error" status="500"/>
        </response>
      </method>
      <method name="PUT">
        <request>
          <representation mediaType="application/xml" element="ord:order"/>
        </request>
        <response>
          <representation status="200"/>
          <fault mediaType="application/xml" element="ord:error" status="404"/>
          <fault mediaType="application/xml" element="ord:error" status="409"/>
          <fault mediaType="application/xml" element="ord:error" status="500"/>
        </response>
      </method>
      <method name="DELETE">
        <response>
          <representation status="200"/>
          <fault mediaType="application/xml" element="ord:error" status="404"/>
          <fault mediaType="application/xml" element="ord:error" status="405"/>
          <fault mediaType="application/xml" element="ord:error" status="500"/>
        </response>
      </method>
    </resource>
  </resources>
</application>
```

The <application> element is the root for the WADL metadata. It acts as the container
for schemas that describe the service's resource representations in the <grammars>
element and the resources that are contained within the <resources> element.
The <grammars> element typically refers to XML Schema schemas (which we have
defaulted to for Restbucks) that describe the structure of the resource representations
supported by the service, though other schema types (e.g., RELAX NG) are supported
too. Consumers of the service can use this information to create local representations
of those resources such as orders and products.

In a WADL description, the <resources> element is where most of the action happens. It provides a static view of the resources available for consumption. It uses a templating scheme that allows consumers to infer the URIs of the resources supported by a service. Calculating URIs can be a little tricky since WADL relies on a hierarchy of resources, with each URI based on the parent URI's template plus its own. In Example 4-34, we have two logical resources: http://restbucks.com/order for POST and http://restbucks.com/order/{orderId} for the other verbs. The resource URIs are computed by appending the path of the <resource> element to the path defined in the base attribute of the <resources> element.

> ——— **NOTE** ———————————————————————————————
>
> In addition to dealing with URI templates and query strings, WADL also has a comprehensive mechanism for building URIs. WADL can deal with form encoding and handling a range of URI structures, including matrix URIs.*

The <method> element allows WADL to bring together the request and response resource representations and HTTP verbs to describe the set of permissible interactions supported by the service. The Restbucks ordering service is described in terms of two separate resource paths. We first define the *order* resource (<resource path="order">), which only allows POST requests (<method name="POST">) and requires that the payload of those requests be XML representations of an order. We also describe the possible ways the Restbucks ordering service can reply to a POST request (in the <response> element) depending on the outcome of processing the submitted order. In this case, the possible response code is 201, 400, or 500.

Using a URI template, a second set of resources—the orders that Restbucks has created—is advertised by the element <resource path="order/{orderId}">. Like the POST method element, each subsequent <method> element describes the possible responses and faults that the ordering service might return. Additionally, the PUT <method> element declares that an XML order representation must be present as the payload of any PUT requests.

While it's helpful that we can read and write WADL by hand (at least in simple cases), the point of WADL is to help tooling automate as much service plumbing as possible. To illustrate how WADL can be consumed by an automation infrastructure, the authors of WADL have created the WADL2Java† tool.‡ WADL2Java allows us to create consumer-side Java that minimizes the code we have to write in order to interact with a service described in WADL. The Java code in Examples 4-35 and 4-36 shows the consumer-side API that Java programmers can use to interact with a WADL-decorated ordering service.

* *http://www.w3.org/DesignIssues/MatrixURIs.html*
† *https://wadl.dev.java.net/wadl2java.html*
‡ Other tools also exist; for example, REST Describe at *http://tomayac.de/rest-describe/latest/RestDescribe.html*.

Example 4-35. *WADL-generated endpoint*

```
public class Endpoint {
  public static class Orders {

    public DataSource postAsIndex(DataSource input)
      throws IOException, MalformedURLException {
      // Implementation removed for brevity
    }
  }

  public static class OrdersOrderId {

    public OrdersOrderId(String orderid)
      throws JAXBException {
      // Implementation removed for brevity
    }

    // Getters and setters omitted for brevity

    public DataSource getAsApplicationXml()
      throws IOException, MalformedURLException {
      // Implementation removed for brevity
    }

    public Order getAsOrder()
      throws ErrorException, IOException, MalformedURLException, JAXBException {
      // Implementation removed for brevity
    }

    public DataSource putAsIndex(DataSource input)
      throws IOException, MalformedURLException {
      // Implementation removed for brevity
    }

    public DataSource deleteAsIndex()
      throws IOException, MalformedURLException {
      // Implementation removed for brevity
    }
  }
}
```

In Java, resources are locally represented by classes such as Order, shown in
Example 4-36, which allow us to inspect and set values in the XML representations
exchanged with the ordering service.

Example 4-36. *Java representation of an order resource*

```java
@XmlAccessorType(XmlAccessType.FIELD)
@XmlType(name = "", propOrder = {
    "location",
    "items",
    "status"
})
@XmlRootElement(name = "order")
public class Order {

    @XmlElement(required = true)
    protected String location;
    @XmlElement(required = true)
    protected Order.Items items;
    @XmlElement(required = true)
    protected String status;

    // Getters and setters only, omitted for brevity

}
```

WADL can be useful as a description language for CRUD services such as the ordering service. It can be used to automatically generate plumbing code with very little effort, compared to manually building clients. Since the client and server collaborate over the life cycle of a resource, its URI, and its representation format, it does not matter whether the plumbing is generated from a metadata description. Indeed, WADL descriptions may help expedite consumer-side maintenance when changes happen on the server side.

NOTE

As we will see in the next chapter, the Web uses hypermedia to provide contracts in a much more loosely coupled way than WADL. But for CRUD-only services, WADL can be a useful tool.

CRUD Is Good, but It's Not Great

Now that we've completed our tour of CRUD services, it's clear that using HTTP as a CRUD protocol can be a viable, robust, and easily implemented solution for some problem domains. In particular for systems that manipulate records, HTTP-based CRUD services are a straightforward way to extend reach over the network and expose those applications to a wider range of consumers.*

---

* Naively exposing systems that have not been built for network access is a bad idea. Systems have to be designed to accommodate network loads.

Since we can implement CRUD services using a small subset of HTTP, our integration needs may be completely satisfied with few CRUD-based services. Indeed, this is typically where most so-called RESTful services stop.* However, it's not the end of our journey, because for all their strengths and virtue of simplicity, CRUD services are only suited to CRUD scenarios. More advanced requirements need richer interaction models and, importantly, will emphasize stronger decoupling than CRUD allows.

To decouple our services from clients and support general-purpose distributed systems, we need to move away from a shared, tightly coupled understanding of resource life cycles. On the human Web, this model has long been prevalent when using hyperlinks to knit together sequences of interactions that extend past CRUD operations. In the next chapter, we're going to replicate the same hypermedia concept from the Web to create robust distributed systems.

---

* We're being generous here, since most so-called RESTful services tend to stop at tunneling through HTTP!

CHAPTER FIVE

Hypermedia Services

EMBRACING HTTP AS AN APPLICATION PROTOCOL puts the Web at the heart of distributed systems development. But that's just a start. In this chapter, we will go further, building RESTful services that use hypermedia to model state transitions and describe business protocols.

The Hypermedia Tenet

When browsing the Web, we're used to navigating between pages by clicking links or completing and submitting forms. Although we may not realize it, these interlinked pages describe a protocol—a series of steps we take to achieve a goal, whether that's buying books, searching for information, creating a blog post, or even ordering a coffee. This is the very essence of hypermedia: by transiting links between resources, we change the state of an application.

Hypermedia is an everyday part of our online activities, but despite this familiarity, it's rarely used in computer-to-computer interactions. Although Fielding's thesis on REST highlighted its role in networked systems, hypermedia has yet to figure significantly in contemporary enterprise solutions.

Hypermedia As the Engine of Application State

The phrase *hypermedia as the engine of application state*, sometimes abbreviated to HATEOAS, was coined to describe a core tenet of the REST architectural style. In this book, we tend to refer to the *hypermedia tenet* or just *hypermedia*. Put simply, the tenet says that hypermedia systems transform application state.

What is application state? If we think of an application as being computerized behavior that achieves a goal, we can describe an application protocol as the set of legal interactions necessary to realize that behavior. Application state is a snapshot of an execution of such an application protocol. The protocol lays out the interaction rules; application state is a snapshot of the entire system at a particular instant.

A hypermedia system is characterized by the transfer of links in the resource representations exchanged by the participants in an application protocol. Such links advertise other resources participating in the application protocol. The links are often enhanced with semantic markup to give domain meanings to the resources they identify.

For example, in a consumer-service interaction, the consumer submits an initial request to the entry point of the service. The service handles the request and responds with a resource representation populated with links. The consumer chooses one of these links to transition to the next step in the interaction. Over the course of several such interactions, the consumer progresses toward its goal. In other words, the distributed application's state changes. Transformation of application state is the result of the systemic behavior of the whole: the service, the consumer, the exchange of hypermedia-enabled resource representations, and the advertisement and selection of links.

On each interaction, the service and consumer exchange representations of *resource* state, not *application* state. A transferred representation includes links that reflect the state of the application. These links advertise legitimate application state transitions. But the application state isn't recorded explicitly in the representation received by the consumer; it's inferred by the consumer based on the state of all the resources—potentially distributed across many services—with which the consumer is currently interacting.

The current state of a resource is a combination of:

- The values of information items belonging to that resource

- Links to related resources

- Links that represent a transition to a possible future state of the current resource

- The results of evaluating any business rules that relate the resource to other local resources

This last point emphasizes the fact that the state of a resource is partly dependent on the state of other local resources. The state of a sales order, for example, is partly a function of the state of a local copy of an associated purchase order; changes to the purchase order will affect the state of the sales order the next time the business rules governing the state of the sales order are evaluated (i.e., the next time a representation of the sales order is generated).

Importantly, the rules that control the state of a resource are *internal* to the service that governs the resource: they're not made available to consumers. In other words, resource state is a function of a private ruleset that only the resource owner knows about: those rules don't leak into the external representation.

Business rules that relate a resource to other resources should refer only to *locally* owned resources, however. This allows us to identify and prevent circular dependencies, whereby the state of resource A is partly a function of the state of resource B, which in turn is partly a function of the state of resource A, and so on. We can always arrange locally owned resources so as to prevent circular dependencies; we can't do the same if the associated resources are governed by another service. If you need to relate the state of a resource to a third-party resource, we recommend making a local copy of the third-party resource using the Atom-based state alignment mechanisms described in Chapter 7.

A service enforces a protocol—a *domain application protocol*, or *DAP*—by advertising legitimate interactions with relevant resources. When a consumer follows links embedded in resource representations and subsequently interacts with the linked resources, the application's overall state changes, as illustrated in Figure 5-1.

NOTE

Domain application protocols (DAPs) specify the legal interactions between a consumer and a set of resources involved in a business process. DAPs sit atop HTTP and narrow HTTP's broad application protocol to support specific business goals. As we shall see, services implement DAPs by adding hypermedia links to resource representations. These links highlight other resources with which a consumer can interact to make progress through a business transaction.

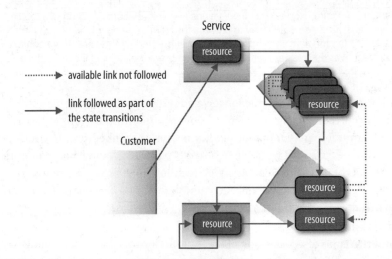

Figure 5-1. *Resources plus hypermedia describe protocols*

Consumers in a hypermedia system cause state transitions by visiting and manipulating resource state. Interestingly, the application state changes that result from a consumer driving a hypermedia system resemble the execution of a business process. This suggests that our services can advertise workflows using hypermedia. Hypermedia makes it easy to implement business protocols in ways that reduce coupling between services and consumers. Rather than understand a specific URI structure, a consumer need only understand the semantic or business context in which a link appears. This reduces an application's dependency on static metadata such as URI templates or Web Application Description Language (WADL). As a consequence, services gain a great deal of freedom to evolve without having to worry whether existing consumers will break.

> **NOTE**
>
> Services should ensure that any changes they introduce do not violate contracts with existing consumers. While it's fine for a service to make structural changes to the relationships between its resources, semantic changes to the DAP or to the media types and link relations used may change the contract and break existing consumers.

Loose Coupling

When developing a service we abstract away implementation details from consumers, thereby decreasing coupling. But no matter the degree of loose coupling, consumers must have enough information available in order to interact with our service. We need to provide some way for them to bind to our service and drive the supported application protocol. The beauty of hypermedia is that it allows us to convey protocol information in a declarative and just-in-time fashion as part of an application's resource representations.*

> **NOTE**
>
> Web contracts are expressed in media types and link relations. Accepting a media type means you understand how to process that format when interacting with a service. Using the media types and link relations supported by the service, we can extend a contract over the Web at runtime by advertising new valid links and state transitions.

For computer-to-computer interactions, we advertise protocol information by embedding links in representations, much as we do with the human Web. To describe a link's purpose, we annotate it. Annotations indicate what the linked resource means to the current resource: "status of your coffee order," "payment," and so on. For annotations we can use microformats or Semantic Web technologies, or we can design our own application-specific formats. We call such annotated links *hypermedia controls*, reflecting their enhanced capabilities over raw URIs.

> **NOTE**
>
> Forms are hypermedia controls too. Though we use links exclusively throughout the remainder of this chapter, forms can also be used to guide a consumer's interaction with linked resources. At the HTTP level, POSTing a representation to a URI in a link is equivalent to submitting a form.

* Most middleware solutions, such as WS-*, emphasize the opposite: imperative contracts presented upfront.

To illustrate the key aspects of hypermedia-driven services, we'll build the ordering and payment parts of Restbucks' service using a custom hypermedia format.

Hypermedia Formats

Hypermedia-driven distributed systems put similar demands on their consumers as the Web docs on humans: consumers need to discover and interact with resources so that they can realize an application's goal. To illustrate how representation formats allow consumers to discover and interact with resources, let's consider XHTML, one of the most popular representation formats on the World Wide Web. XHTML is used to represent information on a page (its business payload) and to link to other pages or content (its protocol description). The inclusion of links to other resources makes XHTML a *hypermedia format*. As humans, we take this property for granted. We use web browsers to move from one page to another without thinking of the underlying mechanics (which is a good thing, of course). Browsers apply the hypermedia tenet and interpret links to show possible transitions from one resource (page) to another.

The Web is agnostic to the representation formats exchanged by consumers and services, which is one of the primary reasons for its success in diverse domains. But when it comes to hypermedia, not all formats are equal.

Hypermedia Dead Ends

Despite the success of hypermedia formats on the Web, today's distributed applications typically use nonhypermedia formats such as plain XML to integrate systems. Although XML is easy to use as a data interchange format, and despite its near ubiquity, it is utterly oblivious to the Web. This is neatly demonstrated by our humble order XML representation from Chapter 4, which we show again in Example 5-1.

Example 5-1. *XML lacks hypermedia controls*

```
<order xmlns="http://schemas.restbucks.com">
  <location>takeAway</location>
  <item>
    <name>latte</name>
    <quantity>1</quantity>
    <milk>whole</milk>
    <size>small</size>
  </item>
  <status>pending</status>
</order>
```

There's nothing intrinsically wrong with this order representation when considered in isolation. After all, it conveys the current state of the order well enough. But it fails to provide any context; that is, it doesn't indicate the current state of the business process, or how to advance it. Informally, we know we need to pay for a drink once ordered, but the representation of Example 5-1 doesn't indicate how to make that payment.

The use of plain XML leaves the consumer without a guide—a protocol—for successfully completing the business transaction it has initiated. Because there are no hypermedia controls in the order representation, the consumer must rely on out-of-band information to determine what to do next. From a loose coupling point of view, that's a poor design decision. Aspects of the service's implementation leak through mechanisms such as URI templates into the consumer's implementation, making change difficult and risky.

We can, of course, communicate protocol information to the developers of a consumer application using written documentation, or static contracts such as Web Services Description Language (WSDL), WADL, or URI templates. But, as we'll see, the Web and hypermedia enable us to do better.

URI Templates and Coupling

Let's consider first how Restbucks might communicate protocol information if it chose the static, upfront approach. As we wrote in Chapter 3, Restbucks could share URI templates with its consumers. For example, it could document and share the template `http://restbucks.com/payment/{order_id}`. The documentation would describe how consumers are expected to PUT a payment representation to a URI generated by replacing the `order_id` part of the template with the ID of the original order. It's hardly rocket science, and with a little URI manipulation it can quickly be made to work. Unfortunately, it can be made to fail just as rapidly.

If Restbucks chose to publish URI templates to consumers, it would then be bound to honor those templates for the long term, or risk breaking existing consumer applications. Publishing URI template details outside a service's boundary exposes too much information about the service's implementation. If the implementation of the ordering and payment services were to change, perhaps as a result of outsourcing the payment capability to a third party, there'd be an increased risk that consumers built to the (now defunct) `http://restbucks.com/payment/{order_id}` template would break. Since that kind of business change happens frequently, Restbucks ought to encapsulate its implementation details as far as possible.

Generally, it's better to expose only stable URIs. These stable URIs act as entry points to services, after which hypermedia takes over. For example, the entry point to the Restbucks ordering service is *http://restbucks.com/order*. Interacting with the resource at that URI generates further resource representations, each of which contains hypermedia links to yet more resources involved in the ordering business process.

This doesn't mean URI templates are a bad idea. In fact, they are an excellent metadata format. But as with all good things, we must learn how to use them in moderation. We believe URI templates are an excellent means for documenting service design.

Restbucks' implementations all embrace URI templates for internal documentation and implementation purposes. However, those same implementations only ever share completed (opaque) URIs with consumers. The templates remain a private design and development detail.

Selecting a Hypermedia Format

Formats provide the means for interacting with a service, and as such they're part of that service's contract. Because a format is part of the service contract, it's important to choose an appropriate hypermedia format at design time.

REST's hypermedia tenet doesn't prescribe a specific representation format, but it does require a format capable of conveying necessary hypermedia information. Different hypermedia formats suit different services. The choice depends on a trade-off between reach and utility—between the ability to leverage existing widely deployed software agents and the degree to which a format matches our domain's needs.

Standard hypermedia formats

Several of the hypermedia formats already in use on the Web today are capable of supporting some of our requirements. Formats such as Atom* (and RSS) and XHTML are widely used and understood. Correspondingly, many software tools and libraries are available to produce, consume, and manage resource representations in these formats. Web browsers, for example, know how to render XHTML representations as pages, and Atom representations as lists of entries.

> ——— **NOTE** ———
> Underlying the Web is a principle of generality, which prefers a few commonly agreed-upon, general-purpose formats to many specialized formats. The principle of generality allows huge numbers of different programs and systems to interoperate using a few core technologies.

However, widespread tool support alone doesn't make a format suitable for every domain. For example, XHTML supports hypermedia (and is therefore capable of describing business protocols) because it implements hypermedia controls such as <a href>. Still, as Example 5-2 shows, it's a verbose format for representing a Restbucks order in a computer-to-computer interaction.

Example 5-2. *Encoding an order in XHTML*

```
<!DOCTYPE html PUBLIC "-//W3C//DTD XHTML 1.0 Transitional//EN"
  "http://www.w3.org/TR/xhtml1/DTD/xhtml1-transitional.dtd">
```

---

* A popular hypermedia format and the focus of Chapter 7.

```
<html xmlns="http://www.w3.org/1999/xhtml">
  <body>
    <div class="order">
      <p class="location">takeAway</p>
      <ul>
        <li class="item">
          <p class="name">latte</p>
          <p class="quantity">1</p>
          <p class="milk">whole</p>
          <p class="size">small</p>
        </li>
      </ul>
      <a href="http://restbucks.com/payment/1234"
        rel="http://relations.restbucks.com/payment">payment</a>
    </div>
  </body>
</html>
```

By encoding our order as XHTML, we are able to render it in a web browser, which is helpful for debugging. We leverage XHTML controls, such as the class attribute, to convey semantics about the contents of an element. The approach of mixing business data with web page presentation primitives has been popularized through microformats, which we'll discuss in Chapter 10. Example 5-2 illustrates, however, how the fusion of business data and presentation primitives comes at the expense of some noisy XHTML markup. In choosing XHTML, we make the conscious decision to trade expressiveness for reach by shoehorning a specific application format into a more general format.

But sometimes, trading expressiveness for reach isn't the right thing to do. Do our consumers really need to understand XHTML and all its verbiage? Given that Restbucks isn't concerned with user-facing software (browsers), XHTML appears more an overhead than a benefit. In this case, it's probably better to devise our own hypermedia format.

Domain-specific hypermedia formats

Because the Web is agnostic to representation formats, we're free to create custom formats tailored to our own problem domains. Whether we use a widely under-stood format or create our own, hypermedia formats are more web-friendly than nonhypermedia formats. A good hypermedia format conveys both domain-specific and protocol information. Domain-specific information includes the values of information elements belonging to a business resource, such as the drinks in an order. Protocol information declares how to make forward progress in a business process—how to move from ordering to payment, for example.

In a hypermedia format, hypermedia controls represent protocol information. A hypermedia control includes the address of a linked resource, together with some semantic markup. In the context of the current resource representation, the semantic markup indicates the meaning of the linked resource.

Creating a domain-specific hypermedia format isn't as difficult as it might seem. In Restbucks' case, we can build on the XML schemas we've already created. All we have to do is to introduce additional elements into the representations. We can add hypermedia controls to these schemas by defining both a link and the necessary semantic markup. Example 5-3 shows a first attempt at adding an application-specific hypermedia control to an order.

Example 5-3. *A coffee order with a custom hypermedia link*

```xml
<order xmlns="http://schemas.restbucks.com">
  <location>takeAway</location>
  <item>
    <name>latte</name>
    <quantity>1</quantity>
    <milk>whole</milk>
    <size>small</size>
  </item>
  <cost>2.0</cost>
  <status>payment-expected</status>
  <payment>https://restbucks.com/payment/1234</payment>
</order>
```

In this format, the order representation contains a proprietary <payment> element. <payment> is a hypermedia control.

If we wanted to represent hypermedia controls in this manner, we would specify in our format description that a <payment> element indicates "a linked resource responsible for payments relating to the current order." A consumer wanting to make a payment now knows which resource it needs to interact with next.

But that's not the only way to add hypermedia controls to our representation format. In fact, we believe it's a suboptimal method because it results in multiple elements with almost identical link semantics, but different protocol semantics. <payment> bears the joint responsibility of being both a link and a semantic annotation. If we added a <cancel> element to our scheme, this new element would have exactly the same link semantic as <payment>, but a wholly different protocol semantic.

Our preferred approach is to separate concerns by distinguishing between the act of linking and the act of adding meaning to links. Linking is a repeatable process. The meanings we attach to links, however, change from context to context. To achieve this separation of concerns, we define a <link> element to convey the domain-agnostic link function, and a rel attribute to represent the application semantics associated with a particular link. Composing this <link> element into Restbucks' representation format is easy, as shown in Example 5-4.

Example 5-4. *A coffee order with hypermedia*

```
<order xmlns="http://schemas.restbucks.com">
  <location>takeAway</location>
  <item>
    <name>latte</name>
    <quantity>1</quantity>
    <milk>whole</milk>
    <size>small</size>
  </item>
  <cost>2.0</cost>
  <status>payment-expected</status>
  <link rel="http://relations.restbucks.com/payment"
    href="https://restbucks.com/payment/1234" />
</order>
```

The Restbucks hypermedia format specification would have to document the meaning of the rel attribute's payment value so that consumers understand the role of the linked resource in relation to the current resource.

NOTE

By incorporating reusable hypermedia controls in our format, we can minimize how much of our representation we need to document and explain to consumers. If we can construct our business documents solely from widely understood and reusable building blocks, so much the better. Indeed, we'll have a closer look at a collection of such building blocks when we discuss the Atom format in Chapter 7 and semantics in Chapter 10.

By adding a `<link>` element to our order schema, we've successfully defined our own custom hypermedia format. Designing our own format allows us to express our specific application needs, yet retain the benefits of hypermedia. Of course, as with any design trade-off, there are downsides. For example, the representations in Examples 5-3 and 5-4 don't have the same reach—the ability to be processed by widely deployed generic clients—as more established hypermedia formats such as XHTML. In essence, we're creating a closed hypermedia ecosystem—one that's specific to Restbucks. This ecosystem is for consumers who are prepared to process our domain-specific payloads. Though this limits an application's reach, for Restbucks and enterprise systems in general, it might be just what we need.

Processing Hypermedia Formats

Introducing a custom hypermedia format feels like a step in the right direction. Now consumers of Restbucks services can receive both business data and the information necessary to drive the ordering and payment protocol, all in a concise and expressive format specific to the business domain.

Still, we need to convey to consumers how to process and reason about these representations. Fortunately, HTTP provides a way of identifying particular *media type* representations using the `Content-Type` header (e.g., `Content-Type: application/xml`, which we have used in previous chapters).

Media types

Grafting hypermedia controls onto XML documents is easy, but it's only half the story. What we really need to do is to create a *media type*. A media type specifies an interpretative scheme for resource representations. This scheme is described in terms of encodings, schemas, and processing models, and is a key step in creating a contract for a service.

A media type name (such as `application/xml`) is a key into a media type's interpretative scheme. Media types are declared in `Content-Type` HTTP headers. Because they're situated outside the payload body to which they're related, consumers can use them to determine how to process a representation without first having to crack open the payload and deeply inspect its content—something that might require relatively heavy processing, such as a decrypt operation, for example.

> ——— **NOTE** ———————————————————————————————
> Media type names may also appear in some inline links and forms, where they indicate the *likely* representation format of the linked resource.

A media type value indicates the service's *preferred* scheme for interpreting a representation: consumers are free to ignore this recommendation and process a representation as they see fit.

For example, we know that XHTML is valid XML and can be consumed by any software that understands XML. However, XHTML carries richer semantics (it supports hypermedia) than plain XML, and so processing it as XML rather than XHTML is lossy—we lose information about linked resources.

If a consumer interprets a received representation ignoring the rules set out by the media type in the accompanying `Content-Type` header, all bets are off.

> ——— **WARNING** ———————————————————————————————
> Willfully ignoring a media type declaration in a `Content-Type` header is not to be taken lightly, and is a rare occurrence.

Media types are one of three key components of DAPs. The other two components are link relation values, which describe the roles of linked resources, and HTTP idioms, which manipulate resources participating in the protocol. Link relation values help consumers understand *why* they might want to activate a hypermedia control. They do so by indicating the role of the linked resource in the context of the current representation.

A media type value helps a consumer understand *what* is at the end of a link. The *how* of interacting with a resource is realized by HTTP constructs such as GET, PUT, and POST (and their conditional counterparts) and the control alternatives suggested by the HTTP status codes.

> **NOTE**
>
> Media types and DAPs are not the same. A media type specification describes schemas, processing models, and link relation values for a representation format. A DAP specification lays out the rules for achieving an application goal based on interactions with resource representations belonging to one or more media types. DAPs augment media type specifications with application-specific link relation values where necessary.

A media type for Restbucks

The media type declaration used in the Content-Type header for interactions with Restbucks is application/vnd.restbucks+xml. Breaking it down, the media type name tells us that the payload of the HTTP request or response is to be treated as part of an application-specific interaction. The vnd.restbucks part of the media type name declares that the media type is vendor-specific (vnd), and that the owner is restbucks. The +xml part declares XML is used for the document formatting.

More specifically, the vnd.restbucks part of the media type name marks the payload as being part of Restbucks' DAP. Consumers who know how to interact with a Restbucks service can identify the media type and interpret the payloads accordingly.*

Why application/xml doesn't help

As we described earlier, we chose to stick with XML for the Restbucks representation formats. This decision allows us to reuse existing schemas/formats in our media type description.† However, this doesn't mean we should use text/xml or application/xml as the value of the Content-Type header, and for good reason. The Content-Type header sets the context for how the payloads should be processed. Suggesting that the payload is just XML gives the wrong indication to software agents about the content and processing model for a representation. Treating Restbucks content and its hypermedia control format as plain XML simply leads to a hypermedia dead end.

For example, in Example 5-5 we see a Restbucks order, which contains two <link> elements advertising other resources of interest to the customer. Using this simple protocol representation format, the service shows consumers how they can make

---

* As more coffee shops bring their business to the Web, it's conceivable to create a common application protocol and a vendor-agnostic media type (e.g., application/coffee+xml). Until such an event, we will assume that Restbucks has the monopoly on coffee on the Web.

† Media types can reference many schemas. When accepting the contract imposed by a media type, you're indicating that you understand the associated schemas.

forward progress through the business process by interacting with the payment and special offer resources.

Example 5-5. *Content-Type dictates how entity bodies are processed*

```
HTTP/1.1 200 OK
Content-Length: 342
Content-Type: application/xml
Date: Sun, 21 Mar 2010 17:04:10 GMT

<order xmlns="http://schemas.restbucks.com">
  <location>takeAway</location>
  <item>
    <name>latte</name>
    <quantity>1</quantity>
    <milk>whole</milk>
    <size>small</size>
  </item>
  <cost>2.0</cost>
  <status>payment-expected</status>
  <link rel="http://relations.restbucks.com/payment"
    href="https://restbucks.com/payment/1234"/>
  <link rel="http://relations.restbucks.com/special-offer"
    href="http://restbucks.com/offers/cookie/1234"/>
</entry>
```

But all is not well with Example 5-5. While the root XML namespace of the payload clearly indicates that this is a Restbucks order (and is therefore hypermedia-friendly, as defined by the Restbucks specification), the Content-Type header declares it should be processed as plain XML, not as the hypermedia-friendly application/vnd. restbucks+xml. When we encounter an HTTP payload on the Web whose Content-Type header is set to application/xml, we're meant to process that payload in accordance with its media type specification, as set out in RFC 3023.

By treating XML hypermedia formats as plain XML, we skip many of their benefits. The interpretative scheme for each format includes hypermedia control definitions that enable programs to identify and process hypermedia controls embedded within a document of that type. These processing imperatives do not exist in the application/ xml media type specification, which means that the payload of Example 5-5 should be treated simply as structured data. The protocol information (the <link> elements) will appear as odd-looking business information.

─── **WARNING** ────────────────────────────────

HTTP is not a transport protocol, it is an application protocol. An HTTP message's body cannot be divorced from its headers, because those headers set the processing context for the entity body payload.

XML thinking encourages us to separate protocol and data—usually to our detriment. Too often, we end up designing containers for data, with no inline provision for protocol information. This leads us to advertise the protocol using an out-of-band mechanism such as URI templates. The burden then falls to consumer applications to keep current with changes in the service implementation (particularly around URIs)—changes that ordinarily the service would not be obliged to share.

Adding hypermedia controls to an XML representation doesn't help much if we then go on to recommend the representation be treated as plain XML. The controls can play their part in a hypermedia system only if the Content-Type header suggests using a hypermedia-aware interpretative scheme. This is the case even if the document's root XML namespace alludes to a useful processing model. Content-Type headers, not XML namespaces, declare how a representation is to be processed: that's the convention on the Web.

NOTE

Services and consumers are bound by the application protocol semantics of HTTP. When a service declares that a payload is in a particular format, consumers should honor that directive rather than second-guess the processing model by deeply examining the payload contents.

A diligent consumer might later examine the XML namespace or associated schema and discover a more specialized type. Activities such as this take place outside the well-understood, predictable mechanisms defined by HTTP. Wrongly inferring the processing model may even harm the application if the originating service explicitly meant for the payload to be interpreted in a specific way—not all representations with angle brackets are well-formed XML, after all.

For example, as part of its monitoring processes, Restbucks may produce a feed of malformed orders: corrupted documents submitted by inept or malicious customers. In the Content-Type header, the service indicates that the representation should be treated as text/plain. Consumers that decide to treat these representations as XML, because they contain angle brackets, had better guard against exceptions arising from malformed XML since the service has made no stronger commitment than to provide plain text.

Media type design and formats

Balancing the number of media types we use against the number of representation formats that our DAP uses can be a tricky affair. On the one hand, it's possible to create a new media type for each representation format hosted by a service. On the other hand, we might choose to create one media type for the entire application domain.

Creating a one-to-one mapping between media types and representation formats, with specialized media type values such as application/vnd.restbucks.order+xml and application/vnd.restbucks.payment.creditCard+xml, can lead to extremely tight coupling between a service's domain layer and its consumers. The interactions in the application protocol might have to be fine-grained since the composition of representation formats will not be possible, given that there can be only one media type per HTTP request or response. At the other extreme, a single monolithic media type can add unnecessary overhead when we want to share a subset of schemas between application domain contexts.

In our case, we've chosen to make application/vnd.restbucks+xml generally applicable to the entire domain of orders and payments in Restbucks. As a result, our media type defines the order, payment, and receipt schemas, and our chosen hypermedia control format and processing model (the <link> element). It also defines a number of link relation values, which our DAP uses to identify the relationship between resources.

> ───── **NOTE** ──────────────────────────────────────
>
> Although Restbucks defined the core functionality for its media type, there's nothing to stop other DAPs from composing our media type with other media types, or adding to our set of link relation values. By composing other media types or layering on other link relations, the Restbucks media type can be easily extended and put to other uses, just like any other good media type.

In the Restbucks application domain, we assume that consumers who understand the application/vnd.restbucks+xml media type are capable of dealing with everything defined by it. However, it occasionally happens that some consumers want to handle only a subset of the representation formats defined in a media type. While there is no standard solution to this issue on the Web, there is a popular convention defined by the Atom community. The application/atom+xml media type defines both the *feed* and the *entry* resource representation formats.* While the vast majority of consumers can handle both, there is a small subset wishing only to deal with standalone entries. In recognition of this need, Atom Publishing Protocol (AtomPub) added a type parameter to the media type value (resulting in Content-Type headers such as application/atom+xml;type=entry). With such a value for the ContentType header, it is now possible to include "entry" resource representations as payloads in HTTP requests or responses without requiring that the processing software agents have a complete understanding of all the Atom-defined formats.

* We will discuss the Atom formats and Atom Publishing Protocol thoroughly in Chapters 7 and 8.

In many of the examples in the remainder of this chapter, we'll omit the HTTP headers
and focus on the hypermedia payloads. These examples assume the Content-Type
header is set to application/vnd.restbucks+xml.

Contracts

Contracts are a critical part of any distributed system since they prescribe how
disparate parts of an application should interact. Contracts typically encompass data
encodings, interface definitions, policy assertions, and coordination protocols. Data
encoding requirements and interface definitions establish agreed-upon mechanisms for
composing and interpreting message contents to elicit specific behaviors. Policies
describe interoperability preferences, capabilities, and requirements—often around
security and other quality-of-service attributes. Coordination protocols describe how
message exchanges can be composed into meaningful conversations between the
disparate parts of an application in order to achieve a specific application goal.*

The Web breaks away from the traditional way of thinking about upfront agreement
on all aspects of interaction for a distributed application. Instead, the Web is a platform
of well-defined building blocks from which distributed applications can be composed.
Hypermedia can act as instant and strong composition glue.

Contracts for the Web are quite unlike static contracts for other distributed systems.
As Figure 5-2 shows, contracts are a composition of a number of aspects, with media
types at their core. Protocols extend the capabilities of a media type into a specific
domain. Currently, there is no declarative notation to capture all aspects of a contract
on the Web. While technologies such as XML Schema allow us to describe the structure of documents, there is no vocabulary that can describe everything. As developers,
we have to read protocol and media type specifications in order to implement applications based on contracts.

---

* In the WS-* stack, these contract elements are typically implemented using XML Schema, WSDL,
  WS-Policy, and BPEL or WS-Choreography, respectively.

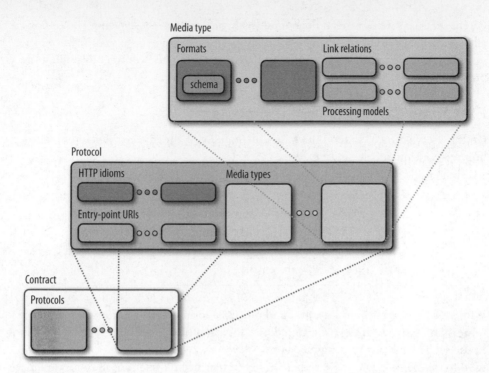

Figure 5-2. *Contracts are a composition of media types and protocols*

Contracts Begin with Media Types

The core of any contract on the Web is the set of media types a service supports. A media type specification sets out the formats (and any schemas), processing model, and hypermedia controls that services will embed in representations.

There are numerous existing media type specifications that we can use to meet the demands of our service. Occasionally, we may create new media types to fit a particular domain. The challenge for service designers is to select the most appropriate media type(s) to form the core service contract.

On entering into the contract, consumers of a service need simply to agree to the format, processing model, and link relations found in the media types the service uses. If common media types are used (e.g., XHTML or Atom), widespread interoperability is easily achievable since many systems and libraries support these types.

We believe an increase in the availability of media type processors will better enable us to rapidly construct distributed applications on the Web. Instead of coding to static contracts, we will be able to download (or build) standard processors for a given media type and then compose them together.*

* Examples of such processors already abound; these include Apache Abdera and .NET's syndication types, both of which implement the Atom Syndication Format.

Often, that's as far as we need to go in designing a contract. By selecting and optionally composing media types, we've got enough collateral to expose a contract to other systems. However, we need not stop there, and can refine the contract by adding protocols.

Extending Contracts with Protocols

On the Web, protocols extend the base functionality of a media type by adding new link relations and processing models.

> **NOTE**
>
> A classic example of protocols building on established media types is Atom Publishing Protocol. AtomPub describes a number of new link relations, which augment those declared in the Atom Syndication Format. It builds on these link relations to create a new processing model that supports the specific application goal of publishing and editing web content.

While media types help us interpret and process a format, link relations help us understand why we might want to follow a link. A protocol can add new link relations to the set provided by existing media types. It can also augment the set of HTTP idioms used to manipulate resources in the context of specific link relations. Service designers can also use independently defined link relations, such as those in the IANA Link Relations registry, mixing them in with the link relations provided by media types and protocols to advertise specific interactions.*

HTTP Idioms

Underpinning all media types and protocols is the HTTP uniform interface, which provides the plumbing through which contracts are enacted at runtime. Even with media types and protocols to describe a contract, consumers still need to know how individual resources should be manipulated at runtime. In other words, contracts define which HTTP idioms—methods, headers, and status codes—consumers should use to interact with a linked resource in a specific context.

Such information can come from several sources. Many hypermedia controls have attributes that describe transfer options. XHTML's <form> element, for example, includes a method attribute that specifies the HTTP method to use to send form data. Occasionally, the current application context can be used to determine which idiom to use next. If the consumer receives a representation accompanied by an ETag header, it's reasonable to assume that subsequent requests for the same resource can be made using a precondition: If-Match or If-None-Match, as appropriate. Similarly, a 303 See Other

---

* IANA defines numerous top-level link relations that are broadly applicable across numerous domains. These relations aren't bound to any particular media type or protocol, and can be freely reused in any service implementation with matching requirements.

status code and accompanying Location header instruct the recipient to perform a GET on the Location header's URI. When neither the current payload nor the processing context indicates which idioms to use, OPTIONS can be used on the linked resource's URI.

NOTE

We should always remember that the OPTIONS method allows us to query for information regarding the communication options currently supported by a resource. However, if we find the need to use many OPTIONS requests or probe linked resources with best-guess requests, we should be concerned about the predictability and robustness of our distributed application.

Using Contracts at Runtime

At runtime, a contract is enacted over the Web as shown in Figure 5-3. The final contract element put into place is a well-known entry point URI (or URIs), which is advertised to consumers so that they can bind to the service.

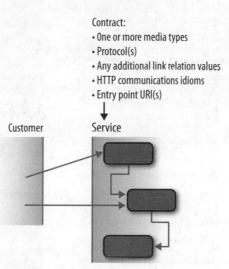

Figure 5-3. *Enacting contracts at runtime*

Although media types, protocols, and link relations are defined orthogonally to any given service, they still constitute a strong contract. A consumer that understands a set of media types, protocols, and link relations can interact with any service that supports them (in any combination).

Since consumers know the service contract, its protocol can be driven entirely by exchanging and processing representations whose content and hypermedia controls are consistent with that contract. This scheme provides loose coupling, and it also allows services to lead their consumers through business protocols.

Hypermedia Protocols

REST introduces a set of tenets that, when applied to distributed systems design, yield the desirable characteristics of scalability, uniformity, performance, and encapsulation. Using HTTP, URIs, and hypermedia, we can build systems that exhibit exactly the same characteristics. These three building blocks also allow us to implement application protocols tailored to the business needs of our solutions.

The Restbucks Domain Application Protocol

As a web-based system, Restbucks supports a DAP for ordering and payment. Figure 5-4 summarizes the HTTP requests that the ordering service supports and the associated workflow logic each request will trigger.

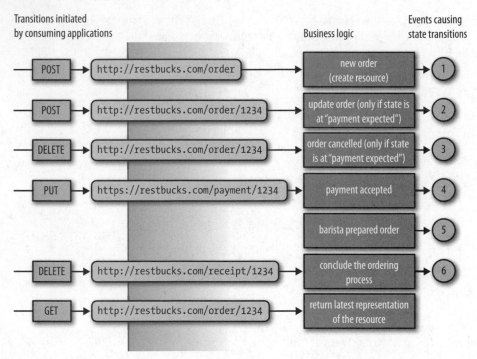

Figure 5-4. *Possible HTTP requests for the Restbucks ordering service*

The permitted interactions shown in Figure 5-4 constitute a complete business protocol for lodging, managing, and paying for an order. Each interaction invokes a workflow activity that changes the underlying state of one or more resources managed by the service.* Modeling Restbucks' business processes as a DAP and then representing that protocol as a state machine in this manner is a useful way of capturing a business process at design time.

Moving from design to implementation, we need to think about the protocol in a slightly different way. In a resource-oriented distributed application, an application protocol can be thought of as a function of one or more resource life cycles and the business rules that connect these resources. Because of its resource-centric nature, the Restbucks service does not host an application protocol state machine. In other words, there's no workflow or business logic for the *application protocol* as such. Rather, the service governs the life cycles of the orders and payments participating in the application protocol. Any workflows in the service implementation relate to *resource life cycles*, not the application protocol life cycle. While we've been explicit in modeling the business process as an application protocol state machine, we've been diligent in implementing it wholly in terms of resource state machines.

Figure 5-5 shows the resource state machine for an order as implemented in the service. From this diagram and Figure 5-4, we can derive the DAP:

- POST creates an order.

- Any number of POSTs updates the order.

- A single DELETE cancels the order, or a single PUT to a payment resource pays for the order.

- And finally, a single DELETE confirms that the order has been received.

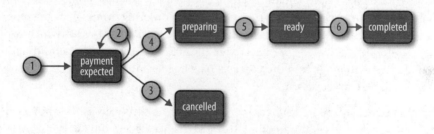

Figure 5-5. *State transitions for the order resource from Figure 5-4*

The state machine diagram in Figure 5-5 is a useful design artifact, but it isn't a good representation format for sharing protocols over the Web. For that, we use hypermedia, which starts with a single, well-known entry point URI.

---

* GET requests are also associated with business logic, but don't cause any state transitions for which the consumer can be held accountable by the service. This is consistent with the use of GET on the Web, and as we will see in later chapters, it is one of the key enablers for massive scalability.

Advertising Protocols with Hypermedia

For our hypermedia service implementation, we'll create an entry point to the ordering service at *http://restbucks.com/order*. To initiate the ordering protocol, a consumer POSTs a request with an order representation to *http://restbucks.com/order*, which results in a new order being created. The payload of the POST request must be a Restbucks order XML representation, and the Content-Type header must contain the value application/vnd.restbucks+xml.

Changing the media type to application/vnd.restbucks+xml from application/xml might seem a modest step, but in doing so we've realized some fundamental goals: the *entry point* to the Restbucks service gives consumers a way of triggering an instance of our DAP. From this point onward, hypermedia takes over, with link relations from the Restbucks media type leading consumers from one step in the business protocol to the next. If all goes well, by the end of the process we will have the set of interactions shown in Figure 5-6.

Figure 5-6 shows the trace of HTTP interactions that occur during a normal, successful interaction with Restbucks. Each interaction is guided by hypermedia links, so it's easy to piece this puzzle together, starting from the beginning.

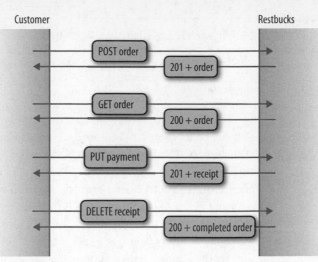

Figure 5-6. *Driving the Restbucks ordering protocol through the happy path*

If Restbucks accepts the POSTed order, the ordering service generates a 201 Created response, which contains a representation of the service's version of the order. So far, this matches the CRUD approach we saw in the preceding chapter. The marked differences are in the use of the Content-Type header, and in the contents of the returned resource representation, which now uses links to advertise the next set of accessible resources.

At this point, the ordering protocol allows the consumer to check the status of the order, cancel it, update it, or pay for it (see Figure 5-7). For example, if the consumer checks the status of the order prior to paying, the service returns a representation with a business payload part depicting the status of the order, and a protocol part indicating payment is still required, as shown shortly in Example 5-6.

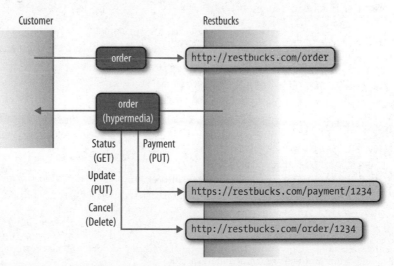

Figure 5-7. *Responses contain links to valid next steps in the interaction*

The semantics of the links in the order representation must be communicated to, and understood by, Restbucks' customers. This is the purpose of the Restbucks media type.* By accepting HTTP responses with the Content-Type header set to application/vnd. restbucks+xml, consumers enter into a contract that requires them to understand Restbucks' representation format and link relation values if they wish to make forward progress. As per the media type description, Restbucks leverages a reusable <link> element to convey business protocol information. We separate the <link> element and its attributes from the rest of the Restbucks representation format elements and we define it in its own http://schemas.restbucks.com/dap namespace:

- <link> elements have a uri attribute whose value indicates a resource with which the consumer can interact to progress the application protocol.

- <link> elements have a rel attribute containing semantic markup. The definitions of the markup values imply which HTTP verb to use when following the link, as well as required HTTP headers, and the structure of the payload.

- If a request requires an entity body, the <link> element will contain a mediaType attribute that declares the format of the request payload. If a request does not require an entity body, the mediaType attribute will be absent.

With the <dap:link> hypermedia control at our disposal, let's see an example order representation. Example 5-6 shows a response representation generated immediately after an order has been accepted.

Example 5-6. *Hypermedia order representation*

```
<order xmlns="http://schemas.restbucks.com"
  xmlns:dap="http://schemas.restbucks.com/dap">
  <dap:link mediaType="application/vnd.restbucks+xml"
    uri="http://restbucks.com/order/1234"
    rel="http://relations.restbucks.com/cancel"/>
  <dap:link mediaType="application/vnd.restbucks+xml"
    uri="http://restbucks.com/payment/1234"
    rel="http://relations.restbucks.com/payment"/>
  <dap:link mediaType="application/vnd.restbucks+xml"
    uri="http://restbucks.com/order/1234"
```

* Since the media type maps entirely to the Restbucks business domain, all link relation values used in the application protocol are defined in its specification.

```
       rel="http://relations.restbucks.com/update"/>
   <dap:link mediaType="application/vnd.restbucks+xml"
     uri="http://restbucks.com/order/1234" rel="self"/>
   <item>
     <milk>semi</milk>
     <size>large</size>
     <drink>cappuccino</drink>
   </item>
   <location>takeAway</location>
   <cost>2.0</cost>
   <status>unpaid</status>
 </order>
```

This order representation shows the different URIs and associated rel values consumers can use to advance the DAP. The semantic markup definitions are shared widely with consumers as part of the media type specification, and are as follows:

payment
> The linked resource allows the consumer to begin paying for the order. Initiating payment involves PUTting an appropriate resource representation to the specified URI, as defined in the Restbucks media type.

self
> The uri value can be used to GET the latest resource representation of the order.

update
> Consumers can change the order using a POST to transfer a representation to the linked resource.

cancel
> This is the uri to be used to DELETE the order resource should the consumer wish to cancel the order.

At this point in the workflow, if the customer GETs the status of the order via *http://restbucks.com/order/1234*, the customer will be presented with the resource representation shown in Example 5-6. Once payment has been PUT to the payment URI, however, subsequent requests for the order will return a representation with different links, reflecting a change in application state and the opening up of a new set of steps in the DAP.

At any point in the execution of the ordering process, the service can inject hypermedia controls into response bodies. For example, if the customer submits a payment via POST, as shown in Example 5-7, the service updates the state of the order to reflect the fact that payment is no longer required.

Example 5-7. *A payment resource representation*

```
<payment xmlns="http://schemas.restbucks.com">
  <amount>2.0</amount>
  <cardholderName>Michael Faraday</cardholderName>
  <cardNumber>11223344</cardNumber>
  <expiryMonth>12</expiryMonth>
  <expiryYear>12</expiryYear>
</payment>
```

The service then injects links to both the order and receipt resources into the response, as shown in Example 5-8.

Example 5-8. *Payment response contains links to order and receipt resources*

```
<ns2:payment xmlns:dap="http://schemas.restbucks.com/dap"
  xmlns="http://schemas.restbucks.com">
  <dap:link mediaType="application/vnd.restbucks+xml"
    uri="http://restbucks.com/order/1234"
    rel="http://relations.restbucks.com/order"/>
  <dap:link mediaType="application/vnd.restbucks+xml"
    uri="http://restbucks.com/receipt/1234"
    rel="http://relations.restbucks.com/receipt"/>
  <amount>2.0</amount>
  <cardholderName>Michael Faraday</cardholderName>
  <cardNumber>11223344</cardNumber>
  <expiryMonth>12</expiryMonth>
  <expiryYear>12</expiryYear>
</payment>
```

In the newly minted representation in Example 5-8, we have two `<link>` elements to consider. The order link takes the customer directly to the order resource (where the customer can complete the ordering protocol) while the receipt link leads to a receipt resource (should the customer need a receipt).

If the customer requires a receipt, a GET on the receipt link returns the representation in Example 5-9. If the customer doesn't want a receipt, it can follow the order link in Example 5-8 directly back to the order. Whichever route is chosen, the customer ends up at a point in the workflow where the order is paid for and we have a representation similar to the one in Example 5-10.

Example 5-9. *Receipt representation with a link to the order resource*

```
<receipt xmlns:dap="http://schemas.restbucks.com/dap"
  xmlns="http://schemas.restbucks.com">
  <dap:link mediaType="application/vnd.restbucks+xml"
    uri="http://restbucks.com/order/1234"
    rel="http://relations.restbucks.com/order"/>
```

```
  <amount>2.0</amount>
  <paid>2010-03-03T21:58:03.834+01:00</paid>
</receipt>
```

Example 5-9 contains two elements that allow us to infer the state of the distributed application. The <paid> element, which contains a timestamp, provides business-level confirmation that the order has been paid for. This sense of application state is reinforced at the protocol level by the presence of a single <link> element, which directs the consumer toward the order resource and the end of the business process. And because the payment link is now absent, the consumer has no way of activating that part of the protocol.

> ──── **NOTE** ────────────────────────────────
>
> While all this is going on in full view of the consumer, behind the scenes an internal process is initiated to add the order to a barista's queue. Restbucks' customers aren't exposed to any of this detail. All they need to know is the next protocol step after payment.

We know that having paid for the order, the customer might GET a receipt—and following that, the latest order representation—or the customer might simply go straight to the latest representation of the order. Either way, the customer eventually ends up with the order information shown in Example 5-10.

There are two things to note here. First, the value of the <status> element has changed to preparing. Second, there is only one possible transition the customer can initiate, which is to request the status of the order through the self link.

Example 5-10. *The updated order resource representation after payment has been accepted*

```
<order xmlns="http://schemas.restbucks.com"
xmlns:dap="http://schemas.restbucks.com/dap">
  <dap:link mediaType="application/vnd.restbucks+xml"
    uri="http://restbucks.com/order/1234" rel="self"/>
  <item>
    <milk>semi</milk>
    <size>large</size>
    <drink>cappuccino</drink>
  </item>
  <location>takeAway</location>
  <cost>2.0</cost>
  <status>preparing</status>
</order>
```

While the order is in this state, every inquiry regarding the status of the order will receive the same response. This is the equivalent of the service saying, "Your order is being prepared; thank you for waiting." Every time the customer GETs the order representation, it will see the same preparing value, until the barista delivers the coffee.

Once a service has exposed information to the outside world, it no longer controls how or when that information might be used. For example, when Restbucks exposes a URI for canceling an order, it can't know when—or if—a customer will use it.

Similarly, customers can't be sure an order (including its hypermedia links) won't change as a result of an internal business process. Even if they try immediately to initiate a transition based on a link in a representation they've just received, they may find the resource no longer supports the transition—the barista may have been even faster!

As with any consumer or service application on the Web, our service implementation must be prepared to deal with any out-of-order request, even if it is just to return an error condition, or to flag conflicting state with a 409 Conflict response.

Once the order is complete, the barista changes the status of the underlying resource to ready. This is an example of how an internal, backend business process can change the state of a resource without consumer intervention. The next time the customer GETs the order resource representation, the response will include the final possible transition in the ordering process, as shown in Example 5-11.

Example 5-11. *Order resource representation after the barista has prepared it*

```xml
<order xmlns="http://schemas.restbucks.com"
  xmlns:dap="http://schemas.restbucks.com/dap">
  <dap:link mediaType="application/vnd.restbucks+xml"
    uri="http://restbucks.com/receipt/1234"
    rel="http://relations.restbucks.com/receipt"/>
  <item>
    <milk>semi</ milk>
    <size>large</size>
    <drink>cappuccino</drink>
  </item>
  <location>takeAway</location>
  <cost>2.0</cost>
  <status>ready</status>
</order>
```

--- NOTE ---

As it stands, there's no way for Restbucks to notify a customer that its order is ready. Instead, the solution uses GET-based polling. We could ask that as part of order submission, customers register a callback URI to which a notification could be POSTed, but this presumes the customer has the means to deploy a service somewhere and accept HTTP requests.

The lack of notification capabilities isn't a big problem. The Web is designed to deal with "impatient" customers who repeatedly try to update their orders. Paradoxical as it might seem, polling and caching enable the Web to scale. Because representations can be cached close to consumers, no additional load needs to be generated on the service. Caching and its implications for service design are discussed in Chapter 6.

The representation in Example 5-11 includes a single, final state transition in the ordering process:

receipt
> Customers can DELETE the linked resource, thereby completing the order.

This DELETE request takes the receipt from Restbucks, at least as far as the consumer is concerned. It's the logical equivalent of physically taking a receipt from the cashier's hand, and in doing so completing the order process.

Inside the service, we probably wouldn't remove the resource, but instead maintain it as part of Restbucks' audit trail. This final resource state transition has the effect of completing the order, and transitions our DAP to its final state.

The response to DELETE transfers a final copy of the order. The representation, as shown in Example 5-12, has no hypermedia constructs, indicating that the resource is not part of an active business process.

Example 5-12. *Representations of completed orders have no links*

```
<order xmlns="http://schemas.restbucks.com"
  xmlns:dap="http://schemas.restbucks.com/dap">
  <item>
    <milk>semi</milk>
    <size>large</size>
    <drink>cappuccino</drink>
  </item>
  <location>takeAway</location>
  <cost>2.0</cost>
  <status>taken</status>
</order>
```

And with that, our protocol instance is complete. But our exploration into hypermedia isn't—at least not yet.

Dynamically Extending the Application Protocol

One advantage of using hypermedia to advertise protocols is that we can introduce new features without necessarily breaking existing consumers. The media type application/vnd.restbucks+xml contains numerous schemas and link relation values, not all of which are required for the basic ordering workflow; some of them are for optional interactions, such as special offers, which Restbucks occasionally runs.

> ──── **WARNING** ──────────────────────────────
> Remember that media types and link relations act as contracts between a service and its consumers. Any additional link relation values that a service adds to its protocols over time must either be supported by existing media types or made optional.

For example, Restbucks might run a loyalty program based on coffee cards: after a customer places nine coffee orders, the tenth drink is free. To allow consumers to create or update a coffee card, Restbucks adds a link to the receipt representation returned after payment has been taken and the drinks dispensed, as shown in Example 5-13.

Example 5-13. *Advertising a coffee card loyalty program*

```
<order xmlns="http://schemas.restbucks.com"
  xmlns:dap="http://schemas.restbucks.com/dap">
  <item>
    <milk>semi</milk>
    <size>large</size>
    <drink>cappuccino</drink>
  </item>
  <location>takeAway</location>
  <cost>2.0</cost>
  <status>taken</status>
  <dap:link rel="http://relations.restbucks.com/coffee-card"
    uri="http://restbucks.com/order/1234/coffeecard"
    mediaType="application/vnd.restbucks+xml"/>
</order>
```

Customers that don't understand the semantics of the coffee-card link are free to ignore it—they just won't get any free drinks. Customers who do understand the semantics of the http://relations.restbucks.com/coffee-card relation but who don't already have a coffee card can issue a simple GET request to the URI identified by the coffee-card link. The response contains the representation of a new coffee card with the coffee that was just purchased already recorded, as shown in Example 5-14.

Example 5-14. *Coffee card GET response*

```
HTTP/1.1 200 OK
Content-Length: 242
Content-Type: application/vnd.restbucks+xml
Date: Sun, 21 Mar 2010 19:04:49 GMT

<coffeeCard xmlns="http://schemas.restbucks.com">
  <link rel="self"
    href="http://restbucks.com/coffeecard/4456afd23" />
  <tamperProof>37d8c227a9e6e255327bb583dd149274</tamperProof>
  <numberOfCoffees>1</numberOfCoffees>
</coffeeCard>
```

The coffee card's resource representation in Example 5-14 contains a self link, which identifies the card; a <numberOfCoffees> element, which records how many coffees have been purchased using the card; and a tamper-proofing mechanism, which allows Restbucks to determine whether malicious customers have adjusted the card's data.*

───── **NOTE** ───

It's safe for us to add links to representations for optional parts of a business process. Nonparticipating consumers will just ignore the optional hypermedia controls and proceed as normal. What's noticeable is how easy it is to add and publish new functionality.

If a customer has a coffee card from a previous purchase, the customer can update it by POSTing it to the identified URI. Doing so updates both the number of coffees purchased and the tamper proofing. In accordance with the business rules around the promotion, if the presented card already carries enough endorsements to obtain a free coffee, a new card will be generated; this new card will then be returned in the response.

───── **NOTE** ───

There is no correlation between the coffee card and a specific order, despite the format of the URI in Example 5-13. Remember, URIs are opaque to consumers. In this case, the link contains information that the Restbucks ordering service uses when updating the count of endorsements in the coffee card.

Upon successfully accepting and updating the customer's coffee card, the service returns the latest representation of the coffee card resource using a 200 OK response, as per Example 5-15.

Example 5-15. *Coffee card POST response*

```
HTTP/1.1 200 OK
Content-Length: 242
Content-Type: application/vnd.restbucks+xml
Date: Sun, 21 Mar 2010 19:07:33 GMT

<coffeeCard xmlns="http://schemas.restbucks.com">
  <link rel=http://relations.restbucks.com/self
    href="http://restbucks.com/coffeecard/4456afd23">
  <tamperProof>fff405268fea556a351459e7368bc1d3</tamperProof>
  <numberOfCoffees>2</numberOfCoffees>
</coffeeCard>
```

Spending fully endorsed coffee cards is simple: at the payment step, customers present their card toward full or partial fulfillment of the bill. While Restbucks is running the promotion, the order's set of hypermedia controls is extended to encompass this activity, as shown in Example 5-16.

---

* This could be something as simple as a hash of the number of coffees and a secret key.

Example 5-16. *Payment by coffee card is available during the promotion*

```
<order xmlns="http://schemas.restbucks.com"
  xmlns:dap="http://schemas.restbucks.com/dap">
  <dap:link mediaType="application/vnd.restbucks+xml"
    uri="http://restbucks.com/order/1234"
    rel="http://relations.restbucks.com/cancel"/>
  <dap:link mediaType="application/vnd.restbucks+xml"
    uri="http://restbucks.com/payment/1234"
    rel="http://relations.restbucks.com/payment"/>
  <dap:link mediaType="application/vnd.restbucks+xml"
    uri="http://restbucks.com/payment/coffee-card/1234"
    rel="http://relations.restbucks.com/coffee-card-payment"/>
  <dap:link mediaType="application/vnd.restbucks+xml"
    uri="http://restbucks.com/order/1234"
    rel="http://relations.restbucks.com/update"/>
  <dap:link mediaType="application/vnd.restbucks+xml"
    uri="http://restbucks.com/order/1234" rel="self"/>
  <item>
    <milk>semi</milk>
    <size>large</size>
    <drink>cappuccino</drink>
  </item>
  <location>takeAway</location>
  <cost>2.0</cost>
  <status>unpaid</status>
</order>
```

Customers that don't want (or are unable) to participate in a promotion simply ignore the coffee-card-payment hypermedia control. Customers that do want to participate simply POST their endorsed card to the coffee-card-payment URI (see Example 5-17).

Example 5-17. *Coffee card POST response*

```
POST /order HTTP/1.1
Host: restbucks.com
Content-Length: 270
Content-Type: application/vnd.restbucks+xml
Date: Sun, 21 Mar 2010 19:08:22 GMT
<coffeeCard xmlns="http://schemas.restbucks.com">
  <link rel=http://relations.restbucks.com/self
    href="http://restbucks.com/coffeecard/4456afd23">
  <tamperProof>19590f1ed86f3b2ecaf911267067e8a8</tamperProof>
  <numberOfCoffees>9</numberOfCoffees>
</coffeeCard>
```

If the coffee card payment covers the bill, the customer receives a payment confirmation as per Example 5-8. If not, the customer receives another order representation with the <cost> element adjusted to reflect the value of the submitted coffee card.

NOTE

The benefit of using a *closed* set of hypermedia control definitions with an *open* set of link relation values is that consumers can recognize the presence of a hypermedia control even if they don't understand what it means. Consumers that can't understand the coffee-card link relation value will nonetheless be able to report the presence of a link. This can encourage the consumer development team to discover the significance of the additional functionality associated with the link.

We recommend that proprietary link relation values take the form of fully qualified URIs, which, if dereferenced, return a human-readable description of the link semantic. That way, processors that report the presence of an unknown link relation value can include the link relation description in any log output, thereby documenting the evolution of the application. <link> elements and rel attributes thus provide a high degree of discoverability.

Data Modeling Versus Protocol Hypermedia

Our discussion to this point has concentrated on using hypermedia to model and implement business protocols. But hypermedia has other uses, including the provision of network-friendly data models.

NOTE

Although we think hypermedia will be used primarily in distributed systems to drive business protocols, we recognize that some systems will need to exchange data in a way that respects and leverages the underlying network. Accessing linked information items over the Web is just as RESTful as interacting with services through DAPs.

On the Web, pages and other media are composed together using links. A web browser fetches a web page and then fetches other resources, such as images and JavaScript. The browser renders the page and exposes links to the user to support page transitions.

This model respects the underlying network. Information is loaded as lazily as possible (but no lazier), and the user is encouraged to browse pages—traverse a hypermedia structure—to access information. Breaking information into hypermedia-linked structures reduces the load on a service by reducing the amount of data that has to be served. Instead of downloading the entire information model, the application transfers only the parts pertinent to the user.

Not only does this laziness reduce the load on web servers, but the partitioning of data across pages on the Web allows the network infrastructure itself to cache information.

An individual page, once accessed, may be cached for up to a year (the maximum allowed by HTTP) depending on how the service developer configures the service. As a result, subsequent requests for the same page along the same network path will be satisfied using a cached representation, which in turn further reduces load on the origin server.

Importantly, the same is true of computer-to-computer systems: hypermedia allows sharing of information in a lazy and cacheable manner. For example, if Restbucks wanted to share its complete menu with other systems, it could use hypermedia to split the menu details across separate resources. This would allow different resource representations to be cached for different lengths of time, depending on the business use. Coffee descriptions, for example, might be long-lived, while pricing might change daily. Examples 5-18 and 5-19 show some of these hypermedia-linked representations.

Example 5-18. Sharing Restbucks' menu in a network-friendly manner

```
<menu xmlns="http://schemas.restbucks.com"
  xmlns:dap="http://schemas.restbucks.com/dap">
  <drink name="latte">
    <dap:link rel="http://relations.restbucks.com/description"
      uri="http://restbucks.com/description/latte"/>
    <dap:link rel="http://relations.restbucks.com/pricing"
      uri="http://restbucks.com/pricing/latte"/>
    <dap:link rel="http://relations.restbucks.com/image"
      uri="http://restbucks.com/images/latte.png"/>
  </drink>
  <!-- More coffees, removed for brevity -->
</menu>
```

Example 5-19. A resource linked from the Restbucks menu

```
<drink xmlns="http://schemas.restbucks.com"
  xmlns:dap="http://schemas.restbucks.com/dap" name="latte">
  <description>
    Classic Italian-style coffee with 1/3 espresso, 1/3 steamed milk,
    and 1/3 foamed milk
  </description>
  <dap:link rel="http://relations.restbucks.com/image"
    uri="http://restbucks.com/images/latte.png"/>
</drink>
```

As Examples 5-18 and 5-19 show, a large information model such as the Restbucks menu can easily be partitioned for network access using hyperlinks.

NOTE ───────────────────────────────────

Structural hypermedia is best suited for read-mostly systems, where the dual benefits of lazy loading of information and caching are available.

It's quite valid to mix structural and protocol hypermedia in a representation. But there are other options: some systems may choose to split hypermedia controls from business payload in their representations. In Restbucks, for example, we could choose to separate the representation of an order from its DAP links. We'd then put the DAP links into a separate resource, as shown in Example 5-20. rel="http://relations.restbucks.com/dap" indicates that the consumer can dereference the link to establish the next legal steps in the DAP.

Example 5-20. *The DAP links for the order are a separate resource*

```
<order xmlns="http://schemas.restbucks.com"
  xmlns:dap="http://schemas.restbucks.com/dap">
  <location>takeAway</location>
  <item>
    <name>latte</name>
    <quantity>1</quantity>
    <milk>whole</milk>
    <size>small</size>
    <dap:link rel="coffee-beans"
      uri="http://restbucks-coffee-beans-supplier.com/beans-no10"
      mediaType="application/xml"/>
    <dap:link rel="coffee-image"
      uri="http://restbucks.com/latte.jpg"
      mediaType="image/jpeg"/>
  </item>
  <cost>2.0</cost>
  <status>preparing</status>
  <dap:link rel="http://relations.restbucks.com/dap"
    uri="http://restbucks.com/order/1234/dap"
    mediaType="application/vnd.restbucks.dap+xml"/>
</order>
```

The decision on what should be decomposed into separate, or even overlapping, resources is part of the design process for a service. In making these decisions, we need to consider numerous design factors:

Size of the representation

How large is the payload going to be? Is it worth decomposing into multiple resources to optimize network access and caching?

Atomicity

Is there a chance that the application might enter an inconsistent state because a resource is in a composite relationship with other resources? Does the entire representation of a resource need to be packaged together in the same payload?

Importance of the information

Do we really need to send all the information as an atomic block? Can we allow consumers to decide which of the linked resources they need to request?

Performance/scalability

Is the resource going to be accessed frequently? Is it computationally or transactionally expensive to generate its representation?

Cacheability

Can resource representations be cached and replicated? Do different information items associated with the resource change at different rates? Which information items are dependent on the request context, and which are agnostic to that context? Answering these questions helps partition the resource by freshness criteria, allowing some of its representations to be cached for long periods of time, others to be regenerated with every request.

Implementing a Hypermedia Service

Implementing a hypermedia service might seem at first to be an intimidating prospect, but in practice, the overhead of building a hypermedia system is modest compared to the effort of building a CRUD system. Moreover, the effort generally has a positive return on investment in the longer term as a service grows and evolves. Although the implementation details will differ from project to project, there are three activities that every service delivery team will undertake throughout the lifetime of a service: designing protocols, choosing formats, and writing software.

We've been describing Restbucks' DAP and formats throughout this chapter, so we're already one step toward a working implementation.

Building the Ordering Service in Java

To build the ordering service in Java, we need only two framework components: a web server and an HTTP library. On the client side, we need only an HTTP library. For these tasks, we've chosen Jersey* (a JAX-RS† implementation), which provides the HTTP plumbing for both the service and its consumers, and the Grizzly web server, because it works well with Jersey. Apart from framework support, all we need is a handful of patterns for services and consumers, beginning with the server-side architecture.

Service Architecture

The Java server-side architecture is split across several layers, as shown in Figure 5-8.

---

* *https://jersey.dev.java.net*
† Java API for RESTful Web Services; see *http://jcp.org/en/jsr/detail?id=311.*

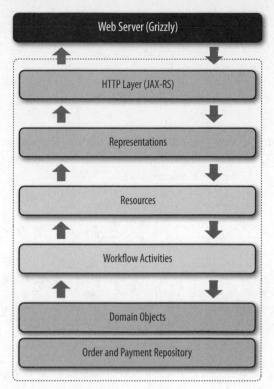

Figure 5-8. *Server-side Java architecture*

Although crucial to the deployment of a working service, the web server implementation is less important architecturally. Fortunately, it is abstracted from the service developer through the JAX-RS layer. The JAX-RS layer—although its name implies much more—simply provides a friendly programmatic binding to the underlying web server.

Using JAX-RS, we declare a set of methods, to which the framework routes HTTP interactions. Inside the service, resources act as controllers for workflow activities, passing through business information extracted from the representations and marshalling results and exceptions into HTTP responses.

Workflow activities implement the individual stages of the Restbucks workflow in terms of resource life cycles: creating orders, updating orders, canceling orders, creating payments, and delivering completed orders to customers. They're also responsible for changing the state of the underlying domain objects, which in turn are persisted in repositories.

Though their value in partitioning work into smaller, more manageable units is obvious, workflow activities provide more than just a unit of work abstraction; they also provide choreography between tasks.

Each activity knows which downstream activities are valid. For example, if payment succeeds, the valid next steps are to ask for a receipt or to check the order status. No other activities are valid, and any attempt to do anything else will result in an error being propagated to the consumer via an HTTP status code. Knowing which activities are valid given the current state of current resources, the service can advertise the next steps in the protocol by embedding hypermedia controls in the representations sent to the consumer.

The hypermedia controls that the service makes available to the consumer describe the parts of the DAP the consumer can use to drive the service through the next stages of its business workflow, as we see in Figure 5-9.

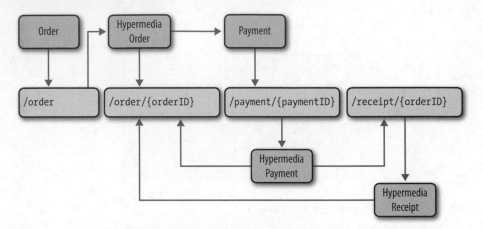

Figure 5-9. Hypermedia resources describe the ordering and payment protocol to consumers

Each resource in Figure 5-9 is internally identified by its URI or URI template. The well-known entry point URI /order is the only URI consumers are expected to know before interacting with the service. The URIs of all other resources (whose templates are used for internal documentation only) are discovered at runtime.

In accordance with Restbucks' DAP, when the service receives a valid order at the entry point URI, it returns a confirmation. This response contains an order representation augmented with additional resource state, including cost and status. Importantly, it also contains links the consumer can use to progress the workflow. In Figure 5-9, the hypermedia-enhanced order representation returned to the consumer contains links to both the order resource and a payment resource.

The pattern repeats for the payment resource. When the service receives a valid payment representation, it generates an enhanced representation containing links to other resources with which the consumer can interact: the order resource (to check status) and a receipt resource (to request a receipt).

Underlying the DAP is code, of course. In the Java implementation, resource behavior is implemented by one or more activity classes, as shown in Figure 5-10.

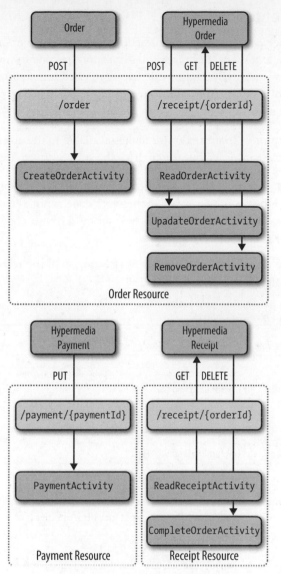

Figure 5-10. *Resources are implemented with workflow activities*

Each activity in Figure 5-10 is bound to a particular URI and verb. For example, the UpdateOrderActivity is triggered by the consumer POSTing a valid order representation to URIs matching /order/{orderId}. Similarly, PaymentActivity is triggered by a PUT with a valid payment representation to /payment/{paymentId} and the protocol is completed with a DELETE request to /receipt/{orderId}.

Here, we're concerned simply that valid representations are transferred via the correct HTTP verb to a resource in the appropriate state. Consumers are corralled toward making the right request at the right time by the semantically annotated hypermedia controls in the representations they receive.

Java Implementation

Jersey helps provide a programmatic abstraction over a web server, but it doesn't help create hypermedia and DAPs. Because of this, most of the code in the service implementation is our own. In writing this code, we've devised some patterns to separate out the concerns of protocols from the concerns of the business activities they coordinate. With that in mind, let's walk through the implementation.

Resources

The resource classes `OrderResource`, `PaymentResource`, and `ReceiptResource` expose the service implementation to the Web through Jersey. In our implementation, all JAX-RS code is localized to the resource classes. Framework code is not allowed to penetrate deeper into the service implementation—we prefer most of our code to be (easily testable) Plain Old Java Objects (POJOs).

The `OrderResource` class shown in Example 5-21 is typical of the resources in the ordering service implementation.

Example 5-21. *OrderResource class*

```
@Path("/order")
public class OrderResource {

    private @Context UriInfo uriInfo;

    @GET
    @Path("/{orderId}")
    @Produces("application/vnd.restbucks+xml")
    public Response getOrder() {
      try {
        OrderRepresentation responseRepresentation = new ReadOrderActivity()
                    .retrieveByUri(new RestbucksUri(uriInfo.getRequestUri()));
        return Response.ok().entity(responseRepresentation).build();
      } catch(NoSuchOrderException nsoe) {
        return Response.status(Status.NOT_FOUND).build();
      } catch (Exception ex) {
        return Response.serverError().build();
      }
    }

    @POST
    @Consumes("application/vnd.restbucks+xml")
    @Produces("application/vnd.restbucks+xml")
    public Response createOrder(String orderRepresentation) {
      try {
        OrderRepresentation responseRepresentation = new CreateOrderActivity()
```

```java
        .create(OrderRepresentation.fromXmlString(orderRepresentation).getOrder(),
                           new RestbucksUri(uriInfo.getRequestUri())));
    return Response.created(
            responseRepresentation.getUpdateLink().getUri())
              .entity(responseRepresentation).build();
  } catch (InvalidOrderException ioe) {
    return Response.status(Status.BAD_REQUEST).build();
  } catch (Exception ex) {
    return Response.serverError().build();
  }
}


@DELETE
@Path("/{orderId}")
@Produces("application/vnd.restbucks+xml")
public Response removeOrder() {
  try {
    OrderRepresentation removedOrder = new RemoveOrderActivity()
                    .delete(new RestbucksUri(uriInfo.getRequestUri()));
    return Response.ok().entity(removedOrder).build();
  } catch (NoSuchOrderException nsoe) {
    return Response.status(Status.NOT_FOUND).build();
  } catch(OrderDeletionException ode) {
    return Response.status(405).header("Allow", "GET").build();
  } catch (Exception ex) {
    return Response.serverError().build();
  }
}


@POST
@Path("/{orderId}")
@Consumes("application/vnd.restbucks+xml")
@Produces("application/vnd.restbucks+xml")
public Response updateOrder(String orderRepresentation) {
  try {
    OrderRepresentation responseRepresentation = new UpdateOrderActivity()
                      .update(
                        OrderRepresentation.fromXmlString(
                         orderRepresentation)
                        .getOrder(), new RestbucksUri(uriInfo.getRequestUri())));
    return Response.ok().entity(responseRepresentation).build();
  } catch (InvalidOrderException ioe) {
    return Response.status(Status.BAD_REQUEST).build();
  } catch (NoSuchOrderException nsoe) {
    return Response.status(Status.NOT_FOUND).build();
  } catch(UpdateException ue) {
    return Response.status(Status.CONFLICT).build();
```

```
      } catch (Exception ex) {
        return Response.serverError().build();
      }
    }
  }
```

The JAX-RS annotations bridge the Web and the service implementation (activities in our case). Methods are invoked in response to a combination of a specific verb and URI or URI template, and each method consumes and produces a representation with a particular media type.

To illustrate, in Example 5-21 the updateOrder method is invoked whenever a representation with media type application/vnd.restbucks+xml is POSTed to the path* /order/{orderId} concatenated with the service URI and web application context (e.g., http://restbucks.com/). The media type, verb, and path elements are associated with the method using the annotations @Consumes, @POST, and @Path, respectively. If the invocation is successful, the service produces a response with media type application/ vnd.restbucks+xml, as declared by the @Produces annotation.

All the public methods in the resource classes follow a similar pattern. For operations that require a received representation, the JAX-RS framework provides one. Domain objects are instantiated from such received representations and passed into a workflow activity for processing. We also pass the request URI into the workflow activity so that the activity can generate response links with the same base path. Once the workflow activity has completed, the representation it generates is packaged as an HTTP response with the appropriate status code and sent back to the consumer.

If an exception occurs during the execution of a workflow activity, an HTTP response is generated to reflect the failure. For instance, if the consumer sends an invalid order representation to the /order or /order/{orderId} URI, an InvalidOrderException is raised in the UpdateOrderActivity. This exception is translated into an HTTP 400 Bad Request response by the OrderResource class. If there's no specific catch block for an exception, the service responds with an HTTP 500 Internal Server Error.

Representations

The representation classes in the service are much like the underlying domain objects, except for two things: they're marked up with JAXB annotations to support XML serialization, and the serialized representations contain links. In our implementation, each representation class inherits from a common parent that stores named links and deals with XML and HTTP metadata such as namespaces and media types. This base Representation class is shown in Example 5-22.

---

* The path for the updateOrder(...) method is a combination of the root path for the resource (/order) and the local path for the method (/{orderId}).

Example 5-22. *Base Representation class*

```java
public abstract class Representation {
  public static final String RELATIONS_URI = "http://relations.restbucks.com/";
  public static final String RESTBUCKS_NAMESPACE =
    "http://schemas.restbucks.com";
  public static final String DAP_NAMESPACE = RESTBUCKS_NAMESPACE + "/dap";
  public static final String RESTBUCKS_MEDIA_TYPE =
    "application/vnd.restbucks+xml";
  public static final String SELF_REL_VALUE = "self";

  @XmlElement(name = "link", namespace = DAP_NAMESPACE)
  protected List<Link> links;
  protected Link getLinkByName(String uriName) {
    if (links == null) {
      return null;
    }
    for (Link l : links) {
      if (l.getRelValue().toLowerCase().equals(uriName.toLowerCase())) {
        return l;
      }
    }
    return null;
  }
}
```

There's only one JAXB annotation in the Representation class, and only one @XmlElement annotation to help serialize the links in the DAP namespace. The solution's other representation classes (OrderRepresentation, PaymentRepresentation, and ReceiptRepresentation) extend the base Representation class, adding in links and business-specific information. The OrderRepresentation in Example 5-23 shows a typical implementation.

Example 5-23. *OrderRepresentation implementation*

```java
@XmlRootElement(name = "order", namespace = Representation.RESTBUCKS_NAMESPACE)
public class OrderRepresentation extends Representation {

  @XmlElement(name = "item", namespace = Representation.RESTBUCKS_NAMESPACE)
  private List<Item> items;
  @XmlElement(name = "location", namespace = Representation.RESTBUCKS_NAMESPACE)
  private Location location;
  @XmlElement(name = "cost", namespace = Representation.RESTBUCKS_NAMESPACE)
  private double cost;
  @XmlElement(name = "status", namespace = Representation.RESTBUCKS_NAMESPACE)
  private OrderStatus status;
```

```
    public OrderRepresentation(Order order, Link... links) {
      try {
        this.location = order.getLocation();
        this.items = order.getItems();
        this.cost = order.calculateCost();
        this.status = order.getStatus();
        this.links = java.util.Arrays.asList(links);
      } catch (Exception ex) {
        throw new InvalidOrderException(ex);
      }
    }  // Remainder of class ommitted for brevity
  }
```

Much of the code in Example 5-23 is simply JAXB annotations. We use `@XmlRootElement` and `@XmlElement` to declare how to serialize fields into root and child nodes in XML. Aside from the framework code, though, `OrderRepresentation` instances are just value objects.

What's more interesting about this code is the way it's used by the workflow activities. Recall that representations are created by activities, and that activities know about subsequent valid activities. Using the constructor `OrderRepresentation(Order order, Link... links)`, activities inject links into the representation. Those links advertise subsequent valid activities to consumers of the representation, informing them of the next steps to take in the DAP.

Workflow activities

The workflow activity classes are units of work that execute some business interaction against the domain model on behalf of a consumer. Each activity knows about the valid activities that follow and is able to map those downstream activities to URIs, thereby rendering hypermedia representations for consumers. To illustrate, consider the `create(...)` method of the `CreateOrderActivity` in Example 5-24.

Example 5-24. CreateOrderActivity implementation

```
public class CreateOrderActivity {
  public OrderRepresentation create(Order order, RestbucksUri requestUri) {
    order.setStatus(OrderStatus.UNPAID);

    Identifier identifier = OrderRepository.current().store(order);

    RestbucksUri orderUri = new RestbucksUri(requestUri.getBaseUri() + "/order/"
                                          + identifier.toString());
    RestbucksUri paymentUri = new RestbucksUri(requestUri.getBaseUri() +
                                      "/payment/" + identifier.toString());
    return new OrderRepresentation(order,
        new Link(Representation.RELATIONS_URI + "cancel", orderUri),
        new Link(Representation.RELATIONS_URI + "payment", paymentUri),
```

```
                    new Link(Representation.RELATIONS_URI + "update", orderUri),
                    new Link(Representation.SELF_REL_VALUE, orderUri));
        }
    }
```

The create(...) method in Example 5-24 works as follows. On receipt of an Order
instance for a given URI, we set the order status to UNPAID and attempt to store it in
the order repository. If the order is successfully stored, we take the internal identifier generated by the repository and use it to compute both a public URI for the
order resource and a corresponding URI for the payment resource.* We then create
a new OrderRepresentation that contains the updated order information and the valid
DAP links. This representation is then returned to the calling JAX-RS code and
dispatched to the consumer. For a newly created order, we return four links marked
up with appropriate rel and mediaType attributes in an OrderRepresentation instance:

rel="http://relations.restbucks.com/cancel"
    The operation requires the order URI, but no media type declarations, because the
    cancel operation uses DELETE.

rel="http://relations.restbucks.com/payment"
    The operation requires a Restbucks payment representation in the entity body to
    be transferred via POST to the payment URI.

rel="http://relations.restbucks.com/update"
    The operation needs a Restbucks order representation in the entity body to be
    transferred by POST to the order URI.

rel="self"
    The operation requires an order URI, with no entity body, and is invoked via GET.

In the other activities (ReadOrderActivity, UpdateOrderActivity, RemoveOrderActivity,
PaymentActivity, ReadReceiptActivity, and CompleteOrderActivity), the pattern is
repeated: domain objects are created from any input representations and the activity
orchestrates an interaction with the underlying domain model. On completion,
activities generate a response representation (if any is needed) and insert links advertising next valid steps in the protocol, along with any media type declarations needed
to advance through those steps.

Consumer-Side Architecture

The consumer-side architecture for a hypermedia service is shown in Figure 5-11. In
this stack, the Jersey client library provides HTTP connectivity and is responsible for
mapping HTTP requests and responses into higher-level abstractions such as domain
objects and exceptions, and dispatching them to workflow activities. The workflow

---

* If Restbucks outsourced payment processing, instead of computing a URI for payment, we'd ask the
  payment provider for a URI.

activities process business payloads while actions handle hypermedia controls. Overall control of the consumer resides in the business logic, which uses the actions to orchestrate interactions with the service through the workflow activities.

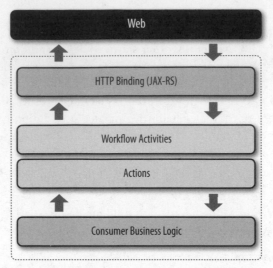

Figure 5-11. *Consumer-side architecture*

Figure 5-12 shows how activities are again at the core of our architecture. Activities take business objects and use them to create representations to transfer to the service. For responses with representations, activities provide access to the business payload in the received data.

Importantly, activities also surface actions to the business logic—abstractions that correspond to future legal interactions with the service. Actions encapsulate the hypermedia controls and associated semantic context in the underlying representation, allowing the consumer business logic to select the next activity in the workflow.

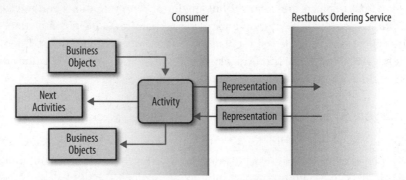

Figure 5-12. *Activities are the key abstraction on the consumer side*

Activities also encapsulate error responses from the service, providing a choice of actions to the consumer business logic. For example, if the service responds with a 500 Internal Server Error message when trying to place an order, the PlaceOrderActivity will yield a retry action—the only valid thing to do at that point in the protocol.

Java Consumer Implementation

Implementing the consumer is nontrivial in the absence of frameworks that understand hypermedia. Nonetheless, with a few simple patterns, we can confidently build consumers for hypermedia services. To illustrate, we'll walk through the code in Example 5-25.

Example 5-25. Actions and business objects in the consumer

```java
public void orderAndPay(Order order, URI entryPointUri) {

    PlaceOrderActivity placeOrderActivity = new PlaceOrderActivity();
    placeOrderActivity.placeOrder(order, entryPointUri);

    // Order processing omitted for brevity...

    Actions actions = placeOrderActivity.getActions();
    if(actions.has(PaymentActivity.class)) {
      PaymentActivity paymentActivity = actions.get(PaymentActivity.class);
      paymentActivity.payForOrder(
        payment().withAmount(readOrderActivity.getOrder().getCost()).build());
      actions = paymentActivity.getActions();
    }
    // Remainder of workflow omitted for brevity
}
```

When building a consumer, we know the service's contractual information is contained in the media types and link relations the service supports, as well as in any entry point URIs the service provider chooses to share with us. Because we already know the processing model for the Restbucks media type, building a consumer for services that support that media type is straightforward.

The orderAndPay(...) method in Example 5-25 shows an ordering and payment implementation that we used in the functional testing of our Java service. The method takes the well-known Restbucks ordering URI (*http://restbucks.com/order*) and uses a PlaceOrderActivity to create and send an order representation to the service via the underlying Jersey client library.

Assuming the order is successfully lodged, the `placeOrderActivity` instance will contain a local `Order` object for the consumer to process and an `Actions` object that encapsulates the legal next activities (if any). Under the covers, the creation of an `Actions` object is parameterized from the link relations that the consumer plumbing finds in response representations.

> **NOTE**
>
> As consumers, we know the link relations that Restbucks uses and can code against that contract. Hence, in our implementation, specific consumer-side actions have been written to correspond to service-side activities advertised through link relations.

From the set of actions returned, the consumer-side business logic can make choices about what to do next. For example, if the consumer discovers an `UpdateOrderActivity` in the `Actions` instance (using the `actions.has(UpdateOrderActivity.class)` call), it retrieves it by calling the `actions.get(UpdateOrderActivity.class)` method and uses it to update the corresponding order resource on the service.

From this point, the workflow proceeds through the remaining activities, updating (or canceling) the order, paying for the order, obtaining a receipt, and acknowledging receipt of the drinks. At each stage, the consumer follows the same pattern: look for the most desirable action to take at the current instant, execute it, and repeat.

Building the Ordering Service in .NET

Like Java, the .NET platform has frameworks, such as Windows Communication Foundation (WCF), that make working with HTTP more pleasant and productive. Again like Java, there's no obvious framework for building hypermedia-aware services, so Restbucks developed one.

The Restbucks .NET Hypermedia Framework

The Restbucks framework decouples hypermedia from business activities, and transparently maps between the service implementation and the DAP advertised to consumers. Figure 5-13 shows a logical view of how a service processes incoming and outgoing resource representations. A similar approach can be used to build consumers with the same framework.

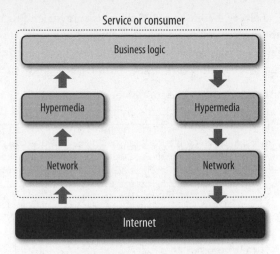

Figure 5-13. *Separating network, hypermedia, and business logic*

In our solution, the network layer deals with HTTP and is provided by the .NET Framework. The hypermedia layer deals with resource state transitions. For incoming representations, it determines whether the request is valid given the current resource state. For outgoing representations, the hypermedia layer injects <dap:link> elements, which advertise the next legal protocol steps, into the response. The business layer, meanwhile, focuses exclusively on application logic and its data.

The hypermedia framework manages resource state transitions by embedding appropriate hypermedia controls into a response based on both the state of the resource targeted by the request and the state of any associated resources. To express this protocol, we have devised a simple, declarative Domain-Specific Language (DSL). Scripts written with the Restbucks DSL choreograph numerous business actions and externalize application state to consumers.

The hypermedia framework and its scripts are hosted on a web server implemented with the HttpListener class.* The server delegates incoming requests to the hypermedia framework's dispatcher. The dispatcher maintains a collection of the currently active state machines, each of which runs an instance of our DSL program.

NOTE

Remember that each workflow in the service implementation represents resource state machines, not a single, overarching application protocol state machine. By implementing the service solely in terms of resource states, we avoid having to save protocol instance state (application state) on the server, which allows us to scale the service horizontally.

---

* Internet Information Server (IIS) on Windows or any other web server that can host the .NET runtime and load SQL Server Modeling's codename "M" language can be used.

Each state machine analyzes incoming HTTP requests and, depending on the state of the resource to which the request relates, dispatches the payload to an appropriate .NET method in the business logic layer. The method deals with XML documents as the input and output, and is unaware of the HTTP and hypermedia details of the interaction.

On the response path, the hypermedia framework receives XML documents from the business layer and augments them with any hypermedia constructs declared in the state machine DSL description. The resultant payload is then passed to the underlying HTTP infrastructure for delivery to the consumer, as we see in Figure 5-14.

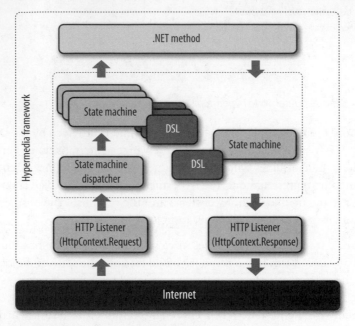

Figure 5-14. The Restbucks .NET hypermedia framework

An External DSL for Hypermedia Interactions

The DSL used for the Restbucks hypermedia framework is a state machine description markup language. This language includes constructs representing hypermedia controls, which are injected into representations as XML <dap:link> elements.

The DSL in Example 5-26 declares the possible states of a Restbucks order resource and the supported transitions from each of those life-cycle states. It's easy to see how tooling could be used to produce such DSL documents, but we think it's easy enough to write by hand too. While the primary focus of the DSL is to describe a resource's state transitions, it also includes those DAP-specific transitions that relate to the particular resource.

```
StateMachine
  UriTemplate http://restbucks.com/order/{id}
  Namespace Restbucks.OrderingService
  MediaType application/vnd.restbucks+xml
  RelationsIn http://relations.restbucks.com


State OrderCreated
  POST NewOrder 201 => Unpaid
    When NotValidOrder 400
End


State Unpaid
  GET GetOrderStatus 200
    When NoSuchOrder 404
  POST UpdateOrder 200
  DELETE CancelOrder 200 => Cancelled
  Links
    latest # When the URI is missing, the active resource's one is assumed
    update
    payment http://restbucks.com/payment/{id}
    cancel
End


State Preparing
  GET GetOrderStatus 200
  Links
    latest
End


State Ready
  GET GetOrderStatus 200
  Links
    latest
    receipt http://restbucks.com/receipt/{id}
End


Final State Delivered End
Final State Cancelled End
```

The state machine description in Example 5-26 consists of a declaration of a set of global properties and a series of states through which the order resource may transition. The first state lexically is considered to be the initial resource state.

- The `UriTemplate` property at the top of the DSL identifies the resource whose life cycle is managed by state machine instances based on this program. To keep things simple, we've assumed that the `UriTemplate` has a specific structure, with the resource identifier at the end being the only variable part of the URI. The service implementation does not expose the URI template to consumers. Outside the boundaries of the ordering service, there is no way to determine which part of the URI is actually used as the internal order identifier.

- The `Namespace` property defines the .NET namespace in which any unqualified method and exception names will reside.

- The `MediaType` property defines the media type that will be used in all HTTP requests and responses based on this DSL.

- The `RelationsIn` property defines the URI prefix for all the relations in the `Links` sections of the DSL.

There are two different subconstructs in each state of Example 5-26:

- The `HTTPVerb` is used to identify valid incoming HTTP requests, given the current state of a resource and what action should be performed upon receipt of such requests. The `MethodName` specifies the .NET method to dispatch followed by the HTTP status code of the response should that method complete normally. An optional `=> StateName` identifies the state to which the resource should automatically transition after successful processing of the incoming request. The optional `When` conjunction allows us to deal with exceptions that the business logic from the invoked .NET method might generate, and the HTTP status code of the response in such a case.

- The `Links` section declares the `<dap:link>` elements that should be included in the payload of the responses to consumers when the resource is at that particular state. The links can point to other resources hosted by Restbucks, or any other resources on the Web.

Using a declarative description of resource state transitions, such as the one shown in Example 5-26, we can modify and evolve a DAP without having to radically change our service's implementation. Most importantly, however, we can rapidly develop and deploy new DAPs.

Implementation Considerations for .NET

When the Restbucks service receives an HTTP request, it routes it to the hypermedia framework dispatcher, which in turn delivers it to the appropriate state machine instance. The dispatcher checks the request's URI against each state machine's URI template to determine which state machine should deal with the request.

Resource creation

The order resource state machine expects the first request to be a POST, as per the initial state of the DSL script in Example 5-26. By activating the initial state of a resource, the framework also creates an instance of the state machine to track the resource's life cycle and its hypermedia interactions. The value of the UriTemplate property, up to but not including the /{id} variable part, is considered the URI for the initial request (*http://restbucks.com/order*). From that point on, requests matching the resource's URI template are checked against the same state machine instance.

> ──── **NOTE** ──────────────────────────────────
>
> Our sample implementation maintains resource state in memory. This solution is not easily scaled horizontally, nor is it resilient to machine failure. In a production environment, we would retrieve resource state on a per-request basis from a shared store or object cache.

If an incoming request doesn't match any of the expected HTTP verbs in the active state, the framework automatically responds with a 405 Method Not Allowed status code. Example 5-27 shows an initial POST request* to the .NET ordering service.

Example 5-27. HTTP request for a new order

```
POST /order HTTP/1.1
Content-Type: application/vnd.restbucks+xml
Accept: application/vnd.restbucks+xml
Connection: keep-alive
Content-Length: 425

<?xml version="1.0" encoding="UTF-8" standalone="yes"?>
<order xmlns="http://schemas.restbucks.com">
  <item>
    <milk>skim</milk>
    <size>medium</size>
    <drink>cappuccino</drink>
  </item>
<item>
  <milk>semi</milk>
  <size>small</size>
 <drink>cappuccino</drink>
</item>
<item>
  <milk>semi</milk>
  <size>large</size>
  <drink>cappuccino</drink>
```

* The XML payload was formatted for readability. The raw XML is unpleasant.

```
        </item>
        <location>takeAway</location>
</order>
```

The web server receives the request and hands it to the dispatcher, which determines from the URI *http://restbucks.com/order* that the order state machine should process the request. Since the URI template and the verb match the conditions for the initial state and the media type is as expected, the state machine extracts the payload from the request and gives it to the NewOrder() method, as per the POST NewOrder definition.

Example 5-28 shows the NewOrder() method. The signatures for methods such as this, which handle requests for the initial state of a state machine, differ from those of the methods for the remaining states in that they return a string that acts as the identifier for the state about to be instantiated. The same string will also be used as the value of the {id} part in the state machine's URI template. The framework maintains an internal dictionary of all the active states based on the unique key returned by the NewOrder() method.

Example 5-28. Implementation of the NewOrder() method

```
namespace Restbucks
{
    public class OrderingService
    {
        public static string NewOrder(XDocument request, XDocument response)
        {
            var order = Database.NewOrderFromXml(request.Root);
            response.Add(order.ToXml());
            return order.Id.ToString();
        }
    }
}
```

As Example 5-28 shows, the hypermedia framework abstracts the HTTP details from the implementation. The application logic only needs to deal with XML payloads for the incoming requests and outgoing responses.

In our service, we create a new business object to represent the order in the database, serialize it back to XML, add it to the response, and return its identifier. The service will embed more information about the order (e.g., its preparation status and cost) in the payload. Remember that the hypermedia framework will add the necessary <dap:link> elements.

The response for this interaction has a 201 Created status code, as shown in Example 5-29, in accordance with the state machine definition in Example 5-26. The payload is the representation of the order resource. This representation includes <status> and

<cost> elements, as well as hypermedia links representing the possible transitions the customer application can initiate. Notice the => Unpaid part following POST NewOrder 201 in Example 5-26; this tells the hypermedia framework to transition the state machine instance for the order to the Unpaid state once the response has been sent.

Example 5-29. *Response sent to the consumer after the successful creation of an order*

```
HTTP/1.1 201 Created
Content-Type: application/vnd.restbucks+xml
Date: Sun, 21 Mar 2010 22:44:11 GMT
Content-Length: 1067

<?xml version="1.0" encoding="UTF-8" standalone="yes"?>
<order xmlns="http://schemas.restbucks.com">
  <item>
    <milk>skim</milk>
    <size>medium</size>
    <drink>cappuccino</drink>
  </item>
  <item>
    <milk>semi</milk>
    <size>small</size>
   <drink>cappuccino</drink>
  </item>
  <item>
    <milk>semi</milk>
    <size>large</size>
    <drink>cappuccino</drink>
  </item>
  <location>takeAway</location>
  <cost>8.00</cost>
  <status>payment-expected</status>
  <dap:link rel="http://relations.restbucks.com/latest"
    mediaType="application/vnd.restbucks+xml"
    uri="http://restbucks.com/order/1" />
  <dap:link rel="http://relations.restbucks.com/update"
    mediaType="application/vnd.restbucks+xml"
    uri="http://restbucks.com/order/1"/>
  <dap:link rel="http://relations.restbucks.com/payment"
    mediaType="application/vnd.restbucks+xml"
    uri="http://restbucks.com/payment/1" />
  <dap:link rel="http://relations.restbucks.com/cancel"
    mediaType="application/vnd.restbucks+xml"
    uri="http://restbucks.com/order/1" />
</order>
```

In this initial state, the order representation contains links that indicate that the customer can get the latest version of the order resource, or update it, or cancel the order, or submit payment. The verbs and the format of the payloads to be used are captured by the rel and mediaType attributes of each <link> element, as per our description of the Restbucks DAP.

Main service logic

Subsequent interactions continue in a similar manner. For example, as long as the order is in the Unpaid state, a GET request sent to *http://restbucks.com/order/1* will result in a call to the GetOrderStatus() method, as shown in Example 5-30.

Example 5-30. *Ordering operations implemented in C#*

```
namespace Restbucks
{
  public class OrderingService
  {
    public static void GetOrderStatus(string id,
                            XDocument request, XDocument response)
    {
      var order = Database.GetOrder(id);
      response.Add(order.ToXml());
    }
  }

  // Other methods elided for brevity
}
```

The GetOrderStatus() method is given the order's identifier and the request/response payloads and interacts with an order repository on the caller's behalf. Correspondingly, the OrderingService class has methods (not shown in Example 5-30) to create, update, and delete an order, each of which follows the same pattern.

Payment

Our next task is to add the payment logic. Without payment, the order won't transition to the Preparing state or be given to the barista. From the moment an order is created, payment is expected. We treat payment as a separate resource, with its own internal state machine. The payment resource state machine is shown in Example 5-31.

Example 5-31. *Payment state machine*

```
StateMachine
  UriTemplate http://restbucks.com/payment/{id}
  Namespace Restbucks.OrderingService
  MediaType application/vnd.restbucks+xml
  RelationsIn http://relations.restbucks.com

State PaymentCreated
  => PaymentExpected
End

State PaymentExpected
  PUT PaymendReceived 201 => PaymentReceived
    When NoValidPayment 400
  Links
    payment
End

Final State PaymentReceived
  GET GetReceipt 200
    When NoSuchPayment 404
  Links
    order http://restbucks.com/order/{id}
    receipt
End
```

Notice that there's no service logic associated with the initial state. The hypermedia framework will not call a method to create a payment resource. Instead, it is expected that the resource will be created out of band, in code. Therefore, once an instance of the state machine is created, the framework will automatically transition it to the PaymentExpected state.*

Because consumers have already been given a payment URI, we have to follow a different pattern here. This requires a consumer to submit a PUT request containing the payment representation, which results in the PaymentReceived() method being called. The implementation of PaymentReceived() is shown in Example 5-32.

---

* It could be argued that PaymentExpected should be the initial state and that the PUT request would create the payment resource. However, the semantics of the initial state in the DSL are such that we expect an HTTP request to be sent to the URI template without the {id} part. Since the payment resource was already created through code, rather than due to a request initiated by a consumer, we need to instruct the hypermedia framework to perform this automatic transition without expecting an initial request.

Example 5-32. *Payment implementation*

```
namespace Restbucks
{
  public static class OrderingService
  {
    public static void PaymentReceived(string id,
                                       XDocument request,
                                       XDocument response)
    {
      var payment = Payment.FromXml(request.Root);
      payment.Paid = DateTime.Now;

      var order = Database.GetOrder(id);
      order.Status = "Preparing";
      Database.UpdateOrder(order);

      Database.PutPayment(id, payment);

      response.Add(payment.ToXml());

      OrderingService.PrepareOrder(id);
    }
  }

  // Other methods elided for brevity
}
```

When the service receives a payment request, it creates a business object from the payload, and then retrieves the order from the database and sets its Status property to Preparing. The service then adds the payment to the database and initiates the preparation of the order. This last step starts an internal process involving the barista. To do this, the service calls ThreadPool.QueueUserWorkItem() to add the work to a queue. The barista receives the order information, prepares it, and then notifies the rest of the ordering service that the order is ready by calling OrderPrepared(), which moves the order into the Ready state.

Notice that the OrderPrepared() method is able to interact with the hypermedia framework without involving a consumer. This allows Restbucks to transition the state machine to the Ready state by binding directly to the state machine instance, rather than through the external HTTP interface.

Delivery

Recall that when the service receives a payment from a consumer, it replies with a 201 Created response. The hypermedia framework adds an order link to that response. In this context, the link indicates to the client that it is expected to GET the latest representation of the order to find out whether it is ready for delivery.

When the barista calls the `OrderPrepared()` method, the order transitions to the Ready state. This change in resource state causes different links to be added to the order's representation the next time it is requested. This is handled by the hypermedia DSL snippet shown in Example 5-33.

Example 5-33. *The Ready state of the order resource*

```
State Ready
   GET GetOrderStatus 200
   Links
      latest
      receipt http://restbucks.com/receipt/{id}
End
```

The DSL here indicates that the receipt link will be included in the payload of any response if the order is in the Ready state. To complete delivery of the order, the consumer only needs to send a DELETE request, as defined by the semantics of `http://relations.restbucks.com/receipt` of the `application/vnd.restbucks+xml` media type, to the receipt URI *http://restbucks.com/receipt/1*. The DSL for the receipt resource is very simple and similar to that of the payment resource, as shown in Example 5-34.

Example 5-34. *Receipt state machine*

```
StateMachine
   UriTemplate http://restbucks.com/receipt/{id}
   Namespace Restbucks.OrderingService
   MediaType application/vnd.restbucks+xml
   RelationsIn http://relations.restbucks.com

State ReceiptCreated
   => ReceiptReady
End

State ReceiptReady
   DELETE ReceiveOrder 200
      When NoSuchReceipt 404
   Links
      receipt
End
```

When the DELETE request is received by the receipt resource, the `ReceiveOrder()` method is called, as shown in Example 5-35.

Example 5-35. *Completing an order*

```
namespace Restbucks
{
   public static class OrderingService
```

```
    {
        public static void ReceiveOrder(string id,
                                        XDocument request,
                                        XDocument response)
        {
            var order = Database.GetOrder(id);
            order.Status = "received";
            Database.UpdateOrder(order);

            response.Add(order.ToXml());
        }
    }
}
```

Like the other methods, the implementation here is very simple. We retrieve the order from the database, update its status, and add its representation to the response. Because the protocol has ended, the representation passes through the hypermedia framework untouched before being dispatched to the consumer.

Ready, Set, Action

With the addition of hypermedia, we've reached the pinnacle of Richardson's service maturity model in Figure 5-15. While we still haven't completed our journey—we have plenty more to learn about using the Web as a platform for building distributed systems—we now have all the elements at our disposal to build RESTful services.

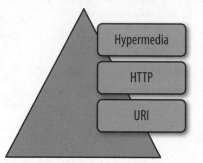

Figure 5-15. *Hypermedia services are level three on the Richardson maturity model*

There's more to the Web than REST, but this milestone is important because of the significant benefits, in terms of loose coupling, self-description, scalability, and maintainability, conferred by the tenets of the REST architectural style.

All of this comes at a rather modest cost when compared to what we did to build nonhypermedia services. This is encouraging, since it means the effort required to build and support a robust hypermedia service over its lifetime is comparable to that associated with building CRUD services. It's certainly a better proposition than tunneling through the Web.

We've now seen how hypermedia services are straightforward to design, implement, and test using familiar tools and libraries. And by augmenting representations with hypermedia controls, we're able to project DAPs over the Web to consumers. We've also seen that computer systems (not just browsers!) use hypermedia links to build DAPs that model (dynamically evolving) business workflows.

From here onward, we'll assume that hypermedia and RESTful services are the norm. In the following chapters, we'll see how scalability, security, and other higher-order protocols such as publish-subscribe can work harmoniously with the Web. Read on!

CHAPTER SIX

Scaling Out

THE WEB IS THE WORLD'S LARGEST ONLINE INFORMATION SYSTEM, scaling to billions of devices and users. Hypermedia documents connect a near limitless number of resources, most of which are designed to be read, not modified. At a grand scale, structural hypermedia rules, helped by the safe, idempotent properties of the ubiquitous GET method, and to a lesser extent some of the other cacheable verbs.

From a programmatic web perspective, the infrastructure that has evolved on the Web—particularly around information retrieval—solves many integration challenges. In this chapter, we look at how we can use that infrastructure and some associated patterns to build scalable, fault-tolerant enterprise applications.

GET Back to Basics

According to the HTTP specification, GET is used to retrieve the representation of a resource. Example 6-1 shows a consumer retrieving a representation of an order resource from a Restbucks service by sending an HTTP GET request to the server where the resource is located.

Example 6-1. *A GET request using a relative URI*

```
GET /order/1234 HTTP/1.1
Connection: keep-alive
Host: restbucks.com
```

The value of the Host header plus the relative path that follows GET together give the complete URI of the resource being requested—in this case, *http://restbucks.com/order/1234*. In HTTP 1.1, servers must also support absolute URIs, in which case the Host header is not necessary, as shown in Example 6-2.

Example 6-2. *A GET request using an absolute URI*

```
GET http://restbucks.com/order/1234 HTTP/1.1
```

The response to either of these two requests is shown in Example 6-3.

Example 6-3. *A response to a GET request*

```
HTTP/1.1 200 OK
Content-Length: ...
Content-Type: application/vnd.restbucks+xml
Date: Fri, 26 Mar 2010 10:01:22 GMT
Last-Modified: Fri, 26 Mar 2010 09:55:15 GMT
Cache-Control: max-age=3600
ETag: "74f4be4b"

<order xmlns="http://schemas.restbucks.com">
  <location>takeaway</location>
  <item>
    <drink>latte</drink>
    <milk>whole</milk>
    <size>large</size>
  </item>
</order>
```

As well as the payload, the response includes some headers, which help consumers and any intermediaries on the network process the response. Importantly, we can use some of these headers to control the caching behavior of the order representation.

As we discussed in Chapter 3, GET is both safe and idempotent. We use GET simply to *retrieve* a resource's state representation, rather than deliberately *modify* that state.

NOTE

If we don't want the entire representation of a resource, but just want to inspect the HTTP headers, we can use the HEAD verb. HEAD allows us to decide how to make forward progress based on the processing context of the identified resource, without having to pay the penalty of transferring its entire representation over the network.

Because GET has no impact on resource state, it is possible to optimize the network to take advantage of its safe and idempotent characteristics. If we see a GET request, we immediately understand that the requestor doesn't want to modify anything. For these requests, it makes sense to store responses closer to consumers, where they can be reused to satisfy subsequent requests. This optimization is baked into the Web through caching.

NOTE

GET isn't the only HTTP verb to yield cacheable responses, though it is by far the most prevalent and useful. We'll focus on GET for now because it's so widespread, but later in the chapter we'll look at caching in the context of other verbs too.

Caching

Caching is the ability to store copies of frequently accessed data in several places along the request-response path. When a consumer requests a resource representation, the request goes through a cache or a series of caches toward the service hosting the resource. If any of the caches along the request path has a fresh copy of the requested representation, it uses that copy to satisfy the request. If none of the caches can satisfy the request, the request travels all the way to the service (or *origin server* as it is formally known).

Origin servers control the caching behavior of the representations they issue. Using HTTP headers, an origin server indicates whether a response can be cached, and if so, by whom, and for how long. Caches along the response path can take a copy of a response, but only if the caching metadata allows them to do so. The caches can then use these copies to satisfy subsequent requests. Cached copies of a resource representation can be used to satisfy subsequent requests so long as they remain *fresh*. A cached representation remains fresh for a specific period of time, which is called its *freshness lifetime*. When the age of a cached object exceeds its freshness lifetime, the object is said to be *stale*. Caches will often add an Age response header to a cached response. The Age header indicates how many seconds have passed since the representation was generated at the origin server.

A stale representation must be *revalidated* with the origin server before it can be used to satisfy any further requests. If the revalidation reveals that the stale representation is in fact still *valid*, the cached copy can be reused. If, however, the resource has changed since the stale representation was first issued, the cached copy must be *invalidated* and replaced. Representations can become invalid during their freshness lifetime without the cache knowing. Unless the consumer specifically asks for a revalidation or a new copy from the origin server, the cache will continue to use these invalid (but fresh) representations until they become stale.

Benefits of Caching

Optimizing the network using caching improves the overall quality-of-service characteristics of a distributed application. Caching significantly benefits four areas of systems operation, allowing us to:

Reduce bandwidth
> By reducing the number of network hops required to retrieve a representation, caching reduces network traffic and conserves bandwidth.

Reduce latency
> Because caches store copies of frequently accessed information nearer to where the information is used, caching reduces the time it takes to satisfy a request.

Reduce load on servers
> Because they are able to serve a percentage of requests from their own stores, caches reduce the number of requests that reach an origin server.

Hide network failures
> Caches can continue to serve cached content even if the origin server that issued the content is currently unavailable or committed to an expensive processing task that prevents it from generating a response. In this way, caches provide fault tolerance by masking intermittent failures and delays from consumers.

Ordinarily, we'd have to make a substantial investment in development effort and middleware in order to achieve these benefits. However, the Web's existing caching infrastructure means we don't have to; the capability is already globally deployed.

Caching and the Statelessness Constraint

One of the Web's key architectural tenets is that servers and services should not preserve application state. The statelessness constraint helps make distributed applications fault-tolerant and horizontally scalable. But it also has its downsides. First, because application state is not persisted on the server, consumers and services must exchange application state information with each request and response, which adds to the size of the message and the bandwidth consumed by the interaction. Second, because the constraint requires services to forget about clients between requests, it prevents the use of the classical publish-subscribe pattern (which requires the service to retain subscriber lists). To receive notifications, consumers must instead frequently poll services to determine whether a resource has changed, adding to the load on the server.

Caching helps mitigate the consequences of applying the statelessness constraint.* It reduces the amount of data sent over the network by storing representations closer to where they are needed, and it reduces the load on origin servers by having caches satisfy repeated requests for the same data.

* Benjamin Carlyle discusses this topic in more detail here: *http://soundadvice.id.au/blog/2010/01/17/.*

In fact, polling is what allows the Web to scale. By repeatedly polling a cacheable resource, a consumer "warms" all of the caches between it and the origin server, pulling data from the origin server into the network where other consumers can rapidly access it. Furthermore, once the caches are warm, any requests they can satisfy mean less traffic to the origin server, no matter how hard a consumer polls. This is the classic latency/scalability trade-off that the Web provides. By making representations cacheable, we get massive scale, but introduce latency between the resource changing and those changes becoming visible to consumers. Of course, individual caches can themselves become overloaded by requests; in such circumstances, we may have to consider clustered or hierarchical caching topologies.

Reasons for Not Caching

We've discussed several of the benefits of caching. But there are at least four situations in which we might not want to cache data:

- When GET requests generate server-side side effects that have a business impact on the service. Remember, GET is safe, but it can still generate side effects for which the consumer cannot be held responsible. These effects may range from simply logging traffic (which is then used to generate business metrics) to incrementing a counter that determines whether a particular class of customer is within a certain usage threshold for the service to which the request is being directed. If these kinds of internal side effects are important, we may want to prevent or limit caching.

- When consumers cannot tolerate any discrepancy between the state of a resource as conveyed in a response and the actual state of that resource at the moment the request was satisfied. As we discuss later in this chapter, caching exacerbates the weak consistency of the Web; the longer a representation of a volatile resource is cached, the more likely it is that a response returned from a cache no longer reflects the state of the resource at the origin server. This is particularly problematic when two or more overlapping resources manipulate the same underlying domain entity. Consider, for example, a service that exposes order and completion resources, where both an order and a completion are associated with the same underlying order domain entity. POSTing a completion changes the state of an order entity. Because of this change, cached order representations no longer reflect the state of the underlying domain entity. Consumers that act on these cached order representations may commit themselves to business transactions that are no longer valid.

- When a response contains sensitive or personal data particular to a consumer. Security and caching can coexist to a certain extent: first, local and proxy caches can sometimes cache encrypted responses; second, as we show later, it is possible to cache responses in a way that requires the cache to authorize them with the origin server with every request. But in many circumstances, regulatory or organizational requirements will dictate that responses must not be cached.

- When the data changes so frequently that caching and revalidating a response adds more overhead than the origin server simply generating a fresh response with each request.

Types of Caches

A whole ecosystem of proxy servers has grown up around GET and its safe and idempotent semantics. Proxy servers are common intermediaries between consumers and origin servers, which we recognize from our human use of the Web. While they can perform various operations on HTTP requests and responses, such as information filtering and security checks, they are most commonly used for caching.

Many of us are familiar with application caches and database caches—two types of caches that can reside behind service boundaries. Nowadays, many systems also explicitly route requests through distributed in-memory caches. But the kinds of caches we're talking about here are those that are already part of the installed infrastructure of the Web:

Local cache
> A local cache stores representations from many origin servers on behalf of a single user agent, application, or machine. A consumer may have a local cache so that frequently accessed resources are stored locally and served immediately. Local caches can be held in memory or persisted to disk.

Proxy cache
> A proxy cache stores representations from many origin servers on behalf of many consumers. Proxies can be hosted both inside the corporate firewall and outside. An organization may deploy caches of its own so that the applications running within its boundaries don't necessarily hit the Internet when accessing cacheable resources. Network providers (e.g., ISPs), organizations with their own virtual networks, and even entire countries may also introduce proxies in order to speed up access to frequently accessed web resources.

Reverse proxy
> A reverse proxy, or accelerator, stores representations from one origin server on behalf of many consumers. Reverse proxies are located in front of an application or web server. Clusters of reverse proxies improve redundancy and prevent popular resources from becoming server hotspots. Reverse proxy implementations include Squid,[*] Varnish,[†] and Apache Traffic Server.[‡]

Figure 6-1 shows the many places in which these caches appear on the Web.

[*] *http://www.squid-cache.org/*
[†] *http://varnish-cache.org/*
[‡] *http://trafficserver.apache.org/*

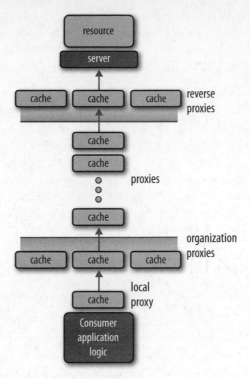

Figure 6-1. *Web caches*

Caches can be arranged in complex topologies. They can be clustered to improve reliability or arranged in hierarchies. Caches in a cache hierarchy forward requests for which they do not have a cached representation to other caches farther up the hierarchy, until a cached representation is found or the request is finally passed to the origin server.

WARNING ————————————————————————————————

A request reaching an origin server is the most expensive operation on the Web. Not only will the request have consumed network bandwidth, but also, once it reaches the server, it may cause computation to occur and data to be retrieved. These are not cheap options at web scale: contention for computational and data resources will be fierce for a typical service. Caching acts as a buffer between the finite resources of a service and the myriad consumers of those resources on the Web.

Making Content Cacheable

Given that caches are designed around the retrieval of resource representations, it shouldn't come as a surprise to learn that they mostly (but not exclusively) work with

GET requests. Responses to GET requests are cacheable by default.* Responses to POST requests are not cacheable by default, but can be made cacheable if either an Expires header, or a Cache-Control header with a directive that explicitly allows caching, is added to the response. Responses to PUT and DELETE requests are not cacheable at all.

The more a service supports GET and the appropriate caching headers, the more the Web's infrastructure can help with scalability. Imagine a situation in which a very inquisitive Restbucks customer repeatedly asks a barista for the status of his coffee. If the barista spends a lot of her time answering questions, her overall output will diminish. Given that the answer stays the same for relatively long periods (e.g., "I'm preparing your medium skim-milk latte"), a lot of effort is wasted for very little benefit. Deploying a cache between the consumer and the Restbucks barista frees the barista from having to answer the same question over and over again. As a result, the overall coffee output of the Restbucks service improves.

Response Headers Used for Caching

There are two main HTTP response headers that we can use to control caching behavior:

Expires
> The Expires HTTP header specifies an absolute expiry time for a cached representation. Beyond that time, a cached representation is considered stale and must be revalidated with the origin server. A service can indicate that a representation has already expired by including an Expires value equal to the Date header value (the representation expires *now*), or a value of 0. To indicate that a representation never expires, a service can include a time up to one year in the future.

Cache-Control
> The Cache-Control header can be used in both requests and responses to control the caching behavior of the response. The header value comprises one or more comma-separated directives. These directives determine whether a response is cacheable, and if so, by whom, and for how long.

If we can determine an absolute expiry time for a cached response, we should use an Expires header. If it's more appropriate to indicate how long the response can be considered fresh once it has left the origin server, we should use a Cache-Control header, adding a max-age or s-maxage directive to specify a relative *Time to Live* (TTL).

Cacheable responses (whether to a GET or to a POST request) should also include a *validator*—either an ETag or a Last-Modified header:

---

* The response should really have either an expiry time, or a validator, as we discuss shortly.

ETag

In Chapter 4, we said that an ETag value is an opaque string token that a server associates with a resource to uniquely identify the state of the resource over its lifetime. When the resource changes, the entity tag changes accordingly. Though we used ETag values for concurrency control in Chapter 4, they are just as useful for validating the freshness of cached representations.

Last-Modified

Whereas a response's Date header indicates when the response was generated, the Last-Modified header indicates when the associated resource last changed. The Last-Modified value cannot be later than the Date value.

Example 6-4 shows a response containing Expires, ETag, and Last-Modified headers.

Example 6-4. *A response with an absolute expiry time*

```
Request:
GET /product-catalog/9876
Host: restbucks.com

Response:
HTTP/1.1 200 OK
Content-Length: ...
Content-Type: application/vnd.restbucks+xml
Date: Fri, 26 Mar 2010 09:33:49 GMT
Expires: Sat, 27 Mar 2010 09:33:49 GMT
Last-Modified: Fri, 26 Mar 2010 09:33:49 GMT
ETag: "cde893c4"

<product xmlns="http://schemas.restbucks.com/product">
  <name>Sumatra Organic Beans</name>
  <size>1kg</size>
  <price>12</price>
</product>
```

This response can be cached and will remain fresh until the date and time specified in the Expires header. To revalidate a response, a cache uses the ETag header value or the Last-Modified header value to do a conditional GET.* If a consumer wants to revalidate a response, it should include a Cache-Control: no-cache directive in its request. This ensures that the conditional request travels all the way to the origin server, rather than being satisfied by an intermediary.

Example 6-5 shows a response containing a Last-Modified header, an ETag header, and a Cache-Control header with a max-age directive.

---

* Choosing between ETag values and Last-Modified timestamps depends on the granularity of updates to the resource. Last-Modified is only as accurate as a timestamp (to the nearest second), while ETags can be generated at any frequency. Typically, however, timestamps are cheaper to generate.

Example 6-5. *A response with a relative expiry time*

```
Request:
GET /product-catalog/1234
Host: restbucks.com

Response:
HTTP/1.1 200 OK
Content-Length: ...
Content-Type: application/vnd.restbucks+xml
Date: Fri, 26 Mar 2010 12:07:22 GMT
Cache-Control: max-age=3600
Last-Modified: Fri, 26 Mar 2010 11:45:00 GMT
ETag: "59c6dd9f"

<product xmlns="http://schemas.restbucks.com/product">
  <name>Fairtrade Roma Coffee Beans</name>
  <size>1kg</size>
  <price>12</price>
</product>
```

This response is cacheable and will remain fresh for up to one hour. As with the previous example, a cache can revalidate the representation using either the Last-Modified value or the ETag value.

Using Caching Directives in Responses

Cache-Control directives serve three functions when used in a response. Some make normally uncacheable responses cacheable. Others make normally cacheable responses uncacheable. Finally, there are some Cache-Control directives that do not affect the cacheability of a response at all; rather, they determine the freshness of an already cacheable response. An individual directive can serve one or more of these functions.

max-age=<delta-seconds>
> This directive controls both cacheability and freshness. It makes a response capable of being cached by local and shared caches (proxies and reverse proxies), as well as specifying a freshness lifetime in seconds. A max-age value overrides any Expiry value supplied in a response.

s-maxage=<delta-seconds>
> Like max-age, this directive serves two functions: it makes responses cacheable, but only by shared caches, and it specifies a freshness lifetime in seconds.

`public`

> This directive makes a response capable of being cached by local and shared caches, but doesn't determine a freshness value. Importantly, `public` takes precedence over authorization headers. Normally, if a request includes an `Authorization` header, the response cannot be cached. If, however, the response includes a `public` directive, it can be cached. You should exercise care, however, when making responses that require authorization cacheable.

`private`

> This directive makes a response capable of being cached by local caches only (i.e., within the consumer implementation). At the same time, it prevents normally cacheable responses from being cached by shared caches. `private` doesn't determine a freshness value.

`must-revalidate`

> This directive makes normally uncacheable responses cacheable, but requires caches to revalidate stale responses with the origin server. Only if the stale response is successfully validated with the origin server can the cached content be used to satisfy the request. `must-revalidate` is enormously useful in balancing consistency with reduced bandwidth and computing resource consumption. While it forces a revalidation request to travel all the way to the origin server, an efficient validation mechanism on the server side will prevent the core service logic from being invoked for a large percentage of requests—all for the cost of a measly 304 Not Modified response.

`proxy-revalidate`

> This directive is similar to `must-revalidate`, but it only applies to shared caches.

`no-cache`

> This directive requires caches to revalidate a cached response with the origin server with every request. If the request is successfully validated with the origin server, the cached content can be used to satisfy the request. The directive only works for responses that have been made cacheable using another header or directive (i.e., it doesn't make uncacheable responses cacheable). Unfortunately, different caches behave in different ways with regard to no-cache: some caches treat no-cache as an instruction to not cache a response (as per an old draft of HTTP 1.1); some treat it correctly, as a requirement to always revalidate a cached response.

`no-store`

> This directive makes normally cacheable content uncacheable by *all* caches.

The HTTP Stale Controls Informational RFC recently added two new directives to this list, which together enable us to make trade-offs between latency, availability, and consistency.* These directives are:

`stale-while-revalidate=<delta-seconds>`

In situations where a cache is able to release a stale response, this directive allows the cache to release the response immediately, but instructs it to also revalidate it in the background (i.e., in a nonblocking fashion). This directive favors reduced latency (caches release stale responses immediately, even as they revalidate them) over consistency. If a stale representation is not revalidated before `delta-seconds` have passed, however, the cache should stop serving it.

`stale-if-error=<delta-seconds>`

This directive allows a cache to release a stale response if it encounters an error while contacting the origin server. If a response is staler than the stale window specified by `delta-seconds`, it should not be released. This directive favors availability over consistency.

Squid 2.7 currently supports these last two directives; support is forthcoming in later versions of Squid and Apache Traffic Server.

The directives we've looked at so far can be mixed in interesting and useful ways, as the following examples demonstrate. Example 6-6 shows how we can make a representation cacheable by local caches for up to one hour.

Example 6-6. Making content cacheable by local caches only

```
Cache-Control: private, max-age=3600
```

Example 6-7 is more interesting, in that it allows caching of representations that require authorization.

Example 6-7. Caching authorized responses

```
Cache-Control: public, max-age=0
```

`public` makes the response cacheable by both local and shared caches, while `max-age=0` requires a cache to revalidate a cached representation with the origin server (using a conditional GET request) before releasing it. (Ideally, we'd use `no-cache`, but because some caches treat `no-cache` as an instruction to not cache at all, we've opted for `max-age=0` instead.) This combination is useful when we want to authorize each request, but still take advantage of the bandwidth savings offered by the caching infrastructure, as we see in Figure 6-2.

---

* *http://www.rfc-editor.org/rfc/rfc5861.txt*

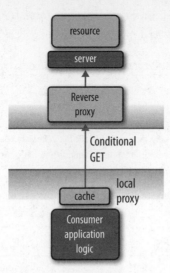

Figure 6-2. *Minimizing traffic for accessing local, consistent, cached representations*

In revalidating each request with the server, the cache will pass on the contents of the `Authorization` header supplied by the consumer. If the origin server replies 401 `Unauthorized`, the cache will refuse to release the cached representation. The combination `public, max-age=0` differs from `must-revalidate` in that it allows caching of responses to requests that contain `Authorization` headers.

Implementing Caching in .NET

Let's see how Restbucks can take advantage of caching to improve the distribution of its menu. The Restbucks menu is an XML document that is consumed by third-party applications such as coffee shop price comparators and customers. The menu resource is dynamically created from the Restbucks product database. Every time the menu service receives a GET request for the menu, it must perform some logic and database access.

Restbucks would like to ensure that its menu service isn't overwhelmed by thousands of requests from external services. But instead of deploying more servers or paying for more bandwidth, Restbucks decides to make use of the Web's caching infrastructure.

This caching infrastructure includes reverse proxies and proxy caches, as well as local caches. Some consumers of Restbucks' menu service may opt to use their local caches to speed up their systems, knowing that consistency with Restbucks' data isn't always guaranteed. Doing so is easy: Example 6-8 shows some simple .NET HTTP client code that uses the WinINet cache provided by Microsoft Windows Internet Services. The WinINet cache is the same local cache that Internet Explorer uses, and so has a large installed base.

To take advantage of local caching, we need only add a `RequestCachePolicy` instance to our request. The policy is initialized with a `RequestCacheLevel.Default` enum value, which ensures that the local cache is used to try to satisfy the request. If the local cache can't satisfy the request, the request will be forwarded to the origin server (or to any intervening shared caches).

Example 6-8. Using the WinINet local cache from consumer code

```
Uri uri = new Uri("http://restbucks.com/product-catalog/1234");
HttpWebRequest webRequest = (HttpWebRequest) WebRequest.Create(uri);
webRequest.Method = "GET";
webRequest.CachePolicy = new RequestCachePolicy(RequestCacheLevel.Default);
HttpWebResponse webResponse = (HttpWebResponse) webRequest.GetResponse();
```

On the server side, the menu service is implemented using an instance of the .NET Framework's HttpListener class.* Example 6-9 shows the code that creates and starts the listener.

Example 6-9. A simple web server

```
private static void Main(string[] args)
{
  Console.WriteLine("Server started...");
  Console.WriteLine();

  HttpListener listener = new HttpListener();
  listener.Prefixes.Add("http://localhost./");
  listener.Start();
  listener.BeginGetContext(new AsyncCallback(GetMenu), listener);

  Console.ReadKey();
}
```

When it receives a request, the listener calls its GetMenu(...) method, passing it an HttpListenerContext object, which encapsulates the request and response context. Each request is handled on a separate thread taken from the .NET thread pool. The implementation of GetMenu(...) is shown in Example 6-10.

Example 6-10. GetMenu(...) satisfies an HTTP GET request

```
public void GetMenu(HttpListenerContext context)
{
  context.Response.ContentType = "application/xml";
  XDocument menu = menuRepository.Get();
  using (Stream stream = context.Response.OutputStream)
  {
    using (XmlWriter writer = new XmlTextWriter(stream, Encoding.UTF8))
    {
```

---

* For this example, we host the HttpListener instance in a console application. For production, we'd host it in IIS to take advantage of management and fault-tolerance features.

```
        menu.WriteTo(writer);
      }
    }
  }
```

First, GetMenu(...) sets the ContentType of the response to application/xml. Then it gets an XDocument representation of the menu from a repository and writes it to the response stream.

This implementation produces the response shown in Example 6-11. Every time a consumer attempts to GET the Restbucks menu, the request is handled by this code. In other words, every request consumes processor time. This is because there are no caching headers in the response that would allow any web proxies on the request path to cache the response and directly serve it in the future.

Example 6-11. Response to a GET request for the Restbucks menu

```
HTTP/1.1 200 OK
Content-Type: application/xml
Date: Sun, 27 Dec 2009 01:30:51 GMT
Content-Length: ...

...
<!-- Content omitted -->
```

According to the HTTP specification, a web proxy can cache a 200 OK response even if the response doesn't include any specific caching metadata.* Still, it'd be helpful if the service explicitly stated whether a response can be cached. Doing so helps to ensure that the caching infrastructure is used to its full potential. Example 6-12 shows how we can change the implementation of GetMenu(...) to include some caching metadata.

Example 6-12. Adding a Cache-Control header to the response

```
public void GetMenu(HttpListenerContext context)
{
  context.Response.ContentType = "application/xml";
  context.Response.AddHeader("Cache-Control", "public, max-age=604800");
  XDocument menu = Database.GetMenu();
  using (Stream stream = context.Response.OutputStream)
  {
    using (XmlWriter writer = new XmlTextWriter(stream, Encoding.UTF8))
    {
      menu.WriteTo(writer);
    }
  }
}
```

---

* Additional responses that can be cached in this fashion include 203 Non-Authoritative Information, 206 Partial Content, 300 Multiple Choices, 301 Moved Permanently, and 410 Gone.

As Example 6-12 shows, we only need to add a single line in order to make the response cacheable. Because we don't expect the menu to change more than once per week, we inform caches that they can consider the response fresh for up to 604,800 seconds. We also indicate that the representation is public, meaning both local and shared caches can cache it. As a result of this change, the response now contains a Cache-Control header, as shown in Example 6-13.

Example 6-13. The response now includes a Cache-Control header

```
HTTP/1.1 200 OK
Cache-Control: public, max-age=604800
Content-Type: application/xml
Date: Sun, 27 Dec 2009 01:30:51 GMT
Content-Length: ...

...
<!-- Content omitted -->
```

That one line of code has the potential to dramatically reduce Restbucks' infrastructure and operational costs. Our menu's representation now gets distributed at various caches around the Web, as Figure 6-3 illustrates.

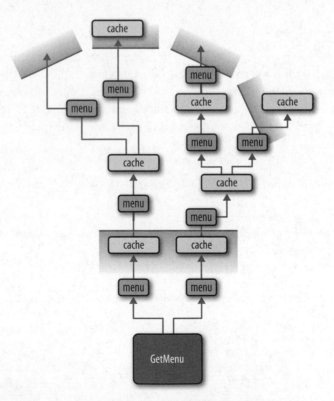

Figure 6-3. The menu representation is cached throughout the Web

Caching doesn't just work for public-facing services. Using these same web caching techniques, we can also improve the scalability and fault-tolerance characteristics of services we deploy within the boundaries of an organization. If we write our applications with caching in mind, and expose most of our business logic through domain application protocols using GET and caching headers, we can offload much of the processing and bandwidth load to caches without any special coding or middleware.

Consistency

Because the Web is loosely coupled, weak consistency is a feature of all web-based distributed applications. As a result of the statelessness constraint, a service has no way of notifying consumers when a resource changes. In consequence, consumers sometimes act on stale data. In an attempt to keep up-to-date, many consumers will repeatedly GET (poll) a resource representation to discover whether it has changed recently. But this strategy is only as good as the polling frequency. In general, we must assume that a consumer's understanding of the state of a resource lags the service's view of the same resource.

Caching only exacerbates the situation. The moment we introduce caching, we should assume that consumers *will* become inconsistent with services, and just deal with it. While there are several techniques for increasing the degree of consistency among consumers, caches, and services, the fact remains that different web actors will often have different copies of a resource representation.

The three techniques for improving consistency are:

Invalidation

Invalidation involves notifying consumers and caches of changes to resources for which they hold cached representations. With server-driven invalidation, the server must maintain a list of recipients to be contacted whenever a resource changes. This goes against the requirement that services not maintain application state.

Validation

To ensure that they have an up-to-date resource representation, consumers and caches can verify a local copy with the origin server. This approach requires the consumer to make a validation request of the service, which uses bandwidth and places some load on the server. Services must be able to respond to validation requests. Unlike server-driven invalidation, however, servers do not have to maintain a list of consumers to be contacted whenever a resource changes. Despite the fact that requests have to travel all the way to the origin server, validation is a relatively efficient, low-bandwidth way of keeping data up-to-date. Validation helps improve scalability and performance, and reduce latency. In so doing, it drives down per-request costs.

Expiration

> Expiration-based consistency involves specifying an explicit TTL for each cacheable representation. Cached representations older than this TTL are considered stale, and must usually be revalidated or replaced. HTTP implements expiration-based consistency using `Expires` HTTP headers and `Cache-Control` directives.

Expiration raises a couple of issues. On the one hand, a long TTL increases the likelihood that at some point a cached representation will no longer reflect the current state of the resource on the origin server, even though it is still fresh in the cache. That is, fresh representations can become invalid. Consumers of such cached representations must be able to tolerate a degree of latency between a resource changing and its being updated in a cache. On the other hand, representations that have become stale in the cache, but whose resources haven't changed since they were issued, will in fact prove to be still valid; revalidating such representations, though necessary, is suboptimal in terms of network and server resource usage.

Expiration and validation can be used separately or in combination. With a pure validation-based approach (using, for example, a `no-cache` directive), consumers and caches revalidate with every request, thereby ensuring that they always have an up-to-date version of a representation. With this strategy, we must assess the trade-offs between increased consistency and the resultant rise in bandwidth and load on the server.

In contrast, an exclusively expiration-based approach reduces bandwidth usage and the load on the origin server, but at the risk of there being newer versions of a resource on the server while older (but still fresh) representations are being served from caches. After a cached representation has expired, a subsequent GET will result in a full representation being returned along the response path, even if the version hasn't in fact changed on the server.

By using expiration and validation together, we get the best of both worlds. Cached representations are used while they remain fresh. When they become stale, the cache or consumer revalidates the representation with the origin server. This approach helps reduce bandwidth usage and server load. There's still the possibility, however, that representations that remain fresh in a cache become inconsistent with resource state on the origin server.

Using Validation

A cache can determine whether a resource has changed by revalidating a cached representation with the origin server. In Chapter 4, we used `ETag` values with `If-Match` and `If-None-Match` headers (and `Last-Modified` values with `If-Unmodified-Since` and `If-Modified-Since` headers) to do conditional updates and deletes. Validation is accomplished using the same headers and values, but with conditional GETs.

A conditional GET tries to conserve bandwidth by sending and receiving just HTTP headers rather than headers and entity bodies. A conditional GET only exchanges entity bodies when a cached resource representation is out of date. In simple terms, the conditional GET pattern says to a server: "Give me a new resource representation only if the resource has changed substantially since the last time I asked for it. Otherwise, just give me the headers I need to keep my copy up-to-date."

Conditional GETs are useful only when the client making the request has previously fetched and held a copy of a resource representation (and the attached ETag or Last-Modified value). To revalidate a representation, a consumer or cache uses a previously received ETag value with an If-None-Match header, or a previously supplied Last-Modified value with an If-Modified-Since header. If the resource hasn't changed (its ETag or Last-Modified value is the same as the one supplied by the consumer), the service replies with 304 Not Modified (plus any ETag or Location headers that would normally have been included in a 200 OK response). If the resource has changed, the service sends back a full representation with a 200 OK status code.

When a service replies with 304 Not Modified, it can also include Expires, Cache-Control, and Vary headers. Caches can update their cached representation with any new values in these headers. A 304 Not Modified response should also include any ETag or Location headers that would ordinarily have been sent in a 200 OK response; including these headers ensures that as well as the cached resource state, the consumer's cached metadata is also kept up-to-date.

NOTE

The Vary header is used to list the request headers a service uses to generate different representations of a resource. Caches store and release responses based on the values of these request headers. Vary: Accept-Encoding, for example, indicates that requests with different Accept-Encoding header values will generate significantly different representations. If the responses can be cached, each variation will be stored separately so that it can be used to satisfy subsequent requests with the same Accept-Encoding value. Be careful using Vary: careless use of the Vary header can easily overload a cache with multiple representations of the same resource.

Example 6-14 shows two request-response interactions: a GET, which returns an entity body, and then a revalidation, which uses the Last-Modified value from the first response with an If-Modified-Since header. The revalidation says "execute this request only if the entity has changed since the Last-Modified time supplied in this request."

Example 6-14. Revalidation using If-Modified-Since with a previous Last-Modified value

```
Request:
GET /order/1234 HTTP/1.1
Host: restbucks.com
```

```
Response:
HTTP/1.1 200 OK
Content-Length: ...
Content-Type: application/vnd.restbucks+xml
Date: Fri, 26 Mar 2010 10:01:22 GMT
Last-Modified: Fri, 26 Mar 2010 09:55:15 GMT
ETag: "74f4be4b"

<order xmlns="http://schemas.restbucks.com">
  <location>takeaway</location>
  <item>
    <drink>latte</drink>
    <milk>whole</milk>
    <size>large</size>
  </item>
</order>

Request:
GET /order/1234 HTTP/1.1
Host: restbucks.com
If-Modified-Since: Fri, 26 Mar 2010 09:55:15 GMT

Response:
HTTP/1.1 304 Not Modified
```

Example 6-15 shows a similar pair of interactions, but this time the revalidation uses an If-None-Match header with an ETag value. This revalidation says "execute this request only if the ETag belonging to the entity is different from the ETag value supplied in the request."

Example 6-15. *Revalidation using If-None-Match with an entity tag value*

```
Request:
GET /order/1234 HTTP/1.1
Host: restbucks.com

Response:
HTTP/1.1 200 OK
Content-Length: ...
Content-Type: application/vnd.restbucks+xml
Date: Fri, 26 Mar 2010 10:01:22 GMT
Last-Modified: Fri, 26 Mar 2010 09:55:15 GMT
ETag: "74f4be4b"
```

```
<order xmlns="http://schemas.restbucks.com">
  <location>takeaway</location>
  <item>
    <drink>latte</drink>
    <milk>whole</milk>
    <size>large</size>
  </item>
</order>
```

Request:
```
GET /order/1234 HTTP/1.1
Host: restbucks.com
If-None-Match: "74f4be4b"
```

Response:
```
HTTP/1.1 304 Not Modified
```

When developing services, we have to decide the best way of calculating entity tags on a case-by-case basis. Consumers, however, should always treat ETags as opaque string tokens—they don't care how they're generated, so long as the tag discriminates between changed representations.

There are two things to consider when implementing ETags in a service: computation and storage. If an entity tag value can be computed on the fly in a relatively cheap manner, there's very little point in storing the value with the resource—we can just compute it with each request. If, however, generating an entity tag value is a relatively expensive operation, it's worth persisting the computed value with the resource.

Computationally cheap ETag values can be generated using quoted string versions of timestamps, as we discussed in Chapter 4. This is generally a "good enough" solution for entities that don't change very often. When a consumer includes an entity tag value generated using this method in a conditional request, evaluating the conditional request is often as simple as comparing the supplied value against a file or database row timestamp. For collections, we can use the timestamp of the most recently updated member of the collection. Using a timestamp in an ETag header rather than— as is more usual—a Last-Modified header allows us to evolve the service validation strategy without requiring corresponding changes in consumers. For example, we might choose to use a timestamp-based strategy in an early version of a service because the business context ensures that resources change relatively infrequently. If the business process later evolves such that resources change twice or more during a single second, we can safely change the service-side entity tag generation and validation strategy without consumers having to evolve in lockstep. If we'd initially used a Last-Modified header, consumers would have to switch to using ETags.

The most expensive ETag values tend to be those that are computed using a hash of a representation. Hashes can be computed from just the entity body, or they can include headers and header values as well. If hashing headers, avoid including header values containing machine identity. This is to avoid problems when scaling out, where many machines serve identical representations. If a representation's ETag value encodes something host-specific, caches will end up with multiple copies of a representation differing only by origin server. Similarly, if we generate ETag values based on a hash of the headers as well as the entity body, we should avoid using the Expires, Cache-Control, and Vary headers, which can sometimes be used to update a cached representation after revalidating with the origin server.

NOTE

Of course, we should remember that before we can hash a resource, we must assemble its representation. When used in response to a conditional GET, this strategy requires the server to do everything it would do to satisfy a normal request, except send the full-blown representation back across the wire. We'll still save bandwidth, but we'll continue to pay a high computational cost—because hashes tend to be expensive algorithms. If assembling a representation is expensive, it may be better to use version numbers, even if it involves fetching them from a backing store. Alternatively, we might simply indicate that an entity has changed by generating a universally unique identifier value (a UUID), which we then store with the entity. If in doubt as to the best strategy, implement some representative test cases, measure the results, and then choose.

As an optimization, we might consider caching precomputed entity tag values in an in-memory structure. Once again, load-balanced, multimachine scenarios introduce additional complexity here, but if computing the value on the fly is especially expensive, or accessing a persisted, precomputed value becomes a bottleneck in the system, a distributed, in-memory cache of ETag values might just be the thing we need to help save precious computing resources.

Most of the work of implementing conditional GET takes place in the service code, which has to look for the If-Modified-Since and If-None-Match headers, evaluate their conditions, and construct a 200 OK or 304 Not Modified response as appropriate. Services that don't set caching headers, or that incorrectly handle conditional GETs, can have a detrimental effect on the behavior of the system.

The bandwidth, latency, and scalability benefits of using conditional GET should be clear by now, but at what expense? It might seem as though to realize these benefits we have quite a bit of work to do on the client and the server—storing entity tags, adding If-Modified-Since and If-None-Match headers to requests, and updating store representations with response header values.

But guess what? Most caches handle this behavior for us for free. Consumer applications don't need to take any notice of ETag and Last-Modified values: validations are dealt with by the underlying caching infrastructure.

Using Expiration

We've already seen how a service can control the expiration of a representation using the Expires header and certain Cache-Control directives in a response. Consumers, too, can influence cache behavior. By sending Cache-Control directives in requests, consumers can express their preference for representations that fall within particular freshness bounds, or their tolerance for stale representations.

max-age=<delta-seconds>
> Indicates that the consumer will only accept cached representations that are not older than the specified age, delta-seconds. If the consumer specifies max-age=0, the request causes an *end-to-end revalidation* all the way to the origin server.

max-stale=<delta-seconds>
> Indicates that the consumer is prepared to accept representations that have been stale for up to the specified number of seconds. The delta-seconds value is optional; by omitting this value, the consumer indicates it is prepared to accept a stale response of any age.

min-fresh=<delta-seconds>
> Indicates that the consumer wants only cached representations that will still be fresh when the current age of the cached object is added to the supplied delta-seconds value.

only-if-cached
> Tells a cache to return only a cached representation. If the cache doesn't have a fresh representation of the requested resource, it returns 504 Gateway Timeout.

no-cache
> Instructs a cache not to use a cached representation to satisfy the request, thereby generating an *end-to-end reload*. An end-to-end reload causes all intermediaries on the response path to obtain fresh copies of the requested representation (whereas an end-to-end revalidation—using max-age=0—allows intermediaries to update cached representations with headers in the response).

no-store
> Requires caches not to store the request or the response, and not to return a cached representation.

These Cache-Control directives allow a consumer to make trade-off decisions around consistency and latency. Consider, for example, an application that has been optimized for latency (by making the majority of representations cacheable). Consumers that require a higher degree of consistency can use max-age or min-stale to obtain representations with stricter freshness bounds, but at the expense of the cache revalidating with the origin server more often than dictated by the server. In contrast, consumers that care more about latency than consistency can choose to relax freshness constraints, and accept stale representations from nearby caches, using max-stale or only-if-cached.

Another situation where these request directives are useful is after a failed conditional PUT or POST. If a conditional operation fails, it's normal for the consumer to GET the current state of the resource before retrying the operation. In these circumstances, it is advisable to use a Cache-Control: no-cache directive with the request, to force an end-to-end reload that returns the current state of the resource on the server, rather than a still fresh but now invalid representation from a cache.

Using Invalidation

There are two types of invalidation: consumer-driven invalidation and server-driven invalidation. Server-driven invalidation falls outside HTTP's capabilities, whereas a form of consumer-driven invalidation is intrinsic to HTTP.

Let's look at consumer-driven invalidation first. According to the HTTP specification, DELETE, PUT, and POST requests should invalidate any cached representations belonging to the request URI. In addition, if the response contains a Location or Content-Location header, representations associated with either of these header values should also be invalidated.

NOTE

Unfortunately, many caches do not invalidate cached content based on the Location and Content-Location header values. Invalidations based on the unsafe methods just listed are, however, common.

At first glance, it would appear that a consumer could invalidate a cached representation using a DELETE, PUT, or POST request, and thereafter be confident that this same representation won't be returned in subsequent GETs. But we must remember that this technique can only guarantee to invalidate caches on the immediate request path. Caches that are not on the request path will not necessarily be invalidated. Once again, we are reminded of the need to deal with the weak consistency issues inherent in the Web's architecture.

In contrast to the necessarily weak consistency model of consumer-driven invalidation, server-driven invalidation would appear to offer stronger consistency guarantees. With server-driven invalidation, the service sends invalidation notices to the caches and consumers it knows are likely to have a cached representation of a particular resource. With this approach, all interested parties—both those on and those off the request-response path—will be invalidated when a resource changes.

But this is not the way the Web usually works. For such an approach to be successful, a service would have to maintain a list of consumers and caches to be contacted when a resource changes. In other words, the service would have to maintain application state. And holding application state on the server undermines scalability.

Server-driven invalidation only works for caches the server knows about. Moreover, its strong consistency guarantees only hold while the caches that need to be notified of an invalidation event are connected to the service. If a network problem disconnects a cache, causing it to miss one or more invalidation messages, the overall distributed application will be in an inconsistent state—at least temporarily.

It should be clear by now that server-driven invalidation can only partly mitigate the weak consistency issues that come with adopting the Web as an integration platform. Because of the generally web-unfriendly nature of server-driven invalidation, expiration and validation are by far the most common methods of ensuring eventual consistency between services and consumers on the Web.

Extending Freshness

Once we have determined that a resource's representations can be cached, we will have to decide which caches to target, together with the freshness lifetimes of the cacheable representations.

When deciding on the freshness lifetime of a representation, we must balance server control with scalability concerns. With short expiration values, the service retains a relatively high degree of control over the representations it releases, but this control comes at the expense of frequent reloads and revalidations, both of which use network resources and place load on the origin server. Longer expiration values, on the other hand, conserve bandwidth and reduce the number of requests that reach the origin server; at the same time, however, they increase the likelihood that a cached representation will become inconsistent with resource state on the server over the course of its freshness lifetime.

Being able to invalidate cached representations would help here; we could specify a long freshness lifetime for each representation, but then invalidate cached entries the moment a resource changes. Unfortunately, the Web doesn't support a general invalidation mechanism.

There is, however, one way we can work with the Web to make representations as cacheable as possible, but no more. Instead of seeking to invalidate entries, we can extend their freshness lifetime.

Cache Channels

Cache channels implement a technique for extending the freshness lifetimes of cached representations.* Caches that don't understand the cache channel protocol will continue to expire representations the moment they become stale. Caches that do understand the protocol, however, are entitled to treat a normally stale representation as still fresh, until they hear otherwise.

* Cache channels are the brainchild of Mark Nottingham; see *http://www.mnot.net/blog/2008/01/04/ cache_channels*.

Cache channels use two new Cache-Control extensions. Caches that understand these directives can use cache channels to extend the freshness lifetime of cached representations. These extensions are:

channel

> The channel extension supplies the absolute URI of a channel that a cache can subscribe to in order to fetch events associated with a cached representation.

group

> The group extension supplies an absolute URI that can be used to group multiple cached representations. Events that apply to a group ID can be applied to all the cached representations belonging to that group.

Example 6-16 shows a request for a product from Restbucks' product catalog. The response includes a Cache-Control header containing both cache channel extensions.

Example 6-16. The channel and group extensions allow caches to subscribe to a cache channel

```
Request:
GET /product-catalog/1234
Host: restbucks.com

Response:
HTTP/1.1 200 OK
Cache-Control: max-age=3600, channel="http://internal.restbucks.com/product-
catalog/cache-channel/", group="urn:uuid:1f80b2a1-660a-4874-92c4-45732e03087b"
Content-Length: ...
Content-Type: application/vnd.restbucks+xml
Last-Modified: Fri, 26 Mar 2010 09:33:49 GMT
Date: Fri, 26 Mar 2010 09:33:49 GMT
ETag: "d53514da9e54"

<product xmlns="http://schemas.restbucks.com/product">
  <name>Fairtrade Roma Coffee Beans</name>
  <size>1kg</size>
  <price>10</price>
</product>
```

The max-age directive specifies that this representation will remain fresh for up to an hour, after which it must be revalidated with the origin server. But any cache on the response path that understands the channel and group extensions can continue to extend the freshness lifetime of this representation as long as two conditions hold:

- The cache continues to poll the channel at least as often as a precision value specified by the channel itself.

- The channel doesn't issue a "stale" event for either the URI of the cached representation or the group URI with which the representation is associated.

If a cache performs a GET on the channel specified in the channel extension, it receives the cache channel feed shown in Example 6-17.

Example 6-17. *An empty cache channel feed*

```
HTTP/1.1 200 OK
Cache-Control: max-age=300
Content-Length: ...
Content-Type: application/atom+xml
Last-Modified: Fri, 26 Mar 2010 09:00:00 GMT
Date: Fri, 26 Mar 2010 09:42:02 GMT

<feed xmlns="http://www.w3.org/2005/Atom"
  xmlns:cc="http://purl.org/syndication/cache-channel">
  <title>Invalidations for restbucks.com</title>
  <id>urn:uuid:d2faab5a-2743-44b1-a979-8e60248dcc8e</id>
  <link rel="self"
    href="http://internal.restbucks.com/product-catalog/cache-channel/"/>
  <updated>2010-03-26T09:00:00Z</updated>
  <author>
    <name>Product Catalog Service</name>
  </author>
  <cc:precision>900</cc:precision>
  <cc:lifetime>86400</cc:lifetime>
</feed>
```

This is an Atom feed that has been generated by the origin server. In the next chapter, we discuss Atom feeds in detail and use them to build event-driven systems. For now, all we need to understand is that this is an empty feed—it doesn't contain any channel events. (Cache channels don't have to be implemented as Atom feeds, but given that there's widespread support for Atom on almost all development platforms it's easy to build cache channels using the Atom format.) The feed's <cc:precision> element specifies a precision in seconds, meaning that caches that subscribe to this feed must poll it at least as often as every 15 minutes if they want to extend the freshness lifetimes of any representations associated with this channel. The <cc:lifetime> element value indicates that events in this feed will be available for at least a day after they have been issued.

> ——— **NOTE** ———————————————————————————
>
> As you can see from Example 6-17, the Atom feed can itself be cached. As we'll learn in the next chapter, event feeds can take advantage of the Web's caching infrastructure as much as any other representation.

As long as the cache continues to poll the channel at least every 15 minutes, it can continue to serve the cached product representation well beyond its original freshness lifetime of an hour. If the resource does change on the origin server, the very next time the cache polls the channel it will receive a response similar to the one shown in Example 6-18.

Example 6-18. *A cache channel feed containing a stale event*

```
HTTP/1.1 200 OK
Cache-Control: max-age=900
Content-Length: ...
Content-Type: application/atom+xml
Last-Modified: Fri, 26 Mar 2010 13:10:05 GMT
Date: Fri, 26 Mar 2010 13:15:42 GMT

<feed xmlns="http://www.w3.org/2005/Atom"
  xmlns:cc="http://purl.org/syndication/cache-channel">
  <title>Invalidations for restbucks.com</title>
  <id>urn:uuid:d2faab5a-2743-44b1-a979-8e60248dcc8e</id>
  <link rel="self"
    href="http://internal.restbucks.com/product-catalog/cache-channel/"/>
  <updated>2010-03-26T13:10:05Z</updated>
  <author>
    <name>Product Catalog Service</name>
  </author>
  <cc:precision>900</cc:precision>
  <cc:lifetime>86400</cc:lifetime>
  <entry>
    <title>stale</title>
    <id>urn:uuid:d8b4cd04-d448-4c26-85a6-b08363de8e87</id>
    <updated>2010-03-26T13:10:05Z</updated>
    <link href="urn:uuid:1f80b2a1-660a-4874-92c4-45732e03087b" rel="alternate"/>
    <cc:stale/>
  </entry>
</feed>
```

The feed now contains a stale event entry whose alternate `<link>` element associates it with the group ID to which the product representation belongs (urn:uuid:1f80b2a1-660a-4874-92c4-45732e03087b). Each event has its own ID, which has nothing to do with the identifiers of any cached representations; it's the `<link>` element's href value that associates the event with a group or particular representation.

> ──── NOTE ────
>
> In practice, we might expect to see additional entries—related to other groups and individual resource IDs—in the feed, with the most recent entries appearing first.

Seeing this event, the cache stops extending the freshness lifetime of any representations belonging to this group. The next time a consumer issues a request for *http://restbucks.com/product-catalog/1234*, the cache will revalidate its stale representation with the origin server.

Cache channels work with the Web because they don't require origin servers to maintain application state in the form of lists of connected caches. Each cache is responsible for guaranteeing the delivery of stale events by polling the cache channel. If a cache can't connect to the channel, it can no longer continue to extend the freshness lifetime of otherwise stale representations.

By associating cached representations with groups, cache channels provide a powerful mechanism for canceling the extended freshness of several related representations at the same time. This is particularly useful when we decompose an application protocol into several overlapping resources that together manipulate the state of an underlying domain entity. POSTing a completion to *http://restbucks.com/orders/1234/completion*, for example, may render any fresh representations of *http://restbucks.com/orders/1234* invalid. This is the kind of consistency issue traditional invalidation mechanisms seek to address and precisely the kind of challenge the loosely coupled nature of the Web makes difficult to solve. Using small freshness lifetimes together with cache channels, we can reduce the time it takes for the overall distributed application to reach a consistent state.

NOTE

Cache channels provide a clean separation of concerns. Cache management can be dealt with separately from designing the caching characteristics of individual resource representations. Cache channel servers can even be deployed on separate hardware from business services.

Of course, cache channels only work for caches that know how to take advantage of the channel and group extensions. Though the HTTP Cache Channels Internet-Draft has now expired, several reverse proxies, including Squid and Varnish, include support for its freshness extension mechanism.* But in an environment where not all cache implementations can be controlled by service implementers, the same difficult truth emerges once again: the Web is weakly consistent.

Stay Fresh

In this chapter, we saw how the safe and idempotent properties of the most popular verb on the Web, GET, are key to building fault-tolerant and scalable systems. The installed infrastructure of the Web includes a caching substrate that we can use to bring frequently accessed representations closer to consumers, thereby reducing

---

* *http://ietfreport.isoc.org/idref/draft-nottingham-http-cache-channels/*

latency, conserving bandwidth, masking transient faults, and decreasing the load on services. Services dictate the caching behaviors of the representations they issue; consumers tighten or relax the expectations they have of caches as they see fit.

We also considered the implications of the Web's weak consistency model. No matter the expiration or validation mechanisms we choose to employ, we must always remember that we cannot guarantee that a representation of resource state as received by a consumer reflects the current state of the resource as held by the service.

In the last section, we looked at how cache channels allow us to extend the freshness lifetimes of cached representations. Our cache channels example used an Atom feed to communicate "stale" events to caches that understand the cache channels protocol.

In the next chapter, we look in more detail at the Atom feed format. Knowing about GET and the caching opportunities offered by the Web, we show how to put these pieces together to create a scalable, fault-tolerant, event-driven system.

CHAPTER SEVEN

The Atom Syndication Format

HTML REMAINS THE MOST POPULAR HYPERMEDIA FORMAT IN USE TODAY, but as the Web extends its reach beyond the browser, we're seeing other useful formats emerge. Of these newer hypermedia types, one in particular deserves our attention: the Atom Syndication Format, or Atom for short.* Atom is an XML-based hypermedia format for representing timestamped lists of web content and metadata such as blog postings and news articles.

NOTE —————————————————————————————

In Chapter 5, we used a custom hypermedia format to expose data and protocols to consumers. By contrast, Atom is a general-purpose hypermedia format.

Atom interests us because it provides a flexible and extensible interoperability format for transferring data between applications. Its success has led to wide cross-platform support, and you can now find Atom libraries in all popular languages, including Java and C#.

The Format

Atom represents data as lists, called *feeds*. Feeds are made up of one or more time-stamped *entries*, which associate document metadata with web content.

* *http://www.ietf.org/rfc/rfc4287.txt*

The structure of an Atom document is defined in the Atom specification (RFC 4287), but the content of a feed will vary depending on our domain's requirements. On the human Web, it might be blog posts or news items, whereas for computer-to-computer interactions, it might be stock trades, system health notifications, payroll instructions, or representations of coffee orders.

To illustrate the Atom format, let's share a list of coffee orders between a cashier, who takes orders, and a barista, who prepares them. Example 7-1 shows an Atom feed produced by the Restbucks ordering service. The feed is consumed by the order management system (we'll see more of the order management system in the next chapter).

Example 7-1. An Atom feed containing two entries

```
<?xml version="1.0"?>
<feed xmlns="http://www.w3.org/2005/Atom">
  <id>urn:uuid:d0b4f914-30e9-418c-8628-7d9b7815060f</id>
  <title type="text">Recent Orders</title>
  <updated>2009-07-01T12:05:00Z</updated>
  <generator uri="http://restbucks.com/order">Order Service</generator>
  <link rel="self" href="http://restbucks.com/order/recent"/>
  <entry>
    <id>urn:uuid:aa990d44-fce0-4823-a971-d23facc8d7c6</id>
    <title type="text">order</title>
    <updated>2009-07-01T11:58:00Z</updated>
    <author>
      <name>Jenny</name>
    </author>
    <link rel="self" href="http://restbucks.com/order/1"/>
    <content type="application/vnd.restbucks+xml">
      <order xmlns="http://schemas.restbucks.com/order">
      <item>
        <milk>whole</milk>
        <size>small</size>
        <drink>latte</drink>
      </item>
      <item>
        <milk>whole</milk>
        <size>small</size>
        <drink>cappuccino</drink>
      </item>
      <location>takeAway</location>
    </order>
    </content>
  </entry>
  <entry>
    <id>urn:uuid:6fa8eca3-48ee-44a9-a899-37d047a3c5f2</id>
    <title type="text">order</title>
```

```
      <updated>2009-07-01T11:25:00Z</updated>
      <author>
        <name>Patrick</name>
      </author>
      <link rel="self" href="http://restbucks.com/order/2"/>
      <content type="application/vnd.restbucks+xml">
        <order xmlns="http://schemas.restbucks.com/order">
          <item>
            <milk>semi</milk>
            <size>large</size>
            <drink>cappuccino</drink>
          </item>
          <location>takeAway</location>
        </order>
      </content>
    </entry>
  </feed>
```

Here, Atom entries represent coffee orders, with the Atom metadata capturing useful business information, such as who took the order and when.

Feeds, like entries, have metadata associated with them. Feed metadata allows us to provide friendly descriptions of content, links to other services or resources, and, most importantly, a means of navigating to other feeds—all in a standard manner.

Atom doesn't attach any significance to the order of entries in a feed. A feed will often be sorted by the `<atom:updated>` or `<atom:published>` value of its constituent entries, but it can as easily be sorted by other elements—by category, or author, or title, for instance. In our example, we've organized the feed based on when coffee orders were placed, with the most recent order appearing at the top of the feed.

Our orders feed is typical of how Atom is used in a computer-to-computer scenario. The feed's metadata sets the context for the enclosed coffee orders, allowing consumers to reason about the list's origin, its purpose, and its timeliness. This feed metadata includes the following elements:

- `<atom:id>` is a permanent, universally unique identifier for the feed.

- `<atom:title>` provides a human-readable name for the feed.

- `<atom:updated>` indicates when the feed last changed.

- `<atom:generated>` identifies the software agent that created the feed, which in this case is the ordering service.

- `<atom:link>` contains the canonical URI for retrieving the feed.

The ordering service feed in Example 7-1 contains two `<atom:entry>` elements, each representing an order (of course, there could have been more). Each entry is a mixture of Atom metadata markup and application-specific XML content. The following elements are included in the `<atom:entry>` metadata:

- `<atom:id>` is a unique identifier for the entry.

- `<atom:title>` provides a human-readable title for the entry.

- `<atom:updated>` is a timestamp indicating when the entry last changed, which in this instance is the time the order was accepted by the system.

- `<atom:author>` identifies who created the entry, which in our example is the cashier who took the order.

- `<atom:link>` contains the URI for addressing this entry as a standalone document.

Each entry also contains an `<atom:content>` element. `<atom:content>` elements can contain arbitrary foreign elements, including elements that share the default namespace. Here, the content includes a piece of Restbucks XML representing an order's details. The `<atom:content>` element's type attribute contains a media type value (`application/vnd.restbucks+xml`) so that the consumers of an entry know how to process the payload.

Common Uses for Atom

In Restbucks, we use Atom feeds to move business information between providers and consumers of coffee operations, exactly as we would using other enterprise integration techniques. This is just one use of Atom in the enterprise; other uses include:

Syndicating content
> Atom is an ideal representation format when the creation and consumption of resources closely mirrors a syndication model, with a producer or publisher distributing content to many consumers.

Representing documents and document-like structures
> Many domain resources are structured like documents; if this is the case, we might consider mapping the resource's attributes to Atom's metadata elements.

Creating metadata-rich lists of resources
> We can use Atom feeds to represent ordered lists, such as search results or events, especially if the Atom metadata is useful in the context of our service. In this scenario, Atom establishes a domain processing context for some other domain content. The event example later in this chapter shows how we can use Atom metadata to represent event metadata, thereby establishing an event-oriented processing context for each Atom entry's payload.

Adding metadata to existing resource representations

We can use feeds and entries to add metadata to existing resource representations. In particular, we can use Atom metadata elements to surface information related to a resource's publishing life cycle: its author, the date it was created, when it was last updated, and so on. Just as importantly, we can attach hypermedia links to existing resource representations by embedding the representation inside an Atom entry and adding one or more `<atom:link>` elements to the entry.

Creating directories of nonhypermedia content

We can use Atom to create entries that link to resources that cannot otherwise be represented in a hypermedia format, such as binary objects. Use the `<atom:content>` element's `src` attribute to link to the resource, and specify a media type using the element's type attribute.

Using Atom for Event-Driven Systems

Now that we've looked at the anatomy of an Atom feed, we're ready to see how such feeds can be used for simple computer-to-computer interactions. As an example, let's see how Atom can be used to implement a staple of enterprise computing: events. Normally with event-driven systems, events are propagated through listeners. Here, however, we plan to publish an ordered list of events that readers can poll to consume events.

> ---- **NOTE** ---
>
> We believe Atom is an ideal format for highly scalable event-driven architectures. But as with any web-based system, Atom-based solutions trade scalability for latency, making Atom often inappropriate for very low-latency notifications.*
> However, if we're building solutions where seconds, or better still, minutes or hours, can pass between events being produced and consumed, publishing Atom feeds works very well.

The Problem

Restbucks' headquarters chooses which coffees and snacks will be served in its stores. HQ is also responsible for organizing promotions across the regions. It maintains product and promotion information in a centralized product catalog, but a number of other business functions within Restbucks depend on this information, including distribution, local inventory management, point of sale, and order management.

This situation is typical of the integration challenges facing many organizations today: systems that support key business processes need access to data located elsewhere. Such

---

* For extremely low-latency notifications, we might consider proprietary middleware designed for that domain. The trade-off is scalability for latency, but with the added complication of lock-in.

shared data may be required to enable end-to-end processing, or it may be needed in order to provide the organization with a single, consistent view of a business resource.

The benefits of data integration include increased consistency and availability of core data. But to get to this state we often have to overcome the challenges of data redundancy, poor data quality, lack of consistency among multiple sources, and poor availability.

Reference Data

As it has grown, Restbucks has evolved its data and application integration strategy to mirror its business capabilities and processes. This strategy has led to independent services, each of which authoritatively manages the business processes and data belonging to a business unit.

Effectively, Restbucks has decomposed its information technology ecosystem into islands of expertise. The product catalog service, for example, acts as an authoritative source of data and behavior for Restbucks' product management capabilities.

Data such as product and promotions data is often called *reference data*. Reference data is the kind of data other applications and services refer to in the course of completing their own tasks.

Sourcing and using reference data are two quite separate concerns. Typically, an application will source a piece of reference data at the point in time it needs to use it. To preserve service autonomy and maintain high availability in a distributed system, however, it is best to maintain separation of concerns by decoupling the activities that own and provide access to reference data from those that consume it. If order management has to query the product catalog for a price for every line item, we'd say the two services were tightly coupled in time. This coupling occurs because the availability of order management is dependent on the availability of the product catalog. By breaking this dependency—separating the sourcing of data from its use—we reduce coupling and increase the availability of the order management service.

> **WARNING**
>
> Temporal coupling weakens a solution because it requires numerous independent systems to be running correctly at a specific instant in time. When multiple servers, networks, and software all need to be functioning to support a single business behavior, the chances for failure increase.

To reduce coupling between producers and consumers of reference data, we generally recommend that reference data owners publish copies of their data, which consumers can then cache. Consumers work with their local copy of reference data until it becomes stale. By distributing information this way, services can continue to function even if the network partitions or services become temporarily unavailable. This is exactly how the Web scales.

To solve the coupling problem between the product catalog and its several consumers, Restbucks replicates its product catalog data. Each consumer maintains a local cache of the reference data, which it then updates in response to notifications from the provider. Each consumer can continue to function, albeit with possibly stale data, even if the product catalog becomes unavailable.

To ensure that updates to the product catalog are propagated in a timely manner, Restbucks uses Atom feeds.

Event-Driven Updates

To communicate data changes from the product catalog service to the distribution, inventory, and order management systems, Restbucks has chosen to implement an event-driven architecture. Whenever a new product is introduced, an existing product is changed, or a promotion is created or canceled, the product catalog publishes an event. The systems responsible for distribution, inventory, and order management consume these events and apply the relevant changes to their reference data caches.

Figure 7-1 shows how Restbucks' product catalog exposes an Atom feed of events. Stores poll this feed at regular intervals to receive updates. When processing a feed, a store first finds the last entry it successfully processed the last time it polled the feed, and then works forward from there.

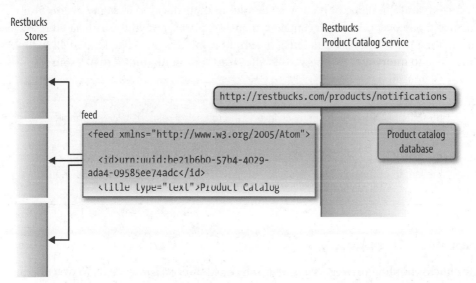

Figure 7-1. *Event-driven architecture using Atom feeds*

Restbucks' underlying business process in this instance isn't latency-sensitive. Products and promotions don't change very often, and when an event occurs, it's OK for stores to find out several minutes later. But while low latency isn't an issue, guaranteed delivery is: price optimization and campaign management depend on HQ's product catalog changes definitely being propagated to stores. It's important, therefore, that we can guarantee that changes reach the stores, and that they are applied by the start of the next business day.

Event-driven systems in general exhibit a high degree of loose coupling. Loose coupling provides failure isolation and allows services and consumers to evolve independently of each other. Restbucks uses polling and caching to loosely couple providers and consumers. This polling solution respects the specific technical and quality-of-service requirements belonging to the challenge at hand (many consumers, guaranteed delivery, but latency-tolerant).

Polling propagates product catalog events in a timely fashion, limited only by the speed with which a store can sustainably poll a service's feeds. But polling can introduce its own challenges: as stores multiply and polling becomes more frequent, there's a danger that the product catalog service becomes a bottleneck. To mitigate this, we can introduce caching. As we saw in Chapter 6, local or intermediary caches help by reducing the workload on the server and masking intermittent failures.

The Anatomy of an Event

An event represents a significant change in the state of a resource at a particular point in time (in the case of the product catalog, the resource is a product or a promotion). An event carries important metadata, including the event type, the date and time it occurred, and the name of the person or system that triggered it. Many events also include a payload, which can contain a snapshot of the state of the associated resource at the time the event was generated, or simply a link to some state located elsewhere, thereby encouraging consumers to GET the latest representation of that resource.

> ——— **NOTE** ———————————————————————————————————————
>
> Interestingly, the polling approach inverts the roles and responsibilities normally associated with guaranteed message delivery in a distributed system. Instead of the service or middleware being responsible for guaranteeing delivery of messages, each consumer now becomes responsible for ensuring that it retrieves all relevant information. Since messages are collocated in time-ordered feeds, there's no chance of a message arriving out of order.

Solution Overview

Restbucks' product catalog feed is treated as a continuous logical feed. In practice, however, this logical feed consists of a number of physical feeds chained together, much like a linked list. The chain begins with a "working" feed, followed by a series of "archive" feeds. The working feed contains all the events that have occurred between the present moment and a cutoff point in the past. This historical cutoff point is determined by the notification source (the product catalog service in our case). The archives contain all the events that occurred before that cutoff point. The contents of the working feed continue to change until the feed is archived, whereupon the feed becomes immutable and is associated with a single permanent URI.

The product catalog service is responsible for creating this series of feed resources. The contents of each feed represent all the changes that occurred during a particular interval. At any given point in time, only one of these feeds is the working feed. The service creates an entry to represent each event and assigns it to the working feed. When the service determines that the working feed is "complete," either because a certain period has elapsed since the feed was started or because the number of entries in the feed has reached a predetermined threshold, the service archives the working feed and begins another.

Each feed relates to a specific historical period. This includes the working feed, which always relates to a specific period. The only thing that differentiates the working feed from an archive feed is the open-ended (the "as yet" not determined) nature of the working feed's period.

In addition to these historical feeds there is one more resource, which we call "the feed of recent events." Unlike the other feeds, the feed of recent events is not a historical feed; it's always *current*. At any given moment, the feed of recent events and the working feed contain the same information, but when the service archives the current working feed and starts a new one, the feed of recent events changes to contain the same data as the new working feed.

As we'll see, consumers need never know about working or archive feeds. Working and archive feeds are implementation details; as far as consumers are concerned, the notifications feed *is* the feed of recent events (the *current* feed). As service designers, however, we've found it useful to distinguish between these three types of feeds because of some subtle differences among them, particularly in terms of caching and links.

Using a linked list of feeds, we can maintain a history of everything that has taken place in the product catalog. This allows Restbucks' stores to navigate the entire history of changes to the catalog if they so wish. Figure 7-2 shows how all these feeds link together, including the feed of recent events, the working feed, and the archive feeds.

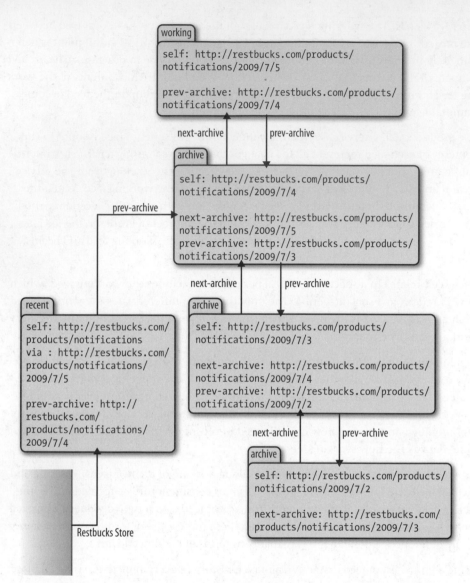

Figure 7-2. *The notifications feed is a chain of connected feeds*

At the Atom level, each feed and entry has its own unique atom:id. A feed's atom:id remains the same for the lifetime of that feed, irrespective of whether it's the working feed or it has become an archive feed. This guarantees that stores can identify feeds even if the addressing (URI) scheme radically changes, further ensuring that the solution is loosely coupled and capable of being evolved.

Link Relations

Because we've split the notifications feed into a series of linked feeds, we need to help stores navigate them. In other words, we need to both link feeds together and describe how they relate to each other. We do this using Atom's `<atom:link>` element.

The `<link>` element is Atom's primary hypermedia control. As we discussed in Chapter 5, connecting resources is an important part of building web-friendly systems. Hypermedia controls allow services to connect and clients to access and manipulate resources by sending and receiving resource representations using a uniform set of operations.

To use a hypermedia control successfully, a client must first understand the control's semantic context. The client must then be able to identify and address the resource with which the control is associated. Finally, it must know which media type to send or what representation formats it can expect to receive when it makes use of the control. These requirements are satisfied by the `<atom:link>` element's `rel`, `href`, and `type` attributes, respectively:

- A `rel` attribute's value describes the link relation or semantic context for the link.

- The `href` attribute value is the URI of the linked resource.

- The `type` attribute describes a linked resource's likely media type.

We say that the type attribute value represents the likely media type because this value can always be overridden by the owner of the resource at the end of the link. The Content-Type header in a response is always authoritative, irrespective of any prior indication of the linked resource's media type. The type attribute remains useful, however, insofar as it allows clients to distinguish between different media type representations of the same resource. Consider a situation in which an entry is linked to JSON and XML representations of a resource. A client interested in only JSON representation would look for links with a type attribute value of application/json.

The Atom specification describes five link relations. Using two of these core link relations, we can now describe the relationships between some of the product catalog feeds, as shown in Table 7-1.

Table 7-1. *The core Atom link relations*

Link relation	Meaning
self	Advertises a link whose href identifies a resource equivalent to the current feed or entry.
via	Identifies the source for the information in the current feed or entry. Restbucks uses this link to indicate the current source for the feed of recent events.

Table 7-2 describes the remaining three Atom link relations.

Table 7-2. *The remaining core Atom link relations*

Link relation	Meaning
alternate	Indicates that the link connects to an alternative representation of the current feed or entry.
enclosure	Indicates that the referenced resource is potentially large in size.
related	Indicates that the resource at the href is related to the current feed or entry in some way. Restbucks uses this link to correlate each entry (which represents an event) with the domain resource to which the event relates (the related link contains the URI of this domain resource).

IANA's Registry of Link Relations contains a larger list of recognized link relation values.* This list has nearly quadrupled since 2008, and now includes values such as payment (for describing links to resources that accept payments), first, last, previous, next, previous-archive, and next-archive (for navigating paged and archived feeds). For the Restbucks product catalog service, we will use several of these values to help navigate between the feeds that compose the overall set of product notifications.

* *http://www.iana.org/assignments/link-relations.html*

Polling for Recent Events

Recall that the feed of recent events is the entry point for all consumers of the list of product notifications. The feed is located at the well-known URI *http://restbucks.com/ products/notifications*. The entries in this feed represent the most "recent" events (relative to the point in time when the feed is accessed). But these entries also belong to a specific historical period, which began when the previous working feed was archived. The feed of recent events therefore includes a link (a via link) to the source of the entries for this specific historical period.

Example 7-2 shows a store polling the feed of recent events.

Example 7-2. *A store polls the feed of recent events*

```
Request:
GET /product-catalog/notifications HTTP/1.1
Host: restbucks.com

Response:
HTTP/1.1 200 OK
Date: ...
Cache-Control: max-age=3600
Content-Length: ...
Content-Type: application/atom+xml;charset="utf-8"
ETag: "6a0806ca"

<feed xmlns="http://www.w3.org/2005/Atom">

  <id>urn:uuid:be21b6b0-57b4-4029-ada4-09585ee74adc</id>
  <title type="text">Product Catalog Notifications</title>
  <updated>2009-07-05T10:25:00Z</updated>
  <author>
    <name>Product Catalog</name>
  </author>
  <generator uri="http://restbucks.com/products">Product Catalog</generator>
  <link rel="self" href="http://restbucks.com/products/notifications"/>
  <link rel="via" type="application/atom+xml"
    href="http://restbucks.com/products/notifications/2009/7/5"/>
  <link rel="prev-archive"
    href="http://restbucks.com/products/notifications/2009/7/4"/>
```

```xml
<entry>
  <id>urn:uuid:95506d98-aae9-4d34-a8f4-1ff30bece80c</id>
  <title type="text">product created</title>
  <updated>2009-07-05T10:25:00Z</updated>
  <link rel="self"
    href="http://restbucks.com/products/notifications/95506d98-aae9-4d34-a8f4-
1ff30bece80c"/>
  <link rel="related" href="http://restbucks.com/products/527"/>
  <category scheme="http://restbucks.com/products/categories/type"
    term="product"/>
  <category scheme="http://restbucks.com/products/categories/status"
    term="new"/>
  <content type="application/vnd.restbucks+xml">
    <product xmlns="http://schemas.restbucks.com/product"
      href="http://restbucks.com/products/527">
      <name>Fairtrade Roma Coffee Beans</name>
      <size>1kg</size>
      <price>10</price>
    </product>
  </content>
</entry>

<entry>
  <id>urn:uuid:4c6b6b57-81af-4501-8bbc-12fee2e3cd50</id>
  <title type="text">promotion cancelled</title>
  <updated>2009-07-05T10:15:00Z</updated>
  <link rel="self"
    href="http://restbucks.com/products/notifications/4c6b6b57-81af-4501-8bbc-
12fee2e3cd50"/>
  <link rel="related" href="http://restbucks.com/promotions/391"/>
  <category scheme="http://restbucks.com/products/categories/type"
    term="promotion"/>
  <category scheme="http://restbucks.com/products/categories/status"
    term="deleted"/>
  <content type="application/vnd.restbucks+xml">
    <promotion xmlns="http://schemas.restbucks.com/promotion"
      href="http://restbucks.com/promotions/391">
      <effective>2009-08-01T00:00:00Z</effective>
      <product type="application/vnd.restbucks+xml"
        href="http://restbucks.com/products/156" />
      <region type="application/vnd.restbucks+xml"
        href="http://restbucks.com/regions/23" />
        </promotion>
  </content>
</entry>
</feed>
```

The response here contains two useful HTTP headers: ETag and Cache-Control. The ETag header allows Restbucks' stores to perform a conditional GET the next time they request the list of recent events from the product catalog service, thereby potentially conserving network bandwidth (as described in Chapter 6). The Cache-Control header declares that the response can be cached for up to 3,600 seconds, or one hour.

The decision as to whether to allow the feed of recent events to be cached depends on the behavior of the underlying business resources and the quality-of-service expectations of consumers. In this particular instance, two facts helped Restbucks determine an appropriate caching strategy: products and promotions change infrequently, and consumers can tolerate some delay in finding out about a change. Based on these factors, Restbucks decided the feed of recent events can be cached for at least an hour (and probably longer).

The feed itself contains three <atom:link> elements. The self link contains the URI of the feed requested by the store, which in this case is the feed of recent events. The via link points to the source of entries for the feed of recent events; that is, to the *working feed*. (Remember, the working feed is a feed associated with a particular historical period. It differs from an archive feed in that it is still changing, and is therefore cacheable for only a short period of time. It differs from the feed of recent events in that at some point it will no longer be current.) The last link, prev-archive, refers to the immediately preceding archive document.* This archive document contains all the events that occurred in the period immediately prior to this one.

> ─── **NOTE** ───────────────────────────
>
> In our example, the Restbucks product catalog service ticks over every day, archiving the current working feed at midnight. Because we use "friendly" URIs for feed links, it looks as if stores can infer the address of an archive feed from the URI structure, but we must emphasize that's not really the case. Stores should not infer resource semantics based on a URI's structure. Instead, they should treat each URI as just another opaque address. Stores navigate the archive not by constructing URIs, but by following links based on rel attribute values.

Moving now to the content of the feed, we see that each entry has a self link, indicating that it's an addressable resource in its own right. Besides being addressable, in our solution every entry is cacheable. This is not always the case with Atom entries, since many Atom feeds contain entries that change over time. But in this particular solution, each entry represents an event that occurs once and never changes. If an underlying product changes twice in quick succession, the product catalog service will create two separate events, which in turn will cause two separate entries to be published into the feed. The service never modifies an existing entry.

---

* The prev-archive link relation value is defined in the Feed Paging and Archiving specification: *http://tools.ietf.org/html/rfc5005*.

Below the self link are two <atom:category> elements. Atom categories provide a simple means of tagging feeds and entries. Consumers can easily search categorized feeds for entries matching one or more categories. (And by adding feed filters on the server side, we can produce category-specific feeds based on consumer-supplied filter criteria.)

An <atom:category> element must include a term attribute. The value of this term attribute represents the category. Categories can also include two optional attributes: label, which provides a human-readable representation of the category value, and scheme, which identifies the scheme to which a category belongs. Schemes group categories and disambiguate them, much as XML and package namespaces disambiguate elements and classes. This allows entries to be tagged with two categories that have the same terms, but belong to two different schemes.

In Restbucks, we use categories to identify the event type (product or promotion), and its status (new, updated, or cancelled). The last entry in the feed in Example 7-2, for example, indicates that the promotion for the product http://restbucks.com/products/156 has been canceled. Using these categories, Restbucks' stores can filter specific kinds of events from a feed.

Navigating the Archive

Navigating an individual feed is straightforward. Feeds are ordered by each entry's <atom:updated> timestamp element, with the most recent entry first.* To process a feed, a Restbucks store steps through the entries looking for the combination of atom:id and atom:updated that belongs to the last entry it successfully processed. Once it has found that entry, it works forward through the feed, applying each entry's payload to its own local copy of the product catalog data.

Atom doesn't prescribe how a consumer should process the entries in a feed. In our example, Atom entries represent event metadata. This metadata provides a processing context for the event's business payload. When an Atom processor encounters an <atom:content> element, it delegates control to a media type processor capable of handling the contained product or promotion representation. The client invokes the specialized handler for the content in the knowledge that it is dealing with a representation of state at a particular point in time. We call this ability to hand off from one media type processor to another *media type composition*.

---

* The value of the feed's <atom:updated> element matches that of the first entry.

If the consumer can't find in the current feed the last entry it successfully processed, it navigates the prev-archive link and looks in the previous archive. It continues to trawl through the archives until either it finds the entry it's looking for or comes to the end of the oldest archive feed (the oldest archive has no prev-archive link). Example 7-3 shows a consumer retrieving a previous archive.

Example 7-3. *The consumer retrieves the previous archive*

```
Request:
GET /product-catalog/notifications/2009/7/4 HTTP/1.1
Host: restbucks.com

Response:
HTTP/1.1 200 OK
Cache-Control: max-age=2592000
Date: ...
Content-Length: ...
Content-Type: application/atom+xml;charset="utf-8"
ETag: "a32d0b30"

<feed xmlns="http://www.w3.org/2005/Atom"
  xmlns:fh="http://purl.org/syndication/history/1.0">

  <id>urn:uuid:be21b6b0-57b4-4029-ada4-09585ee74adc</id>
  <title type="text">Product Catalog Notifications</title>
  <updated>2009-07-04T23:52:00Z</updated>
  <author>
    <name>Product Catalog</name>
  </author>
  <generator uri="http://restbucks.com/products">Product Catalog</generator>
  <fh:archive/>
  <link rel="self" href="http://restbucks.com/products/notifications/2009/7/4"/>
  <link rel="prev-archive"
    href="http://restbucks.com/products/notifications/2009/7/3"/>
  <link rel="next-archive"
    href="http://restbucks.com/products/notifications/2009/7/5"/>

  <!-- Entries omitted for brevity -->

</feed>
```

The first thing to note about this archive feed is that it contains an `<fh:archive>` element, which is a simple extension element defined in the Feed Paging and Archiving specification.* The presence of `<fh:archive>` is a further indication that this archive feed will never change and is therefore safe to cache.

Following the `<fh:archive>` element are three `<atom:link>` elements. As with the feed of recent events, this archive feed contains `self` and `prev-archive` links, but it also includes a `next-archive` link, which links to the feed of events that have occurred in the period immediately following this one—that is, to a feed of more recent events. A store can follow `next-archive` links all the way up to the current working feed.

Again, just like the feed of recent events, the response contains a `Cache-Control` header. Whereas the recent feed can only be cached for up to an hour, archive feeds are immutable, meaning they can be cached for up to 2,592,000 seconds, or 30 days.

Caching Feeds

Feeds can be cached locally by each store, as well as by gateway and reverse proxy servers along the response path. Processing an archive is a "there and back again" operation: a consumer follows `prev-archive` links until it finds an archive containing the last entry it successfully processed, and then works its way back to the head feed— this time following `next-archive` links. Whenever a consumer dereferences a `prev-archive` link, its local cache stores a copy of the response. When the consumer next accesses this same resource, most likely as a result of following a `next-archive` link on the return journey, the cache uses its stored response. Navigating the full extent of an archive is a potentially expensive operation from a network point of view: caching locally helps save valuable network resources when returning to the head feed.

NOTE

This ability to create or reconstruct a local copy of the product catalog based on the entire archive is a great pattern for bringing a new system online or for supporting crash recovery, and is one of the ways the Restbucks infrastructure scales to thousands or even millions of stores if necessary.

To explore the implications of this strategy in more detail, let's assume a store goes offline for a period of time—perhaps because of a problem with its local infrastructure. When the store eventually comes back up, it begins to update its local copy of the product catalog by polling the feed of recent events, and then working its way through `prev-archive` links looking for an archive feed containing the last entry it processed. Figure 7-3 shows the store following `prev-archive` links and working its way back in time through the archives. At each step, it caches the response locally in accordance with the metadata it receives in the HTTP cache control headers.

* *http://tools.ietf.org/html/rfc5005*

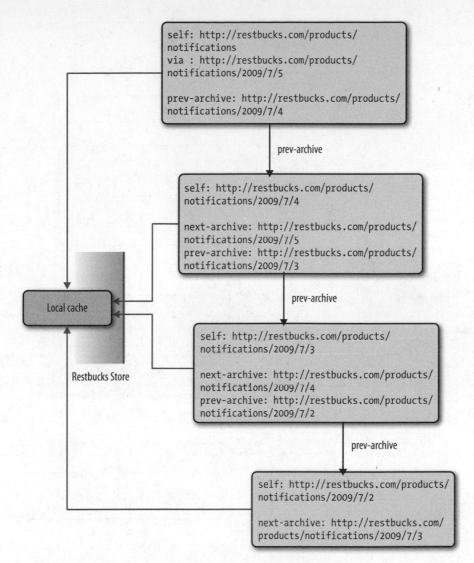

Figure 7-3. *The consumer works its way back through the archives*

At some point, the store finds the last entry it successfully processed. The store can now start working forward in time, applying the contents of each feed entry to its local copy of the product catalog, and following next-archive links whenever it gets to the top of a feed. This forward traversal is shown in Figure 7-4.

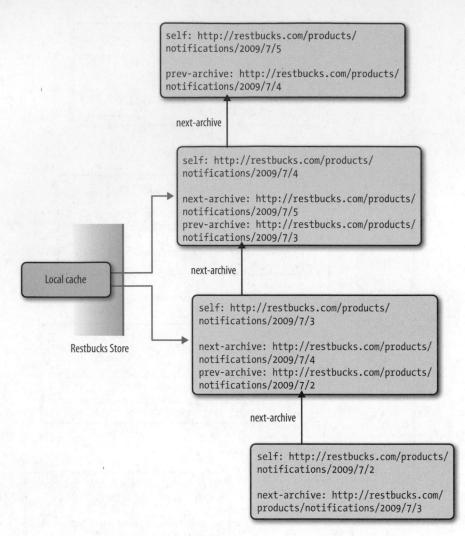

Figure 7-4. *Working forward through the archives*

Every time the store traverses a `next-archive` link, the response is fetched from the local cache (or an intermediary cache somewhere on the Restbucks network). This happens with every `next-archive` link—except the last one, when the request once again goes across the network. This last network request happens because the head of the feed is cached (if it is cached at all) against the well-known entry point URI, *http://restbucks. com/products/notifications*, rather than the working feed URI, which is *http://restbucks.com/ products/notifications/2009/7/5*. Because the store hadn't accessed the working feed while working back through the archives (it went from the feed of recent events to the first archive feed), it now has to fetch the working feed from the origin server.

This linking and caching strategy trades efficiency for generalization. Generalization comes from our being able to build hypermedia clients that can navigate feeds using standardized prev-archive and next-archive link relations. In other words, there's no need to build any special logic to prevent unnecessary end-to-end requests: it's the local caching infrastructure's job to store and return archive feeds at appropriate points in the feed traversal process. To a consumer, a request that returns a cached response looks the same as a request that goes all the way to the product catalog service.

The overall efficiency of this solution, however, breaks down with the final GET, when the consumer has to make one last network request. Assuming we started with empty caches all the way along the response path, navigating forward and backward through N feeds will cause the product catalog service to handle N+1 requests.

In designing this solution, we've assumed Restbucks' stores won't navigate the archive quite as often as they access the head feed by itself. If in practice the stores navigated the archives almost every time they polled the feed, we'd change the solution so that every request for the feed of recent events is redirected immediately to the current working feed, as shown in Example 7-4. Such a change would ensure that the head feed is cached against the current working feed's URI, rather than the entry point URI. An immediate redirect doesn't cut down on the overall *number* of wire requests, since the redirect response itself counts as an over-the-wire interaction, but it does reduce the overall *volume* of data sent in comparison to the first solution.

Example 7-4. Redirecting requests for the feed of recent events to the current working feed

```
Request:
GET /product-catalog/notifications HTTP/1.1
Host: restbucks.com

Response:
HTTP/1.1 303 See Other
Location: http://restbucks.com/products/notifications/2009/7/5

Request:
GET /product-catalog/notifications/2009/7/5 HTTP/1.1
Host: restbucks.com

Response:
HTTP/1.1 200 OK
Date: ...
Cache-Control: max-age=3600
Content-Length: ...
Content-Type: application/atom+xml;charset="utf-8"
ETag: "6a0806ca"

<feed xmlns="http://www.w3.org/2005/Atom">
  ...
</feed>
```

Recall that at some point the current working feed will be archived. When this happens, an `<fh:archive>` element and an `<atom:link>` element with a `rel` attribute value of `next-archive` will be inserted into the feed. The link points to the new current working feed. Responses containing the newly archived feed will include a `Cache-Control` header whose value allows the now immutable feed to be cached for up to 30 days.

Implementation Considerations

What distinguishes the working feed from an archive feed? As developers, we must distinguish between these feeds because the combination of caching strategy and available links differs. The working feed is cacheable only for short periods of time, whereas archive feeds are cacheable for long periods of time.

Using `prev-archive` and `next-archive` links saves us from having to add to each store some specialized knowledge of the product catalog's URI structure and the periodization rules used to generate archives. Because they depend instead on hypermedia, stores need never go off the rails; they just follow opaque links based on the semantics encoded in link relations. This allows the catalog to vary its URI structure without forcing changes in the consumers. More importantly, it allows the server to vary its feed creation rules based on the flow of events.

During particularly busy periods, for example, the product catalog service may want to archive feeds far more frequently than it does during quiet periods. Instead of archiving at predefined intervals, the service could archive after a certain number of events have occurred. This strategy allows the service to get feeds into a cacheable state very quickly. As far as Restbucks' stores are concerned, however, nothing changes. Each store still accesses the system through the feed of most recent events, and navigates the archives using `prev-archive` and `next-archive` links.

> **NOTE**
>
> In low-throughput situations, it's often acceptable to generate feeds on demand, as and when consumers ask for them. But as usage grows, this approach puts increasing strain on both the application and data access layers of the feed service. In high-throughput scenarios, where lots of consumers make frequent requests for current and archive feeds, we might consider separating the production of feeds from their consumption by clients. Such an approach can use a background process to generate feeds and store them on the filesystem (or in memory), ready to be served rapidly with minimal compute cost when requested by a consumer.

At a feed level, links with link relation values of `self`, `alternate`, `next-archive`, and `prev-archive` encapsulate the product catalog service's implementation details—in particular, the service's archiving strategy and the location of its current and archive feeds. This interlinking helps us both size feeds and tune performance. It also establishes a protocol that allows consumers to navigate the set of feeds and consume the event data held within.

The Restbucks product catalog uses many other Atom elements besides links to create an entire processing context for a list of domain-specific representations. In other words, Restbucks uses Atom to implement hypermedia-driven event handlers. To build this processing context, stores use:

- `<atom:id>` and `<atom:updated>` to identify the oldest entry requiring processing
- Categories to further refine a list of entries to be processed
- `related` links to correlate entries with domain-specific resources
- An entry's `<atom:content>` element's type attribute value to determine the processing model to be applied to the enclosed domain-specific representation

Atom helps us separate protocol and processing context from business payload using media type composition. Because the processing context for an event is conveyed solely at the Atom document level, the event-handling protocol itself can be implemented by domain-agnostic client code—that is, by generic Atom clients. The split between event context and business resource state snapshot allows stores to use Atom processors to determine which events to process, and allows domain- or application-specific media type processors to act on an entry's business payload.

Building an Atom Service in Java

For Java solutions, on the server side our basic tools are a web server, an HTTP library, and a feed generator. On the client side, we need only an HTTP library and a feed parser. For our Java implementation, we've chosen Jersey* (a JAX-RS[†] implementation) to provide the HTTP plumbing for the service and its consumers, and ROME[‡] for generating and consuming Atom feeds. For development purposes, we've chosen to use the Grizzly web server because it works nicely with Jersey.

Server-Side Architecture

The server-side architecture follows a classic layered pattern, as shown in Figure 7-5. At the lowest layer is a repository, which holds a history of changes to products and promotions, much like a source repository holds the records of changes to code. The domain objects in the middle layer encapsulate the information in the repository and make it available to the upper layers.

---

* *https://jersey.dev.java.net*
† *http://jcp.org/en/jsr/detail?id=311*
‡ *https://rome.dev.java.net*

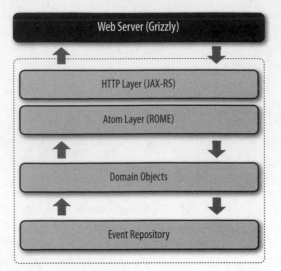

Figure 7-5. *Server-side Java architecture*

The uppermost layers compose the interface to the network. Here we must address two separate concerns: creating Atom feeds and providing access to feeds via HTTP. Generating feeds is a matter of querying and pushing appropriate events from the domain model into feed objects through the ROME library. Exposing feeds to the Web is done through the JAX-RS layer, which provides connectivity to the underlying web server.

> —— **NOTE** ————————————————————————
>
> With our Java solution, we regenerate a feed with each request. As we'll see in the .NET example later in this chapter, it's possible to store feeds in their final form so that instead of being regenerated with each request, they can be served without any transformation.

Managing Feeds

Recall that our strategy for managing the many events the service produces is to partition events across separate feeds, and then to link feeds so that clients can navigate between them. For the Java implementation, rather than archiving on an hourly or daily basis, we split the feeds based on a maximum number of entries per feed. By optimizing the size of feeds, we trade granularity for the number of network interactions needed to read the feed history.

The strategy we use for archiving feeds is application-specific, and has no bearing on the way in which consumers access and navigate the feed.

Service consumers navigate feeds by following next-archive and prev-archive links. While our service has a predictable algorithm for creating these links, to consumers the links are just opaque URIs. Example 7-5 shows a couple of links.

Example 7-5. *Providing links between feeds*

```
<link rel="next-archive"  type="application/atom+xml"
  href="http://restbucks.com/product-catalog/notifications/40,59" />
<link rel="prev-archive"  type="application/atom+xml"
  href="http://restbucks.com/product-catalog/notifications/0,19" />
```

Internally, the Java service generates links according to a simple URI template: `http://restbucks.com/product-catalog/notifications/{start},{end}`. Using this template, the service extracts from the request URI a pair of numerical identifiers, which it then uses to retrieve the appropriate events from the underlying event repository.

> ——— **WARNING** ———————————————————————————
>
> The Java service uses a URI template internally for design and documentation purposes, but it doesn't share this template with consumers. Doing so would tightly couple the service and its consumers; a change to the service's URI structure would break clients.
>
> Consumers who choose to infer URIs based on this structure are treading a dangerous path, because the service isn't obliged to honor them.

The URIs we're using in Example 7-5 look different from the others we've seen so far. This is a result of the different (but equivalent) feed generation strategy we've used for our Java implementation. The changes serve to emphasize that URIs are opaque to consumers, and that it is the link relations that drive the protocol.

Java Implementation

On the Java platform, we have a ready set of components to build out each layer of our service. Some of these (such as Jersey, our JAX-RS implementation) we've seen in prior chapters; others (such as ROME, our Atom library) are new.

Using Jersey for HTTP connectivity

JAX-RS provides a comfortable abstraction over HTTP, especially when compared to lower-level APIs such as the Servlet interface.* Using Jersey as our friendly interface to the HTTP stack allows us to delegate the plumbing details to the framework, and to concentrate instead on the overall design of the service.

Our first task is to expose the feed of recent events at a well-known URI, thereby providing an entry point into the service for consumers. The implementation for this is shown in Example 7-6. To expose the feed, we simply declare the verb (GET), the path where the feed will be hosted (/recent), and the representation format for the resource, which of course is Atom (application/atom+xml).

---

* *http://java.sun.com/products/servlet/*

Once we've got the framework code out of the way, all that's left for us to do is to generate a feed. We do this using our own EventFeedGenerator, which wraps an underlying Feed object from the ROME framework. We then turn the generated feed into a string representation. Finally, using a JAX-RS builder, we build and return a 200 OK response, adding the appropriate caching directive (Cache-Control: max-age=3600, to cache the feed for one hour) and the Atom media type. Any exceptions are handled by Jersey, which generates an HTTP 500 Internal Server Error response.

Example 7-6. *Exposing feeds for recent events and the working feed through JAX-RS*

```
@GET
@Path("/recent")
@Produces("application/atom+xml")
public Response getRecentFeed() {
    EventFeedGenerator generator = new
                                    EventFeedGenerator(uriInfo.getRequestUri(),
                                    ENTRIES_PER_FEED);
    Feed feed = generator.getRecentFeed();

    return Response.ok().entity(stringify(feed))
                .header(CACHE_CONTROL_HEADER,
                 cacheDirective(CachePolicy.getRecentFeedLifetime()))
                .type(ATOM_MEDIA_TYPE).build();
}
```

We follow a similar pattern for archive feeds, though the framework code here is a little more intricate than the code for the feed of recent events. The framework declarations in Example 7-7 include an @Path annotation, which defines the URI template the service implementation uses to extract parameters ("/{startPos},{endPos}"), and which Jersey uses to dispatch requests to the method. Only request URIs matching the template will be routed to this method.

Example 7-7. *Exposing older feeds through JAX-RS*

```
@GET
@Path("/{startPos},{endPos}")
@Produces("application/atom+xml")
public Response getSpecificFeed(@PathParam("startPos") int startPos,
  @PathParam("endPos") int endPos) {

    if (validStartAndEndEntries(startPos, endPos)) {
            // Bad URI - the paramters don't align with our feeds
            return Response.status(Status.NOT_FOUND).build();
    }

    if(workingFeedRequested(startPos)) {
        return getWorkingFeed();
    }
```

```
        EventFeedGenerator generator = new
          EventFeedGenerator(uriInfo.getRequestUri(), ENTRIES_PER_FEED);
        Feed feed = generator.feedFor(startPos);
        return Response.ok().entity(stringify(feed)).header(CACHE_CONTROL_HEADER,
          cacheDirective(CachePolicy.getArchiveFeedLifetime()))
          .type(ATOM_MEDIA_TYPE).build();
    }

    private Response getWorkingFeed() {
        EventFeedGenerator generator = new
                                EventFeedGenerator(uriInfo.getRequestUri(),
                                ENTRIES_PER_FEED);
        Feed feed = generator.getWorkingFeed();

        return Response.ok().entity(stringify(feed))
                        .header(CACHE_CONTROL_HEADER,
                          cacheDirective(CachePolicy.getWorkingFeedLifetime()))
                          .type(ATOM_MEDIA_TYPE).build();
    }
```

Jersey extracts the URI parameters from the URI at runtime and passes them into the method via the two @PathParam annotations in the method signature. From there, we validate whether the parameters fit with our feed-splitting scheme by testing whether the values are divisible by our feed size. If the values from the URI template don't fit our feed scheme, the service returns a 404 Not Found response.

If the URI parameters are valid, we check whether the requested feed refers to the current working feed. If it does, we generate a representation of the working feed and send that back to the consumer. Otherwise, we call into the archive feed generation logic to create a feed using generator.feedFor(startPos). Once the feed has been created, we turn it into a string representation and build a 200 OK response containing the feed plus the Content-Type header, as shown in the final line of the method.

Generating feeds with ROME

The HTTP-centric code is only half the implementation of the service. Under the covers is a great deal of code that generates Atom feeds on demand.

> **WARNING**
>
> ROME can be an awkward library to work with. Many of the API calls in the 1.0 release are weakly typed using String and nongeneric collections. It's helpful to have the Javadoc comments on hand when working with it.*

* *https://rome.dev.java.net/apidocs/1_0/overview-summary.html*

Example 7-8 shows the EventFeedGenerator.feedFor(...) method, which creates a feed by orchestrating several calls into the underlying ROME library.

Example 7-8. *Generating an Atom feed with ROME*

```
public Feed feedFor(int startEntry) {
  Feed feed = new Feed();

  feed.setFeedType("atom_1.0");
  feed.setId("urn:uuid:" + UUID.randomUUID().toString()); // We don't need stable
                                                          // ID because we're not
                                                          // aggregating feeds
  feed.setTitle(FEED_TITLE);
  final Generator generator = new Generator();
  generator.setUrl(getServiceUri());
  generator.setValue(PRODUCING_SERVICE);
  feed.setGenerator(generator);
  feed.setAuthors(generateAuthorsList());
  feed.setAlternateLinks(generateAlternateLinks(startEntry));
  feed.setOtherLinks(generatePagingLinks(startEntry));
  feed.setEntries(createEntries(EventStore.current()
                          .getEvents(startEntry, entriesPerFeed)));
  feed.setUpdated(newestEventDate(events));
  return feed;
}
```

The first few lines in Example 7-8 set the feed metadata: feed type, title, creation date, generator, and authors. These elements are created by the setters setFeedType(...) through to setAuthors(...).

> ── **NOTE** ─────────────────────────────
>
> We're using a randomly generated feed identifier here. This means that consumers receive a different identifier each time they request the feed. If we had multiple feed providers (as Atom supports), the identifier would need to be stable over time, and crash-recoverable, so that consumers could safely merge separate physical feeds into a single logical feed.

The setter methods in Example 7-8 give us the beginnings of the Atom feed shown in Example 7-9. This feed contains all the necessary feed metadata.

Example 7-9. *Generated feed metadata*

```
HTTP/1.1 200 OK
server: grizzly/1.8.1
Cache-Control: max-age=3600
Content-Type: application/atom+xml
```

```
<feed xmlns="http://www.w3.org/2005/Atom">
  <title>Restbucks products and promotions</title>
  <author>
    <name>A Product Manager</name>
  </author>
  <id>urn:uuid:4679956d-b084-48f7-a20f-6e7b3891d951</id>
  <generator uri="http://restbucks.com/product-catalog/notifications">
    Product Catalog
  </generator>
  <updated>2009-08-13T16:42:04Z</updated>
  <!-- Remainder of feed omitted for brevity -->
</feed>
```

Things get more interesting when we have to generate some of the dynamic feed content, particularly links. For the feed, this means identifying the URI through which the feed was accessed (rel="self") and the source of entries for that feed (rel="via"). Both of these are serialized as <atom:link> elements as the feed is constructed. The code in Example 7-10 shows how the dynamic content for the /recent feed is created.

Example 7-10. *Generating self and via links*

```
public Feed getRecentFeed() {
    int startEntry = findStartingEntryForHeadFeeds();
    Feed recent = feedFor(startEntry);
    Link self = new Link();
    self.setHref(requestUri.toString());
    self.setRel("self");
    self.setType(ATOM_MEDIA_TYPE);
    recent.getAlternateLinks().add(self);
    recent.getAlternateLinks().addAll(generatePagingLinks(startEntry));
    Link via = new Link();
    via.setHref(this.generateCanonicalUri(startEntry));
    via.setRel("via");
    via.setType(ATOM_MEDIA_TYPE);
    recent.getAlternateLinks().add(via);
    return recent;
}
```

To generate the self link we take the (previously validated) request URI and add it to the list of Link objects with a rel value of self. If the requested feed is the feed of recent events, as accessed via the well-known URI /recent, we also need to generate the source URI so that a consumer can still access the entries associated with this particular time period when the current feed is archived. That's easily done by adding another Link object with a rel value of via to the list of links for the feed.

With the links added to the feed, we now get the XML shown in Example 7-11 for the feed of recent events, and that in Example 7-12 for an archive feed.

Example 7-11. Generated self and via links in the feed of recent events

```
<link rel="self" type="application/atom+xml"
  href="http://restbucks.com/product-catalog/notifications/recent" />
<link rel="via" type="application/atom+xml"
  href="http://restbucks.com/product-catalog/notifications/160,179" />
```

Example 7-12. Generated self link in archive feed

```
<link rel="self" type="application/atom+xml"
  href="http://restbucks.com/product-catalog/notifications/80,99" />
```

The final feed metadata comprises the links we need to navigate back (prev-archive) and forth (next-archive) through older feeds. In Example 7-13, we generate these links by determining whether there are newer and older feeds relative to the current feed; if there are, we calculate the link values using our algorithm for splitting feeds. Once calculated, we add the paging links to the list of links returned to the feed generator.

Example 7-13. Generating navigation links between feeds

```
private List<Link> generatePagingLinks(int currentFeedStart) {
  ArrayList<Link> links = new ArrayList<Link>();

  if(hasNewerFeed(currentFeedStart)) {
    Link next = new Link();
    next.setRel("next-archive");
    next.setType(ATOM_MEDIA_TYPE);
    next.setHref(generatePageUri(getServiceUri(),
                  currentFeedStart + entriesPerFeed));
    links.add(next);
  }

  if(hasOlderFeed(currentFeedStart)) {
    Link prev = new Link();
    prev.setRel("prev-archive");
    prev.setType(ATOM_MEDIA_TYPE);
    prev.setHref(generatePageUri(getServiceUri(),
                  currentFeedStart - entriesPerFeed));
    links.add(prev);
  }
  return links;
}
```

The code in Example 7-13 gives us the feed-level links shown in Example 7-14.

Example 7-14. *Navigation links in an Atom feed*

```
<link rel="prev-archive" type="application/atom+xml"
  href="http://restbucks.com/product-catalog/notifications/140,159" />
<link rel="next-archive" type="application/atom+xml"
  href="http://restbucks.com/product-catalog/notifications/180,199" />
```

Once the feed-level metadata has been created, it's time to populate the feed with entries. Each entry in a feed represents a business event pertaining to a product or promotion. The createEntries(...) method shown in Example 7-15 is responsible for creating the entries for a given set of events.

Example 7-15. *Populating a feed with entries containing events*

```
private List<Entry> createEntries(List<Event> events) {
  ArrayList<Entry> entries = new ArrayList<Entry>();

  for(Event e : events) {
    final Entry entry = new Entry();
    entry.setId(e.getTagUri());
    entry.setTitle(e.getEventType());
    entry.setUpdated(e.getTimestamp());
    entry.setAlternateLinks(generateLinks(e));
    entry.setCategories(generateCategories(e));
    entry.setContents(generateContents(e));
    entries.add(entry);
  }

  return entries;
}
```

The events provided to the createEntries(...) method are supplied from the underlying event store. For each event, the following metadata is extracted and pushed directly into the entry:

- An identifier from the event's stable, long-lived tag URI*

- The event type, being a product or promotion event

- The timestamp for when the event was generated

Following on from the metadata, we add two links, self and related, to the entry. The self link contains the entry's URI; the related link correlates the entry with the underlying product or promotion's URI in the product catalog service.

---

* Tag URIs are a way of creating a nonaddressable identifier from an addressable URI scheme such as HTTP. We use them here because events only have to be identifiable, whereas entries have to be addressable. See *http://diveintomark.org/archives/2004/05/28/howto-atom-id* for more information.

Finally, we serialize the event payload into XML, and add it to the entry's <content> element. We then add the new entry to the feed. The snapshot of the state of a product or promotion appears as a child of an <atom:content> element, as shown in Example 7-16.

Example 7-16. *Event payloads exposed as entry content in an Atom feed*

```
HTTP/1.1 200 OK
server: grizzly/1.8.1
Cache-Control: max-age=2592000
Content-Type: application/atom+xml

...
<entry>
  <title>product</title>
  <link rel="self"
   href="http://restbucks.com/product-catalog/notifications/notifications/120" />
  <link rel="related" href="http://restbucks.com/products/2012703733" />
  <category term="product"
   scheme="http://restbucks.com/product-catalog/notifications/categories/type" />
  <category term="new"
   scheme="http://restbucks.com/product-catalog/notifications/categories/status" />
  <id>tag:restbucks.com,2009-08-15:120</id>
  <updated>2008-04-04T16:24:02Z</updated>
  <content type="application/vnd.restbucks+xml">
    <product xmlns="http://schemas.restbucks.com/product"
     href="http://restbucks.com/products/2012703733">
      <name>product name 543809053</name>
      <price>2.34</price>
    </product>
  </content>
</entry>
<entry>
  <title>promotion</title>
  <link rel="self"
   href="http://restbucks.com/product-catalog/notifications/notifications/148" />
  <link rel="related" href="http://restbucks.com/promotions/1669488880" />
  <category term="promotion"
   scheme="http://restbucks.com/product-catalog/notifications/categories/type" />
  <category term="new"
   scheme="http://restbucks.com/product-catalog/notifications/categories/status" />
  <id>tag:restbucks.com,2009-08-15:148</id>
  <updated>2008-04-04T16:24:02Z</updated>
  <content type="application/vnd.restbucks+xml">
    <promotion xmlns="http://schemas.restbucks.com/promotion"
     xmlns:ns2="http://www.w3.org/2005/Atom"
```

```
        href="http://restbucks.com/promotions/1669488880">
          <effective>2009-08-15</effective>
          <ns2:product type="application/vnd.restbucks+xml"
            href="http://restbucks.com/products/1995649500" />
          <ns2:region type="application/vnd.restbucks+xml"
            href="http://restbucks.com/regions/2140798621" />
        </promotion>
      </content>
    </entry>
    ...
```

Now that we have exposed interlinked feeds with entries representing business events, clients can traverse and consume those feeds, and use the information in the events to trigger local processing. This leads us to the consumer-side infrastructure.

Java Consumer Implementation

Like the product catalog service, the consumer implementation has been developed using Jersey for HTTP plumbing code, and ROME for parsing Atom feeds. Unlike the service implementation, however, the consumer code—excluding any business logic and error handling—is quite small, with Jersey and ROME providing most of the necessary functionality.

The code to request an Atom feed is shown in Example 7-17.

Example 7-17. *Consuming an event feed with Jersey and ROME*

```
private Feed getFeed(URI uri) {
  // Jersey
  Client client = Client.create();
  ClientResponse response = client.resource(uri)
                            .accept(ATOM_MEDIA_TYPE)
                            .get(ClientResponse.class);

  String responseString = response.getEntity(String.class);

  // Rome code
  WireFeedInput wfi = new WireFeedInput();
  WireFeed wireFeed;
  try {
    wireFeed = wfi.build(new StringReader(responseString));
  } catch (Exception e) {
    throw new RuntimeException(e);
  }

  return (Feed) wireFeed;
}
```

The responsibilities in Example 7-17 are split between Jersey and ROME. The Jersey code creates an HTTP client, and then sends an HTTP GET request with an Accept header of application/atom+xml to the product catalog service.

The get(...) call populates the HTTP response object with the results of the interaction, including an Atom feed if the request was successfully processed. This Atom feed is extracted as a String instance and passed into the ROME library where it is converted to an object representation that can be processed by the consumer's business logic.

Of course, this isn't the end of the story for our consumer. If the consumer can't find the entry it last successfully processed in the current feed, it will have to look through the archives. Fortunately, because feeds are navigable via their next-archive and prev-archive links, the consumer need only follow these links to discover and consume the archive feeds. Programmatically, this is straightforward, since we already have a means to access feeds by URI (Example 7-17), and ROME provides us the means to extract URIs from feeds, as we see in Example 7-18.

Example 7-18. *Navigating feeds from a consumer perspective*

```
private URI getUriFromNamedLink(String relValue, Feed feed)
                                    throws URISyntaxException {
  for (Object obj : feed.getOtherLinks()) {
    Link l = (Link) obj;
    if (l.getRel().equals(relValue)) {
      return new URI(l.getHref());
    }
  }
  return null;
}
private URI getPrevArchive(Feed feed) throws URISyntaxException {
  return getUriFromNamedLink("prev-archive", feed);
}
private URI getNextArchive(Feed feed) throws URISyntaxException {
  return getUriFromNamedLink("next-archive", feed);
}
```

Example 7-18 shows how a consumer extracts links from a feed. Moving forward through a set of feeds is a matter of looking for next-archive links, while moving backward is a matter of acting on the corresponding prev-archive links in each feed. As each feed is discovered, the consumer filters and applies the feed's entries to the objects in its local domain model.

Building an Atom Service in .NET

Our .NET solution serves pregenerated Atom feeds from the filesystem rather than constructing them on the fly. This way, we separate the construction of feeds from the handling of requests. The benefit of this approach is that it conserves computing resources. The downside is that it introduces additional latency between an event occurring and its appearing in a feed. We can tolerate this trade-off because transferring products and offers to Restbucks stores isn't very latency-sensitive, and so any additional delay doesn't prevent the solution from working effectively.

> **NOTE**
>
> Using pregenerated static files for archive feeds is particularly effective at web scale. Most web servers are very good at serving static files; furthermore, public-facing services can use content delivery networks (CDNs) to store copies of archive feeds closer to their globally distributed consumers. Static files allow us to implement additional optimizations, such as storing and serving feeds in a gzipped state.

This separation of concerns between constructing feeds and handling requests is reflected in two core components: `ProductCatalog.Writer`, which generates feeds, and `ProductCatalog.Notifications`, which handles requests.

Writing Feeds to Files

Writing feeds to files is triggered by a timer, which fires periodically. When the timer fires, the feed writer reads new events from a buffer and writes them to the recent events feed file. If during this process the recent events feed becomes full, the service archives it and starts a new one.

Importantly, with this approach, once a file has been written to the filesystem, it's never updated. This is to prevent contention between file readers and writers. Consider, for example, the situation where a client request is being served from a file at the same time as the recent events feed is being updated. If we were to allow file updates, we'd run the risk of blocking consumers while the service obtains a lock on the underlying file and modifies its contents, complicating the solution for little gain.

Making a file unchangeable once it has been published works fine in the case of archive feeds: archives by their very nature are immutable. But things are trickier with the feed of recent events, which continues to grow as more events occur.

One solution to this problem is to publish the feed of recent events as a series of *temporary* files. Each time the feed writing process is triggered, the service creates a *copy* of the recent events feed, and then it adds new events to this copy. The service maintains an in-memory mapping between the resource identifier for the recent events feed and the newest temporary file containing this feed. When the feed updating process completes, the service updates the mapping.

Updating the in-memory mapping is an atomic operation. Until the mapping is updated, requests continue to be served from the older temporary file. Once the mapping has been updated, however, new requests are satisfied from the new temporary file. A reaper process cleans up older temporary files after a short interval.

The feed writing process is controlled by an instance of the FeedWriter class, which hosts a timer. Timer events are handled by the FeedWriter.WriteFeed() method shown in Example 7-19. WriteFeed() stops the timer, loops through and executes the tasks responsible for updating the recent events feed, and then restarts the timer.

Example 7-19. WriteFeed() handles the feed writing timer event

```
private void WriteFeed()
{
  timer.Stop();

  ITask task = new QueryingEvents();
  while (!task.IsLastTask)
  {
    task = task.Execute(fileSystem, buffer, feedBuilder, NotifyMappingsChanged);
  }

  timer.Start();
}
```

Tasks

We've broken down the feed writing process down into a series of discrete tasks. Each task is responsible for a single activity. Once it has completed its activity, the currently executing task creates and returns the next task to be executed. By breaking the process of updating the recent events feed into a number of discrete tasks, we make the solution easier to develop and test.

Each task executed by WriteFeed() implements the ITask interface shown in Example 7-20.

Example 7-20. *The ITask interface*

```
public interface ITask
{
  bool IsLastTask { get; }
  ITask Execute(IFileSystem fileSystem,
    IEventBuffer buffer,
    FeedBuilder feedBuilder,
    Action<FeedMappingsChangedEventArgs> notifyMappingsChanged);
}
```

ITask's Execute(...) method takes four parameters:

fileSystem

> An object that implements the IFileSystem interface, which provides access to the filesystem directories containing the recent events feed, archive feeds, and feed entries.

buffer

> Provides access to new events waiting to be written to a feed. Example 7-21 shows the IEventBuffer interface. In a production system, we might use a persistent queue or database table to back this buffer. In our sample application, the event buffer is implemented as an in-memory queue.

feedBuilder

> Formats feeds and entries. We'll look at the FeedBuilder class in more detail later.

notifyMappingsChanged

> A delegate, which is used to raise an event indicating the feed mappings have changed. Tasks can invoke this delegate when the process of writing a feed has been completed. Doing so notifies other parts of the system that the recent events feed has changed.

Example 7-21. *The IEventBuffer interface*

```
public interface IEventBuffer
{
  void Add(Event evnt);
  IEnumerable<Event> Take(int batchSize);
}
```

Figure 7-6 shows how the tasks responsible for updating the recent events feed are organized into a processing pipeline for events.

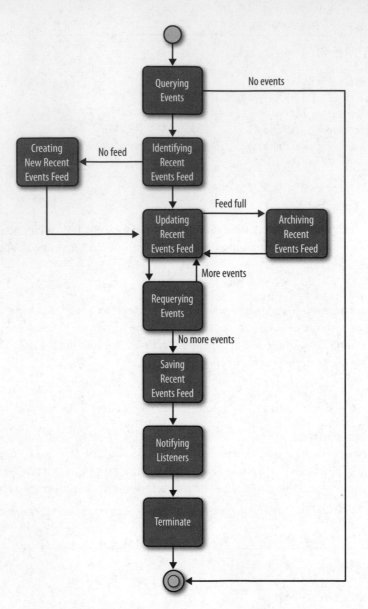

Figure 7-6. *Tasks involved in writing a feed*

These task classes are:

QueryingEvents

Takes a batch of events from the buffer. If there are no new events in the buffer, QueryingEvents returns a Terminate task; otherwise, it returns an IdentifyingRecentEventsFeed task.

IdentifyingRecentEventsFeed

> Identifies the latest recent events feed file. If the file exists, this task uses the feed builder to load the feed into memory. It then returns an UpdatingRecentEventsFeed task, passing the in-memory feed and the new events waiting to be added to the feed to the new task's constructor. If IdentifyingRecentEventsFeed can't find a recent events feed file on the filesystem, it returns a CreatingNewRecentEventsFeed task.

UpdatingRecentEventsFeed

> Iterates over new events retrieved from the buffer and updates the recent events feed. If during this process the feed's entry quota is reached, the task returns an ArchivingRecentEventsFeed task. If, on the other hand, the task gets through all the new events without having to archive the recent events feed, it returns a RequeryingEvents task.

RequeryingEvents

> Gets another batch of new events from the buffer. If there are no new events, this task returns a SavingRecentEventsFeed task; otherwise, it returns a new UpdatingRecentEventsFeed task.

SavingRecentEventsFeed

> Tells the in-memory recent events feed to save itself to the filesystem and then returns a NotifyingListeners task.

NotifyingListeners

> Invokes the notifyMappingsChanged delegate with the latest recent events feed's details and then returns a Terminate task.

CreatingNewRecentEventsFeed

> Is executed when the service can't find a recent events file on the filesystem. This will be the case, for example, when the service starts for the very first time. CreatingNewRecentEventsFeed creates an empty recent events feed and returns a new UpdatingRecentEventsFeed task, passing the newly created feed to this new task. (This new feed is not saved to the filesystem until SavingRecentEventsFeed is executed.)

ArchivingRecentEventsFeed

> Uses the current feed to create a new recent events feed, which is empty. It then archives the old feed and creates and returns an UpdatingRecentEventsFeed task, passing the new recent events feed to the new task's constructor.

Terminate

> Completes the process of updating the recent events feed.

Together, these tasks retrieve batches of new events from the event buffer and update the recent events feed. When the current feed's entry quota has been reached, the service archives the feed and begins a new one. The service then repeats the process of retrieving events, adding them to the recent events feed and archiving where necessary, until there are no more new events in the buffer.

Building Feeds

FeedBuilder creates in-memory representations of feeds and entries. Feeds are of two types: RecentEventsFeed and ArchiveFeed. The feed builder is responsible for creating new recent events feeds and restoring recent events feeds from the filesystem. It can also create a subsequent feed and an archive feed from the current feed.

A feed builder uses a helper class, Links, to generate links. When the service starts, it configures a Links object with some service-specific URI templates. The feed builder parameterizes these templates at runtime with resource Ids to generate URIs for feeds and entries.

RecentEventsFeed and ArchiveFeed objects are initialized with a FeedMapping object. Feed mappings encapsulate the mapping between a resource ID and its filename. An Id is the service's own internal representation of the distinguishing part of a feed or entry's address. Links uses an Id object to generate a feed or entry URI by filling in a URI template. Our sample service is configured at startup with a base address of *http:// restbucks.com/product-catalog/notifications/*, and a URI template for feeds of /?page={id}. An Id object with an integer value of 4, therefore, will result in the following feed URI: *http://restbucks.com/product-catalog/notifications/?page=4.*

By making the creation of temporary filenames private to a feed mapping, we ensure that we generate a different temporary filename every time we create a mapping, thereby guaranteeing that feed files will never be updated once they've been saved. A feed mapping can generate new feed mappings in three different ways. It can create a copy of itself with the same ID but a different temporary filename. It can generate a new feed mapping with an incremented ID (and different filename). Finally, it can create a copy with the same ID and a permanent, archive filename—as opposed to a temporary filename—based on that same ID.

A feed builder's primary responsibility is to create a recent events feed. Its CreateRecentEventsFeed(...) method is shown in Example 7-22.

Example 7-22. Creating an in-memory representation of a new feed

```
public RecentEventsFeed CreateRecentEventsFeed(FeedMapping mapping,
  IPrevArchiveLinkGenerator prevArchiveLinkGenerator)
{
  SyndicationFeed feed = new SyndicationFeed
    {
      Id = new UniqueId(Guid.NewGuid()).ToString(),
      Title = SyndicationContent.CreatePlaintextContent(Title),
      Generator = ServiceName,
      LastUpdatedTime = DateTime.Now,
      Items = new List<SyndicationItem>()
    };

  feed.Authors.Add(new SyndicationPerson {Name = ServiceName});
```

```
      feed.Links.Add(links.CreateRecentFeedSelfLink());
      feed.Links.Add(links.CreateViaLink(mapping.Id));

      prevArchiveLinkGenerator.AddTo(feed, links);

      return new RecentEventsFeed(feed, mapping, this);
   }
```

CreateRecentEventsFeed(...) accepts a feed mapping and an object that implements IPrevArchiveLinkGenerator. Depending on its underlying implementation, this latter parameter will either add a prev-archive link to the generated feed or do nothing. The very first feed to be generated doesn't require a prev-archive link, but all the others do.

CreateRecentEventsFeed(...) uses the .NET Framework's SyndicationFeed to build the feed. SyndicationFeed is one of many classes in the System.ServiceModel.Syndication that together make up a media type library for constructing and parsing Atom feeds. CreateRecentEventsFeed(...) initializes a new syndication feed with some feed-level metadata. It then adds a self link and a via link, and uses the prevArchiveLinkGenerator parameter to add a prev-archive link.

Feed builders are also responsible for creating individual Atom entries. FeedBuilder.CreateEntry(...), which is shown in Example 7-23, initializes a SyndicationItem and sets its Id, Title, and LastUpdatedTime properties. Note that the entry's ID value is computed using the same *Tag* scheme we used in our Java solution. After creating and adding self and related links (the self link is a standalone URI for the entry, the related link the URI of the domain entity to which the event refers), CreateEntry(...) serializes the supplied event to the entry's Content property.

Example 7-23. *FeedBuilder.CreateEntry(...) method*

```
   public Entry CreateEntry(Event evnt)
   {
      SyndicationItem item = new SyndicationItem
        {
           Id = string.Format("tag:restbucks.com,{0}:{1}",
             evnt.Timestamp.ToString("yyyy-MM-dd"), evnt.Id),
           Title = SyndicationContent.CreatePlaintextContent(evnt.Subject),
           LastUpdatedTime = evnt.Timestamp
        };

      item.Links.Add(links.CreateEntrySelfLink(new Id(evnt.Id)));
      item.Links.Add(links.CreateEntryRelatedLink(evnt.Body.Href));

      item.Content = new XmlSyndicationContent(evnt.Body.ContentType,
        evnt.Body.Payload, null as DataContractSerializer);

      return new Entry(item, new Id(evnt.Id).CreateFileName());
   }
```

FeedBuilder exposes three more public methods:

- LoadRecentEventsFeed(...)
- CreateNextRecentEventsFeed(...)
- CreateArchiveFeed(...)

The first of these, LoadRecentEventsFeed(...), uses an IFileSystem implementation to load a feed from the current directory, as shown in Example 7-24. With the file contents loaded into a syndication feed, the method parses out the resource ID from the feed's via link and uses this to create a new feed mapping. It then uses the new mapping to initialize a new RecentEventsFeed. This ensures that the returned feed retains the loaded feed's resource ID, but is given a new temporary filename.

Example 7-24. *Loading a feed from the filesystem*

```
public RecentEventsFeed LoadRecentEventsFeed(IFileSystem fileSystem,
  FileName fileName)
{
  using (XmlReader reader = fileSystem.CurrentDirectory.GetXmlReader(fileName))
  {
    SyndicationFeed feed = SyndicationFeed.Load(reader);
    Id id = links.GetIdFromFeedUri(feed.GetViaLink().GetAbsoluteUri());
    return new RecentEventsFeed(feed, new FeedMapping(id), this);
  }
}
```

CreateNextRecentEventsFeed(...), which is shown in Example 7-25, takes a feed mapping belonging to the current recent events feed and uses it to initialize a PrevArchiveLinkGenerator. This generator can then be used to generate prev-archive links that point to the feed associated with the mapping. It can also be used to generate a new mapping containing the *next* resource ID. The new feed mapping and the link generator instance are used to call CreateRecentEventsFeed(...), which creates a new RecentEventsFeed.

Example 7-25. *Creating the next recent events feed*

```
public RecentEventsFeed CreateNextRecentEventsFeed(FeedMapping mapping)
{
  return CreateRecentEventsFeed(
    mapping.WithNextId(), new PrevArchiveLinkGenerator(mapping.Id));
}
```

Example 7-26 shows the implementation of CreateArchiveFeed(...). This method takes a syndication feed and feed mapping belonging to the feed to be archived, together with a mapping belonging to the next recent events feed, and uses them to create an ArchiveFeed based on a clone of the supplied feed.

Example 7-26. *Creating an archive feed*

```
public ArchiveFeed CreateArchiveFeed(SyndicationFeed feed,
  FeedMapping currentMapping, FeedMapping nextMapping)
{
  SyndicationFeed archive = feed.Clone(true);

  archive.GetSelfLink().Uri = archive.GetViaLink().Uri;
  archive.Links.Remove(archive.GetViaLink());
  archive.Links.Add(links.CreateNextArchiveLink(nextMapping.Id));
  archive.ElementExtensions.Add(new SyndicationElementExtension(
    "archive", "http://purl.org/syndication/history/1.0", string.Empty));

  return new ArchiveFeed(archive, currentMapping.WithArchiveFileName());
}
```

To create an archive feed from a recent events feed, CreateArchiveFeed(...) first clones
the supplied syndication feed. It then copies the cloned feed's via link value into a new
self link and removes the via link from the feed. Next, it adds a next-archive link that
points to the next recent events feed. Finally, it adds an <archive> extension element.

Handling Requests

Requests are handled by a NotificationsService object, which is hosted by an instance
of ServiceHost. The service host encapsulates all the HTTP plumbing. In our implementation, this means using a System.Net.HttpListener object to listen for requests
and send responses.

Example 7-27 shows the service host's HandleRequest(...) method. This method is
dispatched to a thread from the .NET thread pool with each request.

Example 7-27. *ServiceHost.HandleRequest(...) wraps requests and applies responses to the
output*

```
private void HandleRequest(HttpListenerContext context)
{
  Log.DebugFormat("{0} {1}", context.Request.HttpMethod, context.Request.RawUrl);

  IResponse response = service.GetResponse(
    new HttpListenerRequestWrapper(context.Request));
  using (IResponseWrapper wrapper =
    new HttpListenerResponseWrapper(context.Response))
  {
    response.ApplyTo(wrapper);
  }
}
```

`HandleRequest(...)` translates between the requests and responses used by the service logic and the request and response objects belonging to the HTTP plumbing. The method wraps the request and response objects provided by the `HttpListenerContext` with simple wrapper objects so as to prevent `HttpListener` specifics from leaking into the rest of the service code. Doing so supports rapid test-driven development because it allows the service implementation to be tested *without depending on any HTTP plumbing or connectivity*.

The service host itself simply translates between the HTTP infrastructure and the service implementation. The real request handling logic is implemented in `NotificationsService.GetResponse(...)`, as shown in Example 7-28.

Example 7-28. *The notifications service handles requests*

```
public IResponse GetResponse(IRequestWrapper request)
{
  Log.DebugFormat("Received request. Uri: [{0}].", request.Uri.AbsoluteUri);

  try
  {
    IRepositoryCommand command = routes.CreateCommand(request.Uri);
    IRepresentation representation = command.Invoke(repository);
    return request.Condition.CreateResponse(representation);
  }
  catch (ServerException ex)
  {
    Log.ErrorFormat("Server exception. {0}", ex.Message);
    return Response.InternalServerError();
  }
  catch (InvalidUriException ex)
  {
    Log.WarnFormat("Invalid request. {0}", ex.Message);
    return Response.NotFound();
  }
  catch (NotFoundException ex)
  {
    Log.WarnFormat("Invalid request. {0}", ex.Message);
    return Response.NotFound();
  }
}
```

`GetResponse(...)` implements the conditional GET HTTP idiom. To implement a conditional GET, `GetResponse(...)` first fetches a representation from a repository. It then supplies this representation to the condition specified in the request. This condition creates and returns a response, which is handed back to the host for applying to the response stream. We'll look at how this condition is generated, and how it determines whether to return 200 OK or 304 Not Modified, in more detail shortly. Before we do that, let's look at how the repository command is created.

Every feed has a unique URI. The notifications service uses this URI to create a command that can retrieve a feed representation from a repository. The logic for creating a command from a URI is encapsulated in a Routes object, which matches the request URI with some service-specific URI templates. Example 7-29 shows the implementation of Routes in its entirety.

Example 7-29. *Routes creates repository functions based on request URIs*

```
public class Routes
{
  private readonly Uri baseAddress;
  private readonly UriTemplateTable uriTemplates;

  private static readonly Func<NameValueCollection, IRepositoryCommand>
    GetFeedOfRecentEvents =
      parameters => GetFeedOfRecentEventsCommand.Instance;

  private static readonly Func<NameValueCollection, IRepositoryCommand>
    GetFeed =
      parameters => new GetFeedCommand(
        new ResourceId(parameters.GetValues("id")[0]));

  public Routes(UriConfiguration uriConfiguration)
  {
    Check.IsNotNull(uriConfiguration, "uriConfiguration");

    baseAddress = uriConfiguration.BaseAddress;

    uriTemplates = new UriTemplateTable(baseAddress);
    uriTemplates.KeyValuePairs.Add(new KeyValuePair<UriTemplate, object>(
      uriConfiguration.RecentFeedTemplate, GetFeedOfRecentEvents));
    uriTemplates.KeyValuePairs.Add(new KeyValuePair<UriTemplate, object>(
      uriConfiguration.FeedTemplate, GetFeed));
  }

  public Uri BaseAddress
  {
    get { return baseAddress; }
  }

  public IRepositoryCommand CreateCommand(Uri uri)
  {
    UriTemplateMatch match = uriTemplates.MatchSingle(uri);

    if (match == null)
    {
      throw new InvalidUriException(string.Format("Invalid uri: [{0}]",
        uri.AbsoluteUri));
    }
```

```
      var commandFactoryMethod = (Func<NameValueCollection, IRepositoryCommand>)
        match.Data;
      return commandFactoryMethod.Invoke(match.BoundVariables);
    }
  }
```

GetFeedOfRecentEvents and GetFeed are static functions, both of which accept a NameValueCollection parameter and return a command. In the case of GetFeedCommand, this command is initialized with a ResourceId based on an id value in the parameters collection.

The constructor for Routes associates these functions with UriTemplates by adding them to a UriTemplateTable object. When it receives a request, CreateCommand(...) matches the request URI with a template in this table. If it finds a match, it invokes the associated function, passing in any variables parsed out of the request URI. The command returned from this invocation becomes the return value for CreateCommand(...).

At startup, the notifications service is initialized with a repository, which is then passed to this command. With each request, the repository queries the underlying store and returns a representation object, which the notifications service then hands to the condition (If-None-Match) supplied in the request. This condition is responsible for creating a Response object.

Writing the response

In Example 7-27, we saw that the response returned by NotificationsService. GetResponse(...) is applied to a wrapped instance of the HttpListener's outgoing response. This Response wrapper object applies a representation to a ResponseContext object and then flushes this context to the response stream. Example 7-30 shows how this is implemented.

Example 7-30. Response.ApplyTo(…) applies a response context to an outgoing response

```
public void ApplyTo(IResponseWrapper responseWrapper)
{
  ResponseContext context = new ResponseContext();
  context.AddHeader(statusCode);
  representation.UpdateContext(context);
  context.ApplyTo(responseWrapper);
}
```

In our .NET service, representation data is built up using a decorator pattern.* The representation returned from a repository comprises one of three feed instances—WorkingFeed, FeedOfRecentEvents, or ArchiveFeed—plus, in each case, an inner FileBasedAtomDocument instance.

---

* *http://en.wikipedia.org/wiki/Decorator_pattern*

As a result of using the decorator pattern, several representation objects contribute HTTP headers and entity body strategies to the response context:

WorkingFeed

> Adds a short caching policy to the context, plus a response body rewriting strategy that transforms a recent events feed into a working feed

FeedOfRecentEvents

> Simply adds a short caching policy to the response context

ArchiveFeed

> Adds a long caching policy

FileBasedAtomDocument

> Adds Content-Type, Last-Modified, and ETag HTTP headers to the response context, and a strategy that opens the feed file for reading

Entity body strategies are simply functions that open files and apply transformations to file contents. By implementing a strategy as a function, we allow its execution to be deferred until the service is certain it is needed. While a FileBasedAtomDocument object may add a function that opens a feed file to the response context, and a WorkingFeed a function that transforms feed file contents into a working feed, neither function will be invoked until the service determines it is necessary to open a file and write the contents to the response stream. If the service receives a conditional GET and determines that the requested feed has not changed since it was last requested, it skips these functions and writes only the necessary headers to the output.

Implementing Conditional GETs

As we mentioned, our .NET service supports conditional GET operations as a performance and scalability optimization. The FileBasedAtomDocument class generates several representation values, including an entity tag value based on a feed's filename and write time, as illustrated in Example 7-31.

Example 7-31. *Generating HTTP headers based on file properties*

```
public FileBasedAtomDocument(string fileName,
  IChunkingStrategy chunkingStrategy)
{
  fileInfo = new FileInfo(fileName);

  if (!fileInfo.Exists)
  {
    throw new NotFoundException(
      string.Format("File does not exist. File: [{0}].", fileInfo.FullName));
  }
```

```
    eTag = new ETag(
      string.Format(@"""{0}#{1}""", fileInfo.Name, fileInfo.LastWriteTimeUtc.Ticks));
    chunking = chunkingStrategy.CreateHeader(fileInfo.Length);
    lastModified = new LastModified(fileInfo.LastWriteTimeUtc);
}
```

Because they're based on file properties rather than the contents of a file, these entity tag values are relatively cheap to generate. The service can compare an entity tag value supplied in a request's If-None-Match header with a feed's current value, and return 304 Not Modified if the feed hasn't changed since it was last requested—all without once having to open and read a file.

To see how this is implemented, we'll look at the IfNoneMatch class. As we saw when we looked at ServiceHost.HandleRequest(...), every request is wrapped with an object that implements IRequestWrapper. The IRequestWrapper interface exposes an ICondition property. Example 7-32 shows HttpListenerRequestWrapper's implementation of this Condition property.

Example 7-32. Retrieving an entity tag value from a request

```
public ICondition Condition
{
  get
  {
    string eTag = request.Headers["If-None-Match"];
    if (string.IsNullOrEmpty(eTag))
    {
      return NullCondition.Instance;
    }

    Log.DebugFormat("If-None-Match header present. ETag: [{0}].", eTag);

    return new IfNoneMatch(new ETag(eTag));
  }
}
```

The request member variable here is an instance of HttpListenerRequest, which is the request as it comes off the wire. The Condition property parses out the If-None-Match header from this request. If the header value exists, it returns a new IfNoneMatch object; otherwise, it returns a NullCondition instance.

Condition objects are responsible for creating responses. As Example 7-33 shows, an IfNoneMatch condition object will return 304 Not Modified if the supplied representation contains an ETag header and matching entity tag value, or 200 OK if it doesn't.

Example 7-33. *IfNoneMatch creates a response based on evaluating a condition*

```
public IResponse CreateResponse(IRepresentation representation)
{
  HeaderQuery query = new HeaderQuery(eTag);

  if (query.Matches(representation))
  {
    Log.DebugFormat("If-None-Match precondition failed.");
    return Response.NotModified();
  }

  Log.DebugFormat("If-None-Match precondition OK.");
  return Response.OK(representation);
}
```

The IfNoneMatch object uses a HeaderQuery to determine whether the representation the service is about to write contains a specific header and header value. Its Matches(...) method is shown in Example 7-34.

Example 7-34. *HeaderQuery uses a local response context to determine whether a representation includes a header*

```
public bool Matches(IRepresentation representation)
{
  IResponseContext context = new ResponseContext();
  representation.UpdateContext(context);
  return context.ContainsHeader(header);
}
```

IfNoneMatch is an example of using a response context for a purpose other than writing to the output stream. The response context gathers all the headers from the supplied representation parameter. Matches(...) then uses this context to determine whether the header exists. Because it doesn't involve opening a file or transforming a file's contents, the context is cheap to initialize.

Wiring It Up

In our .NET implementation, the feed writer and the notifications service run on separate threads inside the same process. The only time they need to synchronize is when the feed writer has updated the recent events feed. When that happens, the notifications service needs to know the name of the new temporary file associated with the recent events feed.

To achieve this, the feed writer exposes a FeedMappingsChanged event. This event is raised when the NotifyingListeners task calls the notifyMappingsChanged parameter delegate.

When the service starts, it initializes a repository instance and then subscribes the repository's `OnFeedMappingsChanged(...)` event handler to the feed writer's `FeedMappingsChanged` event. The repository's implementation of `OnFeedMappingsChanged(...)` is shown in Example 7-35.

Example 7-35. *A repository's OnFeedMappingsChanged(...) event handler*

```
public void OnFeedMappingsChanged(object sender,
  FeedMappingsChangedEventArgs args)
{
  Log.DebugFormat(
    "FeedMappingsChanged event. ResourceId: [{0}]. StoreId: [{1}].",
    args.RecentEventsFeedResourceId, args.RecentEventsFeedStoreId);

  Interlocked.Exchange(ref feedMappings, new FeedMappings(
    converter, new ResourceId(args.RecentEventsFeedResourceId),
    new StoreId<string>(args.RecentEventsFeedStoreId)));
}
```

A `FeedMappings` object is responsible for creating functions that can retrieve a specific feed file from a backing store based on an understanding of the current working feed's `ResourceId` and the name of the temporary file containing the recent events feed. The `feedMappings` reference changes atomically each time the repository handles a `FeedMappingsChanged` event.

Atom Everywhere?

Atom, as we've seen, can be a powerful tool in our developer toolbox, but it's not an integration panacea. Originally designed for syndicating news articles and blog entries, Atom has since proven to be applicable in many other areas—integration included. Broadly speaking, it can be used to enrich resource representations with general-purpose metadata, allowing consumers to search, sort, and filter representations without needing to understand their details.

> ——— NOTE ———
>
> This separation of concerns between Atom and the resources it encapsulates is helpful. It means we can use Atom-specific software for managing and consuming Atom-formatted lists of resources, and more specialized software for handling embedded content only where necessary. In turn, this allows us to implement protocols based entirely on Atom.

Most development platforms today include an Atom library for creating and parsing feeds and entries. But cross-platform support alone isn't a sufficient reason to choose Atom as a representation format. While it's tempting to use Atom everywhere, to make every list and collection a feed and every item an entry, there are many situations where Atom is not the most appropriate representation format. If all we need is a list, not the feed metadata, we shouldn't burden our application with Atom's information overhead. If we've no real need for an entry's document metadata, we shouldn't use Atom entries. If we find ourselves populating Atom's metadata elements with data that's of no use to clients, or with default or "stub" data, we should consider employing an alternative representation format.

Assuming Atom is appropriate for our integration needs, we may still find we need to extend the format to support some domain- or application-specific requirements. Atom's metadata elements implement the majority of feed syndication and document description use cases, but it's still quite common to discover a requirement to extend the format.

There are a couple of options to choose from when extending Atom. All Atom elements can be extended with new attributes. Many can also be extended with additional elements. Extending Atom with additional elements and attributes is called *metadata extensibility*. In contrast, *content extensibility* involves putting proprietary information inside an entry's `<atom:content>` element. Content extensibility supports media type composition, which tends to enforce a stricter separation of concerns.

Our guidelines for choosing between these options are pretty straightforward: use metadata extensions for adding generally applicable, application-agnostic metadata to a feed, and use content extensibility for domain- or application-specific information. In the majority of cases, you're better off going with content extensibility. The more the Atom format itself is customized for a specific domain, the less the resultant feed and entry documents can be consumed and usefully manipulated by a generic Atom client.

Proprietary extensions to the Atom format can severely limit an application's reach and longevity. A test of a good extension is to ask whether a client *must* understand it before it can process a feed or entry successfully. The best extensions accelerate specialized clients, but do not hinder nonspecialized ones. Clients should be able to ignore proprietary elements when processing a feed or entry and still achieve meaningful and useful results.

Add proprietary metadata to the Atom format only when you're certain it has broad reach and applicability. Evaluate candidate elements in terms of their application agnosticism and their conformance with any existing standards or community initiatives. There's an obvious parallel here with microformats, which draw on prior art and adapt commonly accepted formats.

NOTE

The Feed Paging and Archiving specification is a proprietary metadata extension with precisely this mix of application agnosticism and broad reach and applicability. The specification is set out in RFC 5005.

Content extensibility, on the other hand, forces a cleaner separation of responsibilities: Atom clients handle feed and entry metadata, and specialized processors handle the application-specific content, with content dispatched to specialized processors based on its type.

After the Event

In this chapter, we explored the Atom Syndication Format and used it to develop an event-driven system for propagating product information around Restbucks. In particular, we saw how Atom as a hypermedia format can be used to create a simple protocol that allows consumers to consume both current and historical notifications. We also saw how load can be federated across the network with caches to increase availability and decrease load and response times for the product catalog service and downstream systems.

Atom-based services score highly on Richardson's service maturity model. Atom feeds and entries advertise service-generated URIs that link to other resources; this is a simple but powerful example of the hypermedia constraint, and is considered level three (the highest level) on the Richardson maturity model.

CHAPTER EIGHT

Atom Publishing Protocol

IN THE PRECEDING CHAPTER WE LEARNED ABOUT ATOM, a hypermedia format for publishing timestamped lists of web content. We then successfully applied that format to creating an event-driven system, typical of both enterprise and Internet computing, where events published by one system as an Atom feed were consumed and processed by downstream systems.

In this chapter, we're going to look at Atom Publishing Protocol (AtomPub), a protocol that is built on top of Atom, and which is used for publishing and editing web resources.* As a publishing protocol, AtomPub provides a standard mechanism for creating and editing resources, and resolving any arising conflicts. AtomPub extends the Atom format with a number of new publishing-related elements; at the same time, it specifies the HTTP idioms that can be used to manipulate published content.

Once we've understood AtomPub, we'll look at how it can serve as a foundation for our own domain application protocols. In the second half of the chapter, we show how Restbucks built an order fulfillment protocol and service atop AtomPub.

NOTE --

In Chapter 5, we used custom domain application protocols. AtomPub is a general-purpose domain application protocol, which is widely understood and supported by many software tools.

---

* *http://www.ietf.org/rfc/rfc5023.txt*

Atom Publishing Protocol

Resources can be created on or off the Web. Resources that are generated by a back-end process inserting a row in a database table are created off-Web. Atom Publishing Protocol, in contrast, uses HTTP to create resources on the Web.

AtomPub is a domain application protocol for publishing and editing web content (including binary content) with associated Atom metadata. The protocol is composed of a number of protocol-specific resources, plus the rules governing how a client can manipulate these resources using HTTP verbs, headers, and status codes.

AtomPub addresses issues common to many publishing scenarios: the concurrent editing of resources and the visibility of published resources. It implements an optimistic concurrency control mechanism based on HTTP entity tags and validators. Using an extension to the Atom format, it provides clients with the ability to control the public visibility of published resources.

Overview

AtomPub describes itself as "an application-level protocol for publishing and editing web resources…based on HTTP transfer of Atom-formatted representations." Despite its brevity, this description captures several key points about AtomPub:

It's an application-level protocol
> AtomPub is an application-level protocol, meaning it's implemented in software at the application layer, not the transport or network layer. Being a protocol, it governs the interactions between two applications, a client and a server, in the context of a specific goal. That goal is to publish web resources. AtomPub lays out the rules a client and server use to create and edit web resources.

It's designed for publishing and editing web content
> A web resource is anything that can be put on the Web and given an address. AtomPub is concerned with web resources in general, not just Atom feeds and entries. This may seem a little odd at first, but it makes more sense when we understand that the "Atom" in "Atom Publishing Protocol" refers not to the thing being published, but to the carrier format used to transfer a representation of the thing being published.

It's based on the HTTP transfer of Atom-formatted representations
> AtomPub reuses a more general-purpose application transfer protocol, HTTP, to implement a domain-specific application protocol. To create and edit web resources, clients and servers exchange Atom-formatted representations of these resources using HTTP idioms.

When to Use AtomPub

We can, of course, create and manipulate resources directly using the HTTP idioms discussed in previous chapters, effectively creating our own custom publishing protocols. After all, the CRUD systems we looked at in Chapter 4 also implement simple publishing protocols. So, why would we want to use Atom and AtomPub to do the same thing? As with Atom, reach and interoperability weigh heavily in AtomPub's favor. AtomPub is applicable in many publishing scenarios precisely because it addresses a core set of well-understood activities; it covers the bulk of common publishing use cases much as Atom covers the core elements common to an envelope format.

We recommend using AtomPub for the following:

Creating and manipulating Atom entries
> A web resource published by AtomPub doesn't have to be an Atom entry; it simply needs to be added to the content of an Atom entry while participating in the protocol. But given the prominent role AtomPub attaches to Atom, it makes perfect sense to use the protocol to publish Atom entries. In other words, AtomPub is the ideal means for manipulating the contents of Atom feeds in a standardized manner.

Associating Atom metadata with published web resources
> If we need to record events in a resource's life cycle—when it was published, when it last changed, and so on—or index it by some document attributes (such as author and title), or categorize it, Atom and AtomPub provide a means for associating this information with the resource as part of the publishing process.

Promoting an interoperable publishing protocol
> We can use AtomPub wherever we require an unambiguous, interoperable mechanism for creating and editing resources. Though programming support for AtomPub is not as widespread as it is for Atom, it is still relatively easy to implement the protocol on popular platforms.

Underpinning a domain application protocol
> Besides its intrinsic utility, AtomPub acts as a useful foundation for creating higher-level domain-specific application protocols. In the example at the end of this chapter, we show how Restbucks implements an order fulfillment protocol using AtomPub.

Anatomy of AtomPub

AtomPub servers host collections of published web content. When a client submits a piece of content to a collection, the server creates an Atom-formatted member to contain that content and represent its associated Atom metadata. Clients can then use this new member's URI to further manipulate the web resource and its metadata.

AtomPub services also host service and category documents, which together help clients discover collections and understand how the contents of those collections can be manipulated.

Taken together with the Atom format specification, AtomPub is an excellent example of a hypermedia-driven application protocol. AtomPub's processing model defines four things that are key to building hypermedia applications:

- Resource representation formats

- Hypermedia control markup

- The HTTP idioms clients can use to manipulate resources

- The link relations servers use to advertise legitimate state transitions

A good RESTful protocol can be described in terms of resources, representation formats, methods, and status codes.* Atom Publishing Protocol is described in exactly these terms. Its moving parts include four resources—members, collections, service documents, and category documents—and their representation formats. Members and collections are abstract names for the things targeted by publishing activities. A member encapsulates a representation of a published web resource, or a representation of a resource that is in a draft state, waiting to be published. A collection is a set of members. In AtomPub, a member is represented as an Atom entry, a collection as an Atom feed. The activities used to manipulate these resources are described in terms of HTTP methods, headers, and status codes.

Example 8-1 shows an AtomPub collection with three members.

Example 8-1. *An AtomPub collection with three members*

```
<feed xmlns="http://www.w3.org/2005/Atom" xmlns:app="http://www.w3.org/2007/app">

  <title>Product Catalog</title>
  <link rel="self" href="http://restbucks.com/product-catalog"/>
  <updated>2010-02-01T13:04:30Z</updated>
  <generator uri="http://restbucks.com/product-catalog">
    Product Catalog Service
  </generator>
  <id>urn:uuid:1d0f1a52-31d7-11df-b8ee-f47856d89593</id>

  <entry>
    <title>Fairtrade Roma Coffee Beans</title>
    <id>urn:uuid:7b512808-31d7-11df-aede-127c56d89593</id>
    <updated>2010-01-29T08:22:00Z</updated>
    <app:edited>2010-02-01T13:04:30Z</app:edited>
    <author>
      <name>Product Manager A</name>
    </author>
    <content type="application/vnd.restbucks+xml">
```

* See "How to Create a REST Protocol," *http://www.xml.com/pub/a/2004/12/01/restful-web.html.*

```xml
      <product xmlns="http://schemas.restbucks.com/product">
        <name>Fairtrade Roma Coffee Beans</name>
        <size>1kg</size>
        <price>10</price>
      </product>
    </content>
    <link rel="edit" href="http://restbucks.com/product-catalog/1234"/>
  </entry>

  <entry>
    <title>Fairtrade Roma Coffee Beans</title>
    <id>urn:uuid:08acdbfe-31db-11df-9fa6-839856d89593</id>
    <updated>2010-01-29T08:22:00Z</updated>
    <app:edited>2010-01-29T08:22:00Z</app:edited>
    <author>
      <name>Product Manager A</name>
    </author>
    <summary type="text">Fairtrade Roma Coffee Beans image</summary>
    <content type="image/png"
      src="http://restbucks.com/product-catalog/fairtrade_roma.png"/>
    <link rel="edit-media"
      href="http://restbucks.com/product-catalog/fairtrade_roma.png" />
    <link rel="edit"
      href="http://restbucks.com/product-catalog/5555" />
  </entry>

  <entry>
    <title>Early Riser Promotion</title>
    <id>urn:uuid:3bb346e8-31d9-11df-8999-e78956d89593</id>
    <updated>2010-01-28T10:02:00Z</updated>
    <app:edited>2010-01-28T10:02:00Z</app:edited>
    <author>
      <name>Product Manager B</name>
    </author>
    <content type="application/vnd.restbucks+xml">
      <promotion xmlns="http://schemas.restbucks.com/promotion">
        <effective>2010-03-01T00:00:00Z</effective>
        <product type="application/vnd.restbucks+xml"
          href="http://restbucks.com/products/156" />
        <region type="application/vnd.restbucks+xml"
          href="http://restbucks.com/regions/23" />
      </promotion>
    </content>
    <app:control>
      <app:draft>yes</app:draft>
    </app:control>
```

```
        <link rel="edit" href="http://restbucks.com/product-catalog/9876"/>
    </entry>

</feed>
```

The collection comprises an Atom feed whose default namespace, `http://www.w3.org/2005/Atom`, belongs to the Atom Syndication Format. The collection also includes some AtomPub elements belonging to the AtomPub namespace, `http://www.w3.org/2007/app`. These elements are considered foreign markup, and will be safely ignored by an Atom processor that doesn't understand AtomPub.

The first member in the collection in Example 8-1 has been edited more recently than the other two. The second member is a media link entry whose `<atom:content>` element's `href` value points to an image of some coffee beans. Its `edit-media` link allows the client to delete or replace this image; its `edit` link allows the client to edit the entry (i.e., the image metadata).* The last member in the collection contains an `<app:draft>` element with a status of yes, indicating that this member is not to be made publicly visible.

Now that we have an overall understanding of AtomPub, we'll examine in more detail AtomPub's resources, their representation formats, and the HTTP idioms used to manipulate them.

Collections

Collections are defined in service documents. The protocol doesn't specify how they are created or deleted. Collections support the following operations:

- To list a collection's members, a client sends a `GET` to the collection's URI.

- To create a new member, a client `POST`s a representation of the prospective member to a collection's URI. Different collections support different media types. The set of acceptable media types supported by a collection is typically specified in a service document (described later in this section).

Upon successful creation of a member resource, a service responds with a `201 Created` status code and a `Location` header containing the URI of the newly created member. This URI is called the *member URI*. The body of the response contains an Atom entry representing the new member resource. The new resource's member URI also appears as the value of an `edit` link in this member's entry in a collection.

Although AtomPub establishes the conventions for creating and modifying web resources, the server always determines whether an interaction is permitted. The server mints URIs and controls the URI space and the members identified by these URIs. Clients can create their own ID for a new member, but the server is entitled to modify the member and its representation, and even assign a new ID, as it sees fit.

---

* We describe media link entries in more detail later on.

Servers will not, however, modify any IDs the client assigns to the underlying web resources—that is, the server won't touch the contents of member representations. The entity body in the response to a POST reflects whatever actions the server has applied to a member in the course of handling a request.

Members

Members in a collection are time-ordered based on the value of their <app:edited> elements (we provide details of this new element shortly), with the most recently edited member appearing first. Members support the following operations:

- To get a representation of a member resource, a client sends a GET to the resource's member URI.

- To update a member resource, a client sends a PUT request to its member URI.

- To delete a resource, a client sends a DELETE request to its member URI.

Text-based resource representations can be included directly in a member's <atom:content> element. Images, videos, and executables, on the other hand, can't be included directly. To cover these different situations, AtomPub breaks members down into a couple of subtypes. Members that can be represented using Atom entries are called *entry resources*. Members whose representations can't be included directly in an Atom entry are called *media resources*. Entry resources can be included directly in a collection feed; media resources can't. In place of a media resource, a proxy resource, known as a *media link entry*, is inserted in a collection feed. This media link entry contains the media resource's metadata, plus a link to the media resource itself.

Category and service documents

Whereas collections and members transport representations of web resources, category and service documents describe the overall protocol. In particular, they group collections into workspaces, describe each collection's capabilities, describe which categories and media types belong to each collection, and provide discovery mechanisms based on well-known entry points to collections. AtomPub provides simple XML vocabularies for service and category documents, borrowing elements from the Atom format wherever possible.

Category documents. Category documents contain lists of categories for categorizing collections and members. A category list can be fixed, meaning it's a closed set, or left open, allowing for subsequent extension.

Category documents have their own processing model, with a media type of application/atomcat+xml.

Restbucks' product catalog, which we looked at in the preceding chapter, is updated using AtomPub. Because products can be categorized in a number of different ways, Restbucks' product catalog service exposes several category documents, one of which is shown in Example 8-2.

Example 8-2. *A category document containing a fixed set of categories*

```
<categories xmlns="http://www.w3.org/2007/app"
  xmlns:atom="http://www.w3.org/2005/Atom"
  scheme="http://restbucks.com/product-catalog/categories/status" fixed="yes">
  <atom:category term="new"/>
  <atom:category term="updated"/>
  <atom:category term="deleted"/>
</categories>
```

Example 8-2 shows a closed set of categories. These categories can be used to indicate the status of a product entry in a product catalog feed. The category document's root element belongs to the AtomPub namespace, but the categories themselves are defined using <atom:category> elements.

Service documents. A service document acts as a well-known entry point into the collections hosted by a service. From a service document, a client can navigate to the collections provided by the service. As shown in Figure 8-1, a service groups collections into workspaces. A service document can contain more than one workspace, and a collection can appear in more than one workspace.

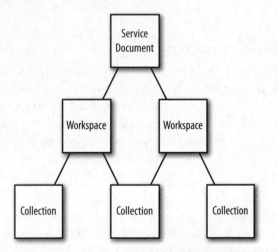

Figure 8-1. *Service documents group collections into workspaces*

Service documents have their own processing model, with a media type of application/atomsvc+xml.

Restbucks' product catalog service has a service document, which acts as a well-known entry point into the catalog, as shown in Example 8-3.

Example 8-3. *Service document for Restbucks' product catalog*

```
<service
  xmlns="http://www.w3.org/2007/app"
  xmlns:atom="http://www.w3.org/2005/Atom">
  <workspace>
    <atom:title>Product Catalog</atom:title>
    <collection href="http://restbucks.com/product-catalog/products">
      <atom:title>Products</atom:title>
      <accept>application/atom+xml;type=entry</accept>
      <categories href="http://restbucks.com/product-catalog/categories/status"/>
    </collection>
    <collection href="http://restbucks.com/product-catalog/promotions">
      <atom:title>Promotions</atom:title>
      <accept>application/atom+xml;type=entry</accept>
      <accept>image/png</accept>
      <accept>image/gif</accept>
      <categories href="http://restbucks.com/product-catalog/categories/status"/>
      <categories href="http://restbucks.com/product-catalog/categories/scope"/>
      <categories scheme="http://restbucks.com/product-catalog/categories/origin"
        fixed="yes">
        <atom:category term="in-house"/>
        <atom:category term="partner"/>
      </categories>
    </collection>
  </workspace>
</service>
```

The product catalog service document contains a single workspace, which represents the editable face of the catalog. This workspace contains two collections: one for products, the other for promotions. Clients interact with these collections by dereferencing the href attribute values associated with each collection.

Collections indicate which media types they support using <app:accept> elements. While the product collection only accepts Atom entries in POSTs to the collection, the promotions collection accepts both Atom entries and two types of images. Each collection also advertises a number of categories. The product collection's <app:categories> element references an external category document (in fact, the category document described earlier). The promotions collection includes an inline set of categories.

AtomPub Extensions to Atom

AtomPub extends Atom in a number of ways:

- It uses Atom extensibility to add three new entry elements: `<app:edited>`, `<app:control>`, and `<app:draft>`. These elements belong to the AtomPub namespace.

- It adds two new link-relation values, edit and edit-media, to the IANA Link Relations registry.

- It adds a type parameter to the Atom media type.

AtomPub also introduces a new HTTP header, Slug. Clients can include a Slug header when creating a new member. The Slug header represents a request that the server include the header value (or a modified version of the header value) in the URI, ID, or title of a new member. A client might use a Slug header to encourage the server to create pretty or human-readable URIs for a particular member.

app:edited

The `<app:edited>` element indicates when a member was created or last edited. Every member in a collection must contain exactly one `<app:edited>` element. Members in an AtomPub collection are ordered by `<app:edited>`, with the most recently created or updated members appearing first in the collection. The server changes the value of `<app:edited>` every time the member's metadata or content changes. `<atom:updated>`, on the other hand, only needs to be updated when a "significant" change occurs, typically in the member content. As we suggested in Chapter 7, in some circumstances we might give clients control of the `<atom:updated>` value. Clients, after all, are best placed to determine which changes are significant. `<app:edited>`, on the other hand, is always under the server's control.

app:control and app:draft

`<app:control>` is an Atom extension used to host publishing controls. Publishing controls are Atom extension elements dedicated to controlling parts of the publishing life cycle. `<app:draft>` is one such publishing control. Both collections and members can incorporate an `<app:control>` element. The `<app:draft>` value represents a client's preference regarding the visibility of a member; the server can always ignore the client's request and publish the submitted feed or entry as normal.

edit and edit-media link relation values

AtomPub adds the edit and edit-media link relation values to the IANA Link Relations registry. Links with these relation values point to editable member entries and editable media resources, respectively. Clients can use edit and edit-media links to GET, PUT, and DELETE the resources with which they are associated.

type parameters

AtomPub extends the Atom media type of application/atom+xml with a type parameter. Using this parameter, feeds can be identified as application/atom+xml;type=feed and entries as application/atom+xml;type=entry. The introduction of the type parameter caters to different client processing capabilities. Clients designed to handle feeds will usually handle entries as well; applications designed to handle just entries, however, won't necessarily cater to feeds. Clients that understand the type parameter can eagerly invoke the appropriate processing model. Clients that don't understand the parameter still have to examine the root element of an Atom-formatted representation to determine which processing model to apply.

Concurrency Control

One of the most important issues AtomPub addresses is how a service coordinates and resolves multiple updates from different clients. Once it has been made available through an edit link, a web resource is potentially subject to concurrent manipulation by several different clients. In these situations, it is possible that instructions from one client can countermand or overwrite the instructions issued by another, often without either party being aware of the conflict until some time later. This can give rise to the "lost update" problem.

The lost update problem is best illustrated with an anecdote. When Restbucks first opened its doors, communications between customers and staff members were uncoordinated. It wasn't unusual for orders to change, sometimes several times. When this happened, all bets were off: no one could be sure what the prepared drinks would look like.

Imagine a situation in which a couple orders two lattes. The pair wanders off—one person to browse a magazine, the other to make a phone call. Moments later, the first customer returns to the counter and asks for a second shot in one of the lattes. Shortly after that, the second customer, her call completed, comes back to the counter and asks to change the order to a latte and a cappuccino. When preparing the drinks, the barista makes a cappuccino and a latte, both with just a single shot.

This example illustrates how, in the absence of an explicit coordination protocol, a sequence of instructions issued by different parties can lead to an incorrect outcome.* Our barista followed the last instruction he received, but from the first customer's point of view, this resulted in the initial correction to the order being lost or overwritten.

---

* The lost update problem is described in more detail in a W3C note from 1999, "Detecting the Lost Update Problem Using Unreserved Checkout," at *http://www.w3.org/1999/04/Editing/*.

To stop this problem from being repeated, Restbucks could require customers to hang on to their order until they see it being prepared by a barista, effectively implementing a pessimistic locking approach. But this solution consumes space at the counter. Moreover, it's extremely inconvenient for customers. Exclusive locking of resources becomes prohibitively expensive when we scale things out on the Web.

Instead of using pessimistic locking to prevent conflicts and lost updates, AtomPub implements an unreserved checkout strategy. Unreserved checkout means that a resource isn't locked while a client is working with it. AtomPub's lightweight alternative to pessimistic locks uses entity tags and validators to identify potential conflicts, thereby implementing an optimistic locking scheme. When a client POSTs an order to the service, the server responds with 201 Created and an ETag header containing a unique identifier for that particular version of the resource:

```
HTTP/1.1 201 Created
...
ETag: "44bd59eeb984c"
```

When a client PUTs a subsequent modification to the server, it adds an If-Match header and the last known ETag entity value to the request:

```
PUT /orders/123 HTTP/1.1
...
If-Match: "44bd59eeb984c"
```

If the resource has changed on the server since the supplied entity tag value was generated, the server responds with 412 Precondition Failed.

Of course, the client could use a conditional GET to determine whether the resource has changed. But even if this conditional GET returns 304 Not Modified, there's nothing to stop a second client from changing the resource before the first finally PUTs its changes—a race condition still exists. Conditional GETs are optional when updating a resource; conditional PUTs aren't.

Based on a 412 Precondition Failed, the client must decide what to do next. The simplest thing is to GET the latest version of the resource (and its new entity tag value), apply the changes all over again, and then conditionally PUT the modified representation back to the server using the new entity tag value. Some clients, however, will want to examine the latest representation of a resource to determine what has changed in the intervening period. The decision as to whether to proceed with another PUT may require manual (human) intervention. It's analogous to a cashier detecting that an order has been changed since he last saw it and questioning the customer to confirm her intentions.

As we will see shortly, Restbucks can *exclusively* use AtomPub to coordinate order fulfillment, avoiding the lost update problem without resorting to out-of-band coordination or fancy middleware.

Implementing Order Fulfillment Using AtomPub

Following its shambolic first few days in business, when fickle customers exposed the flaws in its order fulfillment process (as described in the "lost update" anecdote in the preceding section), Restbucks took a long, hard look at the ad hoc coordination mechanisms behind the counter and decided to implement a more robust process—one designed to guarantee that customers got what they wanted, no matter how many times they changed their minds. In the following sections, we're going to show how Restbucks now implements order fulfillment using AtomPub.

Overview

Before we dive into the details, let's review the steps in the fulfillment sequence:

- A cashier takes an order from a customer.

- The cashier adds the order to a list of orders awaiting fulfillment and takes payment from the customer.

- The store's baristas work their way through the list of unfulfilled orders, usually but not always picking up the oldest first.

- When a barista finishes making all the drinks in an order, he hands them over to the customer.

- Prior to the drinks being prepared, the order can be modified or canceled.

What we're facing here, from an application integration point of view, is a case of competing consumers. In the competing consumer pattern, multiple receivers—baristas in this case—process messages (orders) from a single point-to-point channel.* The success of the pattern relies on there being no temporal dependencies between messages. That is, message B can be successfully processed before message A, even though it arrived after A.

---

* *Enterprise Integration Patterns* by Gregor Hohpe and Bobby Woolf (Addison-Wesley, 2003).

Restbucks' fulfillment protocol structures and coordinates the activities that go into fulfilling an order. The protocol is agnostic to the implementation of the fulfillment activities themselves. This means we won't look in any detail at how any of the individual fulfillment activities (paying, making a coffee, notifying the customer) are implemented. Instead, we'll look at how the protocol guides cashiers and baristas to communicate their intended actions; how it prevents two baristas from tending simultaneously to the same order; and how it allows cashiers to intervene and correct an order when a customer changes her mind. What emerges is a coordination mechanism that's completely agnostic to orders—a mechanism that uses AtomPub alone, rather than the structure or content of an order, to advance the application state to a successful conclusion.

> **NOTE**
>
> The rules that the cashiers and baristas use to coordinate their activities, and the sequence of steps that abide by these rules, are an internal implementation detail of Restbucks' order fulfillment process. Customers are not exposed directly to this process. All customers care about is being able to order, pay, and receive drinks in return, perhaps changing their minds in the process. The systems that implement the order fulfillment protocol are therefore backend systems, which use the `internal. restbucks.com` hostname.

Figure 8-2 shows the interactions that comprise the fulfillment protocol. Use this diagram to follow along as we describe the protocol in more detail.

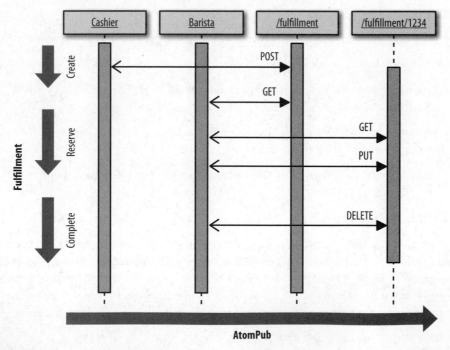

Figure 8-2. *Driving the fulfillment protocol using AtomPub*

Adding an Order to the Fulfillment Pipeline

We'll start by assuming a cashier has just taken an order from a customer. Having taken the order, the cashier adds it to a list of unfulfilled orders. This list functions as a backlog of tasks that supplies the baristas with new work items. Example 8-4 shows what this list looks like just before the cashier adds the new order.

Example 8-4. *An AtomPub collection representing the order fulfillment pipeline*

```
<feed xmlns="http://www.w3.org/2005/Atom" xmlns:app="http://www.w3.org/2007/app">

  <title>Order Fulfillment</title>
  <link rel="self" href="http://internal.restbucks.com/fulfillment"/>
  <updated>2010-03-29T13:00:30Z</updated>
  <generator uri="http://internal.restbucks.com/fulfillment">
    Order Fulfillment Service
  </generator>
  <id>urn:uuid:6d2992ae-ec8a-4dac-91b3-d452186ea409</id>

  <app:collection href="http://internal.restbucks.com/fulfillment">
    <title>Order Fulfillment Service</title>
    <app:accept>application/atom+xml;type=entry</app:accept>
  </app:collection>

  <entry>
    <title>order</title>
    <id>urn:uuid:fc2d3d42-7198-4c59-a936-b9b870ef8469</id>
    <updated>2010-03-29T13:00:30Z</updated>
    <app:edited>2010-03-29T13:00:30Z</app:edited>
    <author>
      <name>Cashier</name>
    </author>
    <content type="application/vnd.restbucks+xml">
      ...
    </content>
    <app:control>
      <app:draft>yes</app:draft>
    </app:control>
    <link rel="edit" href="http://internal.restbucks.com/fulfillment/1234"/>
  </entry>

</feed>
```

As you can see, the order fulfillment pipeline is implemented as an AtomPub collection. To advertise its capabilities, the collection includes an `<app:collection>` element whose child `<app:accept>` element indicates that the collection accepts representations of type application/atom+xml;type=entry.

> `<app:collection>` elements are normally found in AtomPub service documents, but they can also be added to feeds.

The collection currently has one member. This member is in a draft state, as signaled by the presence of an `<app:draft>` element with a value of yes. In the context of the fulfillment protocol, a draft member is simply one that is not visibly in progress. It represents an order that has not yet been picked up by a barista.

To begin the fulfillment process for a new order, the cashier must POST an Atom-formatted representation of a new order to the collection. Example 8-5 shows this POST request.

Example 8-5. *A cashier POSTs an order to the order fulfillment collection*

```
POST /fulfillment HTTP/1.1
Host: internal.restbucks.com
Content-Type: application/atom+xml
Content-Length: ...

<entry xmlns="http://www.w3.org/2005/Atom">
  <title>order</title>
  <id>urn:uuid:b8e77ffa-31b4-11df-a2b3-1a8155d89593</id>
  <updated>2010-03-29T13:01:30Z</updated>
  <author>
    <name>Cashier</name>
  </author>
  <content type="application/vnd.restbucks+xml">
    <order xmlns="http://schemas.restbucks.com/order">
      <consume-at>takeAway</consume-at>
      <items>
        <item>
          <name>latte</name>
          <quantity>1</quantity>
          <milk>whole</milk>
          <size>small</size>
        </item>
      </items>
    </order>
  </content>
</entry>
```

On receiving the new order, the fulfillment server creates a new member and then responds with 201 Created. Example 8-6 shows the response.

```
HTTP/1.1 201 Created
Date: ...
Content-Length: ...
Content-Type: application/atom+xml;type=entry;charset="utf-8"
Location: http://internal.restbucks.com/fulfillment/9876
Content-Location: http://internal.restbucks.com/fulfillment/9876
ETag: "3f2b06f7"

<entry xmlns="http://www.w3.org/2005/Atom" xmlns:app="http://www.w3.org/2007/app">
  <title>order</title>
  <id>urn:uuid:e557e51b-c994-44ef-b06d-5331246cccbe</id>
  <updated>2010-03-29T13:01:30Z</updated>
  <app:edited>2010-03-29T13:01:30Z</app:edited>
  <author>
    <name>Cashier</name>
  </author>
  <content type="application/vnd.restbucks+xml">
    ...
  </content>
  <app:control>
    <app:draft>yes</app:draft>
  </app:control>
  <link rel="edit" href="http://internal.restbucks.com/fulfillment/9876"/>
</entry>
```

The response includes a `Location` header containing the member URI of the newly created entry. Because the response contains a `Content-Location` header as well as a `Location` header, the cashier can treat the entity body as an authoritative representation of the new entry, as per the AtomPub specification.

Below the headers, the entity body contains the AtomPub member representation. In the fulfillment protocol, this member represents an instance of fulfilling an order. The order itself has been encapsulated as a child of the member's `<atom:content>` element. When engaged in coordinating fulfillment activities as part of the fulfillment protocol, cashiers and baristas deal with AtomPub collections and members. When they come to undertake a specific fulfillment activity, such as making a drink, they deal with the order details inside a member's `<atom:content>`.

The server has created a new ID for the new member (replacing the ID supplied by the cashier). This ID serves as an ID for this instance of fulfillment. The cashier can associate this fulfillment ID with the original order ID, thereby reconciling records in different systems and providing full end-to-end auditing of the progress of an order. The server has also added an `<app:edited>` timestamp, an `<app:draft>` element indicating that the order is not yet being actively fulfilled, and an edit link to the new member.

In a happy-path scenario, this is the last a cashier has to do with the order fulfillment process. We'll look later at what happens if the cashier wants to amend or cancel the order.

Beginning Fulfillment

Let's turn now to the baristas. Each Restbucks store employs several baristas, all of whom take work from the same list of unfulfilled orders. That list is the same one we've just been looking at: the AtomPub collection at `http://internal.restbucks.com/fulfillment`.

When a barista needs more work to do, it retrieves the current list of outstanding orders. Example 8-7 shows a typical request and response.

Example 8-7. *A barista GETs the list of outstanding orders*

```
Request:
GET /fulfillment HTTP/1.1
Host: internal.restbucks.com

Response:
HTTP/1.1 200 OK
Date: ...
Content-Length: ...
Content-Type: application/atom+xml;type=feed;charset="utf-8"

<feed xmlns="http://www.w3.org/2005/Atom" xmlns:app="http://www.w3.org/2007/app">

  <title>Order Fulfillment</title>
  <link rel="self" href="http://internal.restbucks.com/fulfillment"/>
  <updated>2010-03-29T13:01:30Z</updated>
  <generator uri="http://internal.restbucks.com/fulfillment">
    Order Fulfillment Service
  </generator>
  <id>urn:uuid:6d2992ae-ec8a-4dac-91b3-d452186ea409</id>

  <app:collection href="http://internal.restbucks.com/fulfillment">
    <title>Order Fulfillment Service</title>
    <app:accept>application/atom+xml;type=entry</app:accept>
  </app:collection>

  <entry>
    <title>order</title>
    <id>urn:uuid:e557e51b-c994-44ef-b06d-5331246cccbe</id>
    <updated>2010-03-29T13:01:30Z</updated>
    <app:edited>2010-03-29T13:01:30Z</app:edited>
```

```
    <author>
      <name>Cashier</name>
    </author>
    <content type="application/vnd.restbucks+xml">
      ...
    </content>
    <app:control>
      <app:draft>yes</app:draft>
    </app:control>
    <link rel="edit" href="http://internal.restbucks.com/fulfillment/9876"/>
  </entry>

  <entry>
    <title>order</title>
    <id>urn:uuid:fc2d3d42-7198-4c59-a936-b9b870ef8469</id>
    <updated>2010-03-29T13:00:30Z</updated>
    <app:edited>2010-03-29T13:00:30Z</app:edited>
    <author>
      <name>Cashier</name>
    </author>
    <content type="application/vnd.restbucks+xml">
      ...
    </content>
    <app:control>
      <app:draft>yes</app:draft>
    </app:control>
    <link rel="edit" href="http://internal.restbucks.com/fulfillment/1234"/>
  </entry>

</feed>
```

The response comprises an AtomPub collection. The collection is ordered by `app:edited`, with the most recent unfulfilled order at its head. This collection of unfulfilled orders currently contains two members, the topmost one being the order we've just seen the cashier submit.

Though not an intrinsic part of the protocol, it's customary for baristas to take the oldest outstanding order, which in this instance is the last member in the collection. As shown in Example 8-8, the barista GETs a full representation of the order using the member's edit link.

Example 8-8. *The barista GETs an unfulfilled order*

```
Request:
GET /fulfillment/1234 HTTP/1.1
Host: internal.restbucks.com
```

```
Response:
HTTP/1.1 200 OK
Date: ...
Content-Length: ...
Content-Type: application/atom+xml;type=entry
ETag: "3877069e"

<entry xmlns="http://www.w3.org/2005/Atom" xmlns:app="http://www.w3.org/2007/app">
  <title>order</title>
  <id>urn:uuid:fc2d3d42-7198-4c59-a936-b9b870ef8469</id>
  <updated>2010-03-29T13:00:30Z</updated>
  <app:edited>2010-03-29T13:00:30Z</app:edited>
  <author>
    <name>Cashier</name>
  </author>
  <content type="application/vnd.restbucks+xml">
    ...
  </content>
  <app:control>
    <app:draft>yes</app:draft>
  </app:control>
  <link rel="edit" href="http://internal.restbucks.com/fulfillment/1234"/>
</entry>
```

The server replies with a member representation whose `<atom:content>` element contains the order details (omitted here to emphasize the parts of the member that are used in the fulfillment protocol). The response also includes an ETag header.

The barista can now use this ETag header to do a conditional PUT back to the member's edit URI (its member URI). Before sending the member representation back to the member URI, the barista removes its `<app:control>` and `<app:draft>` elements. The overall intention of the PUT is to reserve or check out the order, thereby preventing other baristas from working on it at the same time.

NOTE

An AtomPub member without an `<app:draft>` element is treated as though it had an `<app:draft>` element with a value of no. By removing these two elements, the barista announces (or publishes) its intention to fulfill the order. Draft members represent orders waiting to be fulfilled; "published" members represent orders that are currently being fulfilled.

Failed reservation

The barista's PUT takes the form of a conditional PUT to the member's edit URI. By using an If-Match header, the barista effectively says, "Please accept this representation of my intent, but only if the order is in the same state as when I last looked at it." Example 8-9 shows the PUT.

Example 8-9. *The barista does a conditional PUT to reserve an outstanding order*

```
PUT /fulfillment/1234 HTTP/1.1
Host: internal.restbucks.com
Content-Type: application/atom+xml;type=entry
Content-Length: ...
If-Match: "3877069e"

<entry xmlns="http://www.w3.org/2005/Atom" xmlns:app="http://www.w3.org/2007/app">
  <title>order</title>
  <id>urn:uuid:fc2d3d42-7198-4c59-a936-b9b870ef8469</id>
  <updated>2010-03-29T13:03:00Z</updated>
  <app:edited>2010-03-29T13:00:30Z</app:edited>
  <author>
    <name>Cashier</name>
  </author>
  <contributor>
    <name>Barista A</name>
  </contributor>
  <content type="application/vnd.restbucks+xml">
    ...
  </content>
  <link rel="edit" href="http://internal.restbucks.com/fulfillment/1234"/>
</entry>
```

Unfortunately, another barista has already started work on this particular order. The state of the underlying resource, therefore, *has* changed since our barista last looked at it (i.e., between the barista GETting and conditionally PUTting the order). As a result, the conditional PUT fails, as shown in Example 8-10.

Example 8-10. *Response to the conditional PUT*

```
HTTP/1.1 412 Precondition Failed
Date: ...
```

Try again

Not to worry. Our barista simply has to find more work to do. It does so by navigating to the top of the orders list, attempting to reserve unfulfilled orders along the way. As it happens, the list contains only one more outstanding order: the one recently placed by the cashier at the beginning of this example. So, the barista tries that one.

NOTE

Newer orders may, in fact, be present in the system, but the barista is working from a copy of the orders collection that is slowly becoming stale. This isn't really an issue. Once a barista has exhausted the copy of the list it currently holds, it GETs a fresh copy from `http://internal.restbucks.com/fulfillment`. This new copy will contain any orders generated in the intervening period (in fact, it will contain both new orders and all orders currently being fulfilled). As far as is practically possible, baristas try to take a first-in, first-out approach to serving coffees. The oldest orders are dealt with first. Newer orders don't become visible to a barista until the backlog has been cleared.

Example 8-11 shows the barista GETting the topmost member in the collection.

Example 8-11. *The barista looks at another recent order*

```
Request:
GET /fulfillment/9876
Host: internal.restbucks.com

Response:
HTTP/1.1 200 OK
Date: ...
Content-Length: ...
Content-Type: application/atom+xml;type=entry
ETag: "83fd0a03"

<entry xmlns="http://www.w3.org/2005/Atom" xmlns:app="http://www.w3.org/2007/app">
  <title>order</title>
  <id>urn:uuid:e557e51b-c994-44ef-b06d-5331246cccbe</id>
  <updated>2010-03-29T13:01:30Z</updated>
  <app:edited>2010-03-29T13:01:30Z</app:edited>
  <author>
    <name>Cashier</name>
  </author>
  <content type="application/vnd.restbucks+xml">
    ...
  </content>
  <app:control>
    <app:draft>yes</app:draft>
```

```
    </app:control>
    <link rel="edit" href="http://internal.restbucks.com/fulfillment/9876"/>
  </entry>
```

Once again, the barista attempts to reserve the order using a conditional PUT.
Example 8-12 shows the resultant request and response. Note that before PUTting
the member back to the server, the barista updates the member's <atom:updated>
element and adds its name to the list of contributors.

Example 8-12. *Successfully reserving an outstanding order*

```
Request:
PUT /fulfillment/9876 HTTP/1.1
Host: internal.restbucks.com
Content-Type: application/atom+xml;type=entry
Content-Length: ...
If-Match: "83fd0a03"

<entry xmlns="http://www.w3.org/2005/Atom" xmlns:app="http://www.w3.org/2007/app">
  <title>order</title>
  <id>urn:uuid:e557e51b-c994-44ef-b06d-5331246cccbe</id>
  <updated>2010-03-29T13:04:00Z</updated>
  <app:edited>2010-03-29T13:01:30Z</app:edited>
  <author>
    <name>Cashier</name>
  </author>
  <contributor>
    <name>Barista A</name>
  </contributor>
  <content type="application/vnd.restbucks+xml">
    ...
  </content>
  <link rel="edit" href="http://internal.restbucks.com/fulfillment/9876"/>
</entry>

Response:
HTTP/1.1 200 OK
Date: ...
```

This time, the PUT succeeds.

Where are we?

What would the fulfillment backlog look like if a cashier or barista were to do a GET
now? Let's assume neither of the orders we've looked at so far has been completed.
To make matters more interesting, we'll say that the cashier has recently submitted a
third order. Given this state of affairs, Example 8-13 shows the current collection.

Example 8-13. *The orders collection with one new and two in-process orders*

```
<feed xmlns="http://www.w3.org/2005/Atom" xmlns:app="http://www.w3.org/2007/app">

  <title>Order Fulfillment</title>
  <link rel="self" href="http://internal.restbucks.com/fulfillment"/>
  <updated>2010-03-29T13:04:30Z</updated>
  <generator uri="http://internal.restbucks.com/fulfillment">
    Order Fulfillment Service
  </generator>
  <id>urn:uuid:6d2992ae-ec8a-4dac-91b3-d452186ea409</id>

  <app:collection href="http://internal.restbucks.com/fulfillment">
    <title>Order Fulfillment Service</title>
    <app:accept>application/atom+xml;type=entry</app:accept>
  </app:collection>

  <entry>
    <title>order</title>
    <id>urn:uuid:e557e51b-c994-44ef-b06d-5331246cccbe</id>
    <updated>2010-03-29T13:04:00Z</updated>
    <app:edited>2010-03-29T13:04:30Z</app:edited>
    <author>
      <name>Cashier</name>
    </author>
    <contributor>
      <name>Barista A</name>
    </contributor>
    <content type="application/vnd.restbucks+xml">
      ...
    </content>
    <link rel="edit" href="http://internal.restbucks.com/fulfillment/9876"/>
  </entry>

  <entry>
    <title>order</title>
    <id>urn:uuid:1b305ebe-9077-42e5-bd95-00792c33ffbf</id>
    <updated>2010-03-29T13:03:30Z</updated>
    <app:edited>2010-03-29T13:03:30Z</app:edited>
    <author>
      <name>Cashier</name>
    </author>
    <content type="application/vnd.restbucks+xml">
      ...
    </content>
    <app:control>
```

```
        <app:draft>yes</app:draft>
      </app:control>
      <link rel="edit" href="http://internal.restbucks.com/fulfillment/9999"/>
    </entry>

    <entry>
      <title>order</title>
      <id>urn:uuid:fc2d3d42-7198-4c59-a936-b9b870ef8469</id>
      <updated>2010-03-29T13:02:00Z</updated>
      <app:edited>2010-03-29T13:02:30Z</app:edited>
      <author>
        <name>Cashier</name>
      </author>
      <contributor>
        <name>Barista B</name>
      </contributor>
      <content type="application/vnd.restbucks+xml">
        ...
      </content>
      <link rel="edit" href="http://internal.restbucks.com/fulfillment/1234"/>
    </entry>

  </feed>
```

The first and third members represent orders currently being fulfilled (neither contains an `<app:control>` or `<app:draft>` element). The middle member represents the latest order submitted by the cashier. The members are ordered by `<app:edited>`, with the most recently edited member first. The server changes a member's `<app:edited>` value every time the resource changes. Because our barista reserved an order some moments after the cashier POSTed a newer order, it's the in-process order, not the new order, that appears at the top of the collection.

Completing the Protocol

Remember, the process outlined here is responsible solely for coordinating fulfillment activities. It doesn't have anything to do with how each fulfillment activity is actually implemented. This means that once a barista has reserved an order, the barista must step outside AtomPub to make the drinks.

When making the drinks, the barista will peer into the `<atom:content>` element and inspect the order details. In other words, it drops down to a media type processor capable of handling `application/vnd.restbucks+xml` to process the representation transported in the `<atom:content>` element.

After making the customer's drinks, the barista completes the fulfillment protocol by deleting the member, as shown in Example 8-14.

Example 8-14. *Completing the fulfillment protocol*

```
Request:
DELETE /fulfillment/9876 HTTP/1.1
Host: internal.restbucks.com

Response:
HTTP/1.1 200 OK
Date: ...
```

And that's it: coffee's served.

Exceptions

That's the happy path. Now let's look at some exceptional circumstances. First, what happens if a customer changes her mind?

If a customer asks to change her order, the cashier must attempt to modify the relevant member in the fulfillment backlog. Using the member's edit link, the cashier can GET an up-to-date representation of the member, together with a fresh entity tag. The cashier modifies the order details inside atom:content, and then conditionally PUTs the member back to its edit URI. If the member is still in a state that allows it to be updated (it hasn't been reserved by a barista), the PUT will succeed. If the server determines it's too late to modify this instance of fulfillment—perhaps because preparation is already underway—it returns 412 Precondition Failed.

NOTE

Completed orders, of course, can't be changed: they must be thrown away. Whether this is a permitted outcome for an order depends on a business-level trade-off among order throughput, cost, and customer satisfaction.

If the cashier PUTs a changed order back to the server *after* a barista has retrieved a member representation, but *before* the barista has reserved the enclosed order using its own conditional PUT, the cashier's PUT will succeed (thereby modifying the order), and the barista's will fail (because the resource state will have changed in between the barista GETting and PUTting). A barista interprets a failed PUT as meaning another member of the staff has the member and its contained order. This results in the barista discarding the member in favor of a more recent one. Figure 8-3 shows the sequence of requests: you can clearly see that about two-thirds of the way down, the barista skips /fulfillment/1234 and moves on to /fulfillment/9876.

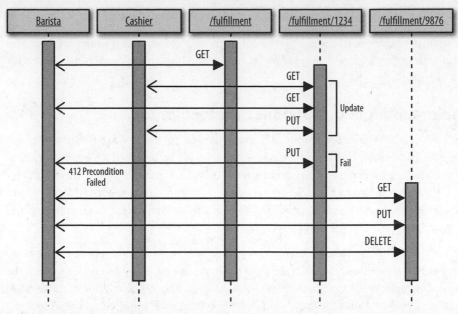

Figure 8-3. *Changing an order while a barista attempts to reserve it*

This isn't really a problem. At some point, one of the baristas will GET an updated version of the orders collection. The modified (but discarded) order will appear somewhere toward the bottom of the collection, waiting to be picked off. It's a somewhat suboptimal solution, but so long as baristas continue polling the orders collection whenever they're ready to take on new jobs, it succeeds in clearing any backlog.

Canceling an order is achieved by sending a DELETE request to the current edit URI. Occasionally, a barista will experience a 410 Gone in response to its attempt to complete the fulfillment protocol; this occurs as a result of the order being successfully canceled (the fulfillment resource deleted) while the drinks were being prepared.

Summary

Let's review the solution and see what we've achieved. We've successfully progressed through a domain-specific protocol—order fulfillment—using a more general, standardized application protocol: AtomPub. At no point have any of the clients—cashiers and baristas alike—had to inspect the domain-specific order XML to determine what to do next.

NOTE

Don't confuse the fulfillment protocol with the steps necessary to implement fulfillment activities. As we saw when it came to the barista making drinks, it is perfectly legitimate and usually necessary to peer into these domain-specific representations when implementing an activity coordinated by the protocol.

To ensure the correctness of the fulfillment protocol, we've had to insist that baristas, whenever they GET a fresh representation of the orders collection, always start at the bottom and work their way up the list until they find the first draft member. This ensures that new orders sitting below recently edited in-process orders are picked up and processed.

Implementing More Complex Protocols

Restbucks' order fulfillment protocol is implemented entirely *in* AtomPub. To participate in the protocol, cashiers and baristas have simply to behave like good AtomPub clients: POSTing an order to the fulfillment collection to create a "draft" member awaiting fulfillment; GETting a member representation, removing its <app:draft> element, and conditionally PUTting it back to "publish" it into an in-process state; and finally, requesting that the server DELETE it to complete the protocol.

But order fulfillment, at least as we've described it here, is a relatively linear three-step process. Few processes are as simple or as straightforward. How would we cope if there were more steps in the protocol, or decisions that an agent—cashier or barista—had to make somewhere along the way? Can AtomPub deal with more complex protocols?

The answer is to compose AtomPub into higher-level protocols. Such protocol implementations still use Atom as a representation format, and AtomPub to coordinate interactions, but they add new link relation values. To progress the protocol, clients need to understand these new values in addition to understanding AtomPub.

We're now going to modify the implementation of Restbucks' order fulfillment protocol to show how AtomPub can be composed into a more complex protocol. While the overall business outcome is the same, the revised implementation shows how such an approach can be used to implement more complex processes.

In this revised solution, the fulfillment service exposes several AtomPub collections, each of which represents one or more states in the application protocol. A member moves from one collection to another as a result of clients activating hypermedia controls provided by the server.

The first thing we're going to do is to create a service document for the new order fulfillment service. This document advertises the collections supported by the service, as shown in Example 8-15.

Example 8-15. A service document advertising the order fulfillment application state space

```
<service
  xmlns="http://www.w3.org/2007/app"
  xmlns:atom="http://www.w3.org/2005/Atom">
```

```
    <workspace>
      <atom:title>Order Fulfillment</atom:title>
      <collection href="http://internal.restbucks.com/fulfillment">
        <atom:title>Order Fulfillment Service</atom:title>
        <accept>application/atom+xml;type=entry</accept>
      </collection>
      <collection href="http://internal.restbucks.com/fulfillment/fulfilled">
        <atom:title>Fulfilled Orders Service</atom:title>
        <accept>application/atom+xml;type=entry</accept>
      </collection>
    </workspace>
  </service>
```

This service document has one workspace, which contains two collections. The first
collection in the workspace is the entry point into the fulfillment process. The second
collection contains members that represent instances of the fulfillment process currently in the fulfilled state. Both collections accept Atom entries.

The first part of the implementation works much as before. Cashiers POST orders to
http://internal.restbucks.com/fulfillment, whereupon the server creates a draft
member that baristas can then reserve using a conditional PUT. Things change, however, once a barista has successfully reserved a member. A fresh GET on a member's
member URI returns the representation show in Example 8-16.

Example 8-16. *A member representing an instance of fulfillment in the in-process state*

```
Request:
GET /fulfillment/9876 HTTP/1.1
Host: internal.restbucks.com

Response:
HTTP/1.1 200 OK
Date: ...
Content-Length: ...
Content-Type: application/atom+xml;type=entry
ETag: "495b0f8f"

<entry xmlns="http://www.w3.org/2005/Atom" xmlns:app="http://www.w3.org/2007/app">
  <title>order</title>
  <id>urn:uuid:e557e51b-c994-44ef-b06d-5331246cccbe</id>
  <updated>2010-03-29T13:04:00Z</updated>
  <app:edited>2010-03-29T13:04:30Z</app:edited>
  <author>
    <name>Cashier</name>
  </author>
```

```
    <contributor>
      <name>Barista A</name>
    </contributor>
    <content type="application/vnd.restbucks+xml">
      ...
    </content>
    <link rel="http://relations.restbucks.com/fulfilled"
      href="http://internal.restbucks.com/fulfillment/fullfilled"/>
    <link rel="edit" href="http://internal.restbucks.com/fulfillment/9876"/>
  </entry>
```

Notice that besides an edit link, this representation includes a second `<atom:link>` element, with a link relation of `http://relations.restbucks.com/fulfilled`.* A link relation of `http://relations.restbucks.com/fulfilled` describes a URI that returns a collection whose members represent fulfilled instances of the fulfillment protocol.

When a barista finishes making an order, it POSTs the member to the fulfilled collection, as shown in Example 8-17.

Example 8-17. *A barista completes the order fulfillment protocol by POSTing a member to the fulfilled collection*

```
POST /fulfillment/fullfilled HTTP/1.1
Host: internal.restbucks.com
Content-Type: application/atom+xml;type=entry
Content-Length: ...

<entry xmlns="http://www.w3.org/2005/Atom" xmlns:app="http://www.w3.org/2007/app">
  <title>order</title>
  <id>urn:uuid:e557e51b-c994-44ef-b06d-5331246cccbe</id>
  <updated>2010-03-29T13:05:00Z</updated>
  <app:edited>2010-03-29T13:04:30Z</app:edited>
  <author>
    <name>Cashier</name>
  </author>
  <contributor>
    <name>Barista A</name>
  </contributor>
  <content type="application/vnd.restbucks+xml">
    ...
  </content>
  <link rel="http://internal.restbucks.com/link-relations/fulfilled"
    href="http://internal.restbucks.com/fulfillment/fullfilled"/>
  <link rel="edit" href="http://internal.restbucks.com/fulfillment/9876"/>
</entry>
```

---

* In accordance with the Atom Syndication Format, this proprietary link relation value is an absolute URI.

Behind the scenes, the server applies some business logic over the internal order resource, modifying the order's state in line with the intentions expressed through the client transfer of a member representation to a particular URI. At the same time, the server determines an appropriate response to the client request based on the current state of the internal order resource. If the order is already in a fulfilled state, POSTing a member containing that order to the fulfilled collection results in the server returning 409 Conflict.

Assuming all goes well, the server adds the member to the fulfilled collection, as shown in Example 8-18.

Example 8-18. *The server adds the member to the fulfilled collection*

```
HTTP/1.1 201 Created
Date: ...
Content-Length: ...
Content-Type: application/atom+xml;type=entry;charset="utf-8"
Location: http://internal.restbucks.com/fulfillment/fulfilled/9876
Content-Location: http://internal.restbucks.com/fulfillment/fulfilled/9876
ETag: "c7be9039"

<entry xmlns="http://www.w3.org/2005/Atom" xmlns:app="http://www.w3.org/2007/app">
  <title>order</title>
  <id>urn:uuid:e557e51b-c994-44ef-b06d-5331246cccbe</id>
  <updated>2010-03-29T13:05:00Z</updated>
  <app:edited>2010-03-29T13:05:30Z</app:edited>
  <author>
    <name>Cashier</name>
  </author>
  <contributor>
    <name>Barista A</name>
  </contributor>
  <content type="application/vnd.restbucks+xml">
    ...
  </content>
  <link rel="edit"
    href="http://internal.restbucks.com/fulfillment/fulfilled/9876"/>
</entry>
```

Figure 8-4 shows the relations among cashiers and baristas, collections, members, and the underlying resources.

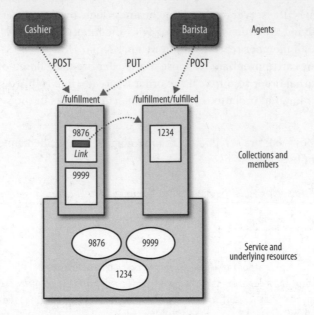

Figure 8-4. *Using multiple collections to implement the order fulfillment protocol*

There's nothing in AtomPub about moving members between collections in this fashion. But that doesn't mean we've departed from the protocol in any way. The solution still uses AtomPub to coordinate activities and constrain the mechanisms used to transfer representations. We use link relations to identify the links a client can use to forward the fulfillment protocol. The client then activates these links using AtomPub. What's important to the client is the relationship between the linked resource and the current representation. That relationship is determined by a link relation value. By matching its intention to its understanding of the link relation values on offer, a client can determine which link to pursue next. This decision is based on the client's current understanding of its own particular roles, responsibilities, and goals, and the current state of the fulfillment activity for which it's responsible.

The server mints links with proprietary link relation values to guide clients down the correct path. It interprets a client's intentions by attaching different pieces of processing logic to each URI. It then activates this logic according to the URI chosen by the client. The server knows which links to mint based on the current and possible next states of an order resource. Taken together, these links form a set of legitimate transitions through which clients can change the application state of the fulfillment process.

Implementing AtomPub in .NET

In this section, we show how Restbucks has implemented a simple version of the fulfillment service using Windows Communication Foundation (WCF). WCF provides a service hosting runtime that takes care of some of the low-level plumbing, allowing us to concentrate on the overall design of our service. Since we tend to work in a rapid, test-driven manner, we've decoupled our service implementation from the WCF runtime. This enables us to deliver functionality quickly by specifying and testing specific HTTP interactions without having to start and stop a service instance.

Because the fulfillment protocol is built on top of AtomPub, our solution needs to implement AtomPub collection and member protocol resources. We'll start by describing how we've built these collections and members using some of the .NET Framework's syndication classes. After that, we'll look at how to add domain logic that instantiates these classes in line with the fulfillment protocol. Next, we'll look at the simple Test Driven Development–centric framework we use to decouple our service implementation from the WCF runtime. Last, we'll examine the commands that we use to handle requests.

Implementing AtomPub Collections and Members

As we mentioned in Chapter 7, the .NET Framework's System.ServiceModel.Syndication namespace contains a number of classes that can be used to implement feeds and entries. For example, by adding a list of SyndicationItem objects to a SyndicationFeed and then outputting that feed using an Atom10FeedFormatter, we can easily generate an Atom feed.

AtomPub, as we've seen, adds several extension elements to Atom's basic feed format. Our fulfillment service uses a member's <app:edited> element and its <app:control> and <app:draft> extension elements to coordinate the fulfillment of coffee orders. In addition, the fulfillment collection itself exposes an <app:collection> element that advertises which media types a cashier can use to initiate the fulfillment process. To use these elements in our solution, we must extend the framework classes.

The .NET Framework allows SyndicationFeed and SyndicationItem classes to be subclassed. To illustrate how we can implement AtomPub extensions by subclassing syndication classes, we'll look in detail at how we extend the SyndicationItem class to provide EditedDateTime and Draft properties corresponding to the <app:edited> and <app:draft> extension elements. Example 8-19 shows the implementation of our Member class.

Example 8-19. *Subclassing SyndicationItem to implement AtomPub extension elements*

```
public class Member : SyndicationItem
{
  private const string EditedElementName = "edited";
  private const string ControlElementName = "control";
  private const string DateTimeFormat = "yyyy-MM-ddTHH:mm:ssZ";

  private static readonly DataContractSerializer ControlSerializer =
    new DataContractSerializer(typeof (ControlExtension));

  private ControlExtension control;
  private DateTimeOffset? editedDateTime;
```

```
public Member()
{
  control = new ControlExtension {Draft = DraftStatus.No};
}

public DraftStatus Draft
{
  get { return control.Draft; }
  set { control.Draft = value; }
}

public DateTimeOffset EditedDateTime
{
  get
  {
    if (editedDateTime == null)
    {
      editedDateTime = LastUpdatedTime;
    }
    return editedDateTime.Value;
  }
  set { editedDateTime = value; }
}

protected override bool TryParseElement(XmlReader reader, string version)
{
  if (reader.LocalName.Equals(ControlElementName) &&
    reader.NamespaceURI.Equals(Namespaces.AtomPub))
  {
    control = (ControlExtension) ControlSerializer.ReadObject(reader);
    return true;
  }
  if (reader.LocalName.Equals(EditedElementName) &&
    reader.NamespaceURI.Equals(Namespaces.AtomPub))
  {
    editedDateTime = reader.ReadElementContentAsDateTime();
    return true;
  }
  return base.TryParseElement(reader, version);
}

protected override void WriteElementExtensions(XmlWriter writer, string version)
{
  writer.WriteStartElement(EditedElementName, Namespaces.AtomPub);
  writer.WriteValue(FormatDateTime(EditedDateTime));
  writer.WriteEndElement();
```

```
    if (control != null)
    {
      ControlSerializer.WriteObject(writer, control);
    }

    base.WriteElementExtensions(writer, version);
  }

  private static string FormatDateTime(DateTimeOffset dateTime)
  {
    return dateTime.ToUniversalTime().ToString(DateTimeFormat);
  }
}
```

Member has two properties, Draft and EditedDateTime, each of which is backed by a
member variable. The first of these, Draft, is of type ControlExtension, which is a simple serializable class, as shown in Example 8-20.

Example 8-20. *ControlExtension represents the app:control and app:draft elements*

```
[DataContract(Name = "control", Namespace = Namespaces.AtomPub)]
public class ControlExtension
{
  [DataMember(Name = "draft")]
  private string draft;

  public DraftStatus Draft
  {
    get
    {
      if (string.IsNullOrEmpty(draft))
      {
        return DraftStatus.No;
      }
      return DraftStatus.Parse(draft);
    }
    set { draft = value.Value; }
  }
}
```

To ensure that these elements are serialized and deserialized correctly, we override
SyndicationItem's WriteElementExtensions(...) and TryParseElement(...) methods, respectively. When serializing a member, WriteElementExtensions(...) writes
the <app:edited> value to the supplied XML writer directly, and then uses a static
ControlSerializer to serialize a ControlExtension instance into <app:control> and
<app:draft> elements. When deserializing a member from an XML document,

`TryParseElement(...)` parses these same elements from the supplied XML reader and instantiates the corresponding .NET classes.

> **NOTE**
>
> `Member` is initialized with a draft status of `DraftStatus.No`. This is to cater to situations where the received XML representation of a member does not include `<app:control>` and `<app:draft>` elements. As per the AtomPub specification, a member without an `<app:draft>` element is assumed to be in a published (not draft) state.

Our `Collection` class extends the `SyndicationFeed` class in a similar manner to `Member`. `Collection` provides a `CollectionExtension` property that indicates which media types a client can use to initiate the fulfillment process.

Using Collections and Members for Order Fulfillment

The fulfillment service uses AtomPub members to represent instances of fulfillment (both outstanding and in-process), and AtomPub collections to represent lists of fulfillment instances. To ensure that collections and members are created with the correct property values according to our domain business rules, we create `Fulfillment` and `FulfillmentCollection` classes. `Fulfillment` encapsulates a single member. It controls access to this member according to our fulfillment business rules. `FulfillmentCollection` does the same for an AtomPub collection.

When a cashier submits a new order to the service, the service creates a new `Fulfillment` object. This fulfillment instance initializes a `Member` object with the Atom and AtomPub metadata used throughout the fulfillment process, as shown in Example 8-21.

Example 8-21. The Fulfillment constructor initializes a Member object with the necessary metadata

```
public Fulfillment(Guid id, DateTimeOffset createdDateTime,
  SyndicationContent content, Uri baseUri, string author)
{
  member = new Member
    {
      Title = SyndicationContent.CreatePlaintextContent("order"),
      Id = new UniqueId(id).ToString(),
      LastUpdatedTime = createdDateTime,
      EditedDateTime = createdDateTime,
      Draft = DraftStatus.Yes,
      Content = content
    };
  member.Authors.Add(new SyndicationPerson {Name = author});
  member.Links.Add(new EditLink(baseUri, id).ToSyndicationLink());
}
```

In a similar fashion, FulfillmentCollection initializes a Collection object with service-specific metadata. After it has been constructed, a fulfillment collection can be populated with AtomPub members by calling its Add(...) method and supplying a list of member objects. The implementation of Add(...) is shown in Example 8-22.

Example 8-22. *FulfillmentCollection's Add(...) method adds members to the underlying collection*

```
public void Add(IEnumerable<Fulfillment> newMembers)
{
  foreach (Fulfillment member in newMembers)
  {
    member.DoAction(i => members.Add(i));
  }

  members.Sort((x, y) =>
    ((Member) y).EditedDateTime.CompareTo(
      ((Member) x).EditedDateTime));

  if (members.Count > 0)
  {
    collection.LastUpdatedTime = ((Member) members.First()).EditedDateTime;
  }
}
```

Add(...) can't assume that the supplied members are in any particular order, so after it has added the new members to the existing list, it sorts the entire list. This ensures that the members are ordered correctly based on their app:edited values. Once the list has been sorted, the collection's LastUpdatedTime property is set to the EditedDateTime of the first (i.e., the most recent) member.

To illustrate how Fulfillment implements some of our domain logic, let's look at what happens when a fulfillment instance is updated. When a cashier or barista PUTs a revised member to the service, the corresponding fulfillment instance is retrieved from a repository and updated via its Edit(...) method, as shown in Example 8-23.

Example 8-23. *Updating a fulfillment instance*

```
public Fulfillment Edit(Member editedMember, DateTimeOffset editedDateTime)
{
  if (member.Draft.Equals(DraftStatus.No))
  {
    throw new InvalidOperationException("Fulfillment can no longer be edited.");
  }

  member.EditedDateTime = editedDateTime;
  member.Draft = editedMember.Draft;
  member.Content = editedMember.Content;
```

```
        return this;
    }
```

In the simplest version of our fulfillment protocol, a fulfillment instance can no longer be modified once it has been claimed by a barista. At the AtomPub level, this means that a member can no longer be edited once it has been published. If the member belonging to an existing fulfillment instance has been published, `Edit(...)` throws an exception; otherwise, it updates the fulfillment instance's member properties with values from the member contained in the request.

Testing WCF REST Services

Before we look at how we've implemented the fulfillment service itself, we'll examine the mechanism we've used to separate the service implementation from the WCF runtime.

The WCF runtime acts as a service factory. This factory creates new service instances based on a declarative (config-, code- or attribute-based) service specification. When a WCF service starts, the runtime assembles a channel stack based on this specification. The channel stack takes care of a lot of common infrastructure tasks, including serializing, encoding, and dispatching messages to .NET methods. Importantly, for web applications, the channel stack also initializes an instance of WCF's `WebOperationContext` helper class, which provides access to the HTTP request and response context. This helper object is available to service instances through the `WebOperationContext.Current` property.

With the HTTP context so tightly coupled to the WCF runtime, to test a service we must first start a service instance and then send it requests using an HTTP client. This adds unnecessary complexity to every test, as well as slowing down the execution of a large suite of tests—both of which hamper development. Because access to the HTTP context is critical to our service implementation, we decided to create our own wrapper around this context so that we could isolate our code from any runtime dependencies.

With this approach, our service logic is written against a request interface that we define, and populates a response object that we own. At runtime, we pass the service an implementation of our request interface that delegates to the WCF request instance. In our tests, however, we use a fake request. This allows us fine-grained control over all parts of the request, including the URI, headers, and entity body. When the service is finished handling a request, it creates a response object, which once again belongs to our decoupling framework. At runtime, this response populates a WCF response context; in our tests, it populates a fake context.

Example 8-24 shows our `IRequest` interface. Note that for requests containing an entity body we've also created a generic interface that derives from this base interface. This latter interface is parameterized with the deserialized type associated with the entity body in the service implementation.

Example 8-24. *IRequest abstracts the runtime HTTP request context*

```
public interface IRequest
{
  Uri Uri { get; }
  IRequestHeaders Headers { get; }
}

public interface IRequest<T> : IRequest
{
  T EntityBody { get; }
}
```

At runtime, service instances are given an instance of WcfRequest, the implementation of which is shown in Example 8-25.

Example 8-25. *WcfRequest wraps the WCF request context at runtime*

```
public class WcfRequest : IRequest
{
  private readonly Uri uri;
  private readonly IRequestHeaders headers;
  private readonly string method;

  public WcfRequest(OperationContext operationContext,
    WebOperationContext webOperationContext)
  {
    uri = GetUri(operationContext);
    headers = GetHeaders(webOperationContext);
    method = GetMethod(webOperationContext);
  }

  public Uri Uri
  {
    get { return uri; }
  }

  public IRequestHeaders Headers
  {
    get { return headers; }
  }

  protected static Uri GetUri(OperationContext context)
  {
    return context.EndpointDispatcher.EndpointAddress.Uri;
  }
```

```
    protected static IRequestHeaders GetHeaders(WebOperationContext context)
    {
      return new WcfRequestHeaders(context.IncomingRequest.Headers);
    }


    protected static string GetMethod(WebOperationContext context)
    {
      return context.IncomingRequest.Method;
    }
}


public class WcfRequest<T> : WcfRequest, IRequest<T>
{
  private readonly T entityBody;

  public WcfRequest(OperationContext operationContext,
    WebOperationContext webOperationContext)
    : base(operationContext, webOperationContext)
  {
    entityBody = GetEntityBody(operationContext);
  }

  public T EntityBody
  {
    get { return entityBody; }
  }

  private T GetEntityBody(OperationContext context)
  {
    var storedMessage = context.Extensions.Find<StoredMessage>();
    return storedMessage.Message.GetBody<T>();
  }
}
```

Most of the implementation of WcfRequest is quite straightforward. The WCF channel stack creates instances of OperationContext and WebOperationContext for each request. These instances are passed to the WcfRequest constructor, where they are used to initialize its property values.

The one piece of code that requires further explanation is the implementation of GetEntityBody(...). Here we retrieve a copy of the entity body from the operation context's Extensions collection. We do this so that we can incorporate the entity body into a cohesive request object.

WCF extensions provide a mechanism for sharing state between different stages in the processing of a message. With our framework, as a message progresses through the message pipeline created by the WCF channel stack, we intercept it and put a copy into a `StoredMessage` extension object. We then attach this extension object to the current operation context. The extension is retrieved by a `WcfRequest` instance once the runtime has handed control to our service implementation.

To copy and store the received message in the operation context, we create a message inspector. WCF provides many extensibility points; message inspectors plug into one of these extensibility points, allowing us to examine or modify messages prior to being handed off to the service implementation. Example 8-26 shows the implementation of our `StoreMessage` message inspector.

Example 8-26. *StoreMessage copies a received message and attaches it to the operation context*

```
public class StoreMessage : IDispatchMessageInspector
{
  public object AfterReceiveRequest(ref Message request,
    IClientChannel channel, InstanceContext instanceContext)
  {
    MessageBuffer buffer = request.CreateBufferedCopy(Int32.MaxValue);
    OperationContext.Current.Extensions.Add(
      new StoredMessage(buffer.CreateMessage()));
    request = buffer.CreateMessage();
    buffer.Close();

    return null;
  }

  public void BeforeSendReply(ref Message reply, object correlationState)
  {
    //Do nothing
  }
}
```

The IDispatchMessageInspector interface here is defined by WCF. As you can see, the interface's methods allow us to handle received messages prior to them being deserialized into our service's typed objects, as well as deal with outgoing responses once they've been serialized into WCF messages. We take advantage only of the former capability, creating a copy of the received message, putting the copy into a new StoredMessage, and adding this stored message to the current operation context's Extensions collection.

We insert the message inspector into the dispatching runtime using a service behavior, which is attached to the service host using a custom class attribute on the service implementation. This custom attribute, WcfDecouplingSupportAttribute, is shown in Example 8-27.

Example 8-27. *WcfDecouplingSupportAttribute attaches a message inspector to the dispatch runtime*

```
[AttributeUsage(AttributeTargets.Class, AllowMultiple = false, Inherited = false)]
public class WcfDecouplingSupportAttribute : Attribute, IServiceBehavior
{
  public void Validate(ServiceDescription serviceDescription,
    ServiceHostBase serviceHostBase)
  {
    //Do nothing
  }

  public void AddBindingParameters(ServiceDescription serviceDescription,
    ServiceHostBase serviceHostBase, Collection<ServiceEndpoint> endpoints,
    BindingParameterCollection bindingParameters)
  {
    //Do nothing
  }

  public void ApplyDispatchBehavior(ServiceDescription serviceDescription,
    ServiceHostBase serviceHostBase)
  {
    IEnumerable<DispatchRuntime> runtimes =
      (from ChannelDispatcher cd in serviceHostBase.ChannelDispatchers
       from EndpointDispatcher e in cd.Endpoints
       select e.DispatchRuntime);

    foreach (DispatchRuntime dr in runtimes)
    {
      dr.MessageInspectors.Add(new StoreMessage());
    }
  }
}
```

Again, IServiceBehavior is an interface defined by WCF. When a service host starts, it calls the behavior's interface methods at the appropriate point in the service startup life cycle. When ApplyDispatchBehavior(...) is called, the attribute instance adds a StoreMessage message inspector to each dispatch runtime.

The last parts of the WCF decoupling framework are the Request.Handle<>(...) and RequestWithEntityBody.Handle<>(...) methods. Each method accepts a function that takes a request object and parameters collection, and which returns a response. The methods are responsible for creating WcfRequest objects, invoking the service logic in the supplied function, and applying the response to the WCF response context.

WCF Service Implementation

With our AtomPub Collection and Member classes and our domain-specific Fulfillment and FulfillmentCollection classes in place, we're ready to implement AtomPub.

NOTE —————————————————————————————

Our solution implements only a subset of AtomPub, because order fulfillment itself requires only a subset of the protocol.

Our first task is to create a C# service contract interface whose methods represent AtomPub transitions, as shown in Example 8-28.

Example 8-28. *IOrderFulfillmentService exposes AtomPub resources and state transitions*

```
[ServiceKnownType(typeof (Atom10FeedFormatter))]
[ServiceKnownType(typeof (Atom10ItemFormatter))]
public interface IOrderFulfillmentService
{
  [OperationContract]
  [WebGet(UriTemplate = "/")]
  Atom10FeedFormatter<Collection> GetCollection();

  [OperationContract]
  [WebGet(UriTemplate = "/{id}")]
  Atom10ItemFormatter<Member> GetMember(string id);

  [OperationContract]
  [WebInvoke(Method = "POST", UriTemplate = "/")]
  Atom10ItemFormatter<Member> CreateMember(Atom10ItemFormatter member);

  [OperationContract]
  [WebInvoke(Method = "PUT", UriTemplate = "/{id}")]
  void UpdateMember(string id, Atom10ItemFormatter<Member> member);
```

```
    [OperationContract]
    [WebInvoke(Method = "DELETE", UriTemplate = "/{id}")]
    void DeleteMember(string id);
}
```

This interface is attributed with two ServiceKnownType attributes. These attributes indicate to the runtime that it can expect to serialize and deserialize Atom10FeedFormatter and Atom10ItemFormatter types when handling requests and returning responses. In addition, each interface method has an OperationContract attribute, and either a WebGet or WebInvoke attribute. WebGet associates the attributed method with GET requests that match the supplied URI template. These requests will be dispatched to that attributed method's implementation at runtime. WebInvoke associates any other HTTP verb (and the specified URI template) with the attributed method.

We now create a service class, OrderFulfillmentService, which implements this interface contract, as shown in Example 8-29.

Example 8-29. OrderFulfillmentService handles requests at runtime

```
[ServiceBehavior(IncludeExceptionDetailInFaults = false,
  ConcurrencyMode = ConcurrencyMode.Single,
  InstanceContextMode = InstanceContextMode.PerCall)]
[WcfDecouplingSupport]
[AllowXmlSubTypeExtension]
public class OrderFulfillmentService : IOrderFulfillmentService
{
  private readonly CommandFactory commands;

  public OrderFulfillmentService(CommandFactory commands)
  {
    this.commands = commands;
  }

  public Atom10FeedFormatter<Collection> GetCollection()
  {
    return Request.Handle(
      (request, parameters) =>
        commands.GetFulfillmentCollection()
          .Execute(request, parameters));
  }

  public Atom10ItemFormatter<Member> GetMember(string id)
  {
    return Request.Handle(
      (request, parameters) =>
        commands.GetFulfillment()
          .Execute(request, parameters));
  }
```

```
public Atom10ItemFormatter<Member> CreateMember(Atom10ItemFormatter member)
{
  return RequestWithEntityBody.Handle<Atom10ItemFormatter,
    Atom10ItemFormatter<Member>>(
    (request, parameters) =>
      commands.CreateFulfillment()
      .Execute(request, parameters));
}

public void UpdateMember(string id, Atom10ItemFormatter<Member> member)
{
  RequestWithEntityBody.Handle<Atom10ItemFormatter<Member>>(
    (request, parameters) =>
      commands.UpdateFulfillment()
        .Execute(request, parameters));
}

public void DeleteMember(string id)
{
  Request.Handle(
    (request, parameters) =>
      commands.DeleteFulfillment().Execute(request, parameters));
}
}
```

This class has been attributed with our framework's WcfDecouplingSupport attribute. It has also been attributed with AllowXmlSubTypeExtension, which is another custom service behavior. AllowXmlSubTypeExtension configures the service to accept representations whose Content-Type header value ends with +xml. Above these two custom attributes, the ServiceBehavior attribute controls the execution behavior of a service instance. As indicated by the PerCall value of the InstanceContextMode property of this ServiceBehavior attribute, WCF creates a new instance of the service class for each request, ensuring that the service doesn't retain any state between requests.

Looking at the body of OrderFulfillmentService, the interesting thing is that it doesn't contain any service logic. Each service method simply creates a command, which it then executes to handle the request. The code that creates and executes a command is written as a lambda expression, which the service method passes to a static Handle<>(...) method from our own WCF decoupling framework. Handle<>(...) is parameterized with the types of the request and response entity bodies.

The service logic, then, is encapsulated in a number of commands, each of which can be developed and tested in isolation from the service infrastructure and runtime. Each command is responsible for validating a request, constructing a domain object (or retrieving one from a repository), and invoking its functionality. Example 8-30 shows the UpdateFufillment command implementation.

Example 8-30. *UpdateFulfillment command*

```
public class UpdateFulfillment
{
  private readonly IRepository repository;
  private readonly IDateTimeProvider dateTimeProvider;

  public UpdateFulfillment(IRepository repository,
    IDateTimeProvider dateTimeProvider)
  {
    this.repository = repository;
    this.dateTimeProvider = dateTimeProvider;
  }

  public Response Execute(IRequest<Atom10ItemFormatter<Member>> request,
    NameValueCollection parameters)
  {
    if (request.Headers.IfMatch == null)
    {
      return new Response(Status.PreconditionFailed);
    }

    if (!MediaTypes.AtomEntry.IsTypeAndSubtypeMatch(
      request.Headers.ContentType))
    {
      return new Response(Status.UnsupportedMediaType);
    }

    try
    {
      ETaggedEntity eTaggedEntity = repository.Get(new Guid(parameters["id"]));

      if (!eTaggedEntity.EntityTag.Equals(request.Headers.IfMatch))
      {
        return new Response(Status.PreconditionFailed);
      }

      Fulfillment fulfillment = eTaggedEntity.Fulfillment.Edit(
        (Member)request.EntityBody.Item, dateTimeProvider.Now);
      repository.Update(fulfillment, request.Headers.IfMatch);
    }
    catch (MemberDoesNotExistException)
    {
      return new Response(Status.NotFound);
    }
    catch (OptimisticUpdateFailedException)
    {
```

```
        return new Response(Status.PreconditionFailed);
      }
      catch (InvalidOperationException)
      {
        return new Response(Status.Conflict);
      }

      return new Response(Status.OK);
    }
  }
```

This command first validates that the request contains an If-Match header and a Content-Type header with the correct content type (application/atom+xml). If either test fails, it returns a response with the appropriate 4XX status code. If both guard clauses pass, the command then retrieves the latest version of the fulfillment instance from the repository.

If the entity tag associated with the latest version doesn't match the value supplied in the If-Match header, the command returns 412 Precondition Failed. If the values do match, it updates the latest version with the member supplied in the request's entity body, and then updates the fulfillment instance in the repository. If at any point an error occurs, the command returns a 4XX status code; otherwise, it returns a response with 200 OK.

A Versatile Protocol

In this chapter, we looked at Atom Publishing Protocol: a standardized mechanism for creating and editing web content. AtomPub addresses many common publishing use cases, and though programming support is not as ubiquitous as it is for Atom, it's still the closest thing we have to a broadly adopted, interoperable publishing protocol. AtomPub should be at the forefront of our minds whenever we need to implement publishing functionality for collections of web resources.

> ──── **NOTE** ────────────────────────────────
>
> There's no need to use AtomPub everywhere, however. If our solution doesn't require Atom metadata, it's simpler to adopt a plain CRUD protocol, as we saw in Chapter 4. We can always implement AtomPub's optimistic locking strategy (based on entity tags and validators) if the need for some form of concurrency control arises.

There's a nice symmetry in being able to publish web resources using collections and members, and then consume them using feeds and entries. In simple cases, the collections we use for publishing resources can also serve as the feeds we expose to other consumers. Our event stream capability, for example, could be outsourced to an AtomPub server. This would allow many applications to publish events to a collection (using AtomPub), from where they could then be consumed by any number of clients.

In other circumstances, however, we might consider separating the publishing of resources from their consumption. In the case of AtomPub, a collection is dedicated to the *publishing* needs of a service and any clients that wish to publish resources. For example, Restbucks' headquarters uses the product catalog AtomPub collection to manage (i.e., publish and edit) the contents of the product catalog. Stores, on the other hand, have no interest in editing catalog entries, nor do they care that feeds have been ordered according to AtomPub's rules.

To meet the needs of stores, we might consider creating more specialized feeds, generated using the same underlying resources but lacking the AtomPub extensions. These feeds would be made available at different URIs from that of the collection. We might even consider exposing product catalog data in a format other than Atom. This highlights the fact that not everything published using AtomPub needs to be surfaced as an Atom feed.

In the second half of this chapter, we looked at ways in which we can build domain application protocols on top of the more general-purpose AtomPub. Here we saw how the server wholly encapsulates the specific knowledge necessary to construct a domain application protocol. In our example, the server maintains a rich domain model of newly created and in-process orders. This model encapsulates the business logic and behaviors controlling the resource life cycles of those domain objects.

Based on its understanding of the current state of a resource, the server constructs AtomPub representations that guide cashiers and baristas to progress the application protocol. As these clients manipulate application state using the legitimate links in the member representations returned by the server, the server changes the underlying resource state, which in turn is reflected in the links made available to the clients in subsequent responses.

This chapter has shown that AtomPub can be used to implement common enterprise integration patterns (e.g., pub/sub) without resorting to specialized infrastructure or writing new code. This is an exciting prospect: the Web's commodity workhorse protocols are already well suited to enterprise heavy lifting.

All we need now is to secure these systems, and we'll have an entire enterprise stack. And the Web provides that too, so read on.

CHAPTER NINE

Web Security

THIS CHAPTER FOCUSES ON SOME EXCITING DEVELOPMENTS in security protocols, which combine the Web's features with mature cryptographic techniques. Yet secure systems need more than just clever cryptography at the network layer to be secure, so throughout this chapter we'll take a systematic view of web security. We'll investigate the following four core pillars of secure computing and show how to apply them to build distributed systems on the Web:

Confidentiality
    The ability to keep information private while in transit or in storage

Integrity
    The ability to prevent information from being changed undetectably

Identity
    The ability to authenticate parties involved in an interaction

Trust
    Authorizing a party to interact with a system in a prescribed manner

The Web has evolved solutions to each of these challenges, and in this chapter, we'll show how those techniques can be adopted for building secure computer-to-computer services.

HTTP Security Essentials

The web community has developed a number of higher-order protocols that address issues such as identity and trust. These protocols sit atop HTTP so as to allow systems to interoperate securely. We'll look at these protocols shortly, but before we do so, we should understand the basics of HTTP security.

HTTP Authentication and Authorization

As we've often seen on the World Wide Web, HTTP natively supports authentication (to establish identity) and authorization (to help establish trust). When a consumer attempts to access a privileged resource, credentials must be provided in an Authorization header, or the consumer will be refused access.

In Restbucks, we can secure access to resources using this capability. For instance, we might allow only authorized consumers to access payment resources. If an unauthorized consumer tries to access a payment resource, it will be refused because it lacks appropriate credentials.

In Example 9-1, the consumer system sends a GET request to the Restbucks payment service. Seeing that there is no WWW-Authenticate header present, Restbucks responds with the challenge shown in Example 9-2.

Example 9-1. *Accessing a payment resource*

```
GET /payment/1234 HTTP/1.1
Host: restbucks.com
```

Example 9-2. *Restbucks challenges the consumer*

```
401 Unauthorized
WWW-Athenticate: Basic realm="payments@restbucks.com"
```

The challenge tells the consumer that Restbucks requires a Basic digest to access some resources in the realm payments@restbucks.com.* If the consumer knows username and password credentials for that realm, it hashes them and embeds them in an Authorization header and retries the request, as shown in Example 9-3.

As an optimization, if a consumer already knows that a resource is protected through Basic authentication, it can provide credentials with the initial request message and so avoid the challenge-response steps.

---

* A *realm* is an identifier that the service generates to describe the resource a consumer is trying to access. It's useful for browser-based systems since it can be presented to a human user for consideration; it's far less useful for machine-to-machine interactions.

Example 9-3. *Attempted authorized access to a payment resource*

```
GET /payment/1234 HTTP/1.1
Host: restbucks.com
Authorization: Basic Zm9vOmJhcg==
```

Unfortunately, HTTP Basic authentication is not secure. Although the username and password are never sent in plain text, the base64-encoded text is easily intercepted and decoded. To make HTTP authentication less susceptible to simple attacks, we need either a secure channel such as HTTPS (which we'll see in the next section), or a mechanism that allows credentials to be passed securely through an insecure channel. Fortunately, this is precisely what HTTP Digest authentication provides.

Example 9-4 shows a Digest challenge from the payment service. Note that this challenge contains far more metadata than a Basic one.

Example 9-4. *Restbucks challenges the consumer*

```
401 Unauthorized
WWW-Athenticate: Digest realm="payments@restbucks.com",
  qop="auth",
  nonce="1e8c46a7d793433490cb8303f18a86e5",
  opaque="ff1eccda9ef442b3b38cabb2435d5967"
```

The Digest challenge metadata shown in Example 9-4 allows the consumer to transmit credentials safely over the Web:

qop

> Quality of Protection metadata that determines whether the consumer's response to the challenge should be based on the HTTP method and digest URI only (qop="auth"), or whether it should include the entity body too (qop="auth-int"). If auth-int is chosen, the entity body can be transferred in a tamper-resistant manner since it is hashed in subsequent interactions.

nonce

> An opaque string used to prevent replay attacks against the service. A nonce is typically created by hashing a representation and a timestamp so that services can uniquely identify requests and reject any suspicious repetitions. Clients are allowed to reuse a nonce until the service generates a 401 Unauthorized response, which may be per request or for several requests within a limited time depending on the security requirements of the service.

opaque

> Information generated by the service that should be returned unchanged in the Authorization header of subsequent requests. The service can use this header to provide context for successive interactions.

Based on the information presented in the challenge, the consumer retries the request with credentials attached to the Authorization header, as shown in Example 9-5.

Example 9-5. *Consumer submits a digest*

```
GET /payment/1234 HTTP/1.1
Host: restbucks.com
Authorization: Digest username="beancounter",
  realm="payments@restbucks.com",
  nonce="1e8c46a7d793433490cb8303f18a86e5",
  uri="/payment/1234"
  qop="auth",
  nc=00000001,
  cnonce="cf45f0087f33bce12332aef430945dff",
  response="ff14aa3457acd60aa2091232a98756ff",
  opaque="ff1eccda9ef442b3b38cabb2435d5967"
```

As you can see in Example 9-5, much of the information in the initial challenge is returned without modification in the response. However, the consumer produces additional metadata to fulfill its part of the authentication protocol:

username
> The identifier of an account authorized to access the resources at the specified URI.

uri
> The URI of the resource to which the request is targeted. This is often identical to the path in the HTTP request, but is repeated since intermediaries (such as load balancers) can rewrite that address.

nc
> A (hexadecimal) count of how many requests the consumer has made using the service's nonce.

cnonce
> The consumer's nonce, generated for each request to prevent replay attacks against the service.

response
> The result of applying a set of hash functions (discussed shortly) to the nonce, nonce count, consumer's nonce, and consumer's password. This is the value the service will ultimately check to see whether the consumer has valid credentials for the realm.

The response is calculated using a three-step process, as follows:

1. The MD5 hash of the username, realm, and password is computed.*

2. The MD5 hash of the method and digest URI is computed.

---

* *http://tools.ietf.org/html/rfc1321*

3. The MD5 hash of the value produced by step 1—the service's nonce, request count (nc), cnonce, and qop—and the result from step 2 is calculated, yielding the consumer's response value.

Since the consumer and service both know the shared secret (the consumer's password) the consumer's request can be checked by the service by repeating the calculation.

> **NOTE**
>
> Unlike Basic authentication, Digest authentication always requires a challenge/response, since the challenge step provides metadata to parameterize the response.

This scheme provides a number of benefits when compared to Basic authentication. First, because passwords are not transmitted over the network, security credentials are far less easily compromised. Second, because the Authorization header's response entry is never repeated (as a result of using nonces) brute force replay attacks are rendered ineffective. Third, passwords no longer have to be transmitted over the network in an easily compromised form.

Despite being more secure than Basic authentication, HTTP Digest authentication can still be broken using a man-in-the-middle attack if transport-level security isn't also used. In Figure 9-1, an interloper mimicking the behavior of the remote service intercepts the initial authentication and responds with a Basic authentication challenge to the consumer. Basic authentication is easily broken; when the consumer responds to the Basic authentication challenge, the man in the middle is able to compromise the credentials.

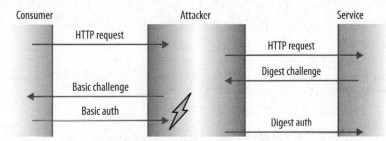

Figure 0 1. *Man in the middle attack on HTTP Digest authentication*

> **WARNING**
>
> If you are going to use HTTP authentication, transport-level security should be considered mandatory.

Critically, the consumer may not know this has happened if the man in the middle presents a faithful reproduction of the target service! To prevent this, transport-level security is *still* necessary, even for Digest authentication. To provide comprehensive defense against man-in-the-middle attacks, we need transport-level mechanisms. Enter HTTPS.

NOTE ───

In addition to Basic and Digest authentication, a third scheme called WSSE
has evolved, driven in part by the desire to secure Atom and AtomPub services.
The WSSE scheme borrows an authentication approach from WS-Security's
UsernameToken profile and maps those features onto HTTP headers.*

WSSE is superior to Basic insofar as it doesn't transmit passwords in clear text,
requiring instead shared secrets between client and server. Like the other authentication mechanisms, WSSE is vulnerable to man-in-the-middle attacks in the
absence of transport-level security.

Transport-Level Confidentiality and Integrity

We often take HTTPS for granted, and yet it supports vast numbers of secure interactions every day on the Web. While it might not be glamorous, humble HTTPS is
mature, widely deployed, and well understood, making it ideally suited to hostile
environments such as the public Internet. Of all the security protocols we could use,
nothing else comes close in terms of ubiquity, maturity, and the huge volume of value
transactions it supports every single minute.

All this gives service developers a degree of comfort: HTTPS is a well-understood and
researched protocol that routinely provides the underlay for secure interactions at
global scale. We can be sure it's fit for purpose.

Conceptually, HTTPS is straightforward. Instead of exchanging HTTP requests and
responses over TCP, we transmit those same requests and responses over Transport
Layer Security, or TLS.† While TLS transparently provides integrity and confidentiality
for HTTP interactions, it's important to understand how it works.

NOTE ───

TLS started life as Netscape's SSL (Secure Sockets Layer). The IETF renamed the
protocol to TLS as it evolved into an Internet RFC.

The TLS protocol has three phases, each of which must be completed before we can
transfer representations via HTTPS:

1. Handshake

2. Secure session

3. Channel setup

---

* *http://docs.oasis-open.org/wss/2004/01/oasis-200401-wss-username-token-profile-1.0.pdf*
† See *http://tools.ietf.org/html/rfc5246* for the latest version (v1.2).

An HTTPS session begins with a normal TCP three-way handshake, which opens a connection to port 443 (the standard TLS port) on the remote server. Once the TCP connection has been established, the secure session can be initiated, as shown in Figure 9-2.

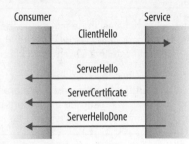

Figure 9-2. *Negotiating parameters for a secure session*

To initiate a secure session, the consumer begins by sending a `ClientHello` message to the remote service. As part of this message, the consumer includes its highest supported TLS version (or SSL version if the consumer is old), the ciphers and hashing algorithms that the consumer understands (in order of preference), and an optional session identifier.* The consumer also sends some pseudorandom data for service-side key generation.

NOTE

TLS is a versatile protocol; besides security, it also supports data compression as an optimization. Compression, however, is not widely used. We favor keeping any compression at the HTTP level using the `Content-Encoding` header so that we can compress representations irrespective of whether we're using TLS or TCP as the transport protocol.

In response, the service sends a `ServerHello` message back to the consumer, indicating the TLS (or SSL) version chosen, the selected cipher and hash algorithms, an optional session identifier, and its own pseudorandom data for consumer-side key generation.†

Following on from the `ServerHello` message, the service transmits a `Certificate` message to the consumer. The `Certificate` message contains the service's public key, and optionally the service name and certificate authority (CA). The consumer uses this information to authenticate the service; it does this by matching the name of the service and the certificate to the name (or domain) of the server. (There's a dependency here on DNS in that we are only as secure as the DNS infrastructure we are using.)

---

* The client provides a session identifier only if it is trying to resume an earlier secure session to avoid paying for setup cost.
† The server responds with an existing identifier only if it is prepared to resume the session. Otherwise, the client must accept that a new session will be initiated.

The final message of the negotiation phase is ServerHelloDone, which the service sends to the consumer to indicate that it's finished negotiating.

> **NOTE**
>
> TLS also supports client-side certificates. If the service sends a Client-CertificateRequest message prior to ServerHelloDone, the consumer should immediately respond with its certificate in a ClientCertificate message.
>
> This is useful because it enables the consumer and service to establish mutual trust at the transport level. Any traffic flowing over a bilaterally certified session has a trusted source and origin, allowing service implementations to authorize or disallow interactions based on the well-known source of an HTTP request.

Having negotiated parameters for a secure session, the service and consumer are now ready to set up a cryptographically secure channel, as shown in Figure 9-3.

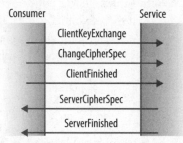

Figure 9-3. *Initializing a secure session*

The consumer transmits a ClientKeyExchange message encrypted using the service's public key. This message typically contains a PreMasterSecret computed from the consumer and service's random data.* If the service is able to decrypt the ClientKeyExchange message, the consumer can be sure the service has the corresponding private key, thereby proving the service's authenticity. To defend against an attacker reverting the session to an earlier and weaker protocol version (known as a *rollback* attack) the service double-checks the protocol version number in the ClientKeyExchange message.

> **NOTE**
>
> The negotiation of a shared secret is secure and cannot be eavesdropped, even by a man-in-the-middle attack. An attacker cannot modify the messages in the hand-shake without being detected, making the negotiation reliable.

The consumer follows with a ChangeCipherSpec message, which indicates to the service that from now on the consumer will use the session key for hashing and encrypting messages. Hashing a message with the session key creates a Message Authentication

---

* Depending on the cipher chosen, the client's public key may be sent instead.

Code (MAC). The MAC provides integrity and authenticity by allowing recipients who know the key to repeat the hash function in order to detect whether the message content has been changed.

As further evidence that nothing has gone awry, the consumer securely transmits a `ClientFinished` message containing a hash of the entire conversation up to this point. The `ClientFinished` message is the first message encrypted and hashed using the shared session key computed by the consumer and service.

To complete the protocol, the service responds first with a `ChangeCipherSpec` message, indicating that it, too, will now use a secure channel using the negotiated keys. The service then sends a `ServerFinished` message that verifies its common understanding of the parameters for the session. The `ServerFinished` message contains a hash of the conversation up to this point for the consumer to verify.

From this point onward, the consumer and service can exchange secure messages using computationally inexpensive shared key methods. That is, we can now transmit HTTP requests and responses whose privacy and integrity are assured.

Network and Performance Considerations

Because HTTPS is so common, we might be tempted to use it liberally in an attempt to provide blanket security. If all a service's resources are secured with HTTPS (particularly with bilateral certificates), its attack surface is significantly reduced. In practice, however, there are drawbacks to such an approach. In particular, forcing every interaction over a secure channel may limit scalability.

The use of a secure channel not only incurs cryptography costs, it also prevents caching in the network; because intermediaries cannot see the representations being exchanged, they cannot understand their caching metadata. Losing the important visibility aspect of HTTP means we only have consumer-side caching (which does not permit cached representations to be shared among many consumers) to help reduce load on servers.

The questions we have to ask ourselves when considering securing resources are "What is the value of the resource?" and "Who should be able to access it?" Only by answering these questions can we determine whether interactions with a resource should be secured, and plan for any performance challenges that arise.

---- **NOTE** ----

Establishing HTTPS requires several network interactions and cryptographic operations before a TLS channel can be used to transfer representations. This overhead makes a single HTTPS call several times more expensive than a single HTTP call. However, if the TLS channel is used for many exchanges, the setup cost and cost of ongoing cryptographic operations becomes less significant and the cost of missed intermediary caching becomes the primary consideration.

To gain the dual benefits of caching and secure interactions, we must turn aside from using encrypted channels to enforce security considerations, and consider instead patterns that allows us to encrypt content on unencrypted (and therefore cacheable) channels. As Figure 9-4 shows, it is possible to publish data on the public Web and still maintain confidentiality and integrity.

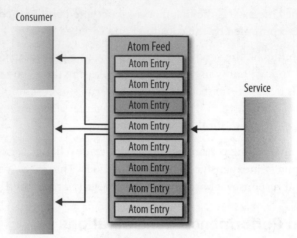

Figure 9-4. *Cacheable and secure representations broadcast over an insecure channel with Atom*

The pattern in Figure 9-4 shows a service publishing an Atom feed onto the Web. The feed and its entries are cacheable, and therefore scale well at modest latencies—as we have come to expect from the Web. However, the content of each atom:entry can be encrypted so that it is meaningless for any consumers that don't have the key to decrypt it.

In Figure 9-4, the top two consumers both access the same (shared) key, while the third accesses a different shared key. This allows the service to broadcast information in the knowledge that only certain recipients will understand it (assuming that any shared keys have already been transmitted and stored securely). Because the content is useless without the decryption keys, the pattern enables the Atom service to publish a highly cacheable feed without worrying about attackers getting hold of the content.

> ──── **WARNING** ──
>
> This technique is not without its drawbacks. Having to share keys increases coupling, and in practice can be tricky to implement and scale.

In the general case, services will expose both secure and insecure resources. It is our duty as service developers to understand the trade-off between security and scalability, and to decide which resources to secure based on their risk/performance profiles.

Identity and the OpenID Protocol

HTTPS provides the foundations of secure computing on the Web. But security doesn't stop at the transport layer. Having looked at how HTTPS provides confidentiality and integrity, we can now begin to address higher-order challenges, starting with identity.

Both HTTP authentication and HTTPS (with client-side certificates) can be used to identify consumers, but they do so in a way that places the burden of identity management on the service itself. Keeping track of consumers is a hard problem, but it shouldn't be *our* problem as business service providers. Instead, we'd like to delegate identity management to services that know how to do identity management well.

One solution to this problem is to decentralize identity management. OpenID is a protocol that allows consumers to present claims about their identity to services such as Restbucks, where an identity provider trusted by Restbucks has authenticated those claims.

NOTE

OpenID doesn't solve trust. A service may accept the identity claims presented by a consumer, but only because it trusts the provider through some out-of-band mechanism. This doesn't, however, mean the consumer is automatically entitled to interact with all aspects of the service.

OpenID allows a service or *relying party* to delegate the responsibility for storing consumer credentials to one or more OpenID *providers*. The providers are responsible for checking OpenID *consumers'* credentials and informing the relying party if an identity claim is valid. OpenID allows consumers to keep their personal details from relying parties, while still being able to present an authenticated identity claim to that party.

OpenID evens the playing field between consumers and services: consumers know the identity of services through their certificates, and services come to know the identity of consumers through their OpenID.*

Protocol Flow

OpenID is compelling because of its simplicity. In just a handful of interactions, a consumer can securely present a claim and have it validated by an OpenID provider, and then interact with a service using the substantiated claim. The end-to-end protocol is shown in Figure 9-5 with the customer playing the *consumer* role, Restbucks as the *relying party*, and the voucher service acting as the *provider*.

---

* We can, of course, use client certificates to provide the identity of the client to the server. However, that approach means the service still has to manage client certificates rather than, as OpenID does, delegating that responsibility to a provider.

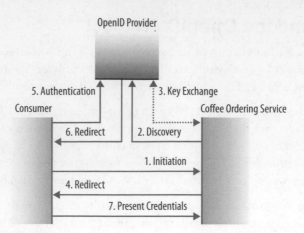

Figure 9-5. *The OpenID protocol*

In Chapter 5, we allowed consumers to keep loyalty cards for Restbucks special offers, but we were never really concerned about customers' identity, and as a result, the cards were anonymous. By allowing consumers to share their identity, Restbucks can track their purchases and reward them when they've bought enough coffee (and begin to gather data for business intelligence as a side effect). We can create a simple loyalty domain application protocol (DAP) based on the following OpenID interactions:

Initiation

A customer submits an OpenID that it claims to own.

Discovery

The coffee ordering service discovers the OpenID provider for the presented OpenID.

Key exchange

Secrets are exchanged between the coffee ordering service and the OpenID provider.

Restbucks redirects to OpenID provider

Restbucks redirects the consumer to its OpenID provider to authenticate.

Authentication

The consumer authenticates with its OpenID provider. (The way in which authentication occurs is out of scope for OpenID.)

OpenID provider redirects to Restbucks

On successful authentication, the OpenID provider redirects the consumer to Restbucks. The redirect includes an OpenID payload.

Present credentials

Finally, the OpenID payload containing the validated identity claim is sent to Restbucks.

In devising this scheme, we've made some pragmatic choices where the OpenID specification allows multiple options. Since we're not limited by the behavior of web browsers, we can reduce the problem to a simple hypermedia application driven by XHTML forms—a popular hypermedia format that is readily amenable to machine processing.

The loyalty protocol starts when a consumer follows a coffee-card link, shown in Example 9-6, contained within an order representation. The link leads to a login resource.

Example 9-6. *A coffee-card link initiates the loyalty protocol*

```
<link xmlns="http://schemas.restbucks.com/dap"
  rel="http://restbucks.com/relations/coffee-card"
  uri="http://restbucks.com/login/1234" mediaType="application/xhtml+xml"/>
```

To process the link, the consumer GETs the representation shown in Example 9-7.

Example 9-7. *Client is directed to the Restbucks OpenID login*

```
GET /login/1234 HTTP/1.1
Accept: application/xhtml+xml
Host: restbucks.com
```

The service responds with the XHTML form shown in Example 9-8. The form contains an <input> element with a well-known name attribute value of openid_identifier (the attribute value is defined by the OpenID protocol). This markup tells a consumer that an OpenID URI is expected in a POST response.

Example 9-8. *The Restbucks OpenID login form is the starting point for authentication*

```
HTTP/1.1 200 OK
Content-Type: application/xhtml+xml
Content-Length: 382
Date: Tue, 18 May 2010 17:36:50 GMT

<!DOCTYPE html PUBLIC "-//W3C//DTD XHIML 1.0 Strict//EN"
  "http://www.w3.org/TR/xhtml1/DTD/xhtml1-strict.dtd">
<html xmlns="http://www.w3.org/1999/xhtml" xml:lang="en" lang="en">
  <head><title>OpenID Login</title></head>
  <body>
    <form action="http://restbucks.com/login/1234" method="post">
      <input type="text" name="openid_identifier"/>
    </form>
  </body>
</html>
```

Following this form-based challenge, the consumer replies with its OpenID URI. The URI the consumer supplies to the service resolves to a discovery document through which the Restbucks service can find an OpenID provider willing to validate the identity claim.

The OpenID URI we've chosen is *http://openid.example.org/jim*, which is transmitted to Restbucks in an application/x-www-form-urlencoded representation, as shown in Example 9-9.*

Example 9-9. *Consumer sends its OpenID URI to Restbucks*

```
POST /login/1234 HTTP/1.1
Content-Type: application/x-www-form-urlencoded
Accept: application/xhtml+xml
Host: restbucks.com
Content-Length: 56


openid_identifier=http%3A%2F%2Fopenid.example.org%2Fjim
```

After receiving the consumer's OpenID URI, Restbucks can discover the provider associated with that URI. It does this by GETting the resource—known as a discovery document—at the URI specified by the consumer. As shown in Example 9-10, Restbucks specifies its preference for an xhtml discovery document (over html or xrds, which OpenID also supports) using the HTTP Accept header.

Example 9-10. *Restbucks discovers the OpenID provider*

```
GET /jim HTTP/1.1
Accept: application/xhtml+xml
Host: openid.example.org
```

In response, the OpenID provider generates an XHTML representation containing the specific URI pertaining to the consumer's OpenID. As we can see in Example 9-11, this information is provided as a link header in the XHTML header space.

Example 9-11. *OpenID provider responds with a discovery document*

```
HTTP/1.1 200 OK
Content-Type: application/xhtml+xml
Content-Length: 271
Date: Tue, 18 May 2010 17:36:50 GMT


<!DOCTYPE html PUBLIC "-//W3C//DTD XHTML 1.0 Transitional//EN"
  "http://www.w3.org/TR/xhtml1/DTD/xhtml1-transitional.dtd">
```

---

* There isn't really an OpenID provider at this URI. For development, we mapped that hostname onto the address of our servers.

```
<html xmlns="http://www.w3.org/1999/xhtml">
  <head>
    <link rel="openid2.provider" href="http://provider.example.org/jim"/>
  </head>
</html>
```

Now that it knows the address of the OpenID provider, Restbucks can use Diffie-
Hellman key exchange* to establish a shared secret key, which can then be used to
sign subsequent interactions. The process of establishing a shared secret key is called
association. Although the association phase is optional, we've elected to adopt it for
Restbucks since we believe it's the canonical use case for OpenID.

There's a modest cost to establishing a shared key as a result of both parties having to
remember the association. The advantage is that from this point onward, there's no
need to verify exchanges between the parties, as would be the case if no association
had been established. Without association, Restbucks would have to validate signatures directly with the OpenID provider every time the provider makes a positive identity assertion, resulting in more network traffic overall.

To establish this association Restbucks POSTs an association request to the association
resource on the OpenID provider, as per Example 9-12. Restbucks sends the OpenID
provider its public key together with the encryption algorithm to be used for the key
exchange (SHA-256 in this example).†

Example 9-12. *Restbucks creates a shared secret with the OpenID provider using Diffie-
Hellman key exchange*

```
POST /jim HTTP/1.1
Host: provider.example.org
Content-Length: 344
Content-Type: application/x-www-form-urlencoded; charset=UTF-8

openid.ns=http%3A%2F%2Fspecs.openid.net%2Fauth%2F2.0&openid.mode=associate&
openid.session_type=DH-SHA256&openid.assoc_type=HMAC-
SHA256&openid.dh_consumer_public=ALs6VTbE6ZrffuOwB1ht%2F5D2XmugZAqCEQtsqLA5GHik9YF2
vx7UU0jWj47zGsqRvK3%2BAcoEWBaE4LNiqutj673UvX98XYCuO3hjEpeiOg%2BHtXAScMd5f7NwMlFw2kR
Xht88dFDo8Fsm2EV9dDYyix%2BI%2BYdEwwDZimbMNPcXQ4li
```

The OpenID provider responds to Restbucks' request, as shown in Example 9-13. The
provider's response contains the provider's public key and an encrypted MAC. Using
the provider's public key together with its own public key, Restbucks can now determine the shared secret key encoded in the MAC.

---

* http://en.wikipedia.org/wiki/Diffie–Hellman_key_exchange

† OpenID association allows key exchange without encryption. Our preference is to secure the representations that services and consumers exchange, irrespective of the underlying channel.

Example 9-13. *OpenID provider fulfills the Diffie-Hellman key exchange*

```
HTTP/1.1 200 OK
Content-Type: application/x-openid-kvf
Content-Length: 375
Date: Tue, 18 May 2010 17:36:50 GMT

ns:http://specs.openid.net/auth/2.0
session_type:DH-SHA256
assoc_type:HMAC-SHA256
assoc_handle:1274204211041-0
expires_in:1800
dh_server_public:cht1xvy3G95qk8SqZuizvA8GBIowaIrj5TMt9OEe9bhNX7G2KPKlxmy398cKJ3NBAa
ZdqHcmy65qU4J5HgpFh+kB89gztAXd4zMKANeaHq3DkRp+isufoqS19cdvlOe/QokylkgN
N/RCfMPrxHa65wNweGlLqHSO1VRxokHUvwc=
enc_mac_key:OCHBkrqdL2JAJ9bUcn8p7Q3gn1lCatkbTe5Y3sKHUq4=
```

Once the association stage has been completed, Restbucks responds to the consumer's original login request (Example 9-9) by generating a form containing several hidden fields, as per Example 9-14. This form is to be submitted to the OpenID provider (as indicated by the value of the form's action attribute) by the consumer.

Example 9-14. *Restbucks responds with authentication data for the consumer to pass through to the OpenID provider*

```
HTTP/1.1 200 OK
Content-Type: application/xhtml+xml
Content-Length: 1086
Date: Tue, 18 May 2010 17:36:50 GMT

<!DOCTYPE html PUBLIC "-//W3C//DTD XHTML 1.0 Strict//EN"
  "http://www.w3.org/TR/xhtml1/DTD/xhtml1-strict.dtd">
<html xmlns="http://www.w3.org/1999/xhtml" xml:lang="en" lang="en">
  <head>
    <title>OpenID Redirection</title>
  </head>
  <body>
    <form name="openid-form-redirection"
      action="http://provider.example.org/jim" method="post">
      <input type="hidden" name="openid.ns"
        value="http://specs.openid.net/auth/2.0"/>
```

```
        <input type="hidden" name="openid.claimed_id"
          value="http://openid.example.org/jim"/>
        <input type="hidden" name="openid.identity"
          value="http://openid.example.org/jim"/>
        <input type="hidden" name="openid.return_to"
          value="http://restbucks.com/authenticate/1234"/>
        <input type="hidden" name="openid.realm"
          value="http://restbucks.com/authenticate/1234"/>
        <input type="hidden" name="openid.assoc_handle" value="1274204211041-0"/>
        <input type="hidden" name="openid.mode" value="checkid_setup"/>
        <input type="Submit" value="Submit"/>
      </form>
    </body>
  </html>
```

In Example 9-14, Restbucks returns an XHTML form with some user-interface markup, namely the element `<input type="Submit" value="Submit"/>`. Consuming applications *can* safely ignore this, but it has the benefit of meaning the whole OpenID workflow can be driven through a browser during development and debugging.

On receiving the form in Example 9-14, the consumer POSTs it to the provider, encoding it as an application/x-www-form-urlencoded representation, as shown in Example 9-15.

Example 9-15. *Consumer transmits Restbucks' OpenID parameters to the OpenID provider prior to logging in*

```
POST /jim HTTP/1.1
Content Type: application/x-www-form-urlencoded
Accept: application/xhtml+xml
Host: provider.example.org
Content Length: 381

openid.realm=http%3A%2F%2Frestbucks.com%3A9998%2Fauthenticate%2F1234&openid.return_
to=http%3A%2F%2Frestbucks.com%3A9998%2Fauthenticate%2F1234&openid.identity=http%3A%
2F%2Fopenid.example.org%3A9999%2Fjim&openid.ns=http%3A%2F%2Fspecs.openid.net%2Fauth
%2F2.0&openid.assoc_handle=1274204211041-
0&openid.claimed_id=http%3A%2F%2Fopenid.example.org%3A9999%2Fjim&openid.mode-
checkid_setup
```

The provider is now in a position to begin authenticating the consumer. OpenID doesn't in fact specify how a consumer authenticates with an OpenID provider. Our provider has been built to respond with a form-based login challenge when consumers try to authenticate against a given service (e.g., Restbucks). This scheme demands that consumers re-POST the OpenID authentication data from Restbucks (or any other relying party) as well as the credentials matching their OpenID URI. It's a simple scheme that adds a single password input, as shown in Example 9-16.

Example 9-16. *The OpenID provider challenges the consumer*

```
HTTP/1.1 200 OK
Content-Type: application/xhtml+xml
Content-Length: 1027
Date: Tue, 18 May 2010 17:36:50 GMT

<!DOCTYPE html PUBLIC "-//W3C//DTD XHTML 1.0 Transitional//EN"
  "http://www.w3.org/TR/xhtml1/DTD/xhtml1-transitional.dtd">
<html xmlns="http://www.w3.org/1999/xhtml">
  <body>
    <form action="http://provider.example.org/jim" method="post">
      <input type="hidden" name="openid.ns"
        value="http://specs.openid.net/auth/2.0"/>
      <input type="hidden" name="openid.identity"
        value="http://openid.example.org/jim"/>
      <input type="hidden" name="openid.claimed_id"
        value="http://openid.example.org/jim"/>
      <input type="hidden" name="openid.mode" value="checkid_setup"/>
      <input type="hidden" name="openid.realm"
        value="http://restbucks.com/authenticate/1234"/>
      <input type="hidden" name="openid.assoc_handle" value="1274204211041-0"/>
      <input type="hidden" name="openid.return_to"
        value="http://restbucks.com/authenticate/1234"/>
      <input type="password" name="password"/>
      <input type="submit" value="submit" />
    </form>
  </body>
</html>
```

As you can see, the form the provider uses to challenge the consumer is the same form that Restbucks sent the consumer, and which the consumer then sent on to the provider. The only difference is that the provider has added the <password> input element to challenge the consumer to authenticate.

Example 9-17 shows how the consumer logs in to the provider by POSTing back the OpenID data together with its password.

WARNING ───────────────────────────────────

Moving a password between the consumer and the OpenID provider in plain text over an insecure channel is not safe for production use—its purpose is only to show the protocol flow. A sensible OpenID provider will use HTTPS to secure the channel over which the plain-text password flows.

Example 9-17. *Consumer logs in to the OpenID provider*

```
POST /jim HTTP/1.1
Content-Type: application/x-www-form-urlencoded
Accept: application/xhtml+xml
Host: provider.example.org
Content-Length: 394

password=jim&openid.realm=http%3A%2F%2Frestbucks.com%3A9998%2Fauthenticate%2F1234&
openid.ns=http%3A%2F%2Fspecs.openid.net%2Fauth%2F2.0&openid.identity=http%3A%2F%2F
openid.example.org%3A9999%2Fjim&openid.return_to=http%3A%2F%2Frestbucks.com%3A9998%
2Fauthenticate%2F1234&openid.mode=checkid_setup&openid.assoc_handle=1274204211041-
0&openid.claimed_id=http%3A%2F%2Fopenid.example.org%3A9999%2Fjim
```

Once the password is accepted, the OpenID provider generates another form for the consumer. This form, shown in Example 9-18, allows the provider to transmit authentication outcomes to Restbucks. It uses hypermedia to drive the protocol by requiring the consumer to POST the form's data to the Restbucks URI specified in the action attribute.

Example 9-18. *OpenID provider responds with data for the consumer to transmit to Restbucks*

```
HTTP/1.1 200 OK
Content-Type: application/xhtml+xml
Content-Length: 1323
Date: Tue, 18 May 2010 17:36:50 GMT

<!DOCTYPE html PUBLIC "-//W3C//DTD XHTML 1.0 Transitional//EN"
  "http://www.w3.org/TR/xhtml1/DTD/xhtml1-transitional.dtd">
<html xmlns="http://www.w3.org/1999/xhtml">
  <body>
    <form action="http://restbucks.com/authenticate/1234" method="post">
      <input type="hidden" name="openid.ns"
        value="http://specs.openid.net/auth/2.0"/>
      <input type="hidden" name="openid.op_endpoint"
        value="http://provider.example.org/jim"/>
      <input type="hidden" name="openid.claimed_id"
        value="http://provider.example.org/jim"/>
      <input type="hidden" name="openid.response_nonce"
        value="2010-05-18T17:36:51Z0"/>
      <input type="hidden" name="openid.mode" value="id_res"/>
      <input type="hidden" name="openid.identity"
        value="http://provider.example.org/jim"/>
```

```
        <input type="hidden" name="openid.return_to"
          value="http://restbucks.com/authenticate/1234"/>
        <input type="hidden" name="openid.assoc_handle" value="1274204211041-0"/>
        <input type="hidden" name="openid.signed"
      value="op_endpoint,claimed_id,identity,return_to,response_nonce,assoc_handle"/>
        <input type="hidden" name="openid.sig"
          value="xQeM1HJEta2KN2jc+rvt856vplMO1MIYY2sSz1zOjk8="/>
        <input type="submit" value="redirect" />
      </form>
    </body>
  </html>
```

The consumer finally presents its authenticated identity claim to Restbucks by POSTing
the form data from Example 9-18, as we can see in Example 9-19.

Example 9-19. *Consumer transmits the OpenID payload to Restbucks*

```
POST /authenticate/1234 HTTP/1.1
Content-Type: application/x-www-form-urlencoded
Accept: application/xhtml+xml
Host: restbucks.com
Content-Length: 577

openid.sig=xQeM1HJEta2KN2jc%2Brvt856vplMO1MIYY2sSz1zOjk8%3D&openid.response_nonce=2
010-05-18T17%3A36%3A51ZO&openid.assoc_handle=1274204211041-
O&openid.claimed_id=http%3A%2F%2Fprovider.example.org%3A9999%2Fjim&openid.mode=
id_res&openid.ns=http%3A%2F%2Fspecs.openid.net%2Fauth%2F2.0&openid.return_to=http%3
A%2F%2Frestbucks.com%3A9998%2Fauthenticate%2F1234&openid.identity=http%3A%2F%2F
provider.example.org%3A9999%2Fjim&openid.op_endpoint=http%3A%2F%2Fprovider.example.
org%3A9999%2Fjim&openid.signed=op_endpoint%2Cclaimed_id%2Cidentity%2Creturn_to%2
Cresponse_nonce%2Cassoc_handle
```

If the consumer has successfully authenticated against the OpenID provider, it receives
a 200 OK response from Restbucks (see Example 9-20) and knows its purchases will be
credited against the loyalty scheme.

If the consumer has not successfully authenticated against the OpenID provider, it
receives a 401 Unauthorized response from Restbucks (see Example 9-21). The consumer can then choose whether to retry authentication or to backtrack through the
Restbucks ordering protocol.

Irrespective of whether authentication has been successful or unsuccessful, Restbucks
provides a link to the current order to help the consumer progress.

Example 9-20. *Consumer logs in successfully to Restbucks*

```
HTTP/1.1 200 OK
Content-Type: application/vnd.restbucks+xml
Content-Length: 188
Date: Mon, 14 Dec 2009 16:04:36 GMT

<link xmlns="http://schemas.restbucks.com/dap"
  rel="http://restbucks.com/relations/order"
  uri="http://restbucks.com/order/1234"
  mediaType="application/vnd.restbucks+xml" />
```

Example 9-21. *Consumer fails to log in*

```
HTTP/1.1 401 Unauthorized
Content-Type: application/vnd.restbucks+xml
Content-Length: 188
Date: Mon, 14 Dec 2009 16:04:36 GMT

<link xmlns="http://schemas.restbucks.com/dap"
  rel="http://restbucks.com/relations/order"
  uri="http://restbucks.com/order/1234"
  mediaType="application/vnd.restbucks+xml" />
```

As you can see from these examples, OpenID is a web-centric protocol. It uses URIs as the basis for a consumer's identity claims, and hypermedia—XHTML forms and POST data—to bind protocol steps together.

Because all mandatory communication happens through the consumer, the protocol preserves loose coupling between OpenID providers and relying parties (such as Restbucks). As long as the service trusts the provider it finds through the discovery mechanism, the protocol allows for decentralized authentication and runtime discovery—all driven by hypermedia.

Although there's some detail in the underlying cryptographic principles and in the security data that's exchanged during OpenID authentication, most of this detail is encapsulated by a variety of freely available toolkits, as we shall see next when we jump into an implementation.

OpenID in Java

Because numerous OpenID toolkits are available on the Java platform, using OpenID is straightforward. All we need to do is wire one of these toolkits into our service to form a working solution, at least in theory.*

---

* In practice, the current crop of Java OpenID toolkits can be difficult to work with. They are tightly coupled to specific underlying HTTP libraries and so resist Test-Driven Development.

Figure 9-6 shows that we chose the Grizzly web server and Jersey as our programmatic layer over HTTP for both the consumer and services. For the cryptographic parts of the solution, we chose OpenID4java.*

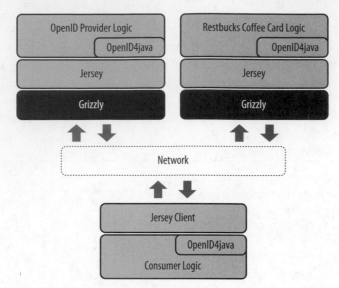

Figure 9-6. *Loyalty card Java solution architecture*

An OpenID-enabled Java consumer

The business goal of the consumer is to identify itself to Restbucks so that any purchases it makes can be reconciled against the generous loyalty program that Restbucks runs.

In the OpenID protocol, the consumer spends most of its time filling in XHTML forms and POSTing form data to Restbucks and its OpenID provider.[†] In Example 9-22, the consumer first retrieves Restbucks' loyalty scheme login form and fills in the openid_ identifier value.

Example 9-22. *Consumer begins the OpenID workflow*

```
public void loginToRestbucks(String id) throws Exception {

    // Get the OpenID Login form from Restbucks
    URI restbucksOpenIdLoginUri = new URI("http://restbucks.com/login/" + id);
    XhtmlForm loginForm = getXhtmlForm(restbucksOpenIdLoginUri);
    FormInput element = loginForm.getElement("openid_identifier");
    element.setValue("http://openid.example.org/RosalindFranklin");
```

---

* *http://code.google.com/p/openid4java/*

† Remember, there's an optional message exchange in OpenID where the provider and relying party exchange keys. The consumer isn't involved in that step.

The consumer subsequently sends the URI of the discovery document for its OpenID provider to Restbucks, and receives back an XHTML form containing opaque information destined for the OpenID provider, as shown in Example 9-23.

Example 9-23. *Consumer receives an XHTML form with opaque information intended for the OpenID provider*

```
// Send the OpenID URI to Restbucks
// Steps 1 & 4 from Figure 9-5; Example 9-9 and Example 9-14
XhtmlForm openIdProviderRedirectionForm = postForm(loginForm);
```

The consuming application duly passes that information on to the OpenID provider by POSTing it in URL-encoded form, as we can see in Example 9-24. The OpenID provider then provides a login form for the consumer to complete and return.

> ——— **NOTE** ———————————————————————————
>
> Remember: the means by which a consumer logs in to an OpenID provider is *not standardized*. This is largely the point of OpenID: the relying party doesn't care how a consumer authenticates with an OpenID provider. In this instance, we use simple forms-based authentication, but any sensible authentication mechanism can be used.

Example 9-24. *Consumer receives and completes a login form from its OpenID provider*

```
// Send Restbucks OpenID data to the OpenID Provider
// Step 5, Figure 9-5; Example 9-15 and Example 9-16
XhtmlForm openIdProviderLoginForm = postForm(openIdProviderRedirectionForm);

// Complete login form (Out of scope for OpenID, Example 9-16)
openIdProviderLoginForm.getElement("password").setValue("scoobydoo");
// Successful login produces redirect form
// Step 6, Figure 9-5; Example 9-18
XhtmlForm openIdProviderLoginResponse = postForm(openIdProviderLoginForm);
```

Once the consumer has successfully logged in to the OpenID provider, it receives another form containing opaque data about the success (or not) of the login; this form is to be relayed back to Restbucks. To complete the OpenID login, the consumer POSTs the form back to Restbucks as per Example 9-25.

Example 9-25. *Consumer relays opaque OpenID login data to Restbucks and receives confirmation of successful (or unsuccessful) identification*

```
// Redirect back to Restbucks
// Step 7, Figure 9-5, Example 9-19, Example 9-20, and Example 9-21
int authenticationResponseCode = postForm(openIdProviderLoginResponse)
                             .getResponseCode();

// Finally check if Restbucks accepted the login
```

```
    if(authenticationResponseCode == 200) {
      // Continue with workflow
      // ...
    } else if (authenticationResponseCode == 401) {
      // Failed to authenticate, try again!
      // ...
    } else {
      throw new RuntimeException(
            String.format("Unexpected response code [%d] from [%s]",
              authenticationResponseCode, restbucksOpenIdLoginUri.toString())));
  }
```

Since the OpenID workflow is predominantly composed from GETting and POSTing forms between Restbucks and the OpenID provider, we have written a few useful convenience methods to deal with transferring XHTML forms and URL-encoded data. These are shown in Example 9-26.

Example 9-26. Exchanging XHTML forms and form-encoded data with Restbucks and the OpenID provider

```
private XhtmlForm toXhtmlForm(ClientResponse response) {
    return new XhtmlForm(response);
}

private XhtmlForm getXhtmlForm(URI loginUri) {
    return toXhtmlForm(client.resource(loginUri)
                        .accept(MediaType.APPLICATION_XHTML_XML)
                        .get(ClientResponse.class));
}

private  XhtmlForm postForm(XhtmlForm form) {
    return toXhtmlForm(client.resource(form.getActionUri())
                        .accept(MediaType.APPLICATION_XHTML_XML)
                        .type(MediaType.APPLICATION_FORM_URLENCODED)
                        .entity(form.toUrlEncoded())
                        .post(ClientResponse.class));
}
```

To provide XHTML form support for the OpenID workflow, we created a simple class that internally represents the form as a set of FormInput elements. These elements represent the various <input> element types allowed in an XHTML form.* The most important aspect of this class is the method that turns XHTML forms into their URL-encoded equivalent via string manipulation, as shown in Example 9-27.

---

* The permissible <input> element types are text, which represents clear text boxes; hidden, for hidden form fields; password, for obfuscated text boxes; and submit, for buttons (which tend not to be used in computer-to-computer scenarios).

Example 9-27. *Converting form content from XHTML form to application/x-www-form-urlencoded format*

```
public String toUrlEncoded() {
  StringBuilder sb = new StringBuilder();
  for (FormInput fi : inputs) {
    if (!fi.isSubmitType()) {
      sb.append(fi.toUrlendcodedFormat());
      sb.append("&");
    }
  }

  // Remove trailing '&' char
  sb.deleteCharAt(sb.length() - 1);

  return sb.toString();
}
```

In Example 9-27, we simply transform each form input element into a name=value pair and insert an ampersand (&) between successive pairs. The method then strips the trailing & character from the last pair.

There is some detail in converting to the application/x-www-form-urlencoded format. Example 9-28 shows how we percent-encode any special characters in the names or values of pairs that we wish to transfer.* As each input item is processed (in the toUrlEncodedFormat(...) method) the names and values are percent-encoded using the values held in a (static) lookup table.

NOTE

Sometimes a piece of base64-encoded text also happens to be legal URL-encoded text. OpenID makes extensive use of base64-encoded text; this text should then be converted into URL-encoded form for transfer. We learned this the hard way: while creating examples for this chapter, we experienced a series of intermittent authentication failures.

Remember to URL-encode all of your OpenID representations, or you'll be caught out too.

Example 9-28. *Converting form content from base64 to application/x-www-form-urlencoded format*

```
private static final HashMap<String, String> percentEncodingSubsitutions =
                      new HashMap<String, String>();

static {
```

---

* *http://en.wikipedia.org/wiki/Percent-encoding*

```
    percentEncodingSubsitutions.put("!", "%21");
    // Several more substitutions removed for brevity...
    percentEncodingSubsitutions.put("]", "%2D");
}

private String percentEncode(String toEncode) {
    toEncode = ensureNotNull(toEncode);
    StringBuilder sb = new StringBuilder();
    for(int i = 0; i < toEncode.length(); i++) {
        String current = new Character(toEncode.charAt(i)).toString();

        if(percentEncodingSubsitutions.containsKey(current)) {
            sb.append(percentEncodingSubsitutions.get(current));
        } else {
            sb.append(current);
        }
    }
    return sb.toString();
}

public String toUrlendcodedFormat() {
    StringBuilder sb = new StringBuilder();
    sb.append(percentEncode(name));
    sb.append("=");
    sb.append(percentEncode(value));
    return sb.toString();
}
```

Although the consumer workflow is simple, there's a reasonable amount of complexity in creating and maintaining our own XHTML forms implementation. Although we sensibly didn't create a fully functioning XHTML form abstraction, we still wrote code.

NOTE ───

It's possible to replace at least some of our custom code with existing, tested software. For example, the web testing tool WebDriver provides automated testing of web pages in code.* While its APIs are designed to support dynamic web applications, it can also be used to drive XHTML forms, thereby reducing the amount of code we have to write (and debug).

Restbucks Java ordering service

To OpenID-enable the Restbucks ordering service, we need to support four activities:

* *http://code.google.com/p/webdriver*

- Accept OpenID URIs identifying customers.

- Create associations with OpenID providers.

- Undertake indirect communication with the OpenID provider through the consumer.

- Finally, if the consumer authenticates, accredit its order against its loyalty card.

Accepting an OpenID is an easy task for Restbucks: we simply expose an XHTML form to the consumer and ask for OpenID URI. The code for this is a JAX-RS method that returns a login form. The method is triggered by a GET request for a URI matching the template /login/{orderId}, as shown in Example 9-29.

Example 9-29. *Exposing an OpenID login form to consumers*

```
@GET
@Produces(MediaType.APPLICATION_XHTML_XML)
@Path(LOGIN_PATH + "/{orderId}")
public Response openIDLogin(@PathParam("orderId") String orderId) {
  return Response.ok().entity(getLoginForm()).build();
}
```

When the consumer receives the form (such as the one in Example 9-8), it looks for an <input> element with an attribute of openid_identifier. It then completes the form by populating this field with its OpenID URI. Once that's done, the consumer converts the form to an application/x-www-form-urlencoded representation (as per Example 9-9) and POSTs it to the form's action URI, which is the service's receiving URI for starting the OpenID authentication process for that order.

On receiving the POSTed form, JAX-RS dispatches to the method shown in Example 9-30. This method triggers the discovery and association interactions with the OpenID provider. It then redirects the consumer to authenticate with its OpenID provider, again using an XHTML form.

Example 9-30. *Discovery, association, and redirecting the consumer to log in to its chosen OpenID provider*

```
@POST
@Path(LOGIN_PATH + "/{orderId}")
@Produces(MediaType.APPLICATION_XHTML_XML)
public Response login(MultivaluedMap<String, String> postBody,
@PathParam("orderId") String orderId) throws Exception {

  String openId = parseOpenIdFromPostBody(postBody);

  Discovery discovery = new Discovery();
  Identifier identifier = discovery.parseIdentifier(openId);

  List discoveries = discovery.discover(identifier);
  DiscoveryInformation discovered = manager.associate(discoveries);
```

```
session(new OrderId(orderId)).add(OPENID_DISCOVERY_KEY, discovered);

String authenticationUri = uriInfo.getBaseUri().toString() +
AUTHENTICATION_URI_PATH + "/" + orderId;

AuthRequest authReq = manager.authenticate(discovered, authenticationUri);

return Response.ok().entity(redirectForm(authReq.getOPEndpoint(),
authReq.getParameterMap())).build();
}
```

The form generated in Example 9-30 allows the consumer to verify its claim with an OpenID provider. When that interaction is completed, the consumer is directed back to Restbucks (again through an XHTML form). This last form is handled by the authenticate(...) method shown in Example 9-31. This method processes the outcome of the authentication between the consumer and its OpenID provider.

Example 9-31. *Processing the OpenID provider's indirect authentication response*

```
@POST
@Path(AUTHENTICATION_URI_PATH + "/{orderId}")
public Response authenticate(@PathParam("orderId") String orderId,
                MultivaluedMap<String, String> params) throws
                  MessageException, DiscoveryException,
                  AssociationException {

ParameterList httpParams = new ParameterList(convertToParameterList(params));

// retrieve the previously stored discovery information
OrderId sessionOrderId = new OrderId(orderId);
DiscoveryInformation discovered = (DiscoveryInformation)
                session(sessionOrderId).get(OPENID_DISCOVERY_KEY);

Identifier verified = manager.verify(uriInfo.getRequestUri().toString(),
                  httpParams, discovered).getVerifiedId();

if (verified != null) {
session(sessionOrderId).add(OPEN_ID_IDENTIFIER_KEY, verified);
return Response.ok().entity(generateOrderLink(orderId).toString())
        .type(RESTBUCKS_MEDIA_TYPE).build();
} else {
return Response.status(Status.UNAUTHORIZED)
        .entity(generateOrderLink(orderId).toString())
        .type(RESTBUCKS_MEDIA_TYPE).build();
}
}
```

Once JAX-RX has dispatched to the code in Example 9-31, the consumer's session is reestablished and the data contained in the POST body is passed in to the OpenID framework code for validation. If the consumer authenticated successfully with the OpenID provider, the login is added to the consumer's session and a representation containing a link to the order is sent back to the consumer, along with a 200 OK status code.

If authentication failed, the consumer still receives a representation containing a link to the original order, but with a 401 Unauthorized status code. Either way, once the consumer has the link and the status code, it can reenter the ordering DAP.

Java OpenID provider

The OpenID provider has to deal with three activities: discovery, association, and authentication. Discovery involves exposing a discovery document on demand. We've chosen XHTML for our discovery mechanism, and we provide links to the OpenID provider for a given OpenID URI, as per Example 9-32.

Example 9-32. OpenID provider discovery

```
@GET
@Produces(MediaType.APPLICATION_XHTML_XML)
@Path("/{userId}")
public Response discover(@PathParam("userId") String userId) {
    StringBuilder sb = new StringBuilder();
    sb.append(generateXhtmlPreamble());
    sb.append("<head><link rel=\"openid2.provider\" href=\"" +
        UriHelper.getBaseUri(uriInfo.getRequestUri()).toString() + "/" +
        userId + "\"/></head>");
    sb.append("</html>");
    return Response.ok().entity(sb.toString()).build();
}
```

Both association and authentication are handled by the associateOrAuthenticate() method in Example 9-33. This method is invoked by JAX-RS whenever any representation encoded as application/x-www-form-urlencoded is POSTed to a URI matching the /{userId} template. The actual association is handled by the OpenID4J toolkit's ServerManager type with the manager.associationResponse() method. To transfer the results of the association to Restbucks, a little more JAX-RS plumbing is used.

Example 9-33. OpenID provider authentication and association

```
@POST
@Path("/{userId}")
@Consumes(MediaType.APPLICATION_FORM_URLENCODED)
public Response associateOrAuthenticate(@PathParam("userId") String userId,
                MultivaluedMap<String, String> params)
                    throws URISyntaxException {
```

```
initialiseManager();
ParameterList requestParams = new ParameterList(convertToParameterList(params));

URI requestUri = uriInfo.getRequestUri();

String mode = requestParams.hasParameter("openid.mode") ?
        requestParams.getParameterValue("openid.mode") : null;

// Association
if ("associate".equals(mode)) {
return Response.ok().entity(manager.associationResponse(requestParams)
        .keyValueFormEncoding())
        .header(HttpHeaders.CONTENT_TYPE,
            MediaType.APPLICATION_FORM_URLENCODED).build();
// Authentication
} else if ("checkid_setup".equals(mode) || "checkid_immediate".equals(mode)) {

if (isPostback(params)) {
  if (!credentialsValid(params, requestUri)) {
  return Response.status(Status.UNAUTHORIZED).build();
  }
} else {
  return Response.ok()
        .entity(generateLoginForm(requestUri,
            requestParams))
        .header(HttpHeaders.CONTENT_TYPE,
            MediaType.APPLICATION_XHTML_XML).build();
}

String usersOpenId = UriHelper.getBaseUri(requestUri) + "/" + userId;
Message response = manager.authResponse(requestParams, usersOpenId,
                  usersOpenId, true, true);

if (response instanceof DirectError) {
  return Response.ok().entity(response.keyValueFormEncoding()).build();
} else {
  // Generate response for Relying Party
  return Response.ok()
        .entity(generateRelyingPartyResponseForm(response
          .getDestinationUrl(false), response.getParameterMap()))
        .header(HttpHeaders.CONTENT_TYPE,
            MediaType.APPLICATION_XHTML_XML).build();
}

// Other error handling elided for brevity...
}
```

Authentication is not within the scope of OpenID, so we've elected to use simple forms-based authentication in our code. In Example 9-33, we check to see if the consumer has authenticated via a POST of the login form back to the URI matching the {/userId} template.

> **NOTE**
>
> Much of the complexity in the OpenID provider and relying party implementations stems from the impedance mismatch between the OpenID4J toolkit and JAX-RS.

Once the consumer authenticates, we're back in OpenID territory. Using the ServerManager.authResponse() method, we compute the authentication information and relay it back to Restbucks via the consumer with some JAX-RS plumbing.

Practical Considerations for OpenID

OpenID is a popular protocol on the human Web, but it is also suitable for programmatic use. Although the toolkits we've used aren't terribly refined, the fact is that OpenID can still be used for managing identity claims for interacting web services.

On the Web, OpenID suffers from a trust issue in that relying parties are under no obligation to accept OpenID URIs from arbitrary providers. However, in the enterprise, where use of a particular OpenID provider can be mandated, the trust problem evaporates (because every system must trust the mandated provider). As such, OpenID is an excellent example of a technology that is useful on the Web, but which can thrive in the enterprise. In the near future, we can expect enterprise security frameworks to support OpenID; Microsoft's Windows Identity Foundation (WIF), for example, already has open source support for OpenID.*

The OAuth Protocol

Once a consumer has been identified, service providers can decide which interactions are allowed. This is known as *authorization*. Authorization is often based on a username and password combination; successfully logging in to a system grants access to some of the functions and data managed by that system. In the enterprise environment, this has worked relatively well because usernames and passwords are often managed centrally in directory services.

> **NOTE**
>
> *Authentication* determines who is interacting with a service, while *authorization* determines what a consumer can do with the resources a service exposes.

* See *http://startersts.codeplex.com/*.

It's not always possible or desirable, however, to centralize and share credentials in the traditional way. When third parties provide services to the enterprise, for example, sharing usernames is normally undesirable and impractical, if not downright impossible. This is where OAuth steps in.* The OAuth protocol enables services and applications to interact with resources hosted securely in third-party services, without requiring the owners of those resources to share their credentials.

The Next Best Thing to Free Coffee?

At Restbucks, we understand that our busy customers don't always have access to cash or cards when they *really* need their coffee. To solve this problem, Restbucks has partnered with a coffee voucher provider. This third-party provider allows customers to buy and manage vouchers that can be used to pay for coffee at Restbucks.

Importantly, Restbucks isn't involved with the day-to-day operations of the voucher provider's service. All that Restbucks needs to know is that it can redeem vouchers when customers pay with them, and that the service will eventually honor those vouchers with cash. Customers own the vouchers and manage their accounts using third-party credentials. These credentials are of no concern to Restbucks. This frees Restbucks from the additional workload of user management.

To support the voucher payment scenario, the system shown in Figure 9-7 has been developed.

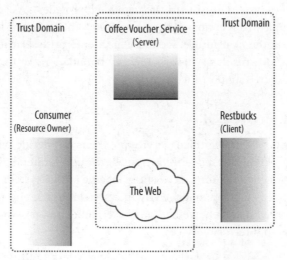

Figure 9-7. *Service provider, consumer, and user roles and existing domains of trust*

The diagram in Figure 9-7 shows the following roles in the OAuth protocol and how they map to Restbucks, its partners, and its customers:

---

* Specifically, OAuth 1.0. See *http://tools.ietf.org/html/rfc5849*.

Server

> The service hosting the protected resources. In our example, the server is the Coffee Voucher service. This voucher service hosts protected coffee vouchers.

Resource owner

> The owner of the protected resources hosted by the server. The resource owner drives the overall workflow. In our example, Restbucks' customers play this role. Trust is established between the resource owner and the server out-of-band, by human agreement, and enforced through mechanisms such as credit cards.

Client

> The service that needs access to the protected resources. Restbucks plays the client role in this example, having first established trust with the voucher service through an out-of-band mechanism.

As the client, Restbucks never sees the credentials that the resource owner shares with the voucher service. Instead, sets of credentials created during the OAuth authorization process are used to access protected resources hosted by the server. OAuth defines three different types of credentials: client, temporary, and token. Each set of credentials comprises a unique identifier and a shared secret. Client credentials are established out-of-band between the server and the client prior to any instance of the OAuth protocol. Temporary credentials are used to bootstrap the OAuth protocol, while token credentials are used to allow access to protected resources once the protocol has completed.

With all the basics in place, it's time to see how it all fits together with an example.

Protocol Example

OAuth is going to play a central role in the vouchers-for-coffee business process, but the process doesn't start with OAuth. Prior to allowing any of its customers to pay with vouchers, Restbucks must establish trust with the voucher service. This trust cuts across two axes. The first is a business-level agreement as to pricing and payment terms. The second is more interesting to us in that it involves Restbucks and the voucher service establishing an electronic domain of trust by sharing a set of client credentials. These credentials comprise a *consumer key* and a *consumer secret*.

> ──── **NOTE** ────────────────────────────────────
>
> Sharing keys and secrets is not part of OAuth. Protocols such as Diffie-Hellman key exchange can be used to establish a shared secret directly between computers. Alternatively, human protocols, such as writing the secret on a piece of paper and sending it by courier, can be used.

Once trust is established, the first business protocol step is the electronic equivalent of looking in our wallets for paper vouchers. In Figure 9-8, we show the customer making an HTTP GET request of the coffee voucher service. Assuming the resource owner is authorized to retrieve a list of vouchers, the service responds with an Atom feed containing a list of valid vouchers for that customer.

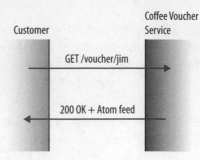

Figure 9-8. *Customer checks for coffee vouchers*

Each Atom entry in the feed contains a link attributed with a coffee voucher link relation, as per Example 9-34.

Example 9-34. *An Atom feed containing available vouchers*

```
<?xml version="1.0" encoding="UTF-8"?>
<feed xmlns="http://www.w3.org/2005/Atom">
 <title>Coffee Vouchers for jim</title>
 <link rel="self" href="http://vouchers.example.org/jim" />
 <author>
  <name>vouchers@example.org</name>
 </author>
 <id>http://vouchers.example.org/jim</id>
 <generator uri="http://vouchers.example.org/">Coffee Voucher Service</generator>
 <updated>2010-04-03T00:20:00Z</updated>
 <entry>
  <title>Coffee Voucher</title>
  <link rel="http://relations.vouchers.example.org/coffee"
  href="http://vouchers.example.org/voucher/jim/1234" />
  <author>
   <name>vouchers@example.org</name>
  </author>
  <id>http://vouchers.example.org/voucher/jim/1234</id>
  <updated>2010-04-03T00:20:50Z</updated>
  <content>Exchange this voucher for a coffee of your choice at your local
  Restbucks store.</content>
 </entry>
 <!-- Many more entries removed for brevity -->
</feed>
```

You may recall from Chapter 5 that Restbucks payments are made by PUTting a credit card payment representation to a URI generated by the service. We use the same approach for vouchers. The customer chooses a voucher from the feed in Example 9-34 and then pays by PUTting the voucher representation to Restbucks, as shown in Example 9-35.

Example 9-35. *Paying with a voucher*

```
PUT /payment/1234 HTTP/1.1
Accept: application/vnd.restbucks+xml
Content-Type: application/vnd.restbucks+xml
User-Agent: Java/1.6.0_17
Host: restbucks.com
Content-Length: 205

<?xml version="1.0" encoding="UTF-8" standalone="yes"?>
<voucherPayment xmlns="http://schemas.restbucks.com">
  <voucherUri>http://vouchers.example.org/voucher/jim/1234</voucherUri>
</voucherPayment>
```

Once the voucher payment has been received, Restbucks can attempt to redeem it with the voucher service. After it's been redeemed, the customer can continue with the order, and Restbucks can instigate a back-office process to bill the voucher service.

This is where OAuth kicks in. Because vouchers are protected with OAuth, Restbucks (the client) must first obtain some temporary credentials from the voucher service (the server). If the customer (the resource owner) and voucher service agree, these temporary credentials can then be exchanged for token credentials, which in turn can be used to redeem vouchers.

Since the OAuth protocol hasn't run at this point, Restbucks has no token credentials with which to redeem the voucher. Because of this, the attempt to redeem the voucher is met with an OAuth challenge from the voucher service, as shown in Figure 9-9.

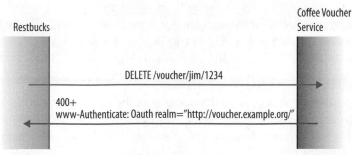

Figure 9-9. *Restbucks fails to authorize and redeem the voucher*

The wire-level view of the failed redemption attempt is shown in Examples 9-36 and 9-37. Restbucks attempts to redeem a voucher by issuing a DELETE against the appropriate voucher resource. The voucher service responds with a 401 Unauthorized response. This response includes a WWW-Authenticate header—a challenge—whose value indicates that the service uses OAuth, and that the realm for which Restbucks must obtain credentials is http://vouchers.example.org/.

Example 9-36. *Restbucks attempts to redeem the voucher*

```
DELETE /voucher/jim/1234 HTTP/1.1
Accept: application/vnd.coffeevoucher+xml
Host: vouchers.example.org
```

Example 9-37. *Voucher service challenges the redemption*

```
HTTP/1.1 401 Unauthorized
WWW-Authenticate: OAuth realm="http://vouchers.example.org/"
Content-Type: application/x-www-form-urlencoded
Date: Sat, 03 Apr 2010 00:27:47 GMT
```

Restbucks answers the voucher service's challenge by POSTing its OAuth client credentials to the service, as shown in Figure 9-10.

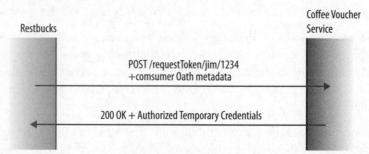

Figure 9-10. *Restbucks responds to authorization challenge by demanding a set of temporary credentials*

The Authorization header value here contains some OAuth metadata. The combination of the metadata and the destination URI triggers the generation of temporary credentials. These OAuth metadata values are important to understand:

oauth_signature *and* oauth_signature_method

> The signature element ensures the integrity of the representation. Using a shared secret (e.g., the consumer secret), the voucher service can determine whether the contents of the request have been tampered with in transit. The signature method

tells the voucher service which algorithm has been used to compute the signature. The service then uses the same algorithm to validate incoming messages.*

oauth_timestamp

The timestamp provides a simple test of message freshness, which the voucher service can use to reject old or out-of-order requests.

oauth_nonce

The nonce is used to uniquely identify the request, thereby preventing replay attacks when transferring representations over insecure channels. The voucher service will honor a request containing a particular nonce only once.

oauth_consumer_key

The client's credentials—comprising a consumer key and consumer secret—were established with the voucher service prior to any OAuth interactions taking place.

oauth_callback

This represents a Restbucks URI to which the voucher service will redirect the customer once the customer has delegated authorization to Restbucks.

oauth_version

This represents an optional entry containing the version of the protocol in use.

The wire-level view of obtaining a set of temporary credentials is shown in Example 9-38.

Example 9-38. Restbucks acquires a set of temporary credentials

```
POST /requestToken/voucher/jim/1234 HTTP/1.1
Accept: application/x-www-form-urlencoded
Authorization: OAuth
oauth_callback="http%3A%2F%2Frestbucks.com%2Fpayment%2F9baea738",
oauth_signature="GHU4a%2Fv9JnvZFTXnRiVf3HqDGfk%3D", oauth_version="1.0",
oauth_nonce="05565e78", oauth_signature_method="HMAC-SHA1",
oauth_consumer_key="light", oauth_timestamp="1270254467"
Host: vouchers.example.org
```

—— NOTE ——

OAuth is permissive about the way protocol messages are transferred between the client and server. Using the HTTP Authorization header is the preferred mechanism, but transferring application/x-www-form-urlencoded data in an entity body or request URI is also permitted (in that order of preference).

Because we're working in a computer-to-computer scenario, we can carefully craft our implementation to follow the preferred approach, which is to use the Authorization header.

---

* In these examples, we have chosen HMAC-SHA-1 to generate signatures. SHA-1 has vulnerabilities that *may* be practical to exploit in the future. There is no problem using SHA-1 for HMAC, however, because the collision-free property isn't important in this use case.

The voucher service determines whether the request in Example 9-38 is valid by verifying the supplied signature using its copy of the consumer secret (which it can find in its trusted store based on the supplied consumer key). If the request can be validated, the voucher service generates a response containing temporary credentials, as shown in Example 9-39.

Example 9-39. *OAuth temporary credentials created*

```
HTTP/1.1 200 OK
Content-Type: application/x-www-form-urlencoded
Content-Length: 79
Date: Sat, 03 Apr 2010 00:27:47 GMT
```

oauth_token=b0c2ec2c&oauth_token_secret=f41eab9d&oauth_callback_confirmed=true

The temporary credentials consist of a temporary token (oauth_token) and a secret (oauth_token_secret). The response also includes an oauth_callback_confirmed parameter, which is there simply to differentiate the response from previous versions of the protocol.

Restbucks stores the oauth_token_secret in case it needs it to sign any future requests for a set of token credentials. Restbucks then redirects the customer to a resource on the voucher service using an HTTP 303 See Other response.

On the wire, this is achieved with an HTTP redirect. Notice how, in Example 9-40, the redirect URI in the Location header contains both the voucher ID (voucher/jim/1234) and the temporary OAuth token (oauth_token=b0c2ec2c) with which Restbucks has just been issued.

Example 9-40. *Redirection for sign-in*

```
HTTP/1.1 303 See Other
Location: http://vouchers.example.org/signIn/voucher/jim/1234?oauth_token=b0c2ec2c
Content-Type: application/vnd.restbucks+xml
Content-Length: 0
Date: Sat, 03 Apr 2010 00:27:47 GMT
```

On receiving the redirect, the customer performs an HTTP GET on the resource identified in the Location header. At this point, the customer must authenticate with the voucher service. Because OAuth does not mandate how services manage login and authorization, we temporarily step outside the OAuth protocol. In our implementation, the response to the redirected GET is an XHTML login form, correctly parameterized for the current resource owner, voucher, and OAuth session, as we can see in Figure 9-11.

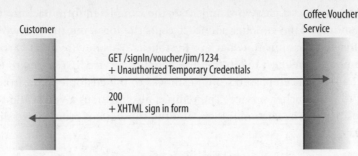

Figure 9-11. *Out-of-band authentication and authorization with the voucher service*

On the wire, the customer's GET request uses an Accept header to request an XHTML representation, as shown in Example 9-41. The voucher service obliges with an XHTML form, as shown in Example 9-42. The form's action attribute contains the URI of the login resource for the voucher that Restbucks wants to access. The form's content includes a hidden <input> element containing the OAuth token to be POSTed back during login.

Example 9-41. *Requesting a sign-in form*

```
GET /signIn/voucher/jim/1234?oauth_token=b0c2ec2c HTTP/1.1
Accept: application/xhtml+xml
Host: vouchers.example.org
```

Example 9-42. *The XHTML sign-in form*

```
HTTP/1.1 200 OK
Content-Type: application/xhtml+xml
Content-Length: 360
Date: Sat, 03 Apr 2010 00:27:47 GMT

<!DOCTYPE html PUBLIC "-//W3C//DTD XHTML 1.0 Transitional//EN"
"http://www.w3.org/TR/xhtml1/DTD/xhtml1-transitional.dtd">
<html xmlns="http://www.w3.org/1999/xhtml">
  <body>
  <form action="http://vouchers.example.org/signIn/voucher/jim/1234"
    method="post">
    <input type="hidden" name="oauth_token" value="b0c2ec2c"/>
    <input type="password" name="password"/>
  </form>
  </body>
</html>
```

The customer provides a password and POSTs the completed form back to the voucher's login resource. If the voucher service accepts the form and the password, it issues another redirect, this time back to Restbucks. This new redirect carries with it the same temporary request token that the voucher service first issued to Restbucks, and which has since been passed from Restbucks to the customer, and from the customer back to the voucher service. The redirect also includes a verification code destined for Restbucks. The customer login and the subsequent redirect are shown in Figure 9-12.

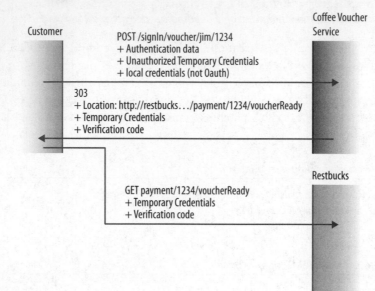

Figure 9-12. *Coffee voucher service authorizes the temporary request token for customer and redirects to Restbucks*

The exchange depicted in Figure 9-12 is shown at the wire level in Examples 9-43, 9-44, and 9-45.

In Example 9-43, the customer sends its credentials to the voucher's login resource, as hosted by the voucher service.* If authorization succeeds, the voucher service responds with a redirect, as shown in Example 9-44.

The redirect is parameterized with the OAuth temporary request token and the verifier that Restbucks will need to obtain a set of token credentials. In Example 9-45, the customer uses the URI in the redirect Location header to GET the notification resource from Restbucks. That GET operation has the side effect of letting Restbucks know the customer has authorized use of the voucher.

---

* In this example, we use HTTP and forms-based authentication for clarity. In a real system on the Web, this interaction should use either HTTPS to guarantee confidentiality, or some other authentication mechanism that is tolerant of insecure channels (e.g., WSSE).

Example 9-43. *Signing in*

```
POST /signIn/voucher/jim/1234 HTTP/1.1
Content-Type: application/x-www-form-urlencoded
Accept: application/xhtml+xml
Host: vouchers.example.org
Content-Length: 68


password=sc00byd00&oauth_token=b0c2ec2c
```

Example 9-44. *Redirecting back to Restbucks*

```
HTTP/1.1 303 See Other
Location: http://restbucks.com/payment/1234/voucherReady?oauth_token=b0c2ec2c
&oauth_verifier=c87677a4
Content-Type: application/x-www-form-urlencoded
Content-Length: 0
Date: Sat, 03 Apr 2010 00:27:47 GMT
```

Example 9-45. *Notifying Restbucks of a successful sign-in*

```
GET /payment/1234/voucherReady?oauth_token=b0c2ec2c&oauth_verifier=c87677a4
HTTP/1.1
Host: restbucks.com
```

The next step in the payment process is for Restbucks to request a set of token credentials from the voucher service. Restbucks does this by POSTing the temporary request token and the verifier it received at its callback URI (in Example 9-45) to the voucher service (see Figure 9-13).

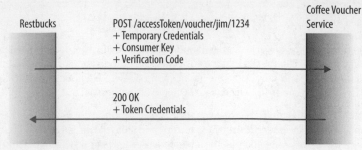

Figure 9-13. *Restbucks exchanges the temporary request token for a set of token credentials*

Restbucks signs its request for a set of token credentials using the oauth_token_secret it received at the outset of the OAuth protocol (the oauth_token_secret is part of the set of temporary credentials received in Example 9-39). On the wire, the request and response are shown in Examples 9-46 and 9-47.

Example 9-46. *Restbucks requests a set of token credentials*

```
POST /accessToken/voucher/jim/1234 HTTP/1.1
Content-Type: application/x-www-form-urlencoded
Authorization: OAuth oauth_signature="m7ials2v0VJuKDO5BrNGISi7Nog%3D",
oauth_version="1.0", oauth_nonce="10d13b8e", oauth_signature_method="HMAC-SHA1",
oauth_consumer_key="light", oauth_verifier="c87677a4", oauth_token="b0c2ec2c",
oauth_timestamp="1270254468"
Host: vouchers.example.org
Accept: application/x-www-form-urlencoded
```

Example 9-47. *Voucher service generates a set of token credentials*

```
HTTP/1.1 200 OK
Content-Type: application/x-www-form-urlencoded
Content-Length: 49
Date: Sat, 03 Apr 2010 00:27:48 GMT

oauth_token=99fe97e1&oauth_token_secret=255ae587
```

The token credentials allow Restbucks to manipulate any of the resources that the voucher service has associated with those credentials. In the general case, sets of token credentials are valid for multiple interactions, which makes sense considering the effort involved in obtaining them! However, our voucher service is restrictive: Restbucks will be allowed to DELETE only a single payment voucher resource per set of token credentials, as we can see in Figure 9-14.

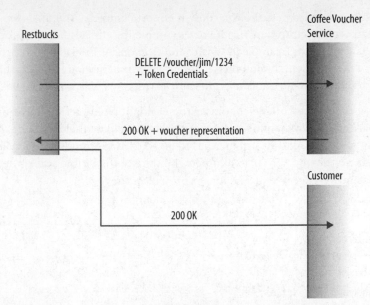

Figure 9-14. Restbucks redeems a voucher and returns control flow to the customer

At the network level, redeeming the voucher in exchange for coffee is a simple DELETE request containing OAuth metadata in the Authorization header. Restbucks computes the signature in Example 9-48 using the token credentials' oauth_token_secret value.

If the voucher service agrees to redeem the voucher, it responds with a 200 OK response and a copy of the voucher state, as per Example 9-49.

Example 9-48. Restbucks redeems a voucher using the access token

```
DELETE /voucher/jim/1234 HTTP/1.1
Accept: application/vnd.coffeevoucher+xml
Authorization: OAuth oauth_signature="k2awEpciJkd2X8rt3NmgDg8AyUo%3D",
oauth_version="1.0", oauth_nonce="9ceea445", oauth_signature_method="HMAC-SHA1",
oauth_consumer_key="light", oauth_token="99fe97e1", oauth_timestamp="1270254468"
Host: vouchers.example.org
```

Example 9-49. Voucher service corroborates the redemption

```
HTTP/1.1 200 OK
Content-Type: application/vnd.coffeevoucher+xml
Content-Length: 252
Date: Sat, 03 Apr 2010 00:27:48 GMT

<?xml version="1.0" encoding="UTF-8" standalone="yes"?>
<link xmlns="http://voucher.example.org/schema"
  mediaType="application/vnd.coffeevoucher+xml"
  uri="http://vouchers.example.org/voucher/jim/1234" rel="voucher"/>
```

With the voucher redeemed, the workflow is almost complete. The final step is to return control to the customer. This involves completing the notification process the customer had started in Example 9-45 (this notification, or callback, had triggered the request for token credentials and the secure voucher redemption). If everything went well, this step is almost an anticlimax: Restbucks responds with a simple 200 OK.

After the workflow has completed, the customer might be interested in seeing how many vouchers it has remaining. It's easy enough to validate that Restbucks has redeemed a voucher. All the customer has to do is GET the Atom feed of available vouchers, as per Example 9-50, and inspect the state of the virtual wallet. Because the voucher has been redeemed, it's no longer present in the feed.*

Example 9-50. *The voucher service has one less voucher*

```
HTTP/1.1 200 OK
Content-Type: application/atom+xml
Content-Length: 977
Date: Sat, 03 Apr 2010 00:27:48 GMT

<?xml version="1.0" encoding="UTF-8"?>
<feed xmlns="http://www.w3.org/2005/Atom">
 <title>Coffee Vouchers for jim</title>
 <link rel="self" href="http://vouchers.example.org/jim" />
 <author>
  <name>vouchers@example.org</name>
 </author>
 <id>http://vouchers.example.org/jim</id>
 <generator uri="http://vouchers.example.org/">Coffee Voucher Service</generator>
 <updated>2010-04-03T00:19:12Z</updated>
 <entry>
  <title>Coffee Voucher</title>
  <link rel="http://relations.vouchers.example.org/coffee"
  href="http://vouchers.example.org/voucher/jim/25983cab" />
  <author>
   <name>vouchers@example.org</name>
  </author>
  <id>http://vouchers.example.org/voucher/jim/25983cab</id>
  <updated>2010-04-03T00:21:20Z</updated>
  <content>Exchange this voucher for a coffee of your choice at your local
  Restbucks store.
  </content>
 </entry>
</feed>
```

---

* Alternatively, we could have added a status flag to the voucher to show that it has been redeemed, or even create a second feed for redeemed vouchers. This is a matter of design taste and doesn't significantly affect the overall solution.

Implementing OAuth in Java

OAuth 1.0a is well supported by vendors and open source efforts across all major development platforms. To demonstrate how to use OAuth, we'll show how to build the example from the preceding section in Java using Jersey* and Jersey-OAuth.[†]

Coffee voucher service

The coffee voucher service plays three roles in the overall solution. Primarily it acts as a virtual wallet, hosting voucher resources that can be used to pay for coffee. It also plays the role of OAuth server, hosting resources for managing temporary and token credentials. Finally, it exposes resources to help customers authorize the use of vouchers. The high-level architecture is presented in Figure 9-15.

Figure 9-15. *Coffee voucher service logical resources*

Each resource in Figure 9-15 is implemented as a Java class with standard JAX-RS annotations. The VoucherResource class shown in Example 9-51 typifies the approach we've chosen.

Example 9-51. *The VoucherResource class*

```
@Path("/voucher")
public class VoucherResource {
  @Context
  private UriInfo uriInfo;

  @GET
  @Path("/{username}")
  @Produces(MediaType.APPLICATION_ATOM_XML)
  public Response vouchersFor(@PathParam("username") String username) {
  String stringifiedFeed = stringify(getVouchersFeedFor(new UserId(username)));
  return addContentLengthHeader(Response.ok().entity(stringifiedFeed),
              stringifiedFeed.getBytes().length).build();
  }
```

---

* *https://jersey.dev.java.net/*

† Jersey-OAuth is a small OAuth library written for Jersey. It provides helpers for signatures and some support for creating client-side filters that inject OAuth metadata into HTTP requests. See *http://download.java.net/maven/2/com/sun/jersey/contribs/jersey-oauth/*.

```
@DELETE
@Path("/{username}/{voucherId}")
@Produces(Representation.COFFEE_VOUCHER_MEDIA_TYPE)
@ResourceFilters(value = {OAuthAuthorizationRequiredFilter.class,
            OAuthAccessTokenRequiredFilter.class,
            OAuthNonceFilter.class})
public Response useVoucher(@PathParam("username") String username,
            @PathParam("voucherId") String voucherId) {
UserId userId = new UserId(username);
Voucher voucher = VoucherStore.current().remove(userId,
                    UUID.fromString(voucherId));

if(voucher == null) {
  return Response.status(Status.NOT_FOUND).build();
}

return Response.ok().entity(voucher.toLink(uriInfo.getRequestUri())).build();
}
    // Other methods elided for brevity
}
```

There are a couple of guards in place to prevent malicious parties from circumventing authorization or subverting the OAuth protocol:

- To obtain a set of temporary credentials, one first needs a shared consumer secret with which to sign requests.

- To obtain a set of token credentials, requests must be signed with the secret from the temporary credentials.

To implement these guards in Jersey, we use the @ResourceFilters annotation to declare preconditions on the execution of various methods within the resource classes. Example 9-51 shows how we've protected the useVoucher(...) method. The @ResourceFilters annotation declares that the OAuth Authorization header (OAuthAuthorizationRequiredFilter), plus a set of token credentials (OAuthAccessTokenRequiredFilter), plus a valid nonce (OAuthNonceRequiredFilter) must be present to trigger dispatch to the useVoucher(...) method.

In general, in our implementation, each resource has zero or more filters associated with it, depending on the protocol preconditions that must be met before the resource can be manipulated. The filters for each resource are shown in Figure 9-16.

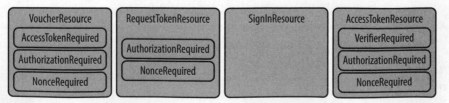

Figure 9-16. *Filters are used to enforce the protocol at runtime*

The OAuthAccessTokenRequiredFilter class shown in Example 9-52 is a typical example of how to separate OAuth protocol concerns from the core business logic using filters.

Example 9-52. *The OAuthAccessTokenRequiredFilter class*

```java
public class OAuthAccessTokenRequiredFilter implements ResourceFilter {

    @Override
    public ContainerRequestFilter getRequestFilter() {
    return new ContainerRequestFilter() {

      public ContainerRequest filter(ContainerRequest cr) {
      HashMap<String, String> oauthValues =
        OauthHeaderHelper.extractOauthParamsFromAuthorizationHeader(
                    cr.getHeaderValue("Authorization"));

      if(!oauthValues.containsKey("oauth_token")) {
        throw new WebApplicationException(
         Response.status(Status.UNAUTHORIZED)
         .type(MediaType.TEXT_PLAIN)
         .entity("No oauth_token in request.").build());
      }

      String oauthToken = oauthValues.get("oauth_token");

      if(!AccessTokenStore.current().containsToken(oauthToken)) {
        throw new WebApplicationException(
         Response.status(Status.UNAUTHORIZED)
         .type(MediaType.TEXT_PLAIN)
         .entity("No matching access token issued.").build());
      }

      return cr;
      }
    };
    }

    // Other methods elided for brevity
}
```

The filter code in Example 9-52 is invoked by Jersey prior to the request reaching a resource class. In the OAuthAccessTokenRequiredFilter class, we check whether the request contains an oauth_token value; if it does, we then check whether that value corresponds to an issued set of token credentials in the access token store. Should either of those tests fail, the request is rejected with a 401 Unauthorized response without being dispatched to the resource for processing.

A similar pattern is used for the OAuthAuthorizationRequiredFilter class. This filter checks that the HTTP Authorization header contains correctly formed and signed OAuth values. The filter code is shown in Example 9-53.

Example 9-53. *The OAuthAuthorizationRequiredFilter class*

```java
public class OAuthAuthorizationRequiredFilter implements ResourceFilter {

  public ContainerRequestFilter getRequestFilter() {
  return new ContainerRequestFilter() {

    public ContainerRequest filter(ContainerRequest cr) {

    String authorizationHeader = cr.getHeaderValue("Authorization");
    ConsumerKey consumerKey = extractConsumerKey(authorizationHeader);
    validateConsumerKey(consumerKey, cr);
    OAuthParameters params = new OAuthParameters();
    OAuthServerRequest request = new OAuthServerRequest(cr);
    params.readRequest(request);

    OAuthSecrets secrets = setupSecretsFor(authorizationHeader, consumerKey);

    try {
      if (!OAuthSignature.verify(request, params, secrets)) {
        throw new WebApplicationException(Response.status(401)
          .entity("Failed to verify signature")
          .type(MediaType.TEXT_PLAIN).build());
      }
    } catch (OAuthSignatureException e) {
      throw new WebApplicationException(e, 500);
    }

    return cr;
    }
    // Other methods elided for brevity
  };
  }
  // Other methods elided for brevity
}
```

Example 9-53 demonstrates the use of some of the server-side Jersey-OAuth components. Specifically, we wrap the underlying request in an OAuthServerRequest instance. This allows us to read the OAuth values into an OAuthParameters instance. We then initialize an OAuthSecrets object with the secrets for the OAuth values in the request, and attempt to validate the signature using the OAuthSignature type.

The Jersey-OAuth components only abstract the underlying cryptographic techniques. This leaves us with quite a bit to implement, including consumer secret storage, policies for token storage and expiration, and the protocol itself.

> **NOTE**
>
> Because implementing a good token store is not trivial, it's common for solutions designers to look to existing middleware to provide OAuth provider functionality. We think this is a sensible thing to do.
>
> Having implemented a basic OAuth provider for the voucher service, however, we can attest that it is possible for regular developers to build and deploy them too.

Restbucks payment service

The payment service is based on the same code we saw back in Chapter 5 in the Restbucks ordering service. This time, however, instead of using credit card details to make payments, we've implemented a voucher version of that code. We've also implemented a notification resource, which allows OAuth callbacks when customers authorize Restbucks to redeem vouchers. The service architecture is shown in Figure 9-17.

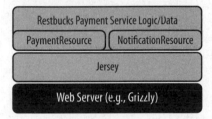

Figure 9-17. *Payment service and its logical resources*

The core of the PaymentResource implementation is shown in Example 9-54. The method's preamble simply validates that there is a corresponding order awaiting payment before then attempting to redeem a voucher.

Example 9-54. *The PaymentResource implementation*

```
@PUT
@Path("/{orderId}")
@Consumes(RESTBUCKS_MEDIA_TYPE)
@Produces(RESTBUCKS_MEDIA_TYPE)
public Response makePayment(@PathParam("orderId") String orderId,
            VoucherPayment voucherPayment) throws Exception {

  Identifier identifier = new Identifier(orderId);
  if (!OrderStore.current().has(identifier)) {
    return Response.status(Status.NOT_FOUND)
```

```
            .type(MediaType.TEXT_PLAIN)
            .entity(String.format("Order [%s] does not exist.",
                uriInfo.getRequestUri().toString())))
            .build();
    }

    Status voucherRedeemed = Status.fromStatusCode(
                    redeemVoucher(voucherPayment).getStatus());

    if (voucherRedeemed == Status.OK) {
        // Unsecured vouchers, free money on the Internet!
        PaymentStore.current().store(identifier, voucherPayment);
        return Response.created(new URI(
            uriInfo.getBaseUri().toString() + "payment/" + orderId))
            .entity(voucherPayment).build();
    } else if (voucherRedeemed == Status.UNAUTHORIZED) {
        PendingPaymentStore.current().store(identifier, voucherPayment);

        URI requestTokenUri = lookupRequestTokenUriFor(voucherPayment);
        RequestToken rt = obtainRequestTokenFor(requestTokenUri);
        RequestTokenStore.current().store(rt);

        URI loginUri = lookupLoginUriFor(voucherPayment);
        URI redirectUri = UriBuilder.fromUri(loginUri)
                        .queryParam("oauth_token", rt.getToken()).build();

        return Response.seeOther(redirectUri)
            .type(MediaType.APPLICATION_FORM_URLENCODED).build();
    }
    return Response.status(Status.BAD_REQUEST).build();
}
```

If Restbucks has not yet started the OAuth protocol for this payment, the attempt to redeem a voucher by DELETEing the voucher resource fails with a 401 Unauthorized challenge. This causes the payment service first to store a new entry in the pending payments store, and then to begin the OAuth protocol.

At the outset of the protocol, Restbucks must resolve the URI where temporary credentials for the current voucher can be requested. This information may come from the voucher itself, or perhaps be stored as part of the trust arrangement that is created when Restbucks and a voucher service choose to partner.

Once the URI for requesting temporary credentials has been resolved, Restbucks calls obtainRequestTokenFor(...) to obtain a set of temporary credentials (we'll look at this method shortly). Having obtained the necessary credentials, Restbucks then redirects the customer to authorize voucher access at the voucher service.

Before we look at what happens after the customer has authorized voucher access, let's examine obtainRequestTokenFor(...), a private method for obtaining a set of temporary credentials as shown in Example 9-55.

Example 9-55. *Requesting a set of temporary credentials*

```
private RequestToken obtainRequestTokenFor(URI requestTokenUri) {
  ClientConfig cc = new DefaultClientConfig();
  cc.getClasses().add(RequestTokenProvider.class);

  Client client = Client.create(cc);

  URI callbackUri = UriBuilder.fromUri(uriInfo.getRequestUri())
              .path("voucherReady").build();

  client.addFilter(
    clientFilterForRequestTokenExchange(requestTokenUri, callbackUri));

  ClientResponse response = client.resource(requestTokenUri)
              .accept(MediaType.APPLICATION_FORM_URLENCODED)
              .post(ClientResponse.class);

  if(response.getStatus() == 200) {
    return response.getEntity(RequestToken.class);
  }

  if(response.getStatus() == 401) {
    throw new WebApplicationException(
        Response.status(Status.UNAUTHORIZED).build());
  }

  throw new WebApplicationException(Response.serverError().build());
}
```

There's a little housekeeping code toward the start of Example 9-55 where we register the RequestTokenProvider class with the Jersey client. Registering this provider means any OAuth temporary credentials we receive from the voucher service will be automatically translated into usable objects.

The next housekeeping task is to register a client filter to handle the creation of the OAuth Authorization header on our behalf. The clientFilterForRequestToken-Exchange(...) method generates such a filter, using the preexisting consumer secret to sign any outgoing requests. Finally, the temporary credentials are requested through a normal Jersey client call to client.resource(...).post(...).

That's the temporary credentials out of the way. Continuing with the payment service's view of the protocol, we can now look at what happens after the customer has authorized use of a voucher (we'll look at the customer's part in the protocol in the next section). As you may remember from the protocol description earlier in this chapter, after the customer has authorized voucher access with the voucher service, the voucher service redirects the customer back to the payment service's notification URI. This triggers the final phase of the OAuth protocol, including voucher redemption, as per Example 9-56.

Example 9-56. *Dealing with the authorization notification*

```
@GET
@Path("/{orderId}/voucherReady")
public Response notifyUserAuthorization(@PathParam("orderId") String id,
                @QueryParam("oauth_token") String requestToken,
                @QueryParam("oauth_verifier") String verifier)
                    throws Exception {

  Identifier orderId = new Identifier(id);
  if (!OrderStore.current().has(orderId) ||
      !PendingPaymentStore.current().has(orderId)) {
    return Response.status(Status.NOT_FOUND).build();
  }

  VoucherPayment pendingVoucherPayment =
          PendingPaymentStore.current().get(orderId);

  OAuthVerifier oauthVerifier = new OAuthVerifier(verifier);
  AccessToken accessToken = obtainAccessToken(
              lookupAccessTokenUriFor(pendingVoucherPayment),
              RequestTokenStore.current()
              .getToken(requestToken), oauthVerifier);
  AccessTokenStore.current().store(accessToken,
                  pendingVoucherPayment.getVoucherUri());

  ClientResponse response = securelyRedeemVoucher(pendingVoucherPayment,
                    accessToken);

  Status voucherRedeemed = Status.fromStatusCode(response.getStatus());

  if(voucherRedeemed == Status.OK) {
    return Response.ok().build();
  } else if(voucherRedeemed == Status.UNAUTHORIZED) {
    return Response.status(Status.UNAUTHORIZED).build();
  } else {
    return Response.serverError().build();
  }
}
```

```
private AccessToken obtainAccessToken(URI accessTokenUri,
                    RequestToken requestToken) {
    ClientConfig cc = new DefaultClientConfig();
    cc.getClasses().add(AccessTokenProvider.class);

    Client client = Client.create(cc);
    client.addFilter(clientFilterForAccessTokenExchange(
            accessTokenUri, requestToken, verifier));
    ClientResponse response = client.resource(accessTokenUri)
            .type(MediaType.APPLICATION_FORM_URLENCODED)
            .accept(MediaType.APPLICATION_FORM_URLENCODED)
            .post(ClientResponse.class);

    return response.getEntity(AccessToken.class);
}

private ClientResponse securelyRedeemVoucher(VoucherPayment voucherPayment,
                                    AccessToken accessToken) {
    URI voucherUri = voucherPayment.getVoucherUri();
    Client client = Client.create();
    client.addFilter(
            clientFilterForSecureRedeemVoucherExchange(voucherUri, accessToken));
    return client.resource(voucherUri)
        .accept("application/vnd.coffeevoucher+xml").delete(ClientResponse.class);
}
```

If the guard logic at the top of this method passes, Restbucks tries to trade its tempo-rary credentials for a set of token credentials. The obtainAccessToken(...) method encapsulates this activity, including the production of the Authorization header signed with the temporary credential's secret.

Once a set of token credentials has been procured, Restbucks uses it to securely redeem the voucher. The securelyRedeemVoucher(...) method encapsulates this activity, taking the token from the token credentials and using it to populate and sign the Authorization header for the DELETE request sent to the voucher's URI.

All that remains once the voucher has been redeemed is to let the customer know the outcome of the notification by returning a 200 OK, 401 Unauthorized, or 500 Server Error status code.

Restbucks customer

In contrast to the client (Restbucks) and server (voucher service) roles in OAuth, the resource owner (customer) role is very straightforward to implement. It just needs to be able to select a voucher and lodge payments with Restbucks, sign in to the voucher service, and deal with any redirections it encounters. The (skeletal) code in Example 9-57 shows an implementation of the necessary resource owner logic.

Example 9-57. *Resource owner implementation*

```
// Choose a voucher, submit it to Restbucks
Identifier orderId = RestbucksServiceHelper.createCoffeeOrder();
URI orderUri = new URI(RestbucksServiceHelper.SERVICE_URI + "payment/" +
                        orderId.toString());

VoucherPayment payment = new VoucherPayment(voucherUri);

Client client = Client.create();
ClientResponse response = client.resource(orderUri).entity(payment)
                            .accept(PaymentResource.RESTBUCKS_MEDIA_TYPE)
                            .type(PaymentResource.RESTBUCKS_MEDIA_TYPE)
                            .put(ClientResponse.class);

// Client will be redirected to an XHTML form

XhtmlForm form = new XhtmlForm(response.getEntity(String.class));
form.getFirstPasswordElement().setValue("supertopsecretpassword");

ClientResponse response = client.resource(form.getActionUri())
                                .entity(form.toUrlEncoded())
                                .type(MediaType.APPLICATION_FORM_URLENCODED)
                                .accept(MediaType.APPLICATION_XHTML_XML)
                                .post(ClientResponse.class);

// Client will be redirected to Restbucks

if(response.getStatus() != 200) {
  // Report the failure
}
```

Although the resource owner code in Example 9-57 is short, it is complete from a protocol perspective. The Jersey `Client` type handles much of the hard work (the redirects) for us, and so all we have to do is to PUT a voucher to pay and complete an XHTML form to authorize access to a voucher. Everything else is handled through HTTP redirection by the Jersey framework.

Practical Considerations for OAuth

OAuth is a popular protocol on the Web. Although it has historically been used for browser-based systems, it is also suitable for programmatic use. The frameworks we used provide the basic cryptography and network plumbing to make OAuth services a reality for regular developers. For those who prefer packages, vendor and open source products are available for OAuth servers.

OAuth 1.0 is now an Internet RFC (RFC 5849). OAuth 2.0 is due toward the end of 2010, with specific flows for web applications, desktop applications, mobile phones, and domestic devices. OAuth 2.0 will not be backward-compatible with version 1.0, however; the parameters are different, and there are many terminological differences.

Service Hacks and Defenses

The protocols we've seen so far in this chapter form an important pillar in securing *interactions* between services. But good security extends not just to the network, but also to service implementations. To be dependable, a service must tolerate various abuses that it is likely to encounter on the Web and deal with those threats gracefully. In the following sections, we outline five important security themes for building dependable services that will survive production.

Denial of Service

It can be hard to distinguish between a genuine consumer interaction and a malicious request. In the normal course of operations, customers submit many successful orders to Restbucks each second, most of which are innocuous.

> **NOTE**
>
> A common attack vector is to overwhelm a service with many requests, thereby causing a denial-of-service attack. Such attacks are best prevented by operations specialists analyzing traffic at the network layer. We're not going to focus any further on the network layer. In this section, we'll cover only those attacks that specifically pertain to service implementations.

While the majority of well-formed requests will likely be legitimate coffee orders, it is possible to craft a perfectly valid order representation that is nonetheless capable of causing mischief. Imagine the problems caused if a malicious consumer crafted a very large representation, such as that in Example 9-58, and POSTed it to Restbucks.

Example 9-58. A large representation crafted to cause denial of service

```
POST /order HTTP/1.1
Host: restbucks.com
Content-Type:application/vnd.restbucks+xml

<order xmlns="http://schemas.restbucks.com/order">
  <location>takeAway</location>
  <item>
  <name>latte</name>
  <quantity>1</quantity>
```

```
    <milk>whole</milk>
    <size>small</size>
    </item>
    <item>
    <name>cappuccino</name>
    <quantity>1</quantity>
    <milk>skim</milk>
    <size>small</size>
    </item>
    <!-- Millions more item elements -->
    <item>
    <name>latte</name>
    <quantity>1</quantity>
    <milk>skim</milk>
    <size>small</size>
    </item>
  </order>
```

At the outset, when the Restbucks ordering service accepts and begins processing the request shown in Example 9-58, everything looks normal. Apart from a missing Content-Length header, the XML appears well formed and valid. The only problem—as the service is about to find out—is that the representation is insanely large! At some point, a sufficiently large representation will consume all the memory available to the service.

NOTE

Whether through sloppy techniques, such as loading an entire XML representation into a DOM representation before processing, or simply by instantiating domain objects in response to processing events, the result of processing a maliciously large representation is the same: out of memory.

If the service runs out of memory, it will cause a slowdown (at best) and a denial of service (at worst) for other consumers. If the implementation has not been developed with such attacks in mind, resuming normal service may even require a restart.

Frustratingly, the Content-Length header might not help defend against these simple attacks, even if it is present. Where it is present and is suspiciously large (this would be rare; hackers aren't normally sloppy), representations can be dropped early in the processing life cycle, before they can do any damage.

A more realistic scenario is one in which the web server drops any representation whose size does not correspond to the Content-Length header. If we establish a policy whereby the service will accept representations up to a reasonable content length (which may be a few megabytes at most for Restbucks), any larger representations can be dropped before they have a chance to do too much damage.

If the Content-Length header is missing, we're in a quandary. The permissive thing to do is to accept the representation and assume it's just a poorly conformant consumer. The secure—and most likely correct—thing to do is to immediately cease processing the representation and respond with 411 Length Required instead.

To make things a little more complex, consumers can also use chunked transfer encoding.* To use chunked transfer encoding, a consumer sets the request header to Transfer-Encoding: chunked. Chunking a message allows the consumer to stream a request of unknown length to the service. Unless your service trusts the consumer, it's wise to reject chunked requests with 411 Length Required.

To defend against large payload attacks, you should test your web server. The HTTP specification says that compliant systems *should* use the Content-Length header—but it's not mandatory. If your web server is ambivalent about these potentially malicious representations, you'll have to code your own defenses at the application layer.

Writing defensive code in modern web frameworks is straightforward. Most frameworks provide hooks into the various processing stages of a request, allowing you to insert checks early in the processing life cycle. If the inbound request seems suspicious, it can be rejected before it does any real damage.

Sometimes, despite your best efforts, an attack will succeed, and a malicious payload will make it into your service. But we're not helpless, even here. Provided our service implementation doesn't allow an exception to be thrown while servicing one request to shut down the entire service, we can always reject the offending consumer and continue processing for others.

> **——— WARNING ———————————————————————————————————————**
>
> Unhandled exceptions should not be allowed to percolate to the top of the stack. Problems such as OutOfMemoryError in Java or OutOfMemoryException in .NET should be handled by the service gracefully—even if that means swallowing the exception and restarting the process.

When dealing with a malicious request, it's important not to leak information to an attacker—even when the service is under severe stress. For example, don't let an exception find its way into a response—that's just more ammunition to an attacker. Instead, either immediately terminate the connection (at the TCP level if at all possible), or return a 400 Bad Request response code. In both cases, you should log the stack trace to help forensic investigations after the fact.

---

* Usually chunking is used by services to efficiently stream large responses to a consumer over a persistent underlying TCP connection.

Keep Secrets Secret

Security through obscurity is a poor strategy by itself, but that doesn't mean a service should be liberal with the information it gives out. We've already discussed how a service should keep its internal structure private by not allowing implementation details (such as exceptions) to be rendered in responses, but we can go further.

Services and consumers coordinate their interactions based on a shared understanding of the semantics of HTTP's status codes. In certain circumstances, however, a service might respond with a more general status code so as to avoid giving too much information away. Consider a scenario in which a possible attacker is probing the resources hosted by a service. Imagine, for example, that by some cunning means an attacker has obtained or reverse-engineered the internal URI templates for the Restbucks payments and ordering services: `http://restbucks.com/payment/{payment_id}` and `http://restbucks.com/order/{order_id}`.

Recall from Chapter 5 that once a payment is lodged, the service no longer allows it to be manipulated by consumers. Instead, the service responds with `405 Method Not Allowed` to requests for a valid payment, and with `404 Not Found` to requests for payments that do not exist. Although this might seem innocuous enough to us, that information is helpful to attackers: a `405` response allows an attacker to infer the URI of orders, and thereafter meddle with them, whereas a `404` response does not.

In these cases, we might choose to trade expressiveness for security. The `405` response indicates that a resource exists, as well as indicating that the consumer can't use any of the HTTP verbs to interact with it at this moment. The information here doesn't help legitimate consumers, but it does give malicious agents a peek into the service. As such, we might consider always responding with `404 Not Found` should *any* consumer try to interact with a payment resource once it's been created.

> **NOTE**
>
> Defaulting to a `404 Not Found` response is commonplace on the Web in situations where a consumer can't make any forward progress. We can adopt the same approach for our web services, using `404` to indicate simply that no further action is allowed; in many circumstances, we'd rather do this than give away more specific details (such as would be conveyed by `401`, `405`, `409`, or `413`), any of which might give an attacker a useful glimpse into the state of the service.

The same principle applies even if we enforce authorization for payment resources. Normally, an unauthenticated consumer receives a `401 Unauthorized` response to a payment request, but this suggests that a resource is available, and it allows an attacker to make inferences about other resources. Again, a `404 Not Found` response is safer in this situation.

─── **NOTE** ───────────────────────────────────────

There's a trade-off here. Sometimes a 401 challenge is used to bootstrap a more secure interaction. For example, HTTP Digest authentication uses information in a 401 response to set up future secure interactions. Similarly, our OAuth example (Figure 9-9) is bootstrapped by a 401 response.

One strategy here is simply to reduce the attack surface by responding with 401 for entry points into a service, and 404 where we want to hide the existence of otherwise secure resources.

All of the above is predicated on an attacker being able to deduce a URI from the Restbucks URI structure. For humans this is quite simple, since we've designed the Restbucks URI structure for expressiveness, and we've even documented it in this book! Nonetheless, it doesn't take a genius to infer Restbucks URI generation rules and then put that knowledge to mischievous uses.

One way of preventing attackers from guessing the URIs associated with a live DAP is to scramble those readable URIs into something much more opaque. Because Restbucks and its customers are agnostic to the actual URI structure, this scrambling can be done transparently. As we can see in Example 9-59, a link's semantics are in the `rel` attribute, not the `uri` attribute; this allows us to supply opaque URIs while maintaining semantic clarity.

Example 9-59. *Using unguessable URIs in the ordering and payment protocol*

```
<order xmlns="http://schemas.restbucks.com/order"
  xmlns:dap="http://schemas.restbucks.com/dap">
  <location>takeAway</location>
  <item>
  <name>latte</name>
  <quantity>1</quantity>
  <milk>whole</milk>
  <size>small</size>
  </item>
  <cost>2.0</cost>
  <status>unpaid</status>

  <!-- Restbucks Domain Application Protocol -->
  <dap:link rel="http://relations.restbucks.com/payment"
    uri="https://restbucks.com/a/d77620fe-9dad-14d1-87bc-de432fdc9841"
    mediaType="application/vnd.restbucks+xml"/>
  <dap:link rel="http://relations.restbucks.com/latest"
    uri="https://restbucks.com/b/8877ef49-774c-11bc-bbce-abf47e0923fe"
    mediaType="application/vnd.restbucks+xml"/>
  <dap:link rel="http://relations.restbucks.com/update"
    uri="https://restbucks.com/b/8877ef49-774c-11bc-bbce-abf47e0923fe"
    mediaType="application/vnd.restbucks+xml"/>
```

```
<dap:link rel="http://relations.restbucks.com/cancel"
    uri="https://restbucks.com/b/8877ef49-774c-11bc-bbce-abf47e0923fe"
    mediaType="application/vnd.restbucks+xml"/>
</order>
```

By using hard-to-guess URIs, we make it difficult for attackers to infer valid URIs.*
In this way, we prevent attackers outside the network path between a consumer
and Restbucks from interrupting other consumers' workflows. However, software
agents (proxies, routers, etc.) that are on the network path between a consumer and
Restbucks will see the opaque URIs; these agents will therefore still be able to interfere
with the service. To thwart this last attack vector, techniques to ensure confidentiality
(e.g., HTTPS) must be used to make the approach robust.

NOTE

Notice that even though we've used UUIDs to generate opaque URIs, we've still
retained a degree of structure. Payment URIs begin with /a/, while order URIs start
with /b/. This small amount of structure allows us to dispatch requests efficiently
inside the service (by matching against the URI templates http://restbucks.com/b/
{payment_uuid} and http://restbucks.com/b/{order_uuid}, respectively).
Alternatively, to dispatch requests to handler code, we might use a mapping table
to map URIs to resource handlers.

Act Defensively

Web-facing services are subject to the most hostile computing environment on the
planet: the Internet. As such, we have to assume the worst, and program defensively
within our services.

We've already discussed how attackers might try to compromise our systems using
large payloads, and thought through some responses to that threat. Dangerous payloads
aren't always so obvious, however—at least to machines, as we can see in
Example 9-60.

Example 9-60. *A representation containing a malicious value*

```
<order xmlns="http://schemas.restbucks.com/order">
  <location>takeAway</location>
  <item>
  <name>latte</name>
  <quantity>2147483648</quantity>
```

---

* If we use a strong UUID generation algorithm (e.g., pseudorandom) as the basis for creating URIs,
the chance of an attacker guessing a URI in use is infinitesimally small. For illustration, if an attacker generates 1 billion UUID-based URIs every second for the next 100 years, the probability of
creating just one matching a Restbucks URI would be about 50%. When you consider that Restbucks URIs are relatively short-lived, they're highly unlikely to be guessed in a useful time frame.

```
<milk>whole</milk>
<size>small</size>
</item>
...
</order>
```

Although an order of just over 2^{16} café lattes would be quite lucrative if true, in all probability this payload is meant to disrupt the ordering service by causing an integer overflow. In this case, the attacker intends to create an order with a negative number of coffees (due to wraparound), hoping to cause unexpected exceptions, which it can then exploit.

Annoying as it is, this attack can be easily prevented with a simple business rule that constrains the valid quantity of coffees to something reasonable (for retail), such as greater than 0 but less than 50.

Representations aren't the only attack vector that attackers might exploit. URIs themselves can present vulnerabilities if we haven't built services defensively. For example, attackers might wish to access our service's configuration files, or worse, the line-of-business databases that support it (which is especially true of the Restbucks payment service). In Example 9-61, we see a GET request that has been crafted to steal the password file from a service hosted on a Unix server.

Example 9-61. *Probing the service with relative URIs*

```
GET /order/../../../../etc/passwd HTTP/1.1
Host: restbucks.com
```

The attack in Example 9-61 will succeed if we are lax on two fronts:

- The service does not validate URI paths, constraining them to legal URIs for resources in the service implementation.

- The user under which the service runs has read access to the file being targeted by the attacker (in this instance, the password file).

This attack is easily thwarted, yet in a pressurized environment, where software must be delivered and deployed rapidly, such obvious security measures are easily missed.

Another attack that uses carefully crafted URIs is one designed to cause a denial of service rather than obtain information.* Imagine that an attacker figures out the relative path of the root directory on a Unix system and issues a GET request such as the one shown in Example 9-62.

---

* See *http://code.google.com/edu/submissions/web_security/listing.html* for a fascinating discussion of this technique.

Example 9-62. *Using relative URIs to cause a denial-of-service attack*

```
GET /order/../../../../dev/random HTTP/1.1
Host: restbucks.com
```

The device /dev/random on Unix systems provides a continuous stream of random(ish) bytes when read. This means that any process—including a service—reading from that location will never stop. In the worst case, this could once again use up available memory on the server and so cause a denial of service.

Although we don't have to use sophisticated frameworks to develop web services, such frameworks help immensely when dealing with this type of threat. WCF and Jersey, for example, validate URIs in ways that typically prevent such attacks from succeeding—all without additional developer effort.

> **WARNING**
>
> Even if we build services atop frameworks that validate URIs on our behalf, it doesn't always mean we're safe. To further reduce risk, we suggest creating some malicious test scripts that mimic the attacks we've outlined. These scripts should be automated and run as part of deployment testing. Executing these tests provides some confidence that at least the simple hacks are defended against.

Less Is Best

Often, the perfect place for a security exploit to hide is deep in mountains of code that is rarely or never used. These are the corners of your codebase that haven't been exposed to the cleansing light of continuous testing and improvement, and have instead been left to fester, waiting for an opportunity to wreak havoc.

But where does this code come from? The answer, unfortunately, is from our own ingenuity. All too often, a feature will be implemented in software that development teams simply *guess* may be useful in the future. The feature is developed and then waits for its moment of glory, at which point all the preplanning miraculously pays off. That's the theory at least. In practice, many speculative features are forgotten about and never used.

This speculative code is like a tumor. It might be benign or remain forever undiscovered. Or it might be malignant and become active when an attacker happens across it. Either way, it constitutes an unnecessary, but entirely avoidable, security risk.

We're not going to extol the virtues of agile software development here, though we tend to favor those techniques. However, in order to reduce the attack surface of a service, the simplest thing we can do is to *write less code*. In writing less code, we still need to meet the service's business objectives. To that end, we advocate building only immediately useful features, while at all times leaving the service implementation in a state that can be rapidly evolved to meet new requirements.*

> ─── **NOTE** ─────────────────────────────────────
> Be agile about delivering against requirements for your service, including validation code to support current requirements. Only deliver what you know consumers want now: build less code, and be more secure.

Security-centric code can itself, ironically, become a weakness in our solutions. Since security code is often complicated and intricate, there's a risk that we regular developers simply get it wrong, and inadvertently create a new attack vector for some malicious party to exploit.

We should be proportionate when securing services. For example, we might apply HTTP-level (HTTPS, OAuth) security widely in a healthcare or financial setting, whereas for Restbucks we might secure only the payment-related resources. In both cases, we still use as little code/infrastructure/configuration as possible to get the job done.

Defend in Depth

Although we maintain that less is better from a security point of view, this doesn't mean we object to classical layered security architectures, simply that we want to maintain simplicity in each layer. Many enterprise systems fall foul of this, believing that HTTPS solves security, and that a large lock on the front door is enough to foil any hackers. Plainly, it is not enough, but such complacency can prove to be an effective attack vector.

> ─── **NOTE** ─────────────────────────────────────
> Remember that SSL (which underpins HTTPS) doesn't concern itself with human notions of security; it only helps with confidentiality and integrity.

Securing certain resources with HTTPS is a good first step toward protecting services. However, good in-depth defense demands more layers. In a production environment, we need to secure all layers of the stack, starting with the network.

For web-based systems, this task can be achieved by using firewalls. Because common web protocols run on well-known ports, a firewall can block traffic on other ports that might otherwise offer attackers a glimpse of less secure services running on the service's servers. The default choice is to open TCP ports 80 (for HTTP) and 443 (for HTTPS), and to block everything else. This applies equally to hardware firewalls, which sit on the physical perimeter of a network, and to software firewalls hosted by servers.

---

* This typically means good unit test coverage to ensure design integrity of the system as it evolves, and a good suite of functional tests to ensure that the functionality—including security provisions—of the service is maintained.

> **WARNING**
>
> Web services can listen on any port. Just remember that when moving from port 80 (or 443) to a service-specific port, you are adding complexity into the firewall configuration. That complexity needs to be managed; otherwise, your firewall becomes a string vest!

Having secured the network, we can turn to the servers. Good system administration hygiene is critically important here. If the service's outer defenses are compromised, we need to restrict access internally so as to limit damage. In practice, this means running the service at the lowest possible user level. In the event of a successful attack, the attacker is sandboxed by lowly privileges on the server.

> **WARNING**
>
> Never run a service as root or administrator. If you do so, successful attackers may be able to cause far more damage than if you had run the service with low privileges.

It's worth reiterating here: good deployment hygiene is important. We have already discussed how attackers might craft URIs to extract useful configuration files or databases through a service interface. To prevent these kinds of attacks, ensure that configuration files and databases are in a separate directory structure to the main service implementation.

Of course, all the other security practices that we know from the WWW are still valid for service-oriented systems. Enforcing strong passwords (or certificates) and checking logs for suspicious activity are sensible procedures. But social engineering techniques need defenses too. Don't allow your production network to be accessed from poorly secured wireless networks; wardrivers *will* thwart your Internet-facing defenses. Don't share knowledge of critical passwords widely or encode them directly into build/deploy scripts. And remind engineers that the free USB key they were given by a nice guy at the drive-through probably shouldn't go anywhere near a computer!

This is all common sense, yet it's easy to forget about the simple, obvious aspects of security while implementing clever things such as OAuth and bilateral certificate exchanges over HTTPS. But attackers will always work toward finding your weakest point, whether that is in the network, in the service, or in the people who run your system.

> **WARNING**
>
> Don't be so blindsided by web security that you neglect physical security and social engineering.

Final Thoughts

Security is a multifaceted problem, and one that constantly evolves in the presence of new threats and countermeasures. While the protocols and strategies outlined in this chapter are a good start, service developers must remain vigilant, particularly if services are exposed outside the relative safety of the enterprise IT environment.

Even in the enterprise, however, we still favor web-based approaches to security. The methods we've studied in this chapter have been forged in the wilds of the Internet by a large community of security specialists, and successfully validated by millions of users over many years. If these techniques can tolerate and thrive in a hostile environment like the Web, there is every reason to believe they will work well in the relatively safe environs behind the corporate firewall!

CHAPTER TEN

Semantics

WHEN BUILDING DISTRIBUTED APPLICATIONS ON THE WEB, you'll see one thing is clear: document formats matter. The meaning, or *semantics*, behind the data and information in a document must be understood by both parties in an interaction in order to successfully achieve a business goal.

This chapter explores some of the possibilities raised by the advent of semantic technologies. It focuses on data, information, and the technologies that have emerged to help in integration scenarios. *Semantics* and *Semantic Web* are popular terms; here we show how they apply both to the example of Restbucks and more generally to building distributed systems on the Web. We'll also briefly explore some popular technologies from the Semantic Web, including RDF and SPARQL.

Syntax Versus Semantics

Most distributed computing models enforce the structural or *syntactic* correctness of a system's APIs and messages using interface or contract definition languages and message schemas. The semantics of these structural elements, however, is usually communicated through some other mechanism—typically a natural language specification. From a syntactic point of view, a `<cost>2.0</cost>` element is as good as an `<a11119eb>2.0</a11119eb>` element, just so long as both conform to the schema defined by the service provider. The difference is that the former is immediately meaningful to a human developer of an application, whereas the latter requires some interpretation—most likely involving reading a specification document.

> ── **NOTE** ───
>
> Of course, the implied semantics of a human-readable document element, opera-
> tion, or operation name can sometimes be misleading—as many of us know all too
> well. How many times have you come across a method whose implementation is
> entirely at odds with its name? What would you make of a document element that
> is entirely in conformance with a message schema, but which reads `<cost>In
> store</cost>`?

Throughout this book, we've suggested that applications need to agree on the way
information is encoded, structured, and represented. With distributed systems, however, individual services need to have a common understanding of how to *interpret* the
(structurally correct) information they exchange so as to ensure meaningful interactions. Our use of link relations to provide semantic context for a hypermedia control
takes us a small way toward creating this common understanding. The introduction of
contracts in Chapter 5 further addressed this requirement, but unsatisfactorily required
some level of human involvement.

We believe there is little chance of real machine automation unless we can somehow
enrich these contracts for machines. Today, there is a great deal of interest in how information can be represented and explicitly exposed in a way that allows (some parts of)
its semantics to be understood and processed by machines. But before we can approach
building systems with Semantic Web technology, we need to understand a little theory.

Structure and Representation of Information

Throughout this chapter, we distinguish between the *structure* and *representation* of information. While the former is about the relationship between the different information
pieces that make up the details of a document, concept, or business entity, the latter is
about choices in representing that information. The choice of representation might have
a significant impact on our ability to share the information in an interoperable manner.

Data, Information, Knowledge

The terms *data*, *information*, and *knowledge* are often encountered in discussions related to
semantics. Here we'll explain what we mean by these terms. Though you may find them
used differently elsewhere, we've tried to align ourselves with more popular definitions.*

We use the term *data* to refer to the raw, uninterpreted bits that make up a business entity (e.g., an invoice, a receipt, the customer details).† We call *information* the
interpretation of data within the context of a particular application domain (e.g., the
contents of the `<milk>` element in a Restbucks order when interpreted as a customer's

---

* *http://en.wikipedia.org/wiki/DIKW*

† We are not just referring to the 0s and 1s of the binary system. A series of characters, or a collection of numbers without any way to interpret them within a particular context, is still "data."

choice of milk). Finally, *knowledge* represents our understanding of a domain after we collect, analyze, and reason over the available data and information.

The result of this reasoning is a set of information facts—knowledge—that we can use to make business decisions. Knowledge can be explicitly recorded, or it can be inferred, or probabilistically assumed, based on analysis such as "Paul is a valued Restbucks customer because he buys coffee every day."

Data can contain different layers of information. For example, a PNG image on the Web is represented as a series of bits in a file. A software agent can interpret the raw data and produce (and manipulate) a visual representation of that image only if it understands the PNG specification. We can interpret the visual depiction of the image as the "information" hidden inside the raw "data" (e.g., a photograph of a car). However, in the context of a different application or user, the same PNG image may convey different information because of some additional context. For example, the statement "this is a photograph of my Ferrari" may be inferred from the same photograph because the person recognizes the car as being a Ferrari, and that it belongs to the person (probably due to a unique characteristic or because of the origin of the photograph).

The cognitive transition from "data" to "information" is dependent on an application's requirements and on the context in which the data is interpreted. That context may be implicit (e.g., a common understanding and experience, such as our familiarity with a sports car's appearance) or explicitly recorded (e.g., the specification of the Restbucks domain application protocol, or DAP). In many cases, the interpretation of data and information may even be subjective.

Turning aside from philosophical discussion about data and information, let's see how semantics might relate to our efforts to build the Restbucks coffee service.* Example 10-1 shows a possible representation of a coffee order.

Example 10-1. *An order as a sequence of characters*

```
ta:latte,q1,m1,s12:cookie,k1,q2
```

Without some additional context or explanation, it's practically impossible for anyone to interpret the data in Example 10-1 as a customer's order (even though we made things easier using ASCII characters instead of binary). At first glance, it looks like a series of meaningless characters. If, however, we were to record the thought process that accompanied the creation of the data, or the algorithmic process that one needs to follow in order to decode the information behind the data, the string of Example 10-1 no longer appears to be a random collection of characters; it becomes instead an order for a take-away coffee and two cookies.

---

* See Sowa's "Knowledge Representation: Logical, Philosophical, and Computational Foundations," and Brachman's and Levesque's "Knowledge Representation and Reasoning" for more information on the subject—or many books on related areas of philosophy such as epistemology.

Structure

As it happens, the string in Example 10-1 represents a Restbucks order:

- The order is to be taken away (ta).

- The first item ordered is a latte with the following details:

  — Quantity: 1 (q1)

  — Milk: whole (m1)

  — Size: 12oz (s12)

- The second item is a cookie with the following details:

  — Quantity: 2 (q2)

  — Kind: chocolate chip (k1)

It's clear that there is a lot of context not explicitly recorded in the order's representation. The set of rules needed to extract information from the string is encoded externally by that representation's specification. If a Restbucks consumer is to meaningfully interact with a Restbucks barista software agent, a common understanding of those rules needs to be in place. Otherwise, any attempt to engage in a meaningful exchange would be unsuccessful.

Besides requiring a common, out-of-band understanding of the rules needed to extract information, a significant problem with data formats such as that of Example 10-1 is that they are very difficult to modify, extend, and evolve without breaking existing applications. Although it is often criticized as being a verbose encoding mechanism, XML explicitly expresses hierarchical structure; furthermore, because of its textual nature, it can often be self-describing. Consider, for example, the same order from Example 10-1, but represented using XML (see Example 10-2).

Example 10-2. *A Restbucks order in XML*

```
<order xmlns="http://restbucks.com">
  <consume-at>takeAway</consume-at>
  <item>
    <name>latte</name>
    <quantity>1</quantity>
    <milk>whole</milk>
    <size>12</size>
  </item>
  <item>
    <name>cookie</name>
    <kind>chocolate-chip</kind>
    <quantity>2</quantity>
  </item>
</order>
```

The XML document of Example 10-2 encodes exactly the same data as the string of Example 10-1, but using more characters (because XML *is* verbose). However, the move to XML brings a shared understanding about how the data is structured. Since we know this is an XML document, we can infer information by simply examining it within that context:

- The <item> tags are contained by (children of) the <order> tag.

- The <quantity>, <size>, and <milk> tags are also children of the <item> tag.

- And so on....

The XML specification does not dictate how an application should take advantage of structure; nor does it determine how to interpret the data. However, because there is a shared understanding of how XML documents look, we can leverage commodity tools to process the order. We can copy, query, or transform the XML document without having to interpret or reason over the information it conveys. XML allows us to maintain a separation between the structured data and the represented information.

—— **NOTE** ————————————————————————————————

In building distributed systems on the Web, we often use XML processing libraries without really having to interpret the contents of the XML documents in the infrastructure layers of our applications (e.g., digital signatures, structure validation, query frameworks, etc.). The interpretation and processing of the data are left to the business layer of our application.

Interpretation

Humans can understand the tag elements in the XML document of Example 10-2, making it possible to infer (some of) the intended use of the captured data. As a result, a technically literate English speaker can assume by inspection that the document describes an order.

However, a software agent usually needs more than just assumptions. We need to be careful how information is inferred. For example, what volume measurement does Restbucks use to express the size of the latte in Example 10-2? Such issues arise in application integration scenarios all the time, as the JPL and the Lockheed Martin engineers will testify.*

As developers, we need to encode the information used by our application's business logic in the document formats we use. We also need to capture and externalize

---

* The Mars Climate Orbiter was sent to its destruction because Lockheed Martin used pounds for measuring thrust while the JPL engineers interpreted the given number as newtons (*http:// en.wikipedia.org/wiki/Mars_Climate_Orbiter*).

the context so as to allow correct interpretation of that information. Services can only interact correctly if this information is shared. Sharing context and interpretation semantics, however, is easier said than done, partly because interactions between distributed services tend to become more intricate as coupling becomes looser. Automation can help us when we need to share interpretation context for both the exchanged information and the semantics of the interactions between the participations in a distributed system.

Shared Understanding

When we deal with the exchange of data in an integration scenario, it's critical that all parties interpret the conveyed information in the same way. Otherwise, a Restbucks customer could order "a latte with whole milk" only for the barista to interpret it as "tea with sugar."

We've already shown how the protocols and formats in use on the Web address the problem of how to exchange data between components. Format it using XML or JSON and coordinate its exchange with HTTP, and suddenly data has been transferred. Data exchange isn't the problem; the key challenge is to actually make sure all parties in an interaction interpret the information consistently.

It's part of every developer's life to read specifications and convert them to working software. In Chapter 5, we suggested that hypermedia application contracts require written specifications. The process of converting a specification written in a natural language to a computer program is difficult and error-prone. Nevertheless, that's the predominant mechanism for implementing a shared understanding of exchanged information.

The web community is trying to address this problem through techniques that automate how applications represent and describe data and information. The goal is for machines rather than developers to reason over the *semantics* of any information in transferred representations.

Semantics

The term *semantics* is overloaded and overhyped, in part thanks to the *Semantic Web*. Since this book is about building distributed systems, we concentrate on the semantics of distributed system components. We use the term *semantics* to refer to the shared understanding defined by a contract, the meaning of a sequence of request-response exchanges, or the manner in which a resource representation should be interpreted. For example, the semantics of the Restbucks ordering protocol defines why we PUT a payment resource representation to a particular URI before allowing the associated order to be given to the barista. Similarly, the semantics attached to the Restbucks media type allows the barista to interpret the <milk> element under <item> as the type of milk to be used.

Representing and sharing semantics makes it possible for humans and computers to *meaningfully* exchange information. For computer systems, we want to automate the mechanics of sharing this understanding as much as possible. The Semantic Web, microformats, and even the humble rel attribute are all techniques that allow us to capture and convey semantics.

The Semantic Web

Human knowledge is captured on the Web in various digital forms: web pages, news articles, blog posts, digitized books, scanned paintings, videos, podcasts, lyrics, speech transcripts, and so on. Over the years, services have emerged to aggregate, index, and enable rapid searching of this digital data. However, the full meaning of that data is only interpretable by humans. Machines are typically incapable of understanding or reasoning about this vast source of information.

The Semantic Web promises to enable machines to meaningfully process, combine, and infer information from the world's data. With the W3C's support, a community was formed to deliver a set of technologies, such as RDF(S) and OWL.

> Machines become capable of analyzing all the data on the Web—the content, links, and transactions between people and computers. A "Semantic Web," which should make this possible, has yet to emerge, but when it does, the day-to-day mechanisms of trade, bureaucracy, and our daily lives will be handled by machines talking to machines, leaving humans to provide the inspiration and intuition. The intelligent "agents" people have touted for ages will finally materialize. This machine-understandable Web will come about through the implementation of a series of technical advancements and social agreements that are now beginning.*

Semantic Web technologies attempt to standardize the mechanics of information sharing so that it can be more easily supported in software. It should come as no surprise that resources and URIs are the building blocks on top of which the Semantic Web is built.

―――― **NOTE** ――――――――――――――――――――――――――――――――

We make a distinction between the general approach of computing based on semantic technologies (machine learning, ontologies, inference, etc.), and the Semantic Web, which is the term used to refer to a specific ecosystem of technologies such as RDF and OWL.†‡ The Semantic Web has gained a lot of attention; however, we consider the Semantic Web technologies to be just some of the many tools at our disposal when we build semantically aware solutions.

――

* Tim Berners-Lee, "Weaving the Web," *http://www.w3.org/People/Berners-Lee/Weaving/*.
† Berners-Lee, T., J.A. Hendler, and O. Lasilla. "The Semantic Web." *Scientific American*, May 2001.
‡ Shadbolt, N., T. Berners-Lee, and W. Hall. "The Semantic Web Revisited." *IEEE Intelligent Systems* 21(3):2006, p. 96–101.

The Semantic Web community has produced many technologies (and an equal number of acronyms) over the past decade—acronyms such as RDF, RDFS, RDFa, OWL, SPARQL, and GRDDL.* While we won't cover all of these technologies in depth, we will look at how Restbucks can utilize RDF and OWL (and, in subsequent sections, SPARQL and RDFa) to offer some additional functionality.

RDF

The Resource Description Framework (RDF) provides a model for describing data as a directed, labeled graph.† RDF's simple structure and resource orientation make it easy for us to evolve data representations, merge different graphs, and reason over the results. For example, part of the Restbucks order can be represented as the graph of Figure 10-1.

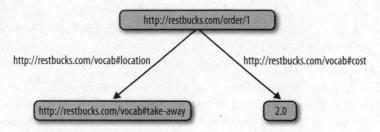

Figure 10-1. *Part of an order as a directed graph*

Note the use of URIs in Figure 10-1. RDF supports statements of the form [subject, predicate, object], also known as triples. The subject and the predicate here are always URIs, whereas the object can be either a URI or a literal (e.g., a string or a number). In the case of an order, we could use a literal object value to define whether the order is "take-away" or "to be consumed in house." A URI, however, allows us to represent the possible locations for consuming a beverage as resources with which we can explicitly associate additional information and processing semantics. For example, we could create a list of textual representations in different languages for "take-away," which can then be automatically used by consuming systems in other countries.

By combining URIs and literals in a structured way, RDF allows us to make statements about resources such as those in Example 10-3. This is because URIs have meaning attached to them, either because there is another RDF graph that describes them (e.g., an OWL description, as we will see shortly), or because they are "well-known" URIs, with well-understood semantics defined by either a natural language specification or a folksonomy.‡

---

* *http://semanticweb.org/, http://www.w3.org/2001/sw/*
† *http://www.w3.org/RDF/*
‡ A collection of terms defined by a community through collaborative tagging: *http://en.wikipedia.org/wiki/Folksonomy*.

Example 10-3. *Statements based on the graph of Figure 10-1*

```
Order 1 is to be taken away
Order 1 costs 2.0
```

As we add more information from a typical Restbucks order to our graph, the graph begins to take on a familiar shape, coming to look like the kind of hierarchical structure we find in XML documents (see Figure 10-2). RDF, however, is not restricted to representing tree structures; it can also represent arbitrary relationships between nodes in a graph.

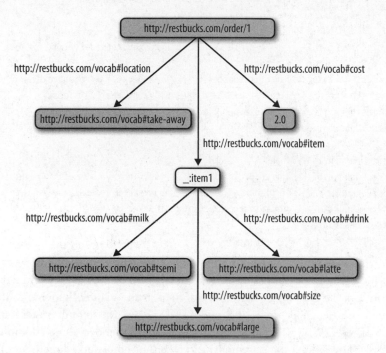

Figure 10-2. *A Restbucks order as a graph*

Please note the "anonymous" node in the graph of Figure 10-2—that is, the one that is not given its own URI. When we don't want all the information in a graph to be identifiable through a URI, we introduce anonymous nodes. For example, we obviously want the Restbucks order to be identifiable as a resource. We also want the predicates and many of the objects in each [subject, predicate, object] relationship to be identifiable—this allows them to be reused across graphs, and their semantics described using machine-readable representations. There are occasions, however, where it is not an application requirement to refer to a node in a graph outside an RDF document. This is the case for all the _:itemN nodes in an RDF Restbucks order, where N is a sequence number. Restbucks doesn't expect individual item entries in an order to be referenced outside the context of an order. Anonymous RDF nodes allow us to build graphs without having to make all its subjects and objects explicitly identifiable outside its context.

There are multiple representation formats for RDF graphs, including Notation 3* and RDF/XML.† We've chosen to use RDF/XML for Restbucks. Example 10-4 shows the graph from Figure 10-2 represented using RDF/XML.

Example 10-4. *A Restbucks order in RDF/XML*

```
<?xml version="1.0"?>
<!DOCTYPE rdf:RDF [<!ENTITY xsd "http://www.w3.org/2001/XMLSchema#">]>
<rdf:RDF xmlns:rdf="http://www.w3.org/1999/02/22-rdf-syntax-ns#"
         xmlns:restbucks="http://restbucks.com/vocab#">

  <rdf:Comment>This graph represents a simple Restbucks order</rdf:Comment>
  <rdf:Description rdf:about="http://restbucks.com/order/1">
    <restbucks:location rdf:resource="http://restbucks.com/vocab#take-away"/>
    <restbucks:cost rdf:datatype="&xsd;decimal">2.0</restbucks:cost>
    <restbucks:item rdf:resource="_:item1" />
  </rdf:Description>

  <rdf:Description rdf:about="_:item1">
    <restbucks:milk rdf:resource="http://restbucks.com/vocab#semi" />
    <restbucks:size rdf:resource="http://restbucks.com/vocab#large" />
    <restbucks:drink rdf:resource="http://restbucks.com/vocab#latte />
  </rdf:Description>
</rdf:RDF>
```

Example 10-4 doesn't contain any more domain information about a Restbucks order than a typical XML representation, with the exception of the @datatype attribute, which conveys the type of the literal. What, then, is the value of moving to RDF? The strength of RDF lies in its processing model and use of URIs to build statements.‡ This means all aspects of a Restbucks order can be further described using additional RDF statements. These additional statements can be either embedded directly in our order representation or delivered to consumers through other means. For example, the current representation contains the price of the order, together with the type of the literal (a decimal), but it doesn't specify which currency is being used. Using RDF, however, we can easily add that information to the representation, as shown in Example 10-5.

Example 10-5. *Capturing the currency for the cost of the Restbucks order*

```
<rdf:Description rdf:about="http://restbucks.com/order/1">
  <restbucks:location rdf:resource="http://restbucks.com/vocab#take-away"/>
```

* *http://www.w3.org/DesignIssues/Notation3.html*

† *http://www.w3.org/TR/REC-rdf-syntax/*

‡ As per the RDF/XML specification, our examples make use of Qualified Names (QNames), which are shorter versions of URIs, for the RDF statements. For example, `restbucks:milk` is the QName for *http://restbucks.com/vocab#milk*.

```
<restbucks:cost rdf:parseType="Resource">
  <rdf:value rdf:datatype="&xsd;decimal">2.0</rdf:value>
  <restbucks:currency rdf:resource="http://restbucks.com/vocab#uk-pounds" />
</restbucks:cost>
<restbucks:item rdf:resource="_:item1" />
</rdf:Description>
```

Adding the `rdf:parseType="Resource"` attribute to the `<restbucks:cost>` property element allows us to add blank nodes to the `restbucks:cost` subgraph. Blank nodes are nodes that aren't explicitly identified through a URI. In this case, we want to describe the value of the cost predicate as being currency in UK pounds. In Example 10-5, the `rdf:value` and `restbucks:currency`* blank nodes describe properties of the `restbucks:cost` node; the `restbucks:cost` node in turn describes a property of http://restbucks.com/order/1.

Adjusting the graph in this way allows a software agent to reason about the value `2.0` and treat it as a currency, not just a decimal. If we were using plain XML, we would have to associate this semantic information with the price value using a natural language specification. Using RDF, the semantic information can be consumed by an application directly. Figure 10-3 shows how the added information changes the order's graph.

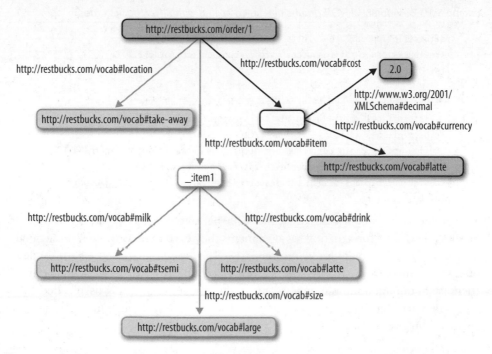

Figure 10-3. *Adding more information to the Restbucks order graph*

---

* We could have reused an existing vocabulary to describe the currency node. For example, Good-Relations (*http://www.heppnetz.de/ontologies/goodrelations/v1*) includes terms to describe the cost of products and the requested currency. In general, the reuse of vocabularies is recommended.

RDF makes it simple to combine information from different graphs, as long as matching URIs are used. This allows software libraries to bring together the known statements about a resource. For example, consider the RDF of Example 10-6, which states that customer `http://restbucks.com/customer/123` has placed the order `http://restbucks.com/order/1`. The document also states that the URI representing the choice "latte" is associated with the "latte" label in English and the "une crème" label in French (using the SKOS* vocabulary); that its origin is Italy (using GeoNames†); and that its milk is hot (using a proprietary coffee vocabulary). Finally, given that Restbucks wishes to be transparent about the ingredients it uses, it declares that its coffee beans come from Brazil.

Example 10-6. Additional RDF graphs can be combined with a Restbucks order

```
<rdf:Description rdf:about="http://restbucks.com/customer/123">
  <restbucks:order rdf:resource="http://restbucks.com/order/1" />
</rdf:Description>

<rdf:Description rdf:about="http://restbucks.com/vocab#latte">
  <skos:prefLabel xml:lang="en">latte</skos:prefLabel>
  <skos:prefLabel xml:lang="fr">une crème</skos:prefLabel>
  <coffee-vocab:origin rdf:resource="http://www.geonames.org/countries/#IT" />
  <coffee-vocab:milk rdf:resource="http://coffee.org/milk#hot" />
  <coffee-vocab:beans-origin rdf:resource="http://www.geonames.org/countries/#BR"/>
</rdf:Description>
```

RDF defines a set of basic rules and constructs that software agents can use as the building blocks for constructing the documents they exchange. However, these building blocks are not enough for all our scenarios. They can be used as the basis for developing vocabularies of concepts, such as "order," "cost," and "drink," which we can then use in our application domains. Due to the absence of a widely used coffee industry vocabulary, Restbucks has defined its own. The Semantic Web community refers to such vocabularies as *ontologies*.

* SKOS Simple Knowledge Organization System: *http://www.w3.org/2004/02/skos/*.
† *http://www.geonames.org/ontology/*

OWL

The Ontology Web Language (OWL) is a family of *knowledge representation* languages. These languages allow us to define, represent, and share the meaning of things, concepts, relationships, and abstractions.* OWL provides the building blocks for creating vocabularies specific to a particular *domain of interest*. Each term in the vocabulary can be associated with semantics in a machine-readable way. OWL's formal underpinnings make it possible for applications to *reason* over the set of facts expressed using one or more defined vocabularies. Developers can use available software libraries, such as Jena,† to incorporate *inferencing* capabilities into their applications, allowing them to generate new information by processing facts captured in OWL and RDF documents.

> ——— **NOTE** ———————————————————————————————————
>
> OWL has evolved a great deal with the move from v1.1 to v2.0. The latter is more expressive and offers different levels of semantics in representing knowledge, depending on our application's requirements.

OWL provides the mechanics for defining classes, relationships, properties/predicates, instances, constraints, and axioms. While there are several ways it can be used on the Web, in this chapter we focus on its potential uses in building distributed systems.

The Restbucks ontology

So far, we haven't defined the vocabulary we've been using to describe Restbucks orders. OWL uses RDF Schema (RDFS) to describe basic class hierarchies, class properties, and type constraints for property values.‡ OWL's own vocabulary includes axioms for defining more sophisticated interclass relationships and the constraints on these relationships, such as cardinalities, existential relationships (e.g., there exists some value), universal relationships (e.g., all values must hold true), and so on. In addition to the description of concepts, OWL's vocabulary can also be used to describe instances of those concepts, known as *individuals*.

Figure 10-4 shows a visual representation of a simple Restbucks ontology. The graph includes concepts such as coffee and ingredient, and their specializations. It also includes the concepts of an order and an item.

---

* *http://www.w3.org/2001/sw/wiki/OWL*
† *http://jena.sourceforge.net/*
‡ *http://www.w3.org/TR/rdf-schema/*

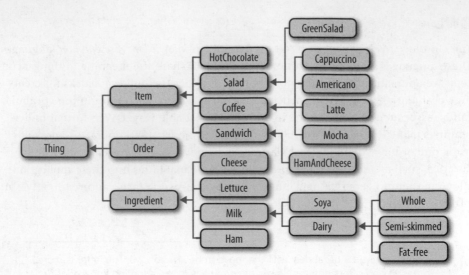

Figure 10-4. *Restbucks concept graph (an arc represents a SubClassOf OWL statement)*

Example 10-7* shows part of the OWL document for the Restbucks ontology. There are multiple renderings of an OWL document: OWL/XML, RDF/XML, Manchester, Turtle, and Functional.† We decided to avoid the XML-based ones given their verbose nature. Instead, we use the Manchester Syntax.‡

Example 10-7. *The Restbucks order and item declarations*

```
Ontology: <http://restbucks.com/vocab#>

Class: <Order>
Class: <Item>

ObjectProperty: <containsItem>
  Domain: <Order>
  Range: <Item>

DataProperty: <quantity>
  Domain: <Item>
  Range: xsd:positiveInteger
DataProperty: <size>
  Domain: <Item>
  Range: {"12oz" , "6oz"}
```

* In all the OWL examples that follow, we are omitting the declarations indicating that some of the concepts are subclasses of owl:Thing, the top-level concept declared by OWL. We have also omitted the http://restbucks.com/vocab# part of the concepts' and properties' URIs in order to make the examples more readable. <Order> should be read as <http://restbucks.com/vocab#Order>.

† *http://www.w3.org/TR/owl2-overview/*

‡ *http://www.w3.org/TR/owl2-manchester-syntax/*

Example 10-7 first declares the classes Order and Item. Next, the object property contains-Item is declared with Order as its *domain* (source of a relationship) and Item as its *range* (target of a relationship). Finally, the quantity and size data properties for the Item class are declared to be an integer and one of "6oz" or "12oz" strings, respectively. Effectively, the OWL of Example 10-7 allows us to make statements of the form "an Order may contain an Item" and "an Item may have the quantity and size data properties."

The links between nodes in graphs are always one-way. Without OWL, we would have to explicitly record a statement such as "an Item may be contained by an Order," which is the inverse of the one we saw earlier. If we were describing individuals, rather than concepts, we would have to record both statements for every pair of individuals.

With OWL, however, we can declare two object properties as being the inverse of each other. As a result, when reasoning over a set of statements, we can assume the existence of one relationship when we encounter its inverse, even if that relationship is not explicitly declared. Example 10-8 shows the declaration of the itemContainedBy property and how it is declared as the inverse of containsItem.

Example 10-8. *The properties containsItem and itemContainedBy are declared to be the inverse of each other*

```
ObjectProperty: <containsItem>
  Domain: <Order>
  Range: <Item>
  InverseOf: <itemContainedBy>

ObjectProperty: <itemContainedBy>
  Domain: <Item>
  Range: <Order>
  InverseOf: <containsItem>
```

Now, let's have a look at one of the Restbucks menu entries—the ones that have been declared as specializations of the Item class (see Example 10-9).

Example 10-9. *The Coffee Restbucks menu item and its hasMilk object property*

```
Class: <Coffee>
  SubClassOf: <Item>
  EquivalentTo: <hasMilk> max 1 <Milk>

ObjectProperty: <hasMilk>
  Domain: <Coffee>
  Range: <Milk>
Class: <Latte>
  SubClassOf: <Coffee>

Class: <Mocha>
  SubClasSOf: <Coffee>
```

Example 10-9 shows the declaration of the Coffee class and two of its specializations, Latte and Mocha. Note that the Coffee class is declared to be equivalent to a class that includes at maximum one instance of the hasMilk object property, whose range is the Milk class. Example 10-9 allows us to make a statement such as "A coffee may have one, but no more, milk individuals." Example 10-10 shows the declaration of some of the Ingredient concepts.

Example 10-10. *The Milk and Dairy concepts*

```
Class: <Ingredient>

Class: <Milk>
  SubClassOf: <Ingredient>

Class: <Dairy>
  SubClassOf: <Milk>
  DisjointWith: <Soya>

Class: <Whole>
  SubClassOf: <Dairy>

Class: <Soya>
  SubClassOf: <Milk>
  DisjointWith: <Dairy>

Class: <Cheese>
  SubClassOf: <Ingredient>
  EquivalentTo: <containsIngredient> some <Dairy>
```

Example 10-10 also shows how the Dairy and Soya concepts are declared to be *disjoint*. In other words, a class or an individual cannot be Dairy and Soya at the same time. Such a declaration allows us to capture the fact that soya milk is not considered dairy and that dairy milk cannot be made out of soya. Furthermore, the example shows how the Cheese class is defined to be equivalent to any class that is declared to contain some dairy as an ingredient.

We now have all the concepts and object properties that we need in order to describe an actual order (see Example 10-11).

Example 10-11. *A Restbucks order using OWL*

```
Individual: <WholeMilk>
  Types: <Whole>

Individual: <WholeMilk>
  Types: <SoyaMilk>
```

```
Individual: <MyDairyOrder>
  Types: <Order>
  Facts: <containsItem> <LatteOrderItem>,
         <containsItem> <MochaOrderItem>

Individual: <LatteOrderItem>
  Types: <Latte>
  Facts: <hasMilk> <WholeMilk>,
         <quantity> "2"^^xsd:positiveInteger,
         <size>  "6oz"

Individual: <MochaOrderItem>
    Types: <Mocha>
    Facts: <hasMilk> <SoyaMilk>,
           <quantity> "1"^^xsd:positiveInteger,
           <size> "12oz"
```

The OWL in Example 10-11 describes an individual order whose identity is
http://restbucks.com/vocab#MyDairyOrder, and which contains the individuals
...#LatteOrderItem and ...#MochaOrderItem. The former is a Latte, has WholeMilk,
has a quantity of 2, and is "6oz" in size. The latter has SoyaMilk, has a quantity of 1,
and is "12oz" in size.

What if a consuming application wanted to determine whether this order contains any
dairy?

A reasoner can use the set of classes and individuals that we have declared in order to
determine the answer to our question. Of course, we need to express our question in
OWL first (see Example 10-12).

Example 10-12. *The ContainingDairy class*

```
Class: <ContainingDairy>
  EquivalentTo:
      <Order>
       and (<containsItem> some (
         (<containsIngredient> some <Dairy>) or (<hasMilk> some <Dairy>)))
```

Example 10-12 shows the declaration of the ContainingDairy class, which can be read
as "ContainingDairy is a class that is an Order and contains an item with some dairy
as an ingredient or some dairy milk." In addition to checking whether a coffee contains dairy milk, the declaration also checks to see if an ingredient used is dairy or not.
Indeed, using the Hermit OWL reasoner* (used as a plug-in to Protégé†), we can determine that MyDairyOrder is indeed of type ContainingDairy. An order that included only

---

* *http://hermit-reasoner.com/*
† *http://protege.stanford.edu/*

THE SEMANTIC WEB   **367**

the `MochaLatteOrder` of Example 10-11 wouldn't be categorized as `ContainingDairy` (see Example 10-13).

Example 10-13. *A Restbucks order that doesn't contain dairy*

```
Individual: <MyNonDairyOrder>
  Types: <Order>
  Facts: <containsItem> <MochaOrderItem>
```

The declaration of the `ContainingDairy` class makes use of the `containsIngredient` object property, which we haven't defined yet (see Example 10-14).

Example 10-14. *The containsIngredient object property and the HamAndCheese order item*

```
ObjectProperty: <containsIngredient>
    Characteristics: Transitive
    Domain: <Item>, <Ingredient>
    Range: <Ingredient>

Class: <HamAndCheese>
    EquivalentTo: <containsIngredient> some <Cheese>,
                  <containsIngredient> some <Ham>
    SubClassOf: <Sandwich>
```

Note the use of the `Transitive` axiom in Example 10-14. A reasoner must now consider the transitive closure of all the classes or individuals that make use of the `containsIngredient` object property. In other words, if an order item A contains ingredient B, and B contains ingredient C, a reasoner can assume that order item A contains ingredient C. We can now declare order items such as ham and cheese and describe their ingredients in detail.

In addition to characterizing object properties (the predicates in relationships) as transitive, OWL allows us to use other mathematical axioms as well. Object properties can be declared to be symmetric, reflective, or functional.

Now that we have an OWL description of the Restbucks vocabulary, we can make it part of our DAP's contract, and so share it with our customers and partners. We can extend the vocabulary to capture the semantics of all the formats and protocols in the DAP so that machines can understand them.

Of course, we've barely scratched the surface of what OWL can do in terms of capturing information and knowledge in a machine-processable manner.

SPARQL

Remember that the RDF and OWL documents can be combined into a single information graph of subject-predicate-object triples. Designed to support the RDF data model, SPARQL is the query language for such graphs. Those familiar with SQL will recognize large parts of its syntax.

Using SPARQL, we can match patterns within a graph or subgraphs. The result may consist of a set of resources and their interrelationships that satisfy the given conditions; answers to true/false questions, given the encoded knowledge; or new graphs that were generated by inferring new triples over the existing set of statements.

As an example, let's assume that Restbucks offers a registry for loyal customers. The registry uses the Friend of a Friend (FOAF) vocabulary.* A service allows customers to register their details; Restbucks then stores all customer information in a large graph at *http://internal.restbucks.com/customers.rdf*, and makes it available to internal services. Example 10-15 shows what a simple query such as "List the Restbucks customers who are over 40" would look like in SPARQL.

Example 10-15. *A simple SPARQL query*

```
PREFIX foaf: <http://xmlns.com/foaf/0.1/>
PREFIX rest: <http://restbucks.com/vocab#>
PREFIX xsd: <http://www.w3.org/2001/XMLSchema#>

SELECT ?name
FROM <http://internal.restbucks.com/customers.rdf>
WHERE { ?x foaf:name ?name;
            foaf:age ?age.
        FILTER (xsd:positiveInteger(?age) > 40) }
```

One of the advantages of Semantic Web technologies is that we can build graphs of information facts without having to fix on a predefined and fixed schema. Sometimes we might not even have a schema for our information model at all. Unlike relational database technologies, RDF allows us to combine information in arbitrary ways, without having to adhere to a data layout defined and fixed in advance of an application's deployment. We saw an example of this earlier in the chapter when we augmented an order's graph with information about how the cost should be interpreted. SPARQL can query these dynamic graphs, thereby supporting an evolutionary approach to data and application design.

RDFa

RDF and OWL are built around the concepts of resources and URIs. Despite the use of web technologies, however, the promise of *linked data* has been difficult to achieve. Today, the machine-driven semantic processing of information is nowhere near as pervasive as the human-driven navigation of linked documents.

---

* See *http://www.foaf-project.org/*. FOAF is an ontology used for representing information about people, such as their name, their email, their workplace, their friends, and much more.

RDF in attributes (RDFa) fills this gap by bringing RDF to the human Web. While it's targeted mainly at the human Web, we believe it's also useful for building distributed web-based applications.

The premise of RDFa is that web documents such as XHTML can convey both presentation and semantic information. Through the use of XML attributes, presentation constructs are annotated with semantic information. This allows software agents other than browsers to process and reason over the embedded information. For example, Example 10-16 illustrates how an XHTML Restbucks coupon can be presented in a way that allows both John Smith and a software agent to process it.

Example 10-16. *A coupon for a free latte in XHTML with RDFa annotations*

```xml
<?xml version="1.0" encoding="UTF-8"?>
<!DOCTYPE html PUBLIC "-//W3C//DTD XHTML+RDFa 1.0//EN"
                  "http://www.w3.org/MarkUp/DTD/xhtml-rdfa-1.dtd">
<html xmlns="http://www.w3.org/1999/xhtml"
      xmlns:restbucks="http://restbucks.com/vocab#"
      xmlns:foaf="http://xmlns.com/foaf/0.1/"
      version="XHTML+RDFa 1.0" xml:lang="en">
  <head>
    <title>Offer to a valued customer</title>
    <!-- Digitally signed thumbprint of a coupon number -->
    <meta property="restbucks:coupon" content="123456" />
  </head>
  <body>
    <h1>Receipt for order 1234</h1>
    <p about="restbucks:coupon-recipient">Dear
      <span property="foaf:name" typeof="foaf:Person">John Smith</span>,</p>
    <p about="restbucks:coupon-product">Thank you for being a Restbucks
      valued customer. Since you have been a valued customer, we would
      like to offer you a complimentary
      <span property="restbucks:name">latte</span>.</p>
  </body>
</html>
```

* *http://linkeddata.org*
† Tim Berners-Lee's design note: *http://www.w3.org/DesignIssues/LinkedData.html*.
‡ *http://en.wikipedia.org/wiki/Linked_Data*

The `<meta>` element in Example 10-16 tells us that "this document represents a coupon with ID 123456." We can also see that the coupon is sent to "John Smith" and is for a "latte." A browser can render this information for a human to read, while a software agent participating in a machine-to-machine interaction can extract the necessary information for making forward progress in a business process involving an offer.

We can leverage RDFa statements in Restbucks' XML documents in order to avoid the expensive transition to RDF and OWL for computer-to-computer interactions. For example, rather than representing a Restbucks order in RDF, as we did earlier in this chapter, we could reuse our familiar XML representation together with RDFa statements to create self-describing documents.

Assuming that recipients of a Restbucks XML+RDFa document understand the Restbucks OWL vocabulary we defined earlier, Example 10-17 shows how the cost of an order can easily be annotated with the currency and the type of the value.

Example 10-17. A Restbucks XML+RDFa order

```
<order xmlns="http://restbucks.com"
       xmlns:rv="http://restbucks.com/vocab#"
       xmlns:xsd="http://www.w3.org/2001/XMLSchema#">
  <location>takeAway</location>
  <cost property="rv:uk-pounds" typeof="xsd:decimal">12.0</cost>
  <item>
    <name>latte</name>
    <quantity>1</quantity>
    <milk>whole</milk>
    <size>12</size>
  </item>
  <item>
    <name>cookie</name>
    <kind>chocolate-chip</kind>
    <quantity>2</quantity>
  </item>
</order>
```

Imagine the possibilities. We could add provenance information for the coffee beans used for the coffee, pointers to the recipe used for the chocolate cookie, or a link to the farmers who supplied the milk. Example 10-18 shows how simple this is.

Example 10-18. A Restbucks XML+RDFa order with more statements

```
<order xmlns="http://restbucks.com"
       xmlns:rv="http://restbucks.com/vocab#"
       xmlns:xsd="http://www.w3.org/2001/XMLSchema#">
  <location>takeAway</location>
  <link about="rv:coffee-beans" rel="rv:origin" href="http://coffeebeans.com" />
  <cost property="rv:uk-pounds" typeof="xsd:decimal">12.0</cost>
```

```
<item>
  <name>latte</name>
  <quantity>1</quantity>
  <milk rel="rv:supplier" href="http://localfarmer.com/">whole</milk>
  <size>12</size>
</item>
<item>
  <name>cookie</name>
  <kind rel="rv:recipe"
        href="http://restbucks.com/recipes/choc-cookie">chocolate-chip</kind>
  <quantity>2</quantity>
</item>
</order>
```

A software agent that understands Restbucks' vocabulary will translate the highlighted RDFa statements of Example 10-18 to the statements of Example 10-19.

Example 10-19. *Machine interpretation of the RDFa statements in Example 10-18*

```
The coffee beans originate from http://coffeebeans.com
The whole milk's supplier is http://localfarmer.com
The recipe for a chocolate cookie is http://restbucks.com/recipes/choc-cookie
```

Note the use of the `<link>` element and `rel` attribute in the order in Example 10-18. We use the `rel` attribute in our hypermedia examples when we want to convey additional information about the referenced resource. RDFa reuses this hypermedia control but allows terms from different vocabularies, rather than just strings, to be used as values.

Microformats

Microformats are a collection of community-driven specifications for conveying machine-processable information.* The goal of this grassroots effort is to design small document formats that can be reused by humans first and machines second. Take, for example, the chocolate cookie recipe referenced by one of the RDFa statements in Example 10-18. Using microformats, we could represent this recipe as an XHTML document containing both human- and machine-processable information, as shown in Example 10-20.

Example 10-20. *A recipe in an XHTML document as a microformat*

```
<div class="hrecipe">
  <h1 class="fn">Restbucks Chocolate Cookies</h1>
  <p class="summary">This is how you can make Restbucks chocolate cookies</p>
  <h2>Ingredients</h2>
  <ul>
```

---

* *http://microformats.org*

```
    <li class="ingredient">
      <span class="value">2.25</span> <span class="type">cups</span> flour.
    </li>
    <li class="ingredient">
      <span class="value">1</span> <span class="type">teaspoon</span> baking soda.
    </li>
    <li class="ingredient">
      <span class="value">1</span> <span class="type">teaspoon</span> salt.
    </li>
    <!-- More ingredients -->
  </ul>
  <h2>Preparation instructions</h2>
  <ul class="instructions">
    <li>Preheat oven to 375° F.</li>
    <li>Combine flour, baking soda, and salt in small bowl... </li>
    <!--  More instructions -->
  </ul>
</div>
```

As you can see from Example 10-20, microformats use existing HTML attributes—the class attribute in particular—to transport machine-readable semantic information. It's this thrifty attitude toward reusing existing HTML presentation attributes, rather than adding new elements and attributes as RDFa does, together with a narrow focus on representing everyday domain entities, such as contact details and calendar events, that makes the microformat movement so appealing to those wanting to add semantic annotations to their representations.

Microformats and RDFa are alike in that they separate semantics from document structure. With plain XML, semantics are bolted to a document's structure: we understand that the value of an <email> element contained within a <user> element signifies a user's email address as a result of our correlating an out-of-band description of the semantics with a part of the document schema. Microformats and RDFa, on the other hand, can insert the very same semantics into many different document structures. An hCard parser, for example, is more interested in identifying any element with a class attribute value of tel, indicating the presence of a telephone number, than it is in navigating a specific XML or HTML structure.

Despite being widely used on the Web today, microformats may soon lose out to RDFa, which will likely be included in future HTML standards. However, it is definitely worth keeping them in mind when designing distributed applications.

Linked Data and the Web

As previously mentioned, the Linked Data effort is all about exposing data and information so that computers, rather than humans, can consume and process it. Companies and organizations are encouraged to make their data available using Semantic Web technologies and link it with other data on the Web.

Structural hypermedia is at the core of this effort. It is used so that all data and information is interconnected in a semantically rich manner. HTTP and URIs, as used by RDF(S), RDFa, and OWL, allow us to create information and knowledge graphs that span organizational and geopolitical boundaries. Tim Berners-Lee has called it the "Giant Global Graph."*

The UK government's initiative to expose the public sector's information using web APIs and Semantic Web technologies is a great example of the Linked Data effort.†

Guidance

As developers of web services, we are all too aware of the importance of contracts and protocols for computer-to-computer interaction. It wouldn't be possible to exchange information among computers if there wasn't an agreement on how that information should be interpreted. Systems can't work if the meaning represented by the exchanged data isn't shared.

NOTE

It is important that a shared understanding of the exchanged information doesn't get translated into a shared way of processing that information. Participants in loosely coupled distributed applications are free to deal with the documents they receive in any way they wish.

Natural language specifications—whether media type descriptions, protocols, or contracts—provide a mechanism for developers to agree on the meaning of the documents they exchange. However, as the complexity and scale of distributed applications grow, it is important to consider the representation of information using machine-processable formats.

Technologies are emerging, especially as part of the Semantic Web effort, to help with the definition of document formats, protocols, and contracts. Semantic technologies are a great asset in our development toolbox whenever we want to represent information that machines can "understand." The intention of a service provider can be captured in semantically rich documents. These documents can be consumed directly by applications, removing the need for humans to read specifications and create programs from them. As a result, the correctness of our distributed system can be improved and the integration process accelerated.

---

* *http://en.wikipedia.org/wiki/Giant_Global_Graph*
† *http://data.gov.uk/*

CHAPTER ELEVEN

The Web and WS-*

THE WEB COMMUNITY HAS QUESTIONED THE WS-* PROTOCOL STACK (SOAP, WSDL, and friends) because of its perceived complexity. In this chapter, we'll take a closer look at the WS-* stack, understand its capabilities, and discuss the reasons the web ecosystem of tools and protocols can provide equivalent, but often more elegant, solutions to many common enterprise and Internet computing problems.

Are Web Services Evil?

In a book about building web-based systems, it's fitting to ask this fundamental question. Of course, the answer is not clear-cut. When SOAP-based Web Services became popular in 2000 they were a disruptive technology. The advent of Web Services changed the enterprise integration landscape utterly by using Internet protocols and XML to connect systems without proprietary middleware, private APIs, or integration specialists. It seems obvious now that open formats and protocols are good for interoperability, but back in 2000 this was a revelation.

Before Web Services, integration middleware had been dominated by uninteroperable technologies such as DCOM, RMI, and CORBA. Even where these technologies had been subjected to standardization, the standards were loose enough to allow integration products that were standards-based on paper yet proprietary in practice. Compounding this, the lack of commoditized and interoperable integration choices meant integration was the sole domain of specialist (costly!) developers.

Today integration is largely a commodity. While we can go out to market and buy specialist integration software, often the development community is finding that the tools built into our everyday development platforms are sufficient. In fact, Web Services did the community a huge service as they became part and parcel of modern development platforms and championed the notion of heterogeneous interoperability.

Since those halcyon days, Web Services—once perceived as disruptive and innovative—have begun to lose some of their glamour and technical credibility in the light of web-friendly approaches to developing distributed systems. It also hasn't helped the Web Services cause that numerous political battles have been fought over the standards, and many incompatibilities, inconsistencies, and some outright mistakes found in the WS-* stack.

The WS-* stack has been the butt of some cruel jokes across the Web, and given names such as WS-DeathStar, an amusing if dramatic reference to its perceived heavyweight and destructive nature. But the questions remain, aside from the hilarity and religious arguments that wage: are Web Services really so bad? Are they in fact evil? The short answer is "not entirely" because, like Darth Vader, there is good in Web Services too.

SOAP: The Whole Truth

The irony of the Web Services stack is that its core specification—SOAP—is lightweight and devoid of much of the bloat that its adversaries detest. All it describes is an XML envelope and a processing model for transferring messages across a network. It also provides some guidance for SOAP implementers on how underlying transport protocols can be used to transfer SOAP messages.

SOAP doesn't try to solve larger problems such as security or transactions and it doesn't try to impose application-level semantics or messaging patterns on SOAP messages. In fact, it's a whole lot lighter than the HTTP specification in that respect.

The SOAP Processing Model

Much like the HTTP envelope, the SOAP envelope consists of a placeholder for headers that contain metadata for setting processing context (e.g., security context, routing) for the message. Headers can also be used to convey information specific to a higher-level protocol (e.g., transactions). At runtime, SOAP envelopes are transferred across arbitrary transport protocols, with bindings defined by the various SOAP binding specifications, of which SOAP over HTTP is the only widely accepted binding to date.

NOTE

SOAP treats all protocols that it binds to as transport protocols, including HTTP, much to the annoyance of the web community. WS-Addressing introduces SOAP headers that, when included in a message, capture binding information. In a sense, SOAP and WS-Addressing together provide the complete transport-independent, end-to-end model for SOAP message processing.

SOAP messages can be routed through any number of intermediaries (both on the network and within services), which process SOAP headers as each message passes through. This is where the similarities end, however.

As we've become accustomed throughout this book, HTTP is an application protocol. As an application protocol, HTTP supports a uniform interface through which operations are applied to resources. We've come to expect that the verbs GET, POST, PUT, and so on are application-level constructs that a program can use to interoperate with another system over the network. Participants share an understanding of the semantics of an interaction, which is defined by the Web in an end-to-end model that covers the behaviors of both services and intermediaries (such as caches).

Conversely, SOAP (plus WS-Addressing) is much more akin to message-oriented middleware since it only defines an envelope and a means of transferring that envelope over the network. Application semantics are maintained entirely within service boundaries and are determined by message payloads (both the header and body content). In other words, SOAP is a low-level messaging protocol* that does not impose any application semantics on transferred payloads, leaving the interpretation of messages to the services that receive them.

Make Love, Not War

Since SOAP is normally used to transport an HTTP-like envelope over an HTTP connection, it has caused a great deal of angst in the web community. It has been argued that since the Web already provides an extensible envelope, metadata, entity body, and support for intermediaries, SOAP merely adds verbosity, latency, and complexity to the stack. Furthermore, web advocates are enraged that SOAP messages are tunneled through HTTP POST, which means the benefits of the existing web infrastructure (particularly caching) are lost.

Clearly, we think the Web is a robust platform too, or we wouldn't have written this book. Yet there are so few ways to build interoperable solutions over the Internet that we shouldn't be surprised that two popular approaches share a few concepts. In fact, it's useful to see just how similar they are before we get into any more mudslinging.

Envelope

Let's start with the envelope. The envelope is the fundamental structure of both the SOAP and HTTP worlds and provides a placeholder for data and metadata. In both SOAP and HTTP, the envelopes are similar. The structure of the HTTP envelope shown in Example 11-1 should look familiar; it's just a set of headers (metadata) and possibly a body containing data. As we can see in Example 11-2, the SOAP envelope is similar if a little more angle-brackety. In this case, both messages have similar intent: to lodge a new purchase order with a remote service.

* SOAP started its life as an interobject RPC protocol and, sadly, is still often used as such.

Example 11-1. *An HTTP envelope*

```
POST /orders HTTP/1.1
Host: restbucks.com
Content-Type: application/vnd.restbucks+xml
Content-Length: 32064


<order xmlns="http://..." .../>
```

Example 11-2. *A SOAP envelope*

```
<soap:Envelope xmlns:soap="http://...">
  <soap:Header>
    <wsa:To xmlns:wsa="http://...">http://restbucks.com/orders</wsa:To>
  </soap:Header>
  <soap:Body>
    <order xmlns="http://..." .../>
  </soap:Body>
</soap:Envelope>
```

Headers

Headers are like labels that we stick on an envelope to ensure that it's delivered to the right place and to set processing context for the contents. For example, if we want to send a paper letter across the planet, we'd attach an "Airmail/Par Avion" sticker to the outside of the envelope to help route it via airmail. Similarly, if we wanted to send potentially hazardous material through a courier, we'd probably want to stick "HazMat" warning stickers to our package so that it can be identified as a particular type of chemical and handled accordingly.

In Example 11-1, we start with the verb (POST), the target path (/orders), and the HTTP version. The HTTP headers that follow are, of course, familiar by now. We have the destination host and some metadata, such as the content type and length to help the recipient process the body. In a real application, there may be any number and combination of headers to set the interaction context.

The SOAP envelope in Example 11-2 also contains its addressing information in a header; in this example, it uses a WS-Addressing To header, which helps the underlying SOAP stack bind the message to an appropriate transfer channel.

Body

In both cases, the business payload is an XML document representing an order. In the HTTP case, we see the corresponding match with the Content-Type header (application/vnd.restbucks+xml) in the HTTP envelope.

In the SOAP envelope, the <order> element is the only child of the <soap:Body> element. The receiving service will typically extract this order from the <soap:Body> and route it internally to some business logic. The body of both the HTTP and SOAP envelopes is application-specific. In the HTTP case, we're carrying resource state representations; with SOAP, we're carrying a payload that the interacting parties must interpret.

Intermediaries

Both HTTP and SOAP processing models support intermediaries between the sender and receiver of messages. For instance, in the Web we are used to caches acting as intermediaries between a client and a resource to help with scalability and reliability. In the SOAP world, we have the notion of *nodes*, which process messages as they flow from the sender to the ultimate recipient. As with HTTP, these SOAP nodes may use metadata stored in the headers to process the messages along the transfer path. In practice, SOAP nodes are implemented by handlers inside the SOAP server and are typically used to set security context or encrypt/decrypt messages as they progress through the server stack to the network or vice versa. It is not uncommon to also see enterprise-wide message routers, which decouple an organization's client applications from enterprise services.

NOTE

The SOAP specification is decoupled from the WS-* protocols that utilize SOAP headers to perform their work. The SOAP processing model treats all headers as equal and does not impose a processing order on them. This allows any set of WS-* technologies to be cleanly interleaved without side effects.

But some technologies, such as WS-Security, have side effects, which means that the ordering of encryption/decryption operations is critical with respect to other headers in the same message. In practice, this means adopting conventions outside the scope of the SOAP specification for ordering encryption and decryption of messages.

Faults

We've seen throughout this book how the Web deals with faults using the 4xx and 5xx response codes from HTTP. This fault model is intrinsic to the Web and is one of the reasons web-based integration is so robust—this metadata provides coordination to help applications make progress or take compensating action at every interaction.

By comparison, SOAP has a very basic fault mechanism, called the SOAP fault, which conveys whether it was the consumer, the service, or an intermediary that caused the fault, plus some information about why the fault happened. Unlike the Web, SOAP faults don't convey enough standardized information to allow for recovery from failed interactions. In other words, we don't have the equivalent of the HTTP status codes or hypermedia links to guide us through an interaction. Instead, the WS-* world leaves such coordination and life-cycle issues to the rarely used WS-Coordination family of protocols.*

---

* WS-Coordination, WS-AtomicTransaction, and WS-BusinessActivity provide context and coordinated outcomes for collaborating services, effectively allowing status codes to be shared among services once a set of operations has completed. This is a different model from HTTP's since coordination happens on a per-activity basis rather than a per-operation basis, but it remains an effective strategy for improving reliability of distributed systems.

While SOAP faults are widely used, they rarely convey SOAP processing faults as the name suggests. Instead, they are often used to transfer programming exceptions between services and consumers. In the process, encapsulation is broken and unhelpful internal implementation errors are delivered to a consumer that has no business knowing them.

As we see in Example 11-3, although the SOAP fault is used syntactically correctly, the consumer receiving the message can't do much with it. The fault doesn't describe a problem with the service's protocol, but instead with its internal implementation. There's no way a consumer can take any meaningful action on receiving this fault other than to propagate the exception.

Example 11-3. *Misusing SOAP faults*

```
<?xml version="1.0" ?>
<env:Envelope
    xmlns:env="http://www.w3.org/2002/06/soap-envelope">
  <env:Body>
    <env:Fault>
      <env:Code>
        <env:Value>env:Receiver</env:Value>
      </env:Code>
      <env:Detail>
        java.io.FileNotFoundException: db.txt
          at java.io.FileInputStream.<init>(FileInputStream.java)
          at java.io.FileInputStream.<init>(FileInputStream.java)
          at Service.main(Service.java:15)
      </env:Detail>
    </env:Fault>
  </env:Body>
</env:Envelope>
```

> **NOTE**
>
> SOAP faults don't compare favorably with the Web, where standard failure status codes are used to coordinate applications.

Unfortunately, most of the popular Web Services toolkits tend to follow this approach. This, as we shall now see, is linked to the unhelpful role that WSDL plays in developing Web Services.

WSDL: Just Another Object IDL

From the preceding section, you'd think that SOAP and HTTP are similar enough that the outbreak of WS-Peace would be imminent. After all, both define envelopes, both have an end-to-end processing model that includes intermediaries, and both rely on metadata. If there is complexity in the Web Services stack, it doesn't come from SOAP.

But we don't have to go far into the Web Services stack to find the source of most complexity: the Web Services Description Language, or WSDL. While WSDL pays lip service to SOAP's message-oriented processing model, in fact it is mostly used as nothing more than a verbose object interface definition language (IDL), which forces an unsuitable RPC-like model of parameters, return values, and exceptions onto Web Services.

Center stage in WSDL 1.1 is the portType (the equivalent in WSDL 2.0 is the more honestly named interface), which is where all of the operations (!) that a Web Service supports are declared. Even to the casual observer, it's clear how the WSDL in Example 11-4 maps directly onto the equivalent Java code in Example 11-5, or indeed how easy it would be to go from Java to the corresponding WSDL—both encouraging unhelpful tight coupling between the service's contract and its implementation.

Example 11-4. *Typical WSDL use*

```
<wsdl:portType name="ordering">
  <wsdl:operation name="placeOrder">
    <wsdl:input message="restbucks:Order"/>
    <wsdl:output message="restbucks:OrderConfirmation"/>
    <wsdl:fault name="fault" message="restbucks:OrderException"/>
  </wsdl:operation>
  <wsdl:operation name="cancelOrder">
    <wsdl:input message="restbucks:Cancellation"/>
    <wsdl:output message="restbucks:Cancelled"/>
    <wsdl:fault name="fault" message="restbucks:NoSuchOrderException"/>
    <wsdl:fault name="fault" message="bank:OrderAlreadyServedException"/>
  </wsdl:operation>
  ...
</wsdl:portType>
```

Example 11-5. *Typical Java Web Service implementation*

```
public class OrderingService {
  public OrderConfirmation placeOrder(Order order)
                                  throws OrderException {

    ...
  }

  public Cancelled cancelOrder(Cancellation cancellation)
                          throws NoSuchOrderException,
                                  OrderAlreadyServedException {

    ...
  }
}
```

Parameters, return values, and exceptions may be great abstractions for Java or .NET programming, but on the Internet these abstractions don't make much sense. We know from experience that using a method-centric model to hide distribution boundaries is brittle, despite its immediate convenience for developers.*

Tight coupling between a service's WSDL and its internal implementation occurs because Web Services tools try to hide the perceived implementation complexity of building service-oriented systems. Tools encourage us to apply an attribute or property to a class or method in order to make it available as a Web Service. Such ease of use tends to make us quite generous in what we expose from our services. Furthermore, the same tools allow us to very easily bind to a Web Service through its WSDL and hide its remote nature by making the interactions with it appear as invocations against any other local object.

Existing consumers may find that our service no longer works for them because the WSDL contract that the service exposes has changed. This is an awkward situation since we'd like to be given freedom to implement and evolve our domain model as the business requirements for our service evolves, yet we're tightly coupled to a service contract, and by extension, external consumers, which inhibits such change. In fact, we'd inadvertently started to share a domain model between systems that should be decoupled!

---

* Waldo et al. were more diplomatic in their seminal paper, "A Note on Distributed Computing," but the underlying message is the same: you can't hide distribution and still have a reliable system. See *http://research.sun.com/techrep/1994/smli_tr-94-29.pdf*.

Figure 11-1 shows the tight coupling that arises when the normal tooling-centric approach is used for developing Web Services. Encapsulation is violated as the service's internal domain model is exposed via WSDL to the outside world. Any consumers that in turn use this WSDL to generate their own domain model become tightly coupled to the service's implementation. In turn, this makes changes significantly more difficult, expensive, and risky.

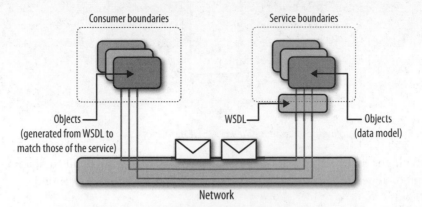

Figure 11-1. *Unintentional RPC with Web Services*

We don't have to create tightly coupled solutions with Web Services, though most tools make implementing that anti-pattern frighteningly easy. It's straightforward to design loosely coupled services by building a "service model" between the domain model and the framework code that connects services to the network.

The service model provides a faithful view of the underlying messaging behavior of the system so that we can explicitly code for high latencies and low reliability in the network. It also provides a mechanism to map information from messages into and out of domain objects, as shown in Figure 11-2.

This model is most prominent in the Spring Web Services approach where developers are expected to interact with SOAP messages via an XML-based API that forces loose coupling between the messages and domain model. Unfortunately, this approach tends to lack metadata (such as WSDL, poor as it is) to support the generation of client- and server-side bindings, and so places a programming burden on the developer. The Windows Communication Foundation (WCF) platform also supports the concepts of "service and data contracts" in an attempt to decouple implementation details from the interaction contract exposed through a service's endpoint, although through judicious use of attributes, WSDL can still be produced.*

---

* It's unfortunate that WCF still creates contracts that tightly couple consumers and services. By default, the tooling produces consumer-side stubs that syntactically match the service-side contract. If a service changes, the consumer breaks too.

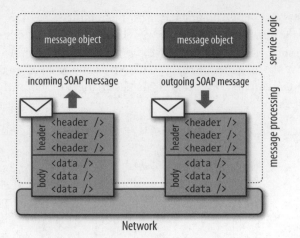

Figure 11-2. *Decoupling domain model from WSDL contract*

Following the approach in Figure 11-2, we have an extra tier to build compared to the naïve tool-generated approach, but the benefits of creating the service model tier are manifold:

- We explicitly decouple our external contract and internal domain model.

- We explicitly code for messages and so take time to understand the latencies and failure modes so that we can handle them gracefully and produce a robust service.

- Proper separation of concerns makes the codebase maintainable for the long term.

Once we've decoupled the domain model from the SOAP messages, WSDL interface changes become significantly more straightforward. Changes to the domain model will not affect service consumers because they are instead bound to the service model. Similarly, changes to the outwardly facing WSDL contract of the service may not require changes to our domain model since our contract and domain model are decoupled via the service model. In short, we have sensible separation of concerns.

Unfortunately, mainstream WSDL tooling promotes poor practices that discourage the design philosophy outlined earlier—SOAP messaging and the SOAP processing model are simply not well supported.*

To make matters a little more confusing, WSDL allows for a number of different encoding styles for the payloads of operations. Confusingly, these styles share overloaded names with other concepts in distributed computing. For example, the serialization styles *Document/Literal* and *RPC/Encoded* in WSDL are easily confused with Remote Procedure Call (RPC).

---

* This is partially because WSDL is a lowest common denominator description language. It takes the abstract notion of operations and binds them onto physical network exchanges. Whether it is an RPC mechanism like Java RMI or a messaging format like SOAP, everything is reduced to fit the operation abstraction.

Encoding messages with your own schema (Literal) and placing the resultant XML directly in the SOAP body (Document) or encoding your content with the SOAP schema* (Encoded) and wrapping it with a parent element before placing it in the SOAP body (RPC) merely changes how the XML looks on the wire. The underlying convention is still request-response plus fault that—in the presence of poor tooling—promotes brittle RPC that has dogged Web Services since their inception.

Both the Web and the explicit messaging model supported by SOAP with WS-Addressing embrace the idiosyncrasies of distributed systems, without trying to hide them. Unfortunately, WSDL's conceptual model and the naïve tooling based around it attempt to hide distribution as though programmers need to be protected from it.† In hiding the remote aspects of a distributed system, we hide necessary complexity to the extent that we can't build services that are tolerant of their inherent latencies, failure characteristics, and ownership boundaries.

Let's call it out, explicitly, just in case you're in any doubt.

As if being an RPC description format wasn't bad enough, it turns out that WSDL is metadata-poor in many other respects. Even though WSDL can support interactions up to a single request and a response (or fault), more sophisticated message exchange patterns are beyond its capabilities. This means WSDL is unable to cope with the typical use case where services exchange messages in arbitrary ways to match the problem at hand, and move beyond trivial request-response plus faults.

---

* The SOAP encoding schema (also known as "Section 5" encoding after part of the original SOAP specification) is now deprecated.

† Nothing could be further from the truth. We need to know about distribution boundaries so that we can write code that deals gracefully with failures outside our control.

WSDL's limited metadata means you can't tell in which order the operations defined in a WSDL interface should be invoked, since those operations convey only a single request, single response, and faults—with no dependencies among them. The conversation state of the Web Service is hidden, so any consumers looking to understand in what order to invoke operations have to be directed to an external source for conversation such as an abstract BPEL or WS-Choreography description. Not only does this add complexity to the solution, but also, most Web Services toolkits simply don't support it.

The final nail in WSDL's coffin is that it is able to support any transfer/transport protocol combination. In theory, capability to support a wide range of envelope formats and transport protocols should be useful, but in practice, Web Services habitually use SOAP over HTTP.* Unfortunately, this means we pay the price in terms of verbosity and complexity for the perceived added flexibility of binding to different envelope formats and transport protocols even though we'll never use it.

> **NOTE**
>
> WSDL is tremendously difficult to write and debug without tool support, and much of that tool support is actively harmful because it hides necessary complexity.

The Web Services stack has been dogged by the inadequacies of WSDL for far too long. WSDL makes doing the wrong things easy and makes doing the right things difficult, especially for frameworks that support WSDL generation from code (and vice versa). However, even in the web world, this mindset lingers on.

Two Wrongs Don't Make a Right

The techniques we've discussed in this book for APIs for web-based services have been uncontroversial. We think that links and careful use of URI templates with the HTTP uniform interface make sensible web-friendly APIs.

The kinds of APIs we see on the Web aren't necessarily isomorphic to Java or .NET classes. Even so, there exists a moral equivalent to WSDL in the web space: WADL, the Web Application Description Language, which we saw in Chapter 4, *can* be used to describe CRUD web services.

> **NOTE**
>
> WADL isn't the only game in town for describing HTTP-centric services. In fact, WSDL has bindings for HTTP GET and POST. Unfortunately, those bindings still promote the operation rather than resource abstraction, which is a poor fit for web-based services.

---

* There is at least a chance of being interoperable this way, unlike proprietary SOAP over JMS bindings, for example.

WADL was created with the best of intentions: to make building and consuming web-based services accessible to a wide community of programmers. However, it falls foul of many of the same problems as WSDL, in addition to some of its own making, specifically:

- WADL takes a static view of the web application by presenting the available resources, schemas, operations, and faults upfront, where the Web uses media types and links for contracts.

- WADL tooling promotes tight coupling of client and service-side abstractions. Resources advertised from the service become the client's domain model with frightening ease, allowing service-side changes to readily ripple through all client applications, leading to fragile, brittle systems just as WSDL-based tooling does in the WS-* world.

- WADL offers no clues about ordering of interactions with resources it advertises. A consumer of a WADL description doesn't know from WADL alone how the service expects interactions to occur. On the Web, we use hypermedia for this.

- WADL often duplicates the metadata that is available from the resources them-selves (e.g., via OPTIONS, HEAD). Thus, WADL introduces an opportunity for incon-sistency where resource metadata and WADL are different.

Perhaps the saving grace for web-based services is that there is comparatively little tooling based around WADL at the moment, and so it doesn't have the same momen-tum in the web space that WSDL enjoys in the Web Services space. The truth of the matter is that the Web has its transgressions just like Web Services—WADL being a case in point. But just like Web Services, the Web can handle sophisticated distrib-uted computing scenarios including security, reliability, and transactions, but without resorting to unsustainable architectural patterns.

Secure, Reliable, Transacted

We can forgive the Web Services stack some of its transgressions (like WSDL) provid-ing the stack can deliver some value that the Web cannot. Security, reliability, and transactions were values deeply enshrined in the Web Services psyche early on by some of its more influential corporate backers* to make interactions between Web Services as robust as traditional enterprise middleware.

This was a worthy and important goal, and it's interesting to see how these fundamen-tal tenets are supported in the WS-* stack. It's also useful to understand how the Web achieves similar outcomes with quite different means.

* Specifically, IBM and Microsoft.

Security

Web Services security encompasses a suite of XML cryptographic techniques to provide a secure end-to-end mechanism for transferring SOAP messages between services. WS-Security allows the sender of a message to sign and/or encrypt any part or the whole of the outgoing message so that it can't be tampered with and/or read while it's in transit, while higher-order protocols allow us to establish domains of trust, negotiate credentials, and so on.

End-to-end model

What's interesting about the WS-Security model is that it is truly end-to-end, based on public key cryptography. The WS-Security components are installed and configured inside a service's SOAP stack, and the security capabilities that the Web Service supports can be advertised in the WS-SecurityPolicy document associated with the service's WSDL. Once a consumer locates some service metadata, it can find out how to securely bind to the service via the WSDL and policy metadata and begin exchanging messages.

WS-Security works at the *transfer* protocol (message) level rather than the *transport* protocol level, so confidentiality and tamper proofing are supported from the sender through to the ultimate recipient. This is not merely between an enterprise gateway and receiving socket in the demilitarized zone (DMZ), but truly an end-to-end approach. In practical terms, this approach reduces the attack surface of the system considerably.

The architecture in Figure 11-3 is typical of many enterprise situations where the services (and their valuable business logic and data) are kept safely away from the Internet inside a protected network zone. A gateway server sits inside the DMZ and provides managed and secured communications between the Internet and the local network, as well as mediating connectivity to the Web Services. Any compromised systems in between the sender and receiver won't be able to view or tamper with the messages in transit. Given the realities of distributed ownership and governance in typical enterprises, this is a sensible defense-in-depth approach.

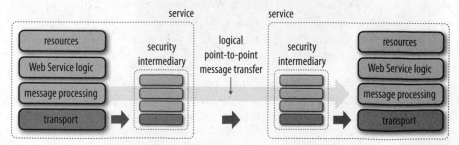

Figure 11-3. *Secure end-to-end message transfer*

WS-Security doesn't have to be applied only at the SOAP envelope level. Unlike transport-level security such as HTTPS, applying cryptographic techniques at the message level makes it possible to sign and/or encrypt only certain parts of the message. Not only can this be more computationally efficient than encrypting all of a message, but it also allows headers to be seen by intermediaries for routing and so on. Any visible headers can, of course, be signed to prevent tampering while keeping data meant for the ultimate recipient of the message private, end to end.

NOTE

Although encryption and signatures can be applied to individual message elements, in practice they are often applied at the envelope level, preventing processing by intermediaries.

Securing long-lived conversations

While WS-Security works well for single message exchanges, the cost of public key cryptography for multiple message exchanges can become expensive very quickly. While we could scale out the number of physical servers to deal with the additional computational workload, a better solution comes in the form of WS-SecureConversation, which uses WS-Security to bootstrap a secure, long-lived conversation with a Web Service.

WS-SecureConversation allows communicating Web Services to establish a shared key using a single public key exchange and then subsequently use that shared key to transfer multiple messages. To make the channel more secure, WS-SecureConversation allows the services to mutate the key as each message is exchanged, which all but circumvents attacks on the key, at a very low computational cost. A typical WS-SecureConversation scenario is shown in Figure 11-4.

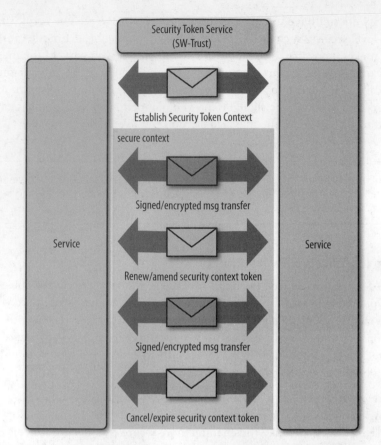

Figure 11-4. *WS-SecureConversation*

The secure session starts when the consumer and Web Service establish a Security Context Token (SCT). The Web Service has three choices in creating the SCT: the SCT can be requested from a WS-Trust Security Token Service, the service can generate its own, or the service can negotiate an appropriate SCT using the WS-Trust protocol (which we will see later).

As the conversation proceeds, the shared key used to secure the messages will mutate to maintain security. These mutated keys (known as derived keys) are computed with (pseudo) random number generators. Finally, the WS-SecureConversation specification provides the capability for renewing an SCT (via WS-Trust) where the SCT has expired before the conversation has completed, or conversely terminate the secure session immediately.

Issuing security tokens

At the heart of Web Services security is the notion of a token that represents a claim in respect of the sender's identity. We see such tokens in everyday life—video store membership cards, driver's licenses, passports, and OpenID URIs are all examples of tokens with varying degrees of strength in various domains. Sometimes tokens are interchangeable; for example, the video store will accept your passport as proof of identity. Sometimes they aren't—just try boarding an international flight with your video store card!

In the Web Services security world, we are exposed to many kinds of tokens too. The same tokens that we use in existing network security protocols are reused by Web Services, including the commonplace X.509 certificate and Kerberos ticket. Since Web Services make no assumptions about any specific token type, we may need to trade tokens when we're interoperating between domains of trust using the WS-Trust protocol.

WS-Trust defines extensions to WS-Security that provide methods for issuing, renewing, and validating security tokens, and ways to establish and broker trust relationships. The cornerstone of establishing trust is the WS-Trust Security Token Service or STS (itself a Web Service), which is able to exchange tokens of one type (in the requesting service's domain) for appropriate tokens of another type (in the receiving service's domain), as shown in Figure 11-5.

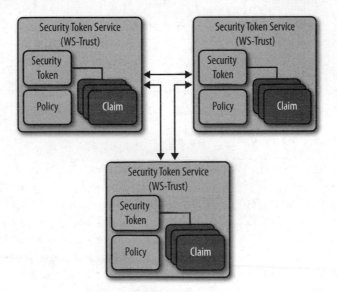

Figure 11-5. *WS-Trust in action*

The security model defined by WS-Trust allows a Web Service to specify that an incoming message must provide a set of claims (e.g., name, key, permission, capability, etc.) via its associated WS-Policy description. If a message arrives without having the required proof of claims, the service will typically ignore or reject the message.

If the requesting service doesn't have the necessary token to support the required claims for a service, it can contact an STS* (indicated in the service's policy) and request those tokens with the proper claims. Once the new tokens have been issued, the service consumer can resume its conversation with the responding service.

Federating identities

The pinnacle of Web Services security is federated identity, where services in one organization may access Web Services in other organizations, using local credentials to access remote services. This is the scenario supported by WS-Federation.

A typical scenario for WS-Federation is shown in Figure 11-6. While this pattern is simple, it can easily be used to build larger trust systems.

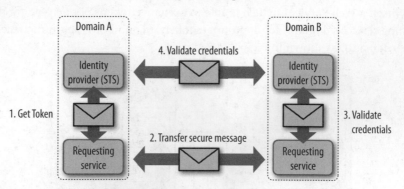

Figure 11-6. *Single sign-on with WS-Federation*

In Figure 11-6, the requesting Web Service obtains its credentials from its local identity provider using WS-Trust. The requesting service sends a message to the receiving service with evidence of its identity from its local domain using WS-Security. On receipt of this message with its foreign identity credentials, the receiving service asks its local identity provider to authenticate the sender of the message using WS-Trust. The identity provider in Domain B uses the foreign credentials to authenticate the sender with the identity provider from Domain A, which it already trusts (via WS-Federation). Once authenticated, the identity provider in Domain B informs the receiving Web service (using WS-Trust) and processing of the message may proceed. Whew!

* The STS may, in turn, require its own set of claims—it is, after all, just another Web Service.

This pattern, where a receiving service calls back to an identity provider, has the benefit
that the credentials are only stored in and validate at a single authority. If business part-
nerships change and Web services from Domain A are no longer to be serviced, only the
STS in Domain B needs to be updated, which reduces cost and complexity in operations.

Similarly, if an employee in Domain A is no longer trusted to perform tasks, a change
is made in Domain A and it immediately impacts Domain B. This pattern eliminates
the problems of defining and coordinating identities in multiple places.

Web services security: Sophisticated and robust, or complex and opaque?

It seems obvious that simple systems tend to be secure. There are just fewer places for
potential bugs to hide in a simple system, and so correspondingly, there's less for the
malicious hacker to exploit. Yet it's with trepidation that developers approach the Web
Services security stack.

The WS-Security stack is smart enough not to reimplement cryptographic primitives
such as hashing functions, random number generators, and encryption algorithms.
Instead, it reuses mature cryptography techniques from the XML security arena.

WS-Security also delivers more powerful techniques such as conversations, trust, and
federated identity. These techniques add to the sophistication of WS-Security and
make federated domains of trust feasible at interenterprise scales.

However, the sophistication of the WS-Security stack comes at a cost in terms of complexity. Each higher-level security specification is itself a specialist protocol that has
been designed by experts and in turn hidden by tools. Being opaque to developers like
this can be risky. If developers are so baffled by the technologies we're using, we're
prone to make mistakes and reduce the overall trustworthiness of our services.

Web Security

Compared with the sophisticated set of protocols we've just seen that compose the
WS-Security stack, the HTTPS solution used by the Web seems pitiful. Yet from
the human Web, we know that HTTP has the ability to support client-to-server

authentication using anHTTP Basic or Digest approach. Furthermore, TLS—the underlay for HTTPS—provides other critical functionality, such as strong authentication (even bilaterally with client certificates) and integrity for message exchanges, that allow us to establish mutually authenticated, confidential, session-based channels between a client and server using widely adopted Internet protocols.

Unlike WS-Security, which can be used in a fine-grained manner, HTTPS creates a secure transport channel and so obfuscates the entire HTTP envelope (including headers). For secure web traffic, this means transferred representations bypass web intermediaries like proxies, and the HTTP metadata is only available to the client and server and not to the underlying web infrastructure.

On the one hand, this is sensible since sensitive information shouldn't be cached or seen by intermediaries. On the other, it does inhibit scalability because a vital part of the Web (caching by intermediaries, and particularly reverse proxy servers) doesn't work for secure traffic, leaving us with client-side caching only. This means HTTPS should be used thoughtfully to ensure that most of the heavy lifting is still delegated to the Web.

NOTE

Although HTTPS is a (relatively) simple point-to-point mechanism for transport security, and is not as sophisticated as the WS-Security stack, it is worth remembering that huge amounts of value—including monetary transactions—are realized every day using this approach. It may be simple, but it is widespread, highly interoperable, and trusted.

Federated authentication on the Web

In the same way that the Web Services community has layered sophisticated security mechanisms such as WS-Trust atop WS-Security, the web community has begun to develop its own security protocols to support more sophisticated secure interactions over the Web.

Since the Web has a collaborative mindset, OpenID seems to have captured the zeitgeist for identity. We covered OpenID in depth in Chapter 9. To recap, its underlying philosophy is to enable an individual (or a computer system) to own a single long-lived identity across the Web—decoupled from any specific identity provider. The OpenID model is relatively simple. A service consumer makes a claim to a service that it owns a particular identity referenced by a URI. That identity enables an OpenID provider to be discovered, which will authenticate the consuming application. The service then authenticates the consumer by delegating the authentication to that OpenID provider—provided the service *trusts* the provider. Underpinning OpenID are the same mature cryptographic algorithms that are used by the WS-Security stack, so we have the same degree of confidence in OpenID.

A similar argument can be made for OAuth (which we also covered in Chapter 9). OAuth provides authorization to interact (read, update, remove) with resources on the Web for a given authenticated user (who may be authenticated through OpenID) for a certain time period. This scheme has allowed some services to evolve into open platforms whose third-party security is implemented through an open and widely used protocol.*

It's telling that protocols such as OpenID and OAuth prosper in a harsh environment like the public Internet, whereas the equivalent WS-* protocols seem to have made little impact even in the safe, law-abiding havens that are enterprise networks. It's paradoxical that techniques that have proven themselves on the public Internet are so downplayed in enterprise computing!

Reliable Messaging

One of the pains inherent in building distributed applications is failure of the communications infrastructure that links components together. At Internet scale, transient communication failures are commonplace, and although TCP does a good job of masking these failures in most cases, application-level mechanisms that deal with delivery of messages are a useful technique to have in our toolbox.

In the Web Services arena, WS-ReliableMessaging is the dominant protocol supported by the major platforms and vendors.† WS-ReliableMessaging offers four schemes for reducing message delivery errors between Web Services:

At most once
 Duplicate messages will not be delivered, but messages may still be dropped.

At least once
 Every message will be delivered, but duplication may occur.

Exactly once
 Every message will be delivered once and once only.

In order
 Messages will be received in the same order they were sent.

Each of these is supported by WS-ReliableMessaging. From a developer's perspective, a Web Service's SOAP stack is configured with components that implement the protocol. On good Web Services stacks, declaring that a service supports the WS-RM protocol will also cause the capability to be advertised via a WS-Policy document associated with the service's WSDL. In turn, consumers of the service know they can use the protocol to communicate reliably with the service from those policy declarations.

---

* For example, Twitter and LinkedIn.
† Like so many of the interesting WS-* specifications, the vendor community has spent several years fighting with proprietary and incompatible versions of reliable messaging protocols. WS-Reliable-Messaging 1.1 finally became an OASIS standard in June 2007, some six years behind the first SOAP specification.

At runtime, the reliable messaging protocol establishes a reliable session by tagging sequence numbers into the SOAP headers of messages, as shown in Figure 11-7.

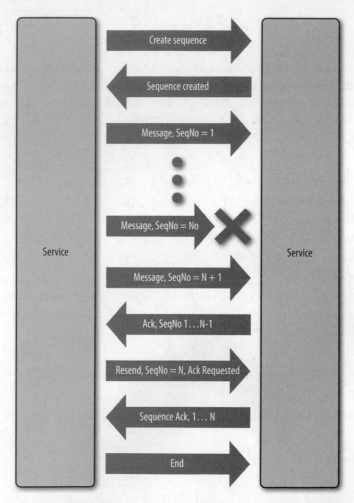

Figure 11-7. *WS-ReliableMessaging in action*

Figure 11-7 shows a typical use case for WS-ReliableMessaging. The consumer negotiates with the service to set up a sequence that is used to identify the order of messages exchanged between the sender and recipient. As each message is received, the WS-ReliableMessaging components on the service side examine the sequence number and request retransmission of messages from the consumer by omitting a confirmation for the missing message in its response ACK message.

On the consumer side, the WS-ReliableMessaging components respond to protocol messages by resending any messages that have gone missing. To make things more reliable, the consumer may request an acknowledgment of the re-sent (and any other) message too, and may persist outgoing messages ready for retransmission in the event of a failure.

Reliability on the Web

The Web is quite different from Web Services when it comes to reliable transfer between clients and servers. Not only are operations such as GET and PUT idempotent and therefore safe to retry in failure cases, but the stateless, synchronous request-response interaction model of the Web ensures ordering by default—there just isn't any asynchrony to mess things up. In fact, the Web deals with many of the same requirements as WS-ReliableMessaging, but does so using HTTP verbs, headers, and status codes to coordinate interactions and implement retries. To recap, we are specifically interested in the following interaction patterns:

- In order

- At least once

- At most once

- Exactly once

The first of these, in order, is actually baked right into the web model—the Web is inherently synchronous. Only if the HTTP status code of an interaction suggests it was successful would we go ahead with the next interaction. If a status code indicates a failure, we might try again or divert to another strategy to make forward progress. The Web embraces distribution rather than trying to hide it beneath an RPC façade.

NOTE

When building web-based systems, we need to know the results of a prior interaction with a resource, because they contextualize future interactions. For example, if we get a 500 or 404, we may take different actions compared to receiving a 200 or 201. Understanding HTTP and the implicit coordination it provides is a prerequisite for building reliable web-based systems.

HTTP does in fact allow asynchrony in the form of pipelined requests. Pipelining allows a client to send multiple requests over a persistent connection without waiting for each response. By convention, however, pipelined requests should only include safe requests. If an error occurs during a sequence of safe pipelined requests, the entire sequence can be retried.

The other three requirements (at most, at least, and exactly once) are just as easily handled by the Web, and actually collapse down to a single exactly once case. If we PUT a representation, it's safe to retry the operation until we get a 200 or 201 response. If we get something like a 409 Conflict, we know to take appropriate recovery action.* The other idempotent verbs, such as GET and DELETE, follow a similar scheme.

---

* Which is to GET the latest state of any resources involved in the computation and compute whether forward progress can be made, or whether some kind of compensation will be required.

The exception to this scheme is, as we might expect, the POST verb. Since POST isn't guaranteed to be idempotent, when we're POSTing to create a new resource or add to an existing resource, we need an additional safeguard. Again we will use the HTTP status codes to reason about the outcome of our POST and react accordingly to success or failure. However, we also need to prevent multiple POST operations from creating unintended side effects. In this case, we can either rely on some unique identifier within the payload, or add an HTTP header with a unique value as per Mark Nottingham's "POST Once Exactly"* scheme where the server will return a 405 Method Not Allowed in response to duplicate POST requests. Either way, there is an expectation that our service implementation will not process any operations for that unique value more than once, which delivers our exactly once semantics.

This means we can achieve the same level of reliable messaging on the Web as WS-* services achieve with XML-based protocols. However, this is not the end of the story as far as reliability goes. Though it's a useful pattern, reliable delivery only applies to a single set of interactions between a consumer and a service. To achieve reliability across a system composed of services, we need (transactional) coordination.

Transactions

To achieve end-to-end reliability in a distributed system, we need to be confident that at the end of an application scope or business process (known as a context) each service involved has a consistent view of the outcome. Classically, to achieve consistent outcomes across parties we use coordination/transaction protocols to drive consensus.

As enterprise developers, we're completely at ease with the notion of database transactions. We have probably experienced distributed transactions across systems using a transaction manager and two-phase commit. In either case, we use transactions to ensure a consistent outcome even in the event of failures. This classic transactional architecture is shown in Figure 11-8.

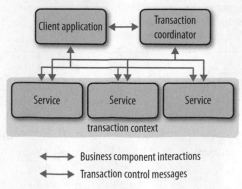

Figure 11-8. *Classic transactions architecture*

* See Mark's website at *http://www.mnot.net/drafts/draft-nottingham-http-poe-00.txt*.

All of the transaction protocols that we know from the Web Services world (and indeed their precursors in J2EE, CORBA, MTS, etc.) are based on the classic model shown in Figure 11-8. It follows that a typical distributed transaction scenario proceeds along these lines:

1. Some part of a distributed application's work needs a globally agreed outcome, so the application requests a transaction context from the transaction manager.

2. The transaction manager returns a reference to a transaction context back to the application. On each subsequent interaction with a transactional service, the client application passes context along in some out-of-band mechanism (e.g., SOAP header).

3. When the service receives the message containing the transaction reference, it may choose to register itself with that transaction. It then goes on to complete any work asked of it. It must have some mechanism such as database rollback, or compensation logic to undo any work in the event that it is instructed to do so by the transaction coordinator.

4. Once all the application work has been completed, the client signals to the transaction manager that the transaction is ready to be completed.

5. The transaction manager then runs the consensus protocol, where it asks each registered service to vote whether it wants to proceed with the work it has performed or whether it wants to cancel that work.

6. After gathering all the votes, the transaction coordinator instructs the services to either commit the work they had provisionally completed, or cancel the work, which forces a rollback or compensation in each service.

Transactions involve a lot of work to arrive at an agreed-upon outcome between components, and implementing the necessary infrastructure to support them can be nontrivial. Transactions are a deep computer science discipline,* and the techniques we take for granted as developers are often the results of significant R&D investments. And there are myriad variants and optimizations for transaction models that suit particular domains.

In the Web Services arena, we've seen a number of competing transaction protocols from Business Transaction Protocol and WS-CAF through to the (finally) broadly accepted WS-BusinessActivity protocol. Although each protocol differed in the details, their lineage derives from the two-phase commit pattern, which is an approach that can make sense in an asynchronous messaging system like Web Services.

---

* See Chapter 7 of *Developing Enterprise Web Services: An Architect's Guide* by Chatterjee and Webber (Prentice-Hall, 2003) for a more thorough explanation of transactional coordination in loosely coupled systems.

Web Transactions

Applying two-phase transactions to the Web is straightforward, though as we will show, we don't believe it is necessary. Although the Web lacks any standard transaction models or media types to support transactions natively, we could choose to reuse the same two-phase pattern with HTTP interactions. For example, at their OOPSLA 2007 session,* Baker and Charlton outlined a model for dealing with transactional coordination across the Web, using a traditional model where all parties in the transaction are modeled as web resources. They also advocate the same kind of two-phase protocol for driving out consensus between distributed resources at the end of the transaction's scope.

As we would expect, web-based service transactions begin with the creation of a transaction by a client application. In this case, we POST a request for a new transaction to a transaction manager to request the creation of a new transaction context as a resource, as in Figure 11-9.

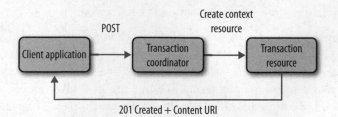

Figure 11-9. *Creating a transaction resource*

Once we have created a resource to represent our transaction, the next stage is for the URI of that transaction to be shared with other (transactional) resources. To achieve this, we embed a transaction context in the form of a URI in an HTTP header that is propagated to any resources we interact with in the scope of the transaction. Something simple like `Transaction-Id: http://transaction.example.org/1234` will suffice here, with the benefit that any resources that don't want to be part of the transaction (or are unable to) can simply ignore the header.

---

* *http://www.slideshare.net/StuC/oopsla-2007-the-web-distributed-objects-realized*

Once a transaction identifier has reached a resource, the next step for the receiving resource is to register as a participant resource in the transaction. It does this by POSTing to the transaction resource with its participant resource URI, as shown in Figure 11-10.

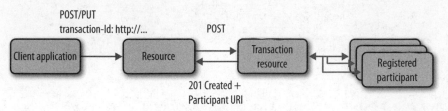

Figure 11-10. *Registering participants under a transaction*

As the application proceeds, a participant resource is created for each transactional resource that has registered. Ultimately, the client application will attempt to finish the transaction, at which point it will initialize the outcome protocol with the registered participants by updating the status of the transaction resource, as we can see in Figure 11-11.

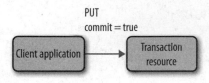

Figure 11-11. *Initiating transaction completion*

Once the client application has initiated transaction completion, the transaction resource gathers votes from its registered participants by PUTting the prepare state onto each, as in Figure 11-12. In response, the participants may answer with a 200 OK status indicating that the resource is happy to go ahead with the work (perhaps along with a copy of the to-be resource representation) or a 409 Conflict to indicate that it is not able to honor the unit of work and wishes to roll back or compensate.

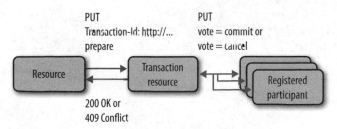

Figure 11-12. *Gathering votes*

Once all the votes have been gathered, the transaction resource PUTs the final outcome of the transaction to each participant and informs the client application of the outcome, as shown in Figure 11-13. On receipt of the outcome, each resource either makes permanent any state changes that have occurred during the transaction or undoes them (by rolling back or compensating, depending on its implementation strategy).

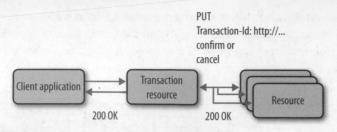

Figure 11-13. *Resolving a consistent outcome*

Of course, transactional scenarios aren't always as straightforward as we've described so far. For example, participants may deregister from the transaction or may want to know (security permitting) who else is participating in the distributed unit of work. Fortunately, the Web allows us to support both of these easily using DELETE and GET. To deregister from a transaction—assuming that it hasn't yet voted and the security policy is not violated—a resource owner or client application can simply DELETE the participant, as we can see in Figure 11-14.

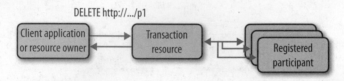

Figure 11-14. *Deregistering a participant with DELETE*

Similarly, to discover which resources are registered with a transaction at any point, we can GET the parent transaction resource and expect to see a set of URIs for each registered participant (or an Atom or RSS feed), as per Figure 11-15. Likewise, if we GET a particular participant resource, we can reasonably expect to see its current status (whether it has yet to vote or whether it has voted to proceed or cancel).

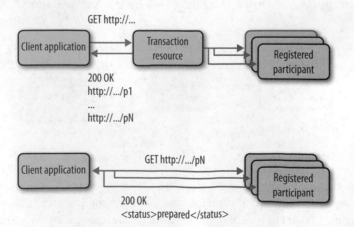

Figure 11-15. *Listing current participants and participant statuses with GET*

In terms of robustness, the pattern we've shown is solid. If the transaction manager and its participant resources are able to recover from crashes (by writing all pertinent resource information to a database or disk), we can be confident we'll get a coordinated outcome even in the presence of all but the nastiest of failures, just like enterprise transaction systems.

Crash recovery for any participant in the transaction is straightforward because the participant can simply GET the status of the transaction as a whole and its own participant status. The means transactional services have to remember (and therefore code for) little transactional state of their own, which is a *very* good thing.

The downside of this pattern is that it is precisely that: simply a pattern, not a standard or implementation. To transact in an interoperable way, convention may not be sufficient, at least not until a sufficiently large community lends its weight to that convention and appropriate media types and link relations emerge. So, in order to transact in the classical sense over the Web, we might need to resort to the same standards committees and politics that have dogged the evolution of Web Services standards in the past few years.

Un-transactions

Fortunately, as we are discovering, the Web tends to have its own answer to enterprise problems, and as it happens transactions aren't necessary when dealing with web-based services. The Web provides feedback in the form of HTTP status codes about every interaction with resources, which means that web-based business processes build consensus as they execute rather than waiting until the end. A consumer driving a protocol through hypermedia spanning any number of services knows at each step in that protocol whether it's safe to continue, or whether it needs to attempt some kind of error recovery *after every interaction*.

NOTE

Receiving a 200 or 201 status code as the result of an interaction with a resource is an invitation to continue, whereas responses in the 400 or 500 range are an immediate signal that some part of the system has refused to go any further and some corrective or compensating action may be needed.

Even though compensating activities may be nontrivial to develop, they are coordinated via the Web just like any other interaction. That is, in order to repeat or undo a unit of work, the same verbs, status codes, hyperlinks, servers, and libraries are used; no additional frameworks or middleware are necessary.

Status codes are coordination metadata, and are as valuable to the Web as transactional coordination is to the enterprise. But unlike the enterprise distributed transaction models, the Web doesn't rely on a shared, trusted coordinator. Since coordinators have to be available for the entirety of the work (just so they can run a consensus algorithm at the end), they risk becoming a scalability and reliability bottleneck. Instead, the Web's model requires only that the consumer makes sensible decisions with respect to the application state and metadata it knows. This is a much more loosely coupled approach.

Respecting boundaries

The fact is that the Web already provides coordination between services. While there are those in the community who will maintain that classic consensus-at-the-end-of processing protocols are necessary for systems composed from web services to be enterprise quality, we disagree.

We understand that in some cases, transactions—even classic two-phase commits—might be used within a service implementation. Not all projects will be greenfield developments, and some services will be built by composing existing transactional systems. In these cases, we have just one plea: respect the autonomy of service boundaries.

While it might make sense for a service implementation to use transactions for its own internal consistency, that's an implementation detail. Don't be tempted to involve consumers in your transactions by allowing such life-cycle information to leak past your service boundary. Not only is it largely unhelpful for your consumers, but also you'll be inviting them to tightly couple to your service's implementation.

In brownfield service development, the challenge of a designer is to minimize the time that transactions spend holding resources, and to map the execution of transactions cleanly onto the steps in the DAP(s) that your service supports.

In Figure 11-16, we show a typical strategy for encapsulating transactions behind service boundaries. The consumer of a service knows nothing of the transaction it triggers when it interacts with a resource. However, when the resource processes the consumer's request, it may trigger a transaction on the domain model and underlying datastore. The scope of the transaction is limited to the backend, and runs for as short a duration as possible to avoid causing contention. Once the transaction completes, a status code mapping to the outcome of the transaction (a domain-specific mapping) and perhaps a representation of the resource will be sent back to the consumer. At no point is the consumer aware that the service executed a transaction on its behalf, since that is the service's implementation detail and not something that needs to be shared.

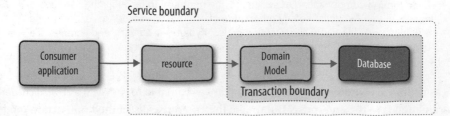

Figure 11-16. *Relationship between service and transaction boundaries*

Backend processes may have to be changed to allow for smaller transactions to be chained together as part of a larger workflow that the service exposes. Allowing transactions to span multiple interactions with a consumer is not a good idea since it effectively allows those consumers to control when resources are released. Poorly written or malicious consumers may cause inadvertent denial-of-service attacks, leaving the service with a mess to clean up.

A Requiem for Web Services?

If we take the entire WS-* stack, it's a large body of work and deserves its heavyweight reputation. Moreover, WS-* services are categorized in Richardson's maturity model at level zero as per Figure 11-17. SOAP and friends leverage very little from the Web, save the odd URI for service endpoints and HTTP as a firewall-friendly transport protocol. This doesn't mean that WS-* itself lacks sophistication, but all of this ingenuity has been built afresh atop and around SOAP, ignoring the value that the Web brings.

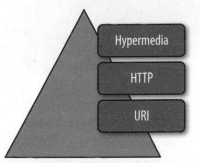

Figure 11-17. *WS-* is a level zero strategy from a web point of view*

Yet much as the web community may like to celebrate the demise of the Web Services stack, it's not yet the end of the road for that platform. The WS-* stack is both comprehensive and modular. If we need reliable messaging, we deploy and use that protocol only. We don't need to worry about the facilities for security or transactions.

The SOAP model means we can focus on the capabilities we need now and defer introducing any other protocols until we are driven to do so. Interoperability among popular WS-* stacks has become substantially better over time, and bridging the Java and .NET worlds (at least) is a reality for most of the mature parts of the stack.

Yet the WS-* stack has failed to leave WSDL behind and move to more sophisticated metadata formats. This has left a legacy of WSDL-centric tooling, which limits the approach to RPC-like communication between services. So much time and effort has been invested in these tools that it is difficult to deviate from this anti-pattern and frustratingly simple to expose domain objects outside of service boundaries.

But as the developer community becomes more confident in embracing the Web, there will be fewer and fewer things that WS-* can do that cannot be achieved by the Web with common patterns and technologies. Of course, there's no guarantee that the Web will have any less of a political and factional aspect when multiple solutions for the same problem are suggested, particularly when those same WS-* vendors become involved, but it is certainly an interesting time to be a web developer!

CHAPTER TWELVE

Building the Case
for the Web

THROUGHOUT THIS BOOK, we hope we've shown how the Web can be used to build real distributed systems, even "enterprise class" solutions for business-critical computing. But there's a great deal of skepticism in computing circles about the "next big thing" because all the previous "next big things" haven't lived up to expectations.

No More Silver Bullets

Think of the various panaceas we've been sold in recent memory: model-driven development, object request brokers, SOA, and Enterprise Service Bus—all have failed to deliver on their promise to make building robust systems easy and repeatable. If we position the Web as another silver bullet, it is similarly doomed to fail. So it's important to understand that even though web-inspired systems are often an excellent solution, *the Web is not a silver bullet and is not suitable for each and every problem domain.*

Far from being an admission of failure, taking the time to understand when the Web will be helpful, and when it will not, is key to successfully deploying web services into your distributed computing environment.

Building and Running Web-Based Services

As system designers and developers, our primary concern is to deliver a working system that satisfies the functional and nonfunctional requirements placed upon it. In satisfying those requirements, we have to select frameworks and components to support our implementation and accelerate delivery.

Using commodity components and contemporary software processes, we've seen how the Web successfully delivers simple remote data access, complex business protocols, and even event-driven systems. In fact, we'd go so far as to say that unless you're building real-time or safety-critical systems, the Web has a high probability of being a great choice as a platform for business information systems.

The high probability of the Web being a good fit for our purpose does not arise by chance. The intrinsic nature of the Web makes it so. For example, if a solution requires numerous components to be wired up, the uniform interface substantially reduces plumbing complexity.

If services need to advertise sophisticated protocols to consumers, the Web's focus on hypermedia and hypermedia-friendly media types allows services to declare contracts that include protocol behavior. Not to mention that such protocol behavior can be readily changed and versioned by changing the links that join resources.

Should our requirements drive us toward creating a secure service, we can rely on extremely mature web standards (such as HTTPS) for channel-level privacy and integrity. Or we can adopt security protocols such as OpenID and OAuth—originally intended for human-facing systems—to support computer-to-computer interactions, *reusing the very same web infrastructure that already drives the human Web*.

The middleware that we use to deliver web-based systems is mature. Web servers, caches, and proxy servers are some of the most widely deployed middleware servers on the Internet. They are commoditized (and sometimes free), and they don't require product specialists to build, configure, and run them.

Similarly, the frameworks we use to produce web services are commoditized—they're the same frameworks web developers use every day. And since the web community is now at the forefront of developing testable, modular software (influenced by the success of Ruby on Rails and the like), development tends to be rapid, incremental, low-risk, and, ultimately, great fun. There really is little comparison to the middleware monoliths of yesteryear, with their heavyweight servers, restrictive licensing, administrative bureaucracy, and frustrating development cycles.

Web development is a mature discipline, and as developers of web services we're piggybacking on all that prior effort. When building a web-based solution, we can use contemporary software engineering practices such as Test/Behavior-Driven Development to write our software. QAs in particular will be thrilled when they discover that even complex web-based systems can be tested with something as familiar and simple as a web browser.*

Nothing is hidden or untestable. There's no (necessary) dependence on proprietary software or protocols, no need for the accounting department to purchase licenses so

---

* Exploratory testing and debugging with simple tools such as Firefox and the Poster add-on (*https:// addons.mozilla.org/en-US/firefox/addon/2691*) is extremely powerful.

that developers can run middleware on their desktops. Even where production environments use proprietary web or application servers, we can still use commodity (even free and open source) software for development. Of course, we'll still need to do realistic testing with the proprietary environments, but most of our developer activities won't be hampered.

No Architecture Without Measurement

Though the Web almost always wins out against traditional middleware-driven solutions, software architecture on any platform remains a notoriously subjective discipline. Architects argue vehemently over design issues expressed using whiteboard sketches or stacks of UML diagrams. Whether a solution's architecture is fit for purpose often depends on the sensibilities of the architect and a good measure of gut instinct based on prior experience.*

The Web doesn't change any of this. A web-based system designed in the absence of careful measurements and empirical data is as likely to fail as any other solution designed without diligence. But the Web encourages the decomposition of systems into interacting services. This means it's easy to measure and evaluate each service, as well as the entire system. Compared to traditional enterprise approaches—particularly those where integration brokers hide necessary complexity—the Web offers *visibility*, which supports effective planning and design.

Like any serious engineering project, building a web-based system is a diligent and disciplined endeavor. We can't shirk our responsibilities as computer scientists; we must tackle difficult issues in distributed systems design head-on using the abstractions the Web provides. While delegating responsibility for so-called "heavy lifting" to middleware services is appealing, it's misguided, since it encourages us to ignore fundamental design considerations and trust an unknown black box.

WARNING

The classic paper by Waldo et al. emphasizes that distribution cannot be safely hidden from developers.[†] If you try to hide distribution in a distributed system, the abstractions will leak at inconvenient times and cause significant problems. It's best to acknowledge the distribution in distributed systems—it is necessary complexity— and to plan accordingly. Correspondingly, the Web does not try to hide distribution. Instead, HTTP offers a universal application protocol for coordinating interactions among distributed resources.

Distributed systems tend to have much more intricate failure characteristics and nonfunctional requirements than centralized systems (though completely centralized

---

* Unfortunately for architects, humans process information using their brains rather than their stomachs, so gut instinct isn't always an accurate measure.

† *http://research.sun.com/techrep/1994/abstract-29.html*

systems are becoming rare in the 21st century). Taking control of nonfunctional requirements is a critical factor in making a solution successful. But to take control, we need to measure and adapt throughout the development cycle, not just in a panic-stricken phase moments before a delivery deadline.

The nonfunctional characteristic that is most obvious and easiest to measure is performance. We must ask hard questions about the loads a service will be subject to and how that load profile changes over time. We have to learn the permitted latencies a service can reasonably operate within, and understand trade-offs between latency and throughput as volumes rise. Importantly, we must understand how the service is expected to react under large loads, *and how it is expected to fail once its parameters are exceeded*.

> ——— **NOTE** ———
>
> Although the Web is an excellent choice for high-throughput systems, low latency is not a strong point. If you are considering the Web for a low-latency service (millisecond scale), test the response times of your chosen server under a representative load first.*

In the 21st century, none of this is controversial. Business (and technical) stakeholders must be able to describe loads and performance expectations to the development team. Enterprise architects should be able to determine how the service should fail. (Should it fail gracefully or noisily? Should it degrade or halt? And so on.) All of this can be combined into a service-level agreement (SLA) for the service, and in turn, this SLA can be used *to continually test the service as it is being built*.

In modern software delivery, continuous integration (CI; an automated build approach) is commonplace. CI servers handle the drudgery of repeatedly building and deploying code, and running tests against the software. Importantly, the CI process can be used to run performance tests against a service to ensure that the established SLAs are being met as the software is built. When the SLA is contravened, the build breaks and the development team figures out which *recent* addition or change to their system caused the failure.[†]

For example, we've used commercial and open source load generation tools (and even crafted our own simple test harnesses) to run realistic performance tests as part of our CI build. We've graphed those results with visualization tools to show to our business and technical stakeholders and to help solve performance problems, as shown in Figure 12-1.

---

* As a rule of thumb, our experience suggests that average latencies of less than 100 ms can be sustained under high loads—thousands of requests per second—for a tuned web server on typical blades. This is surprisingly good for a synchronous, text-based, request-response protocol!

† You won't remember the $O(n3)$ algorithm you accidentally wrote in the depths of a critical part of your service code by the time the project is almost over. It'll take forever to track it down during the panicky test and optimization period. Measuring and optimizing at the end of software delivery is much harder and riskier than incrementally optimizing just enough during development.

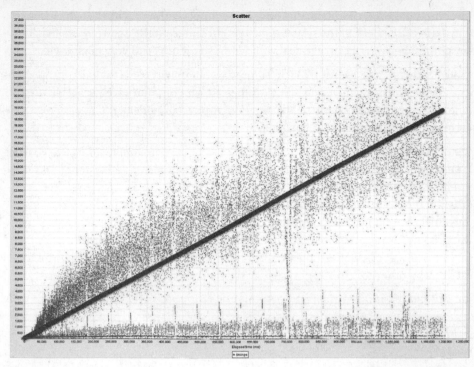

Figure 12-1. *Visualizing performance data to isolate latency problems under sustained high load*

Should we breach our SLA, the Web gives us numerous options to correct the behavior of the service. Developers and system administrators can optimize code, runtime, and server configuration without resorting to arcane (and expensive) specialists to perform the work. The troubleshooting process of understanding the performance data, forming a hypothesis, making changes, running the performance tests, and solving the problem is basic science (and quite therapeutic).

Outside the implementation of an individual service, the Web provides numerous opportunities for performance enhancements. Since good services are built to be stateless, they can scale horizontally just like regular web farms (a tried and trusted pattern). And once a good caching strategy is devised,* load on servers and latency for consumers are both reduced.

Even with caching, horizontal scaling, and careful tuning, a service has limits, and it's important to incorporate those limits into the service design. Constant measurement helps greatly in this effort and provides a great deal of confidence in a service's ability to manage predicted loads.

---

* Not all interactions are amenable to caching, so don't rely on this as your only performance-improving option.

But sometimes even careful predictions can be upset by a successful TV advertisement or by faults elsewhere in the system (or even in connected third-party systems). The question then arises of how we deal with failures and how the Web might help.

In such cases, we use the Web to flag failures and highlight services that are approaching their measured engineering limits (or their SLA). For failure scenarios, we use the standard server status codes (the 500 range) that HTTP provides—it's an easy case that can be solved with out-of-the-box tools.

Where we want to flag services that are approaching their tolerable limits, we've used HTTP status codes to implement *crumple zones*.* For example, in one compute-intensive system, we used the HTTP status code 413 Request Entity Too Large to reject a representation on the basis that it probably wouldn't be processed within the agreed SLA. Consumers of that particular service then push the workload through an alternative "safety valve" route and avoid overloading a service that is working near capacity. This isn't some unexpected afterthought; this behavior was built into the service and tested just like any other feature.

By considering nonfunctional characteristics as part of the service development, we tend to build very robust solutions. Going into production with a high level of confidence from testing services to destruction *and watching them cope* is a great feeling.

Selling the Web

It's perhaps a little disappointing that the Web still needs to be sold to stakeholders, but if we want to build web solutions it's a necessary evil. There's a grain of truth to the anecdote that IT purchasing decisions are rarely based on technical merit. Indeed, some middleware vendors have every reason to fear commoditization, and will raise concerns about any technology that jeopardizes their relevance. They're good at getting that message across to management too.

If you want to build successful web-based systems, you first have to sell the Web to your managers. Managers have different drivers from technologists, and more than anything they want to reduce the risk of their projects going off the rails (it makes them look bad).

Patiently explaining to a typical IT manager why all the "computer science stuff" is important and shouldn't be hidden won't win them over. Telling them that the Web is where all systems are converging won't win them over. The mindset of middleware encapsulating and solving hard information engineering problems is hard to shift.

---

* A crumple zone is designed to remove some of the energy during car collisions. In his wonderful book *Release It!* (Pragmatic Programmers), Michael T. Nygard uses the metaphor to prevent cascade when one component in a system fails. We like this pattern hugely, and are really pleased that it's so easy to implement with HTTP.

Fortunately, IT managers aren't (typically) foolish. And while they'll glaze over at any deeply technical reasons why the Web is a great software platform, they intuitively understand two factors in software delivery: cost and risk.

Cost

Anecdotally, the Web wins out on cost versus any other approach. Given the wide availability of free servers and sophisticated development frameworks, it's hard to imagine a scenario where software costs could be less. Nothing needs to be locked in to proprietary platforms or frameworks; instead, we used commodity technology that doesn't get in the way of delivering business functionality.

Furthermore, since the Web has a rich, extensive, and commoditized set of tools, developers feel at home. Not just expert developers with niche skills in proprietary middleware, but regular developers like us who build everyday systems.

Since people costs are often the most significant factor in any software delivery, by choosing the Web, we can curtail those costs. We don't need to (but can) call in specialist integration consultants since developers with a good understanding of distributed systems and a modern web framework can get the job done.

But cost savings don't stop at development, and importantly, they are overshadowed by the returns that software delivers in the long term. Since successful software spends much more of its lifetime in production than development, the costs of operating a service impact the total cost of ownership.* Given that web servers are commonplace in most production environments, operations staff are quite used to managing them. This means we don't need ongoing support from operational specialists for middleware products just keeping the system ticking over. The same standard tools for monitoring and maintenance that operations staff use for websites can be directly reused for web services. Given that web servers are a commodity,† the cost of software infrastructure to run the service is usually modest.

Mitigate Risk and Release Value, Early and Often

Large system projects are like trophies for IT managers. Bagging a multiyear, multimillion-dollar project brings kudos and the prospect of a career boost. It's not our role to argue with this; we don't want to deny the sense of achievement associated with this behavior. But we do want to make it less risky.

---

* Some IT managers are corralled into a project-centric view of the world where success is defined as getting something over the wall into production. We do not agree with that view, and see production as a normal part of the full software delivery life cycle.

† Web servers are either free or covered as part of the cost of an operating system license. We like both types.

Agile software development follows a mantra whereby working software is the only measure of a successful IT investment. In agile teams, working software is placed into production as soon as it is useful, rather than waiting for an entire solution to be finished. A similar mindset is evident with Internet Software-as-a-Service companies (e.g., Google, Salesforce.com) where functionality is released incrementally and constantly rather than waiting for the whole system to be finished, whenever that might be.*

The Web helps us to follow a similar pattern. Since we're not dependent on any shared middleware frameworks, licenses, specialist developers, or any other impediment, we can choose to deploy any completed features from our service into production early and add to them *incrementally over time* without disturbing other systems.

This removes significant project risk, and gives the opportunity for other stakeholders to get early access to a subset of the final functionality *and to provide feedback at a useful point in the delivery cycle*. It also gives the operations staff early experience in running the software.

For our IT manager, deploying to production provides hard data about project progress. It also gives a certain sense of satisfaction that something is live. The recognition will still be there at the end of the project when all the required functionality is in production, but the manager receives constant reassurance that the software will succeed because it has been deployed many times in the interim. Reducing risk, like reducing cost, makes managers happy, and happy managers are much more amenable to input from software practitioners than stressed, unhappy ones.

Go Forth and Build

Over the past few years, we've seen (and helped to build) numerous web-based distributed systems. They've been fun to build, easy to test, and straightforward to deploy and manage in production. The techniques we've distilled into this book have served us well, and we hope you'll have as much success (and fun) using them as we have. Now, go build something wonderful.

---

* It can be a long wait for a system to be complete. Complex enterprise projects have durations of years. Even Google's Gmail application was in beta for an awfully long time!

Index

demilitarized zone (DMZ), 388
denial-of-service attacks, 339–341
Diffie-Hellman key exchange, 299, 317
Digest authentication, 287–290, 394
DMZ (demilitarized zone), 388
DNS (Domain Name System), 6
documentation, URI templates as, 37
domain application protocol. *See* see DAP
    (domain application protocol)
domain models, 382–383
Domain Name System (DNS), 6
DSL (Domain-Specific Language), 141–145

E

entity body strategies, 231
ETags
    aligning resource state, 79–83
    caching and, 163–164, 173
    polling for recent events, 199
    timestamps in, 175
    validation and, 174–176
event-driven systems
    anatomy of events, 192
    Atoms feeds and, 189
    caching feeds, 202–206
    implementation considerations, 206–207
    link relations, 195–197
    navigating archive, 200
    polling for events, 197–200
    problem overview, 189
    reference data, 190
    update considerations, 191–192
exception handling, 262–263
expiration-based consistency, 172, 177–178
Expires header (HTTP), 162, 173, 176

F

federated authentication, 394
federated identity, 392

Feed Paging and Archiving specification
    about, 235
    fh:archive element, 201, 202, 206
Fielding, Roy, 12, 14, 20, 93
File Transfer Protocol (FTP), 6
FOAF (Friend of a Friend), 369
forms
    action attribute, 323
    as hypermedia controls, 96
    media types and, 103
freshness lifetime (caching), 157
Friend of a Friend (FOAF), 369
FTP (File Transfer Protocol), 6

G

GeoNames website, 362
GET (HTTP) verb
    advertising protocols, 122
    building Atom service, 209
    caching support, 16, 17, 155–157, 169
    conditional, 173, 228, 231–233, 248
    idempotency and, 38, 78
    polling considerations, 120
    reading resource state, 57, 63–68
    reliable transfers and, 397
    URI tunneling and, 38, 41–42
    voucher payment system and, 324
    web transactions, 402
GoodRelations website, 361

H

HATEOAS acronym, 93
hCard format, 29
headers. *See* HTTP headers
HEAD (HTTP) verb, 156
HMAC-SHA-1 algorithm, 321
Hohpe, Gregor, 21
Host header (HTTP), 45
HTML, microformats and, 373
HTTP Basic authentication, 287–290, 394
HTTP Cache Channels Internet-Draft, 183
HttpClient class, 50, 83

HTTP Digest authentication, 287–290, 394

HTTP headers. *See* specific headers

HTTP (HyperText Transfer Protocol)
  AtomPub support, 238, 246
  authentication support, 286–290
  authorization support, 286–290
  building CRUD services, 57
  caching support, 16, 17, 155–157,
    162–164
  envelope structure, 377
  idempotency and, 38, 72, 78
  network considerations, 293–294
  performance considerations, 293–294
  remote procedure calls, 43–44
  Richardson maturity model, 19
  security essentials, 286–294
  transport-level considerations, 290–293
  uniform interface and, 11, 110, 386
  URI tunneling and, 39
  web architecture and, 2

HttpListener class (.NET)
  caching and, 168
  DELETE verb and, 77
  handling requests, 227
  hypermedia service and, 141

HTTP response/status codes. *See* specific
    response/status codes

HTTPS protocol, 290–293, 393–395

HTTP Stale Controls Informational RFC,
    166

HTTP verbs. *See* specific verbs

hypermedia controls
  atom:link element, 195
  defined, 96
  HTTP idioms and, 110
  in hypermedia formats, 100, 101
  implementing hypermedia service,
    130, 141
  semantic context for, 352
  XML and, 97, 105

hypermedia formats
  dead ends, 97
  defined, 97

domain-specific, 100–102
  hypermedia controls in, 100, 101
  processing, 102–109
  selecting, 99–102
  standard, 99–100
  URI templates and coupling, 98

hypermedia protocols
  advertising, 114–121
  AtomPub as, 240
  binding contracts and, 29
  DAP support, 112–113, 121–125
  data modeling versus, 125–128
  extending contracts with, 110

hypermedia services
  building in Java, 128–140
  building in .NET, 140–152
  consumer-side architecture, 137–140
  contracts and, 29, 108–111
  defined, 13
  hypermedia formats, 97–108
  hypermedia protocols, 112–128
  implementing, 128
  loose coupling and, 96–97
  protocols and, 29, 110
  Richardson maturity model, 20, 152
  server-side architecture, 128–131
  state machine illustration, 13
  URI templates and, 35

HyperText Transfer Protocol. *See* HTTP
    (HyperText Transfer Protocol)

I

IANA Link Relations registry, 110, 196,
    246

idempotency
  HTTP verbs and, 38, 72, 78
  reliable transfers and, 397

identifiers, resources and, 5–7

identity
  federated, 392
  HTTP security and, 286–290
  OpenID protocol and, 295–315
  as security pillar, 285

S

W

W3C (World Wide Web Consortium), 2, 13

WADL2Java tool, 88

WADL (Web Application Description Language)
about, 386
consuming services automatically, 86–90
POX implementations and, 49
reducing dependency on, 96
as static contracts, 98

WCF (Windows Communication Foundation)
implementing AtomPub, 268
implementing hypermedia service, 140
implementing services, 279–283
POX support, 46, 49
security considerations, 346
service and data contracts, 383
testing services, 274–279
updating resources, 72

Web Application Description Language. *See* WADL (Web Application Description Language)

web-based services
building/running, 407–409
cost considerations, 413
measurement considerations, 409–412
risk mitigation, 413
as silver bullets, 407

web friendliness
about, 18–20
hypermedia formats, 100
link relations and, 195
URI tunneling and, 41

web integration
coffee ordering system, 32–35
middleware solutions, 31–32
POX over HTTP, 42–54
URI templates, 35–37
URI tunneling, 37–42

Web Services Description Language (WSDL)
about, 380–386
metadata support, 35
as static contracts, 98

wildcards, headers and, 83

Windows Communication Foundation. *See* WCF (Windows Communication Foundation)

WinINet cache, 167

working feed
building Atom service, 209, 211
comparing archive feed and, 206
defined, 199
mutable nature of, 200

World Wide Web
as application platform, 15–18
architectural style, 2–4, 12
as building platform, 1
business processes, 17
consistency and uniformity, 17
loose coupling, 9, 16
scalability and performance, 15
simplicity and reach, 18
technology support, 15
web friendliness and, 18–20

World Wide Web Consortium (W3C), 2, 13

WS-Addressing protocol, 376, 377, 385

WS-Addressing To header, 378

WS-AtomicTransaction protocol, 379

WS-BusinessActivity protocol, 379, 399

WS-CAF protocol, 399

WS-Choreography protocol, 386

WS-Coordination protocol, 379

WS-DeathStar, 376

WSDL (Web Services Description Language)
about, 380–386
metadata support, 35
as static contracts, 98

WS-Federation protocol, 392

WS-ReliableMessaging protocol, 395, 396

About the Authors

Jim Webber is a director with ThoughtWorks, where he works with clients around the world to deliver dependable service-oriented systems tailored to business needs.

Savas Parastatidis is an architect at Microsoft working on large-scale distributed computing platforms for compute- and data-intensive applications and services. Previously he was part of Microsoft's Bing group, where he focused on semantic and knowledge representation technologies.

Ian Robinson is a principal consultant with ThoughtWorks, where he specializes in helping clients create sustainable service-oriented development capabilities that align business and IT from inception through to operation.

Colophon

The cover fonts are Akzidenz Grotesk and Orator. The text font is Adobe's Meridien; the heading font is Akzidenz Grotesk; and the code font is LucasFont's TheSansMonoCondensed.

Get even more for your money.

Join the O'Reilly Community, and register the O'Reilly books you own. It's free, and you'll get:

- $4.99 ebook upgrade offer
- 40% upgrade offer on O'Reilly print books
- Membership discounts on books and events
- Free lifetime updates to ebooks and videos
- Multiple ebook formats, DRM FREE
- Participation in the O'Reilly community
- Newsletters
- Account management
- 100% Satisfaction Guarantee

Signing up is easy:

1. Go to: oreilly.com/go/register
2. Create an O'Reilly login.
3. Provide your address.
4. Register your books.

Note: English-language books only

To order books online:

oreilly.com/store

For questions about products or an order:

orders@oreilly.com

To sign up to get topic-specific email announcements and/or news about upcoming books, conferences, special offers, and new technologies:

elists@oreilly.com

For technical questions about book content:

booktech@oreilly.com

To submit new book proposals to our editors:

proposals@oreilly.com

O'Reilly books are available in multiple DRM-free ebook formats. For more information:

oreilly.com/ebooks

Spreading the knowledge of innovators   oreilly.com

©2010 O'Reilly Media, Inc. O'Reilly logo is a registered trademark of O'Reilly Media, Inc. 00000

Buy this book and get access to the online edition for 45 days—for free!

REST in Practice
By Jim Webber, Savas Parastatidis & Ian Robinson
September 2010, $44.99
ISBN 9780596805821

With Safari Books Online, you can:

Access the contents of thousands of technology and business books

- Quickly search over 7000 books and certification guides
- Download whole books or chapters in PDF format, at no extra cost, to print or read on the go
- Copy and paste code
- Save up to 35% on O'Reilly print books
- **New!** Access mobile-friendly books directly from cell phones and mobile devices

Stay up-to-date on emerging topics before the books are published

- Get on-demand access to evolving manuscripts.
- Interact directly with authors of upcoming books

Explore thousands of hours of video on technology and design topics

- Learn from expert video tutorials
- Watch and replay recorded conference sessions

To try out Safari and the online edition of this book FREE for 45 days, go to **www.oreilly.com/go/safarienabled** and enter the coupon code HJXTOXA. To see the complete Safari Library, visit safari.oreilly.com.

Spreading the knowledge of innovators

safari.oreilly.com